SELF-EVIDENT TRUTHS

Self-Evident Truths

Contesting Equal Rights from the Revolution to the Civil War

RICHARD D. BROWN

Yale

UNIVERSITY PRESS

NEW HAVEN AND LONDON

Yale University Press books may be purchased in quantity for educational,
business, or promotional use. For information, please e-mail sales.press@yale.edu
(U.S. office) or sales@yaleup.co.uk (U.K. office).

Set in Electra type by Newgen North America.
Printed in the United States of America.

Library of Congress Control Number: 2016943623

ISBN 978-0-300-19711-2 (hardcover)

A catalogue record for this book is available from the British Library.

This paper meets the requirements of ANSI/NISO Z39.48-1992
(Permanence of Paper).

10 9 8 7 6 5 4 3 2 1

CONTENTS

John Trumbull, *The Declaration of Independence*, N. Currier, 1835–56.
Currier's print represents the heightened popular admiration for the
Revolution and especially the Declaration during the generation
preceding the Civil War. Courtesy, Library of Congress.

The bold, inspiring promise of the Declaration of Independence has long possessed a powerful grip on Americans' political imagination. The idea that the United States must be a land of equality, where every person should realize equal opportunities for life, liberty, and the pursuit of happiness—with privilege banished—is fundamental to the nation's modern creed. Yet it would be naive to suppose that this ideal has ever accurately reflected American reality. Privilege, sometimes written into law and sometimes merely customary, is a historical fact of life. Statutes have privileged men, property holders, whites, adults, citizens, Protestants, and heterosexuals. Custom has extended these and subtler forms of privilege, like class, ethnicity, and education, into American society broadly. As a result, some have come to regard the Declaration's promise as hollow rhetoric—merely Patriots' propaganda. Why should anyone take these words—"all men are created equal"—seriously when they came from the pen of a slave master and were adopted by a Congress of privileged gentlemen, many of whom were also slaveholders?

The point is debatable. We should not allow the patriotic mythologies that wash over us from childhood to cloud our vision. But neither should we interpret the Declaration to make a weapon in the political battles of our own time. Considering the Declaration's "self-evident truths" maturely requires us to examine their origins and trajectories across the centuries. It is possible that the language of the Declaration was propaganda. Certainly it was an explicitly political text intended to arouse popular support. But, for it to succeed, the ideas it invoked must have been meaningful—even inspiring—for many Americans. Viewing the Congress of gentlemen with full-blown skepticism could be a mistake. Maybe their political machinations were propelled not only by ambition and selfish interests but by ideas and ideals as well.

However critics have judged the founding fathers, they have never accused them of ignorance or stupidity. Obviously Patriot leaders recognized slavery and class privileges in their own time: yet they embraced egalitarian rhetoric. In the short term that rhetoric may have been the key to mobilizing common men to fight; but could John Adams, Thomas Jefferson, George Washington, and their colleagues have been so short-sighted and so confident of their power as to suppose that their language of equality would have no consequences? Among the founding fathers and their constituents, some, we do not know how many, took the language of the Declaration to heart. Dwelling as they did in a society of rank and privilege, some continental congressmen and their descendants expressed egalitarian hopes.

This study aims to investigate the proposition that the self-evident truths proclaimed in the Declaration were not simply rhetorical window-dressing but inspired serious aspirations from the moment they were proclaimed. The constitutions, laws, and politics of the decades between independence and the Civil War reveal the ways that Americans embedded the Revolution's egalitarian impulse in their discourse. Equal rights are the central concern of this study because the Revolution promised equal rights, not any broader form of equality. So our investigation begins with constitutions and bills of rights.

But it also moves into courtrooms, because courts were often a place where rights were defined with precision, where criminal trials and divorce cases tested whether reality matched the rhetoric of equal rights. Because capital trials especially displayed the most intense and uninhibited arguments, they permit us to glimpse collisions between equal rights principles and customary prejudices and privileges. Here, too, the impact of popular opinion on legal procedures challenged the principle of equal justice under law.

The chapters that follow examine contests over equal rights in six central arenas of public concern—religion, nationality and ethnicity, race, gender, age, and social class. Each chapter explores the ways in which Americans came to realize, in whole or in part, the ideal of equal rights expressed in the Declaration—or to disavow that ideal. Though evidence is drawn from all parts of the early Republic, it is weighted toward the Northeast and New England. That is partly owing to the availability of sources and to my familiarity with that region's history. Given the broad scope of this study, even with extensive research in every state, the insights and answers provided in these pages could never be definitive and must rely on some mixture of empirical and impressionistic evidence.

This inquiry cannot treat the entire United States thoroughly in the era from independence to the Civil War, but I hope that it provides a useful beginning. No region was more committed to the realization of equal rights than New England and the Northeast, so if anything, the information drawn from this region may overstate the impact of Revolutionary equal rights doctrine. Bearing that in mind, readers will make their own judgments in light of evidence that cannot be comprehensive. Because I treat a broad range of experiences in North and South and the Old West, especially as revealed in court cases, I aim to provide insights into the practical, everyday complexities of contests over equal rights. Taken together they illuminate the ways in which Americans struggled with one another over recognizing the principle that "all men are created equal."

This book contends that the Declaration's fateful phrase was not merely high-flown rhetoric. For many Revolutionaries it expressed their profound commitment to a new political and social contract. In the words proclaimed by the Continental Congress in 1782, the independent United States was to be a *novus ordo seclorum*, a new order of the ages. But in a country where inequality was customary and often written into law, where people of different religions, ethnicities, nationalities, and races competed with one another, the distance between their declaration and its fulfillment was bound to be arduous and conflict-ridden. Moreover, Americans' all-but-unanimous commitment to private property—and to its heritability across the generations—provided a structural impediment to the full realization of equal rights that few were ready to confront, prompting William Dean Howells to remark, in *Impressions and Experiences* (1896), that "inequality is as dear to the American heart as liberty itself." Nevertheless, this study reveals that the ideal Congress proclaimed on July 4, 1776, remained a talisman for reformers who sought to make their country a *novus ordo seclorum*. And if they were not wholly successful in shaping the United States to fit the ideal, they did sustain its principles in the face of powerful opposition, so as to make critical strides along the path toward the realization of equal rights.

SELF-EVIDENT TRUTHS

ONE

The Declaration of Independence and the Mystery of Equality

We hold these truths to be self-evident, that all men are created equal, that they are endowed by their Creator with certain unalienable Rights, that among these are Life, Liberty and the pursuit of Happiness.
—*Declaration of Independence, July 4, 1776*

Simple words, so direct, so transparent: "We hold these truths to be self-evident, that all men are created equal." No one rose to challenge them when they were put to a vote in the Continental Congress in July 1776. Why should they? Just three weeks earlier Virginia's Revolutionaries avowed much the same credo, proclaiming in their Declaration of Rights "all men are by nature equally free and independent." Patriots throughout the American colonies, outraged by what they saw as *un*equal treatment by British authorities, readily embraced the principle of equality. When they declared themselves to be a people distinct from Britain, they believed that though they were not as powerful or populous as the United Kingdom, nevertheless "the Laws of Nature and of Nature's God" entitled them to an "equal station" with English subjects.[1]

But the meaning of the words and their underlying principle, Americans would learn, were neither simple nor transparent. In July 1776 "all men are created equal" seemed clear enough—every right belonging to politically active men must be preserved, including government by consent. But in the coming months and years men and women throughout the United States came to construe the Declaration's words differently. In fact, the idea

1

that "all men are created equal and endowed by their creator with certain unalienable rights" was more a statement of aspiration—a promise for the future—than an actual guarantee of equal rights. Equal rights would not prove to be self-evident after all; but nowhere in Americans' political lexicon was there a more potent or explosive ideal.[2]

For years, decades actually, colonial political leaders had claimed the "rights of *English*men," an assertion of equal rights resembling the Declaration. But their old formulation differed critically because it was not universal. According to their traditional formula the boundaries of equality followed those of the United Kingdom. In the past no one supposed that the rights of Englishmen could be universal; indeed, Englishmen boasted that their liberty was unique, making them the freest people in the eighteenth-century world. In reality, of course, their vaunted English liberty was both fact and fiction. Leaving aside distinctions created by English, Scots, Irish, and Welsh descent, or residence in communities "grandfathered" in or out of parliamentary representation—wealth and lineage, as well as religious confession and sex, made inequality the rule among English people, not the exception. That a nation of roughly 9 million people possessed—as Thomas Jefferson pointed out in 1774—only 160,000 eligible voters for its House of Commons displayed the unequal structure of English liberty.[3] That British law did not positively recognize race or color distinctions owed chiefly to the rarity of nonwhites in the kingdom, not the universality of British rights. Britons had long connected equal rights to English and Anglican identity—membership in a singular national and cultural community—not the mere fact of being human.[4] Because "the rights of Englishmen" carried this traditional hue, the Declaration's inclusive assertion of *natural equality* was bold.

I

Why, then, did patriots turn away from the old standby "the rights of Englishmen" to "all men are created equal" if they merely sought equality with enfranchised Britons? The older language might be outmoded, but it was comfortable. In contrast, the new emphasis on universal equality was radical. Yet Americans embraced the new language widely and easily; indeed the Continental Congress did not debate this phrase or make the effort to explain it explicitly. Since John Locke's *Second Treatise on Government* helped shape the Declaration, and Locke rested his arguments on natural rights, generations of scholars have, reasonably enough, interpreted the shift to natural equality as an expression of the Revolutionaries' Enlightenment ideology as well as the necessity of moving beyond English legal precedent in proclaiming independence.[5]

The chronology of Americans' appeals to natural rights is revealing. For although the language of natural rights was fully articulated in seventeenth-century political theory, when colonists opposed parliamentary acts before the 1770s they seldom based their claims on natural rights. Instead they made more legalistic arguments, linked especially to taxation and representation. But in a few short years, 1772 through 1775, they made natural rights appeals commonplace. When, for example, the Boston Committee of Correspondence sought to awaken and instruct "the Inhabitants of Massachusetts" in 1772, they proclaimed "the Rights of the Colonists . . . as Men, as Christians, and as Subjects."[6] Although the committee called attention to voters' English rights as subjects, their claims rested on natural rights, particularly the first law of nature, "the Duty of Self-Preservation." Following Locke, they declared that rights to life, liberty, and property were inherent in natural law. Coequal with these rights, they asserted, was inhabitants' right as Christians to liberty of conscience. Their understanding of liberty of conscience excluded "tyrannical" Roman Catholicism and accepted discrimination, even among Protestants; but they believed that something called religious freedom was a natural right.[7]

Colonists recognized the overlap between natural rights and the rights of Englishmen; but English rights were more particular and applied to the English state. Accordingly, royal and legislative power must not be arbitrary, and courts independent and impartial. Natural rights, the rights of Englishmen, and egalitarian belief converged in Locke's oft-invoked maxim: *"There should be one Rule of Justice for Rich and Poor; for the Favourite at Court, and the Countryman at the Plough."*[8] Before the law, "all" should stand equal—regardless of wealth or social rank. Whether that equality should extend to outsiders such as Protestant Dissenters, Catholics, Jews, and Muslims, to foreigners dwelling in British jurisdictions, or to racial outsiders, women, and children, was not generally discussed. In reality, rich and poor, courtiers and countrymen all recognized that *"one Rule of Justice"* was a cultural ideal, not everyday practice. Moreover, among all the grievances in all the protests of 1774 through 1776, the only complaints against the imperial judicial system concerned an independent judiciary, prerogative courts, and the trial venues of British officials and colonists. However rebellious their rhetoric and resolutions, colonists never protested the unequal treatment of rich and poor or other inequalities of British jurisprudence.

Natural rights thinking first led colonists to assert equality among themselves and other Britons only, not a more inclusive ideal of equality. Whatever inequalities Britons "at home" accepted, colonial Patriots accepted as well, excepting only disabilities on dissenting English Protestants. As Bernard Bailyn long ago noted, Patriot radicals sought to purify the British constitution, not "to recast the social order" or confront "the problems of economic inequality and the injustices of stratified societies."[9] Nevertheless, the more they grounded their arguments on natural rights, the harder they found it to draw boundaries around rights claims.

Americans first asserted natural rights collectively when the Continental Congress laid out remarkably bold principles of resistance in its October 1774 "Bill of Rights and List of Grievances." Though this statement would be overshadowed by the Declaration of Independence, its inclusive language seemingly recognized no distinctions of class, religion, race, sex, or nationality. In it Congress professed that "the inhabitants of the English Colonies in North America, by the immutable laws of nature, the principles of the English constitution, and the several charters" possessed a dozen specific rights—the first being the rights "to life, liberty and property."[10]

Tellingly, Congress immediately qualified this literally egalitarian pronouncement with another hereditary assertion of rights: "Our ancestors, who first settled these colonies, were at the time of their emigration from the mother country, entitled to all the rights, liberties, and immunities of free and natural born-subjects within the realm of England." Nominally this claim remained egalitarian, at least for descendants of early English settlers; but the fact that Congress confined its assertion of rights to equivalence with English "free and natural-born subjects" meant that Congress tacitly accepted seventeenth- and eighteenth-century English limitations on equal rights—certainly including restrictions based on property, religion, sex, and nationality. In reality, congressmen were only asserting their own and their constituents' equality with their counterparts in the English political class. As the Virginia legislature had earlier instructed its delegates to Congress, "British subjects in America are entitled to the same rights and privileges as their fellow subjects possess in Britain."

Yet remarkably, the very lawyers in Congress who normally chose words carefully tended to revert to inclusive language, and nowhere more than in the closing paragraph of their October 1774 Declaration and Resolves. Here, after a long list of complaints, they proclaimed that "to these grievous acts and measures *Americans* cannot submit."[11] They did not specify "white, male, property-holding Americans," only "Americans" without distinction. Inadvertently, almost two years before the Declaration of Independence, the Congress was employing language that a truly radical colonist might construe to imply equal rights for all Americans.

One must not make too much of this fact. Then, as now, it was not unusual to use inclusive language reflexively, almost by default, even when a common meaning was generally narrow. Moreover, terms like "mankind" could be understood as unbounded or not, depending on context. Still, repeated use of inclusive terms—calculated or spontaneous—would lend legitimacy to those who chose to interpret such language literally. In the Congress's July 1775 "Declaration of the Causes and Necessity of Taking Up Arms," the delegates had denied that God "intended a part of the human race to hold an absolute property in, and unbounded power over others," a denial aimed at British rule over the colonists but which could also be reasonably interpreted as a repudiation of chattel slavery. "Government," Congress proclaimed in the most inclusive language, "was instituted to promote the welfare of mankind."[12] Fully a year before the Declaration of Independence supplied its simple affirmation of equal natural rights, the language of equal rights enjoyed wide currency among Patriots.

When Thomas Paine's *Common Sense* scornfully dismissed the legitimacy of the British constitution in January 1776 he rendered appeals grounded merely on the rights of Englishmen obsolete. Paine's pamphlet, a popular primer in natural rights and social compact theory, embraced natural egalitarianism while mocking the whole English system of monarchy, aristocracy, and hereditary privilege. Judging from the reactions of Patriot leaders like Washington, elite Patriots chose to overlook the indiscriminate egalitarianism embedded in Paine's text. John Adams conscientiously protested Paine's attack on the balanced English constitution and decried his simple, unicameral constitution, but not even Adams challenged the broad, natural rights egalitarianism of *Common Sense*.[13]

When George Mason drafted Virginia's Bill of Rights in June 1776, natural rights supplanted the rights of Englishmen. This awkwardly worded template for the Declaration's great egalitarian mantra began by stating:

> 1. That *all men* are by nature equally free and independent, and have certain inherent rights, of which, when they enter into a state of society, they cannot, by any compact deprive or divest their posterity; namely, the enjoyment of life and liberty, with the means of acquiring and possessing property, and pursuing and obtaining happiness and safety.
>
> 2. That all power is vested in, and consequently derived from, *the people*; that magistrates are their trustees and servants, and at all times amenable to them.[14]

The fact that Virginia's revolutionary convention—a body of privileged, slaveholding aristocrats—endorsed such apparently egalitarian language seems astonishing in retrospect, sometimes leading present-day historians to treat this passage as blatant hypocrisy. But it was not. By limiting equal rights to recognized members of society, southern delegates believed that they excluded slaves. In the context of 1776, their expression of universal, natural rights idealism is best understood as an aspirational statement of principles.[15]

A decade earlier, in 1767, when the Virginia legislature adopted a law to discourage slave importation, the Patriot Arthur Lee's "Address on Slavery" in the *Virginia Gazette* denounced the slave trade as "a violation of justice and religion." Earlier still, Virginia's royal lieutenant governor Francis Fauquier had proffered the egalitarian pronouncement that "White, Red, or

Black; polished or unpolished; . . . Men are Men." Jefferson's 1774 instructions to the Virginia delegation to the Continental Congress had plainly affirmed that slavery "deeply wounded . . . the rights of human nature" and declared that "the abolition of domestic slavery is the great object of desire" in the colonies. Later that year, when the Congress adopted its Continental Association boycott of trade with Britain, the colonies pledged to "wholly discontinue the slave trade" and to end business with "those concerned in it." Indeed, by the time Virginia leaders passed their Bill of Rights in June 1776, they had repeatedly voted to end slave imports, a measure they hoped would speed slavery toward extinction. The plantation gentry's votes against the slave trade suggest that natural rights idealism sustained the language of equal rights. Hypocrisy cannot be ruled out, as critics like Thomas Hutchinson and Samuel Johnson loudly proclaimed. But they erred in dismissing Patriot declarations as empty rhetoric.[16]

Today, obviously, we cannot re-create the political and ideological context that gave meaning to "We hold these truths to be self-evident, that all men are created equal." Nor should we assume that this talismanic assertion carried only a single meaning in 1776. Yet notwithstanding the absence of any explicit reference to chattel slavery in the Declaration, scholars have long understood that many in that era—Patriots as well as Loyalists—recognized that the natural equality Patriots claimed to justify American independence also condemned holding slaves.

This contradiction was evident in the work of the Declaration's drafting committee. Congressmen John Adams, Benjamin Franklin, Robert R. Livingston, and Roger Sherman all approved Jefferson's draft, endorsing what Adams later called "the vehement philippic against negro slavery." This particular grievance claimed that the king had "waged cruel war against human nature itself, violating its most sacred rights of life & liberty in the persons of a distant people . . . captivating & carrying them into slavery in another hemisphere." George III, Jefferson's draft continued, was "determined to keep open a market where *Men* should be bought & sold."[17] Here the committee proposed blaming His Majesty personally for the slave trade—now prohibited by the Continental Association and condemned for the past decade in several colonial legislatures.

But the whole Congress, more astute than passionate, chose to delete this grievance, not because it approved slavery and the slave trade, but because, as Jefferson noted, South Carolina and Georgia still chose to import Africans and some of "our Northern brethren" had transported and sold such captives. Moreover, to attack George III for acquiescence in this sordid business would only draw attention to some Patriots' own culpability and would divide the colonies at a moment when unity was critical. Patriots remarked on the inconsistency of their own position. As the Reverend William Gordon of Massachusetts wrote in a October 1776 newspaper essay, citing the Virginia Declaration of Rights as well as the Declaration of Independence, "If these . . . are our genuine sentiments . . . let us apply earnestly and heartily to the extirpation of slavery among ourselves."[18] Contemporaries recognized that the idea that "all men are created equal" carried ramifications.

In retrospect it is clear the Declaration's great assertion of natural equality was partly tactical—Congress preferred a source above English law to justify separation—and partly an optimistic, forward-looking profession of faith that served the collective interest at a moment of soaring Revolutionary idealism. Congress's vote for this statement was unanimous; but actual beliefs about equality—religious, political, social, and what was called "race"—were both fluid and divided. Moreover, everyone recognized that the newly created United States' government in 1776 would not and could not revise political and social institutions in the states. Whatever goals reformers like Gordon hoped to achieve regarding slavery, freedom of conscience, or other aspects of personal equality, they would have to pursue in the states.

II

The struggles over slavery in Massachusetts, where only a small fraction of residents held their fellows in hereditary bondage, and in Virginia, where tens of thousands of slaves comprised nearly 40 percent of the inhabitants, reveal the complexity and magnitude of the challenge the new egalitarianism posed for the Patriot generation. In the seventeenth century New Englanders enslaved Indians as well as Africans, so Massachusetts abolition traced its pedigree to Boston and to Samuel Sewall's 1701 pamphlet, *The*

Selling of Joseph. But until the 1760s slavery enjoyed general acceptance. In 1765, for example, John Adams, exploited common negrophobic prejudices in his "Humphrey Ploughjogger" essays against British impositions. In Yankee farmer dialect he declared: "We won't be their negroes. Providence never designed us for negroes, I know, for if it had it wou'd have given us black hides, and thick lips, and flat noses, and short wooly hair, which it han't done, and therefore never intended us for slaves." In contrast, James Otis, in the *Rights of the British Colonies Asserted and Proved* (1764), linked the colonial cause to a vivid condemnation of African slavery. "The Colonists," Otis declared, "are by the law of nature free born, as indeed all men are, white or black." He went on to ridicule racial justifications of slavery: "Does it follow that it is right to enslave a man because he is black? Will short curl'd hair like wool . . . help the argument? Can any logical inference in favour of slavery be drawn from a flat nose, a long or a short face?"[19]

Otis's arguments reveal an emerging abolition consciousness, stated explicitly by the 1765 Worcester town meeting which directed its representative to seek "a law to put an end to that unchristian and impolitic practice of making slaves of the human species." The next year Boston, too, instructed its delegates not merely to prohibit further importation of slaves but to pursue "the total abolishing of slavery among us."[20] Thereafter antislavery essays and sermons appeared almost annually in Massachusetts, Connecticut, and Rhode Island.

In 1771 both houses of the Massachusetts legislature passed a bill to end slave imports, but the governor refused to sign it. Explaining his action, Governor Thomas Hutchinson called the bill "new and unusual," saying that it seemed to be based on "a scruple upon the minds of the People in many parts of the Province of the lawfulness . . . of so great a restraint of Liberty." But this objection was "*meerly* [sic] *moral.*" Two years later in 1773, some Massachusetts slaves collaborated with legislators to form a committee of their own to petition the legislature for freedom. If slavery was abolished they offered to depart for Africa. Half a dozen towns published resolutions opposing slavery or the slave trade, and Harvard College's commencement featured a debate on the legality of enslaving Africans. In January 1774 the house ordered consideration of the "Negro petition." The legislature maintained masters' property rights in slaves; but again it approved a law to end slave importation, a bill that died because neither Governor Hutchinson nor his successor, Thomas Gage, would sign it. The next year Philadelphia Quakers launched the Pennsylvania Society for Promoting the Abolition of Slavery and for the Relief of Free Negroes Unlawfully Held in Bondage.[21]

During the eighteen months leading to the Declaration of Independence the issue of African slavery never dominated Patriot discussion; but neither was it forgotten. Essays and sermons continued to attack slavery on grounds of religion and natural rights, and in the two-month interval between the Battles of Lexington and Concord and Bunker Hill in 1775, one Massachusetts county passed a resolution calling for emancipation.[22] Voters recognized masters' property rights in their slaves and so hesitated to endorse abolition, but none defended slavery publicly. No one resurrected the old argument that enslavement was the proper status for captives of just wars or followed Locke's reasoning that enslaved captives were fortunate to possess their lives. Nor did Massachusetts defenders of the status quo argue the color, physiognomy, or personal traits of Africans fitted them for bondage. Instead, a consensus was emerging that slavery was contrary to Christianity and natural rights. But these nascent abolition beliefs were offset by a profound commitment to property rights coupled with widespread antagonism toward blacks—people whose different appearance, customs and behavior, and poverty made them seem more likely than whites to become tax liabilities requiring public assistance.

Soon after the Declaration a maritime case tested Massachusetts's policy toward slavery and captives. The owners of a Salem privateer sought to sell as cargo two black men captured at sea. Slavery opponents challenged this sale in the House of Representatives and in September 1776 won a resolution declaring that "the selling and enslaving of the human species is a direct violation of the natural rights alike vested in all men by their Creator, and utterly inconsistent with the avowed principles on which this and the other United States have carried their struggle for liberty." The house deleted this antislavery preamble, but it finally directed that the "two Negro Men" not be sold but be "brought as Prisoners into this State."[23] Legislators believed that slavery contradicted Revolutionary principles and so decided the two blacks must not be sold as slaves. But with competing natural rights in play—to liberty and property—they could not agree on how to deal with slavery more broadly.

During 1777 petitions from slaves would spearhead abolition efforts in the legislature, though when representatives proposed an abolition bill, the house voted to table it. Only a few thousand families, white and black, would be affected and slavery had lost all legitimacy; still, the delegates would not act. Ultimately, legislators never voted to abolish slavery; that determination would be made by the state's highest court, an appointive body, in freedom suit judgments in the 1780s. Retroactively the Massachusetts Supreme Judicial Court would rule that the state's 1780 Declaration of Rights made slavery unconstitutional because "all men are born free and equal, and have certain natural, essential, and unalienable rights."[24] The court applied the Declaration of Independence's natural equality motto to chattel slavery directly.

III

If the Massachusetts legislature did not abolish slavery during the climax of Revolutionary enthusiasm, it is no surprise that voters and officials in Virginia, where the entire economy and social and political order rested on slavery, did not either. Yet Virginians, too, connected their assertions of natural equality to slavery and voiced similar concerns about inconsistencies between idealistic professions and actual practice. Notwithstanding Virginia's engagement in the African slave trade and chattel slavery, similarly divided opinions were operating in the Chesapeake and Massachusetts. And if Virginia did not have an early abolitionist to match Samuel Sewall, one great slaveholder, William Byrd, recognized that however bondage might be justified, arguments of race would not serve. Two generations before George Mason's and Thomas Jefferson's declarations he wrote: "All nations of men have the same natural dignity, and we all know that very bright talents may be lodged under a very dark skin. The principal difference between one people and another proceeds only from the different opportunities of improvement."[25] Byrd referred to Indians, not Africans, but he expressed his belief in Lockean natural equality and in an environmentalism like that of Montesquieu.

During the 1760s, before Massachusetts, Virginia's legislature voted to curb slave importation. Nonimportation of British goods in 1767 aimed generally to persuade Parliament to repeal the Townshend taxes on imports, but opposing slave imports served larger purposes. Placing a duty on imported slaves when prices of domestic slaves were soft was a factor, as was frugality; but antislavery sentiment, expressed by the Tidewater lawyer Arthur Lee's assertion that slavery was "a violation of justice and religion," was growing. Five years later, during the 1772 lull in the controversy between Parliament and the colonies, Virginia's lower house vainly petitioned the Crown to allow the colony to discourage slave imports by levying duties on slaves. The argument was moral, not economic: "The importation of slaves," the legislators declared, "hath long been considered as a trade of great inhumanity." Moreover, they feared, continued importation "will endanger the very existence of your Majesty's American dominions."[26] The petition never challenged domestic slavery, but by emphasizing the cruelty of the slave trade and a fear of rising numbers of African Americans, Virginia's elite expressed alarm over a system that, not long before, only fringe religious voices like Quakers dared criticize.

Two years later Thomas Jefferson advised Virginia's Continental Congress delegates that "the abolition of domestic slavery is the great object of desire"; he even anticipated a future with "the infranchisement of the slaves we have." This last suggestion, "infranchisement of the slaves," stamped the thirty-one-year-old Jefferson as visionary in 1774; indeed, for a decade his was among the most outspoken voices on natural equality and slavery in Virginia. Like his mentor and fellow signer of the Declaration, George Wythe, dean of Virginia's bar, Jefferson advocated natural equality and supported manumission.[27]

Virginia prohibited importing slaves in 1778 and enacted a general manumission law in 1782 that opened a path toward civil equality for African Americans in Virginia. The next year Jefferson drafted a plan to free Virginia's slaves and proposed a ban on slavery for all new states after 1800. By the 1780s Baptists joined Quakers in calling for an end to slavery, and in the 1790s a few great planters, notably Robert Carter of Nomini Hall and Richard Randolph, liberated dozens, then hundreds of their African American workers. In time, even George Washington became an advocate for emancipation, freeing his own slaves in his will.[28]

By the early 1790s Virginia's elite decided that slavery was undesirable because, as Ferdinando Fairfax, scion of a great family explained, slavery contradicted "natural right and justice." The state's rulers never agreed on any plan to end slavery, but for a time they considered proposals. In 1790 the twenty-four-year-old Fairfax published his "Plan for Liberating the Negroes within the United States" in a national magazine. Voluntary manumission by planters was the first stage, to be succeeded by African colonization. Later, as American prosperity mounted, the Congress should finance a slave "buyout" with transportation to Africa. But planters' property rights must always come before African Americans' "natural right and justice." Fairfax expressed white Virginians' all-but-unanimous view when he declared, "To deprive a man, at once, of all his right in the property of his negroes, would be the *height of injustice*, and such as, in this country, would never be submitted to."[29]

Several years later St. George Tucker submitted his abolition plan to the Virginia General Assembly. Like Jefferson and Fairfax, Tucker explicitly denied the legitimacy of slavery according to the Revolution's doctrine of natural equality. But like other planters he could not imagine a biracial Virginia in which blacks and whites dwelled as civil and political equals. Tucker's solution was not African colonization; instead, he proposed holding blacks in a subordinate "free" status and thereby encouraging their migration to Spanish Florida and Louisiana. Alert to the interests of slaveholders and other white Virginians, his plan would stretch across a century in which blacks as bound labor would continue to provide agricultural production.[30] That the 1796 legislature finally rejected Tucker's "proposal for the gradual abolition" of slavery demonstrates that when the doctrine "all men are created equal" conflicted with the principle of property rights and fear of African American citizenship, nearly every white Virginian chose to maintain slavery.

Ten years after Tucker's plan failed in the legislature, an 1806 freedom suit in Virginia's court of chancery, *Hudgins v. Wrights*, displayed how judicial authorities tackled the conflict over the meaning of "all men are created equal." Here three pauper children, the Wrights, sued their master, Hudgins, for holding them wrongfully in slavery. Tracing descent from a free Indian grandmother, they claimed freedom. According to Chancellor George Wythe, one of the children "was perfectly white," and he ruled the children free. But Wythe did not base his judgment on lineage. Instead, this signer of the Declaration of Independence defended the principles of 1776, proclaiming, "Freedom is the birth right of every human being, which sentiment is strongly inculcated by the first article of our [Virginia's] 'political catechism,' the bill of rights." Accordingly, the burden of proof was not on the children or their lineage because "whenever one person claims to hold another in slavery," the claimant must prove ownership. For the eighty-year-old Wythe, natural equality remained a guiding principle.[31]

But in 1806 the Virginia Supreme Court of Appeals determined otherwise. Ironically, it was Justice St. George Tucker who directly contradicted Chancellor Wythe, noting that his "principles . . . has [sic] been loudly complained of." Race, not the Bill of Rights, ruled the case. The fact that the Wrights appeared white, Tucker said, made them free because "all *white persons* are and ever have been FREE in this country." In contrast, as another justice pointed out, "in the case of a person visibly appearing to be a negro, the presumption is, in this country, that he is a slave, and it is incumbent on him to make out his right to freedom."[32]

Tucker's court overruled the eighty-year-old signer of the Declaration, rejecting the older man's "reasoning on the operation of the first clause of the Bill of Rights, which," Tucker asserted, "was notoriously framed with a cautious eye to this subject, and was meant to embrace the case of free citizens, or aliens only; and not by a side wind to overturn the rights of property, and give freedom to those very people whom we have been compelled from imperious circumstances to retain, generally, in the same state of bondage that they were in at the revolution, in which they had no *concern, agency,* or *interest.*" Tucker here embraced a restricted reading of the Virginia Bill of Rights, whereas ten years earlier he had aligned with Mason and approvingly quoted Montesquieu's belief that "Slavery not only violates the Laws of Nature, and of civil Society, it also wounds the best Forms of Government: in a Democracy, where all Men are equal, Slavery is contrary to the Spirit of the Constitution."[33] Now, in 1806, property rights were paramount. Tucker recognized that natural rights principles contradicted property in persons, but he disavowed the equal rights principle championed by the signer of the Declaration, George Wythe.

Tucker's shift was emblematic of a broad retreat from natural equality by planters in the early 1800s. Alarmed by an increasingly bloody Haitian Revolution that led white planters to take refuge in Virginia with their slaves, Chesapeake slaveholders feared their own uprising. Gabriel's Conspiracy in 1800 threatened Virginia masters with fiery destruction and murder. "Liberty and equality" were appealing doctrines "in a land of freemen," one Virginian commented; but "where every white man is a master and every black man is a slave," such ideals were "dangerous and extremely wicked." By late 1806, when Tucker and his fellow Supreme Court justices reversed Wythe's ruling on the meaning of Virginia's Bill of Rights, the legislature, too, had reversed course on slavery. Worried not only by Gabriel's violent plans but by increasing numbers of free blacks—twelve thousand in 1790, twenty thousand in 1800, and more than thirty thousand in 1810—legislators reversed course on manumission by requiring newly freed persons to leave Virginia or face reenslavement.[34]

By the first decade of the nineteenth century, even before the cotton boom revitalized slavery and slave prices, the doctrine of natural equality was losing its appeal. When African American citizenship moved from a theoretical future to become present reality, many whites embraced a different natural law, one that reinforced old prejudices. They came to justify unequal policies by invoking inherent natural characteristics ranging from physiognomy and skin color to mental aptitudes—a science of race. As with the ideal of natural equality, Thomas Jefferson stood in the vanguard.

In 1782, when Jefferson composed his *Notes on the State of Virginia*, he had begun to collect observations leading to his "scientific" theory of white superiority and black subordination. "The first difference which strikes us is that of color," Jefferson remarked, a "difference fixed in nature." Color, he believed was "the foundation of a greater or less share of beauty in the two races," and he disparaged the "eternal monotony" of black faces, "that immoveable veil of black which covers the emotions." These he contrasted to the "fine mixtures of red and white" complexion, the beauty of "flowing hair," and the "more elegant symmetry of form" possessed by whites. Blacks themselves preferred whites to their own kind, just as "the Oranootan" preferred "the black woman over those of his own species." Since beauty was worth propagating in "horses, dogs, and other domestic animals; why not," he asked, "in . . . man?"[35]

Jefferson also claimed moral superiority for white people who, though they might not claim greater "faculties of memory," were clearly superior in "reason" and "imagination"; blacks, by contrast, were "dull, tasteless, and anomalous." Blacks were, he acknowledged, "at least as brave and more adventuresome" than whites, but this, he explained, "may perhaps proceed from a want of forethought, which prevents their seeing a danger till it be present." And although black men were "more ardent after their female," he was convinced that "love seems with them more an eager desire, than a tender delicate mixture of sentiment and sensation." When blacks were disappointed, he pronounced, "their griefs are transient." Only regarding black musical faculties and African Americans' capacity "to require less sleep" would Jefferson accept unqualified black superiority. Compared with American Indians, whose environmental condition was similarly primitive, the Virginian naturalist judged African Americans inferior.[36]

Jefferson expressed the prejudice he and many of his generation felt in the 1790s and later. When the black savant Benjamin Banneker sent Jefferson the almanac he had prepared in 1791, hoping to convince the secretary of state of black intellectual ability, Jefferson replied evasively: "No body wishes more than I do to see such proofs as you exhibit, that nature has given to our black brethren, talents equal to the other colors of men, and that the appearance of a want of them is owing merely to the degraded condition of their existence both in Africa & America."[37] Jefferson hoped his skepticism toward blacks would prove erroneous, but he believed that it was valid. In claiming that "no body" wanted favorable outcomes more than he, Jefferson could only have meant other elite Virginians like himself, certainly not the African Americans and Quakers whose efforts on behalf of blacks he would have acknowledged were manifestly more vigorous and consistent than his own.

Almost twenty years later, when Jefferson was leaving the White House, he again expressed deep ambivalence on natural equality and race. Responding to the French Revolutionary abolitionist Abbé Henri Grégoire, who sent Jefferson his new book defending black intellectual achievements, Jefferson declared, "No person living wishes more sincerely than I do, to see a complete refutation of the doubts I have myself entertained and expressed on the grade of understanding allotted to them ['Negroes'] by nature and to find that in this respect they are on a par with ourselves." He reaffirmed belief in equal natural rights to the old revolutionary Grégoire, declaring: "whatever be their degree of talent it is no measure of their rights. Because Sir Isaac Newton was superior to others in understanding, he was not therefore lord of the person or property of others." But privately he dismissed Grégoire's book and Banneker, who possessed "a mind of very common stature indeed." The sixty-five-year-old Jefferson had once seemed to reaffirm his mentor George Wythe's understanding of Virginia's Bill of Rights. But by 1809 race thinking had undermined natural equality, and Wythe's principles were "loudly complained of." Jefferson's doubts respecting the natural equality of blacks were becoming the fixed convictions of younger generations.[38]

IV

Regarding Indians, the question of natural equality was largely moot. Because most lived outside the jurisdiction of the states, there was little need to define their place in society or government. And if in 1782 Jefferson was prepared to view them as more nearly equal to whites than blacks, declaring, Indians "astonish you with strokes of the most sublime oratory; such as prove their reason and sentiment strong, their imagination glowing and elevated," prejudices against them were powerful. In 1775 while Congress formulated Indian policy, John Adams described them as "Savages . . . blood Hounds" ready "to scalp Men, and to butcher Women and Children." Congress addressed them as *"Brothers, Sachems, and Warriors"* and *"Brothers and Friends"* when seeking Indian neutrality in July 1775; but the following year Jefferson's words in the Declaration of Independence used Adams's language, calling them "the merciless Indian savages" who made war on persons "of all ages, sexes and conditions." Twenty years later another signer of the Declaration, Benjamin Rush, published a catalog of Indian vices: "uncleanness," "Nastiness," "Drunkenness," "Gluttony," "Treachery," "Cruelty," "Idleness," "Theft," and "Gaming." Rush, a champion of abolition and African American equality, concluded, "The infamy of the Indian character is completed by the low rank to which they degrade their women."[39] Since leading champions of natural equality embraced derogatory beliefs about Indians and African Americans, fulfillment of the ideal of equal rights for these "outsiders" was bound to remain problematic.

The central question posed by the ideal of natural equality was to identify the outsiders in Revolutionary era America. Most Indians had been outsiders literally; and though enslaved blacks lived for generations among white settlers, they had been seen as outsiders, no matter how close their personal connections. So, too, according to English law, were those who did not profess allegiance to the Church of England. But in the colonies settlers of wealth and power often breached the religious boundary between inclusion and exclusion in social participation. The largest New England colonies had drawn different sectarian boundaries than England's, while Rhode Island and Pennsylvania leaders had deliberately rejected religious barriers to political and social equality. Strictly speaking, the English religious boundary applied only in Virginia, Maryland, Delaware, the Carolinas, and, to a lesser degree, New York, where wealthy and powerful Dutch Reformed settlers compromised the formal Anglican establishment. Nevertheless, until 1776 the principle of established religion ruled. A privileged, government-supported religion was normal.[40]

But in the war for independence Americans had to choose between religious privilege and the principle of equality. Revolutionary leaders recognized that if they grasped religious privilege too tightly they might doom their cause. Congress itself included all sorts of Christians—even the Catholic John Carroll—as did the Continental Army; and Congress called on everyone, churched or unchurched, Christian or Jew, to support the cause. As a result, the Revolutionary War itself pressed the case for natural equality on practical grounds.

One vivid example is the Patriots' effort to engage French Canadians and, later, the French monarchy in their struggle. Notwithstanding their own long history of warfare against French Canada and American Patriots' deep anti-Catholicism—expressed in October 1774 when Congress excoriated Catholicism as having "deluged" Britain "in blood, and dispersed impiety, bigotry, persecution, murder and rebellion through every part of the world"—in May 1775 Congress courted "the Oppressed Inhabitants of Canada." Expressing "pity" for their Canadian "friends," Congress proclaimed "the fate of the protestant and catholic colonies to be strongly linked together." Though Patriots had recently protested the Quebec Act because Parliament had "established" Roman Catholicism in Canada, Congress now warned Québécois that "the enjoyment of your very religion . . . depends on a legislature in which you have no share, and over which you have no controul, and your priests are exposed to expulsion, banishment, and ruin."[41]

This opportunistic appeal failed to persuade French Canadians to join their Anglo-American neighbors; but it expressed a new amity toward Roman Catholicism and inclusion of Catholics who supported the American cause. After the French alliance in 1778 the Boston clergyman Samuel Cooper—supported by a secret French subsidy—would actively promote friendship with France and displaced *Canadiens*. And if in the name of equality Patriots could suppress anti-Catholicism, the same pragmatic idealism applied to Protestant inequalities. Here, as with slavery, there was little scope for congressional action, but even before 1776, reform pressure was mounting in some colonies. The movements for religious equality in Virginia and Massachusetts, large colonies that were preeminent in their regions, are revealing.

Massachusetts had led the way in applying the doctrine of natural equality to slavery, but Virginia's legislature set the pace in religion. There, Anglicans and dissenting Baptists had been chafing under their Church of England establishment since the 1750s, when the legislature's conflict with Anglican clergy over salaries erupted in battle with London over Virginia's TwoPenny Act of 1758. Thereafter Dissenters sought religious liberty, and in 1769 the legislature named a "Committee for Religion" to draft a toleration law. But establishment supporters blocked action, and in 1772 when the committee finally presented its bill, the discriminatory religious establishment remained. Now Baptists mounted new protests, but the larger conflict with Parliament pushed religious questions aside until the Virginia convention adopted its momentous Bill of Rights on June 12, 1776.[42]

The first provision of this bill had asserted the natural equality of "all men." The last declared equal freedom of religion: "Religion, or the duty which we owe to our Creator, and the manner of discharging it, can be directed only by reason and conviction, not by force or violence; and therefore all men are equally entitled to the free exercise of religion, according to the dictates of conscience; and that it is the mutual duty of all to practice Christian forbearance, love, and charity towards each other."[43] On its face, just as the Bill of Rights seemed to forbid the inequality of slavery, so it seemed to prohibit inequality of religious establishments.

That was how Baptists, Presbyterians, and Lutherans understood it, but not the Anglican clergy. They accepted toleration but claimed that preserving their establishment was important for "peace and happiness" because beliefs necessary for social virtue "can be best taught and preserved in their purity by an established church." Although most Virginians were Dissenters, most legislators were Anglican, so while legislators debated disestablishment in the fall 1776, they preserved the establishment until 1779—when the British invaded Virginia and the state needed all the help it could muster from Dissenting citizens. Still, Church of England supporters blocked Governor Jefferson's statute for religious liberty until 1786, when Dissenters finally realized the promise of the 1776 Virginia Bill of Rights. Henceforward, natural equality included matters of conscience. Religion would be no part of government oversight or responsibility—belief or nonbelief would "in no wise diminish, enlarge, or affect" civil rights.[44]

Massachusetts did not travel so far so fast. A colony that hanged Quakers in 1661 and witches in 1692 did not, as a state, quickly accept complete disestablishment or terminate blasphemy prosecutions. As in Virginia, Baptists led protests against paying taxes for Massachusetts' established orthodox Calvinist church. By 1770 Baptists charged Patriots with hypocrisy. Patriots, they said, were quick to berate Parliament for taxation without consent, but they remained determined to "impose cruelly upon their neighbors, and force large sums from them to uphold a worship which they [their neighbors] conscientiously dissent from." Patriot churchmen saw it otherwise. Because the law made allowances to excuse Baptists from church taxes if they paid to support Baptist clergy, orthodox leaders claimed that charges of religious persecution were false. As one tax-supported clergyman put it: "I hate every species of persecution."[45]

The radical character of Jefferson's Virginia Statute of Religious Liberty is evident in comparison to the religious provisions in the 1780 Massachusetts Declaration of Rights, written by John Adams, Jefferson's quasi-Deist partner on the Declaration of Independence. In its opening line Massachusetts proclaimed that "all men are born free and equal, and have certain natural, essential, and unalienable rights," guaranteeing everyone the right "to worship the SUPREME BEING . . . in the manner and season most agreeable to the dictates of his own conscience." But Massachusetts decreed that public worship was "the duty of all men in society," in order to secure "the happiness of the people, and the good order and preservation of civil government." Consistent with the top-down ethos of the Puritan commonwealth, religion must not be left purely to the voluntarism of citizens as in Virginia.

Accordingly, Massachusetts's Bill of Rights balanced religious equality with an assertion of the state's right to "require" all communities to provide "support and maintenance of public *protestant* teachers of piety, religion and morality." Forgetting, revealingly, that Massachusetts people were now *citizens* of a republic, the Bill of Rights authorized the legislature "to enjoin upon all the *subjects* an attendance upon the instructions of the public teachers." All taxpaying "subjects" must pay for "support of public worship" and must maintain the "public teacher" of the taxpayer's "own religion." If the locality possessed no such teacher, the taxes of the Dissenter or unchurched citizen would support the local established clergyman. Proclaiming the principle of equality to "every denomination of Christians, demeaning themselves peaceably, and as good subjects of the Commonwealth," the 1780 Bill of Rights asserted that all would "be equally under the protection of the law."[46]

Unlike Virginia, Massachusetts rejected separation of church and state, preferring a plural Protestant establishment that favored existing established churches and clergymen. For the minority who supported no religion actively or whose sects did not employ a clergyman—as well as the handful of Catholics, Jews, and Muslims—the provision of "equality" was false. Baptists, who were supposed to be protected by the Massachusetts Bill of Rights, complained that compelling them to attend services and pay religious taxes interfered with religious freedom.

John Leland, the Massachusetts native who led Virginia Baptists to join Madison and Jefferson to reform Virginia's laws, dismissed the principle on which Massachusetts and Connecticut based their "religious freedom" statutes. It was not everyone's duty "to support the worship of God." This presumption, Leland argued, was flat wrong: "Is it the duty of a deist to support that which he believes to be a threat and an imposition? Is it the duty of a Jew to support the religion of Jesus Christ, when he really believes that he was an imposter [sic]? Must the papists be forced to pay men for preaching down the supremacy of the pope, whom they are sure is head of the church? Must a Turk maintain a religion opposed to the alcoran, which he holds as the sacred oracles of heaven?" Leland looked beyond the Protestant consensus to advocate a state that steered clear of religion. As townspeople in Ashby, Massachusetts, explained, legislatures had no business meddling with religion: "He that made us reasonable Creatures and Conferd upon us the Blessing of the Gospell has . . . laid us under the strongest Obligation to the practice of Piety, Religeon, and Morality that can possibly be conceived, & if this wont impress our minds to doe our Duty nothing will." In the same spirit, the Virginia Statute of Religious Liberty provided that "no man shall be compelled to frequent or support any religious worship, place or ministry whatsoever."[47] Not only did Virginia terminate religious establishment, but it created a virtually level playing field for religions.

Yet even though the Virginia statute approached full equality of religion, it retained assumptions of the Protestant Enlightenment. "Almighty God hath created the mind free," the statute began, and declared as an undeniable truth that "the Holy author of our religion . . . chose not to propagate it by coercions" on either "body or mind." Jefferson's and Virginia's vision recalled the seventeenth-century Dissenter John Milton, who declared, "Truth is great and will prevail if left to herself."[48] As one might expect, even the most radical revolutionary pronouncements remained bound by their political and intellectual context.

V

Cultural inertia was nowhere more evident than on the possession and disposition of property. Here the meaning of equality in the Declaration's motto was opaque. Jefferson and his congressional colleagues replaced Locke's "life, liberty and property" with "Life, Liberty and the pursuit of Happiness," but neither Locke nor Congress ever imagined that natural equality meant anything like equal distribution of property. Unlike England's revolution, the American Revolution never produced Levelers. Locke argued that in the state of nature men had an equal right to acquire property, but he expected that they would do so unequally and he defended unequal possession as he also defended enslavement of captives of war. American leaders did not embrace Locke's views on slavery, but they shared his understanding of property ownership as a requisite for personal independence and freedom. Where property was concerned, Parliament and imperial administrators had learned that Americans were hypersensitive but certainly not egalitarian.

Yet traces of the seventeenth-century Leveler impulse remained in Revolutionaries' ideas of natural equality and their beliefs about moral and political economy. Observing Virginia, one British officer noted, "The spirit of independency was converted into equality, and every one who bore arms, esteemed himself upon a footing with his neighbour." Similar views prevailed in New England, where the once honorific title "Mister" replaced common social ranks like "yeoman" and "husbandman"; and a Yale-educated clergyman reported, "Every man thinks himself at least as good as his neighbors, and believes that all mankind have, or ought to possess equal rights."[49]

As Virginia's repeal of primogeniture and entail suggested, many believed that the wealthy should not monopolize ever-greater shares of wealth and power. Small property owners had a stake in society to defend, and the state must keep property ownership open to the "people"—many of whom were impoverished war veterans or the sons and brothers of veterans. In Pennsylvania some went so far as to declare that greedy men must not be allowed to accumulate unlimited real estate, because "an enormous Proportion of Property vested in a few individuals is dangerous to the Rights and destructive of the Common happiness of Mankind."[50] Still, except for the landholdings of some Loyalists and the important movement to end primogeniture and entail, Revolutionaries showed no interest in dispossessing the wealthy. Instead, when they looked at the undeveloped lands in their own states from Maine to Georgia and in United States territories stretching to Florida, the Mississippi, and the Great Lakes, elites battled Revolutionary War veterans for advantage from the 1780s onward.

Most of all Americans valued equal opportunities to acquire property, not equal distribution. When Jefferson declared that Isaac Newton's superior intellect did not make him "lord of the person or property of others," he was expressing a widespread American belief. This type of egalitarian doctrine was compatible with social and economic inequality and their resulting disparities in political influence. Jefferson's celebrated "democratic" public school plan for Virginia embraced hierarchy explicitly. He was proud that his system would select "twenty of the best geniuses . . . from the rubbish annually." Jefferson regarded ordinary minds as "rubbish," and even John Adams, who wrote "all men are born equal" in 1766, later spoke of the "common Herd of Mankind," the very same people Washington called "the grazing multitude."[51] As Gordon Wood explained, when the framers of the Declaration of Independence and state constitutions spoke of equality in relation to property, "they meant most obviously equality of opportunity."[52]

One aspect of natural equality that they never seriously contemplated was equality for women or children. Nature, they believed, dictated permanent, insurmountable inequality. Though Abigail Adams and a handful of other elite women would assert some form of equal rights in the 1770s, Revolutionary leaders declined to address the subject. Because their concept of equality began with their own equivalence to British subjects whose rights were bound up with property ownership, to conceive of women or children as naturally possessing equal rights seemed absurd. When women or children did own property, by law men normally controlled it; nature dictated women's and children's dependency on husbands, fathers, or their surrogates. When Jefferson and his congressional colleagues employed the words "all men" to express the boundaries of natural equality, they used the words reflexively, not literally—as we have seen for men who were "outsiders."

But if the meaning of their language could be construed to include slaves and Dissenters, why not women or even children? In less than a generation the boundary of sex, as with religion and race, would be challenged. Some read the Declaration's promise of natural equality symbolically; but others read it literally. In time, interested people would assert its meaning both ways.[53] Yet in the years after 1776 the Declaration of Independence, having served its purpose, faded from political discourse.

Revolutionaries had to fight the war, develop foreign relations, and launch state governments, as well as frame constitutions. They had no need for the Declaration as a guide. But often questions of equality came to the fore. Every discussion of representation, apportionment, and taxation revolved around arguments of "fairness," keeping the ideal of equality in play. Although competing beliefs such as the "stake in society" principle—basing representation on possession of property, as well as wealth requirements for high office—often carried the day, natural equality remained a core principle. When the states had to formulate policies on the relation of church and state and on civil rights during the 1770s and 1780s, citizens and lawmakers contested their understandings of natural equality.

In 1775 a Loyalist had denounced the Revolutionaries and their "popular, dangerous, and fallacious" notion "that the whole human race is born equal; and that no man is naturally inferior, or in any respect subjected to another, and that he can be made subject to another only by his consent." Basing government on ideas like consent and equality, he said, was "fantastic."[54] A year later the Declaration proclaimed otherwise. But whether its grand principle was true or could be realized, even partially, remained to be seen. Revolutionary leaders had embarked on nation-founding by proclaiming ideals that were far from describing the world in which they actually dwelled.

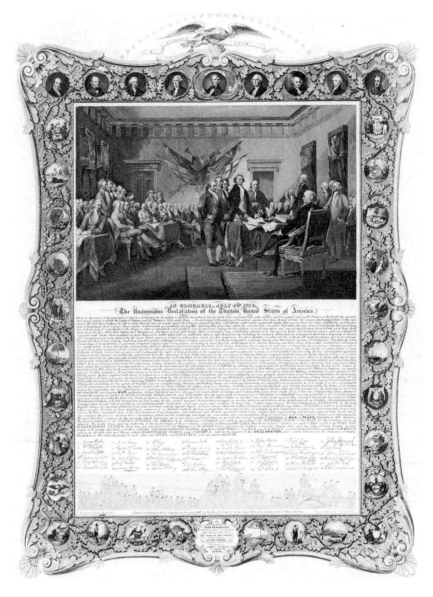

John Trumbull's "Signing of the Declaration" with text reproduced in ornate frame, Boston, 1841. The engraving of the formal painting and the document itself within an elaborate frame elevate the Declaration to sacred status. Courtesy, American Antiquarian Society.

In 1788 one founder portrayed his fellow Americans as "one united people—a people descended from the same ancestors, speaking the same language, professing the same religion, attached to the same principles of government, [and] very similar in their manners and customs." John Jay, the New Yorker who penned this vision in advocating ratification of the Constitution, was the grandson and great-grandson of Huguenot and Dutch immigrants who had married a descendant of Scots, English, and Dutch immigrants. Jay and his sons would go on to embrace the abolition of slavery and equal rights for African Americans, advancing an ideal of equality as well as unity. Though Jay recognized that Americans were divided into "orders and denominations," he claimed "to all general purposes we have uniformly been one people [,] each individual citizen everywhere enjoying the same national rights, privileges, and protection."[55] The notion of equality had captivated this college-bred gentleman's imagination; and he was not alone. But whether his generation and their successors could or would fulfill that ideal was a mystery.

The chapters that follow explore the extent to which Jay's sublime assertion, that Americans were "one people . . . everywhere enjoying the same national rights, privileges, and protection," was accurate or at least prophetic. In a land where people of many origins, many hues, and many faiths dwelled together—divided as well by social class and gender—the realization of Jay's ideal was hard to imagine. It was, perhaps, what never was and never will be.[56] But the struggles and contests generated by this presumption of equal rights have shaped the history of the United States from the Revolution to the Civil War, and beyond.

TWO

Contending for Religious Equality

That religion, or the duty which we owe to our Creator, and the
manner of discharging it, can be directed only by reason
and conviction, not by force or violence; and therefore all men
are equally entitled to the free exercise of religion, according to the
dictates of conscience; and that it is the mutual duty of all to practice
Christian forbearance, love, and charity towards each other.
—*Virginia Declaration of Rights, June 12, 1776*

R eligious equality is not mentioned in the assertion "All men are created
equal and endowed by their creator with certain unalienable Rights,
that among these are Life, Liberty and the pursuit of Happiness," but for the
men who wrote the Declaration of Independence and voted for it in July
1776, the equal right to one's personal religious belief was axiomatic.[1] Like
enlightened people all over the Atlantic world, they believed that faith must
always be a matter of choice, not coercion, and that this freedom to choose
one's beliefs was a natural right. Nevertheless most delegates came from
colonies that, though they allowed choice, also maintained established
churches. By allowing Dissenting Protestants to worship, they practiced toleration, not religious equality. So whether the new states and the United
States should move from toleration to full-fledged equality was a question
dividing Americans from Maine to Georgia.

Most American states began their movement toward religious equality
easily. Two colonies, Rhode Island and Pennsylvania, had at their founding
opposed church establishments on principle. Rhode Island practiced equal-

ity among Protestants, and Pennsylvania equality among Christians even before Parliament made toleration of Protestant Dissenters and Roman Catholics imperial policy in 1689. Subsequently, to encourage commercial development Parliament allowed naturalization of foreign Protestants in 1709 and enabled Jews to become citizens in the American colonies in 1740. In 1753 Parliament even passed a law permitting Jews to apply for naturalized British citizenship. In Britain, however, these liberal Whig policies were short-lived—Parliament repealed naturalization of foreign Protestants after three years and naturalization of Jews after just a single year—but colonial eagerness to encourage trade enabled foreign Protestants and Jewish merchants to settle.[2]

Consequently, by the time the Continental Congress met in 1774 the colonists were comfortable with a degree of toleration—and a measure of religious equality—unknown in Britain. Whereas statutes barred dissenting Protestants and Catholics from both Houses of Parliament, Congress never contemplated religious tests, and its members included Congregationalists, Presbyterians, and even a Catholic in addition to the Anglican majority. Moreover the imperial conflict led American patriots to downplay their religious differences conspicuously; so when Congress opened its proceedings, the staunch Congregationalist Samuel Adams proposed the Anglican Reverend Jacob Duché to serve as chaplain. Adams sought to reassure delegates from the middle colonies and the south that New Englanders, once known for persecuting Quakers, were not religious zealots. His ecumenical gesture was symbolic, however; with seven colonies supporting the Church of England and three maintaining Congregational establishments, the patriot cause needed bridge building.[3]

As such, the issue of religious equality was never central to the Patriot cause. From time to time colonists had chafed under Church of England policies, such as requiring ordination of priests in London and locating an Anglican mission church beside dissenting Harvard College. And Virginia's legislature battled imperial authorities over the Crown's plan to pay Anglican priests according to the 1758 Two-Penny Act. But the core of the independence movement was taxation and colonial governance, not religious liberty.

Yet when Congress declared independence and rested its claims on natural equality, commitment to liberty of conscience was understood. The June 12, 1776, Virginia Declaration of Rights—drafted almost simultaneously with the Declaration of Independence, chiefly by the Anglicans George Mason and James Madison—proclaimed "that religion, or the duty which we owe to our Creator, and the manner of discharging it, can be directed only by reason and conviction, not by force or violence; and therefore all men are equally entitled to the free exercise of religion, according to the dictates of conscience."[4] New Jersey, acting on July 2, 1776, the same day Congress voted independence, similarly declared, "No person shall ever, within this Colony, be deprived of the inestimable privilege of worshipping Almighty God in a manner, agreeable to the dictates of his own conscience; nor, under any pretence whatever, be compelled to attend any place of worship, contrary to his own faith and judgment." And Pennsylvania echoed Virginia's bill of rights in September 1776, declaring, "All men are born equally free and independent," and concurring that "all men have a natural and unalienable right to worship Almighty God according to the dictates of their own consciences and understanding." At the end of the year North Carolina proclaimed the same belief in its declaration of rights.[5]

I

These declarations joined Patriots of different faiths, uniting Baptists especially with the Revolutionary cause. For their time, such enlightened assertions of religious equality were radical. Even when qualified by the requirement of belief in God, as in Pennsylvania, or faith in "Protestant religion," as in North Carolina, these broad statements of natural equality undermined the standing religious order based on toleration. According to the toleration policy prescribed by Parliament in 1689, equality was never intended among Dissenting Protestants, Catholics, and the established, tax-supported Church of England. Anglican bishops sat in the House of Lords; Anglican ecclesiastical courts possessed jurisdiction over everyone; and only members of the Church of England enjoyed access to public office and the universities. In North America, it is true, the toleration regime had been looser than Britain's and religious establishment diminished. Not a single colony housed a resident bishop, possessed ecclesiastical courts, or maintained a hereditary legislature. But ten colonies operated tax-supported churches, and most prescribed religious tests for office holding. When Patriots moved toward independence, they cried, "No taxation without representation," not "Religious equality and no establishment." But their bold natural rights pronouncements of 1776 encouraged religious minorities to challenge the American establishments and to claim equal treatment.

So when the new governments considered religion in their states, the policies they would adopt were not predetermined. Dissenters, usually led by Baptists both in the South, where the Church of England reigned, and in New England, where Congregationalism was established, had long argued for separation between church and state. Compulsory tax payments to support clergymen and churches, they said, must end. But many Revolutionaries supported their relatively relaxed establishments all the more strongly now that the colonies had broken free from Britain. Social order and morals, they feared, could collapse without the reinforcement of state-aided religion.

But under demographic and political pressure defenders of the status quo yielded. In 1760 over 60 percent of churches belonged to established denominations—Anglican or Congregational—but by 1790 these denominations comprised fewer than 30 percent of all churches, and Dissenters won relaxation of establishment restrictions or outright disestablishment. Though religious taxes might still be required, Dissenting Protestants, for example, could now direct them to their own church. Another compromise provided for multisect religious support, whereby the state would require (with a few exceptions) inhabitants to pay tithes to the Christian religion of their choice. Only when residents designated no choice would their taxes default to the established church. A third response was to accept the radical logic of the natural religious equality argument, "no coercion of conscience," and end all religious taxes. Usually this radical solution allowed indirect subsidies to all religions equally, such as tax exemptions for church property and for clergymen. Though the playing field was not strictly level, sects could freely compete so long as they respected the rights of others.[6]

Each state determined questions of religion because state governments alone possessed authority to regulate religion. Sometimes legislators boldly created a religious equality regime. Elsewhere disagreements turned policy in a zigzag pattern, as twists, turns and compromises revealed the complexities of people's sentiments about religion and equality. In the province of New-York, where the prewar status quo had resembled Britain, Revolutionaries made a clean break.

They began with an established Anglican Church and a 1691 royal instruction on toleration—unchanged through 1771—directing New-York's governor to "permit liberty of Conscience to all persons except Papists," not as a right but as a privilege.[7] Though Huguenots and Jews could settle freely and worship publicly like Quakers and other Protestant dissenters, New-York forbade Catholic worship. The Quebec Act in 1774, whereby Parliament formally established Roman Catholicism in the newly conquered colony of French Catholics, set off a fresh storm of colonial anti-Catholic rhetoric. But it was papered over by Congress's appeal to the inhabitants of Canada in May 1775—the Americans declaring "the fate of the protestant and catholic colonies to be strongly linked together." The next year, hoping to gain Canadian support, Congress sent a Maryland Catholic, Father John Carroll, as emissary to Montreal.[8] Still, Protestant suspicions of Catholics remained. When Thomas Paine sought to mobilize the colonists, he called on the everyday Protestant reservoirs of anti-Catholic and anti-Jewish sentiment. He proclaimed in *Common Sense*, "Monarchy in every instance is the Popery of government" and "ranked in scripture as one of the sins of the Jews, for which a curse in reserve is denounced against them."[9]

So when the New York State Constitutional Convention rejected not only established religion but also shifted toward religious equality in 1777, the move was radical. Three articles in the New York Constitution of 1777 laid out the new regime. First, disestablishment: all laws "as may be construed to establish or maintain any particular denomination of Christians or their ministers, . . . are repugnant to this constitution, . . . and they hereby are, abrogated and rejected." New Yorkers terminated all support for the Church of England; and no other would take its place. Second, to reinforce the separation of church and state, the constitution excluded all "ministers of the gospel . . . or priest of any denomination" from "holding, any civil or military office."[10] Most dramatic, the constitution expressed broad commitment to religious equality:

> We are required, by the benevolent principles of rational liberty, not only to expel civil tyranny, but also to guard against that spiritual oppression and intolerance wherewith the bigotry and ambition of weak and wicked priests and princes have scourged mankind, this convention doth further . . . declare, that the free exercise and enjoyment of religious profession and worship, without discrimination or preference, shall forever hereafter be allowed, within this State, to all mankind: *Provided,* That the liberty of conscience, hereby granted, shall not be so construed as to excuse acts of licentiousness, or justify practices inconsistent with the peace or safety of this State.[11]

Despite the province's long record of anti-Catholic regulation and mistrust, and notwithstanding the opposition of the prominent Huguenot and Dutch-descended Patriot leader John Jay, who argued in the convention against toleration for Catholics—even advocating that they be denied the right to hold land, vote, or hold office—New York moved decisively toward religious equality. Now Catholics could worship in public and possess all civil rights. At war's end the legislature repealed New York's now defunct ban on Catholicism.[12]

Nevertheless enduring fears of the papacy—"weak and wicked priests and princes"—surfaced in New York's new policy. Voters could now be required to swear (or affirm) allegiance to New York. For immigrants, whose naturalization included a loyalty oath, John Jay succeeded in adding a barrier to block Catholics. Every new citizen and voter must renounce all loyalty to foreign kings or officials, both civil and ecclesiastical. Quakers could "affirm" rather than swear, and no faith barrier blocked Jews from citizenship. But Catholics, mostly immigrants who recognized the pope as head of their church, could not conscientiously refuse loyalty to him and so were denied equal access to citizenship and political rights. New York City Catholics petitioned Congress for relief in 1783, but Congress, lacking jurisdiction, referred them to the author of their disability, New York's legislature. For a generation the state's exclusionary oaths undermined the grand principles of New York's 1777 constitution. Not until 1802 would a Catholic be allowed to hold office in New York City, and it would take four years and the petitions of thirteen hundred Catholics and their supporters before the legislature removed the barrier word "ecclesiastical" from the loyalty oath so that Catholics could sit among its members. One further egalitarian consequence of this step was allowing state funds to subsidize a New York City Catholic school, just as the state subsidized Protestant schools. In 1821, when the state revised its constitution, delegates erased all traces of religious discrimination from New York's highest law.[13] Several years later a Jewish immigrant from Germany claimed, "Here we are all the same, all the religions are honored and respected and have the same rights."[14]

In New York the revolutionary momentum of overthrowing royal government and fighting British troops brought an early proclamation of religious equality, followed by backsliding before a reassertion of equal rights. Virginia, like New York, possessed a British-style Anglican establishment and followed a path that was similar in some ways yet distinctive in others. Moreover, from Virginia came broadly influential pronouncements that have echoed through American history.

One central reason for the difference is the exceptional stature of Thomas Jefferson and the prominence of James Madison, two future presidents whose seminal voices on the subject of natural religious equality have mattered far more than any thoughts on religion uttered by New Yorkers John Jay and Alexander Hamilton. Another reason was the Baptists' role in creating Virginia's model for religious liberty. Unlike Catholics, Baptists were a large and growing presence in nearly every state, so Virginia's intense struggles and ultimate religious arrangements were representative and influential. Several years later both Kentucky and Tennessee followed Virginia's lead.[15] And timing mattered: ten years after the Declaration, with independence assured and republican governments taking root, after extended debate a broad range of citizens were ready to resolve the issue of religious equality—which had not been true in wartime. Consequently, Virginia achieved a preeminent role in the decentralized history of religious equality in the United States.

Virginia Patriots enunciated the principle of religious liberty early. Article 16 of their June 1776 Declaration of Rights had laid down the principle that "all men are equally entitled to the free exercise of religion"; and while Jefferson was drafting the Declaration of Independence he also composed a Virginia constitution, asserting, "All persons shall have full and free liberty of religious opinion; nor shall any be compelled to frequent or maintain any religious institution." But Virginia lagged behind New York owing to fierce opposition to disestablishment, mounted by established clergymen and their Patriot allies, sometimes including Methodists. Anglican priests and their gentry collaborators, men who defended priestly salaries in the late 1750s, had long resisted challenges by dissenting Presbyterians and Baptists. Virginia, they claimed, would drown in immorality, infidelity, and chaos if the state withdrew church support. Not so, answered the Dissenters. Besides, they should not be required to pay taxes for a church they did not accept when their own sects required money. Rejecting all establishments, Christian or otherwise, Hanover County Presbyterians declared—in a petition that expressed James Madison's identical belief—that if the state could establish one religion, it could establish any religion, even Islam or Roman Catholicism. From Prince Edward County came the Deist-sounding call for "an asylum for free inquiry, knowledge, and the virtuous of every denomination."[16] Article 16 of the Virginia Bill of Rights possessed momentum.

The 1776 General Assembly responded: the delegates vacated all parliamentary statutes privileging the Church of England, suspended fixed salaries for Anglican priests, and exempted dissenters from church taxes. The established church still commanded taxes from everyone else, including Deists and nonbelievers, so-called Nothingarians, and it retained control over revenues from glebe lands set aside to support the parish poor. But these concessions to the growing number of Dissenters brought relative peace for several years. Dissenters and Nothingarians nevertheless resented the Church of England's preferred position; and when Deist Thomas Jefferson succeeded Anglican Patrick Henry as governor in June 1779, the struggle over religious liberty resumed. Later Jefferson remembered that controversy as the most bitter of his conflict-ridden career.[17]

Jefferson rejected the argument that disestablishment would promote chaos and infidelity, since nearby Pennsylvania, known for sobriety, virtue, order, and productivity, had flourished under religious liberty. Influenced by John Locke's *Essay concerning Toleration* (1667), Jefferson believed that since God did not compel people to seek salvation, it was wrong for the state to try. So in 1779, with the assistance of James Madison in the General Assembly and in league with Presbyterians and Baptists, Jefferson moved to end the Anglican establishment. But while the House of Delegates tabled Jefferson's statute of religious liberty, the delegates ended Anglican tax support.[18] Fighting a rear-guard battle, the Church of England retained designated land rentals and exclusive control over marriage fees.

Several years later, in 1784 and 1785, with Patrick Henry as governor and with Jefferson in France and his statute for religious liberty lying dormant on the table, the Anglicans, joined by some Methodists and Dissenters, brought forward a "Bill establishing a Provision for Teachers of Religion." Led by Henry, they proposed a multiple establishment whereby a general tax assessment would pay salaries of "Teachers"—that is, clergy—of the leading denominations. For Virginians who believed that maintaining clergymen and churches was essential for a virtuous, orderly republic, this quasi–religious equality seemed a reasonable compromise between the alternatives of support for a single preferred religion and no support for religion. In addition to Patrick Henry, prominent Revolutionaries such as Richard Henry Lee and John Marshall favored the bill, and George Washington, a nominal Anglican with Deist beliefs, found the plan reasonable.[19] Washington explained to George Mason that he accepted "making people pay towards the support of that which they profess, if of the denomination of Christians, or declare themselves Jews, Mahometans, or otherwise, and thereby obtain proper relief." Yet Washington refused to champion the plan, wishing that "the bill could die an easy death; because I think it will be productive of more quiet to the State."[20]

This proposal for tax-supported clergy had indeed raised determined opposition. John Leland, a transplanted New England Baptist elder, argued that if the law awarded salaries to Baptists like himself, it would violate the principle of voluntary support. Coercion must have no place in religion. Discovering an articulate Christian advocate in Leland, Deists like Jefferson and Madison made common cause. They insisted that religious liberty was a natural right and that citizens' first allegiance was to God and then society; hence the state, as agent of society, must not interfere. So ardent was Madison in opposing the "Teachers of Religion" initiative that he prepared an anonymous broadside, "The Memorial and Remonstrance against Religious Assessments," for circulation as a petition. His fellow Virginians returned over a dozen of his printed petitions to the assembly, bearing more than fifteen hundred signatures.[21]

Madison's statement was a landmark of Enlightenment advocacy for natural equality of religions and for separation of church and state. Beginning by quoting Jefferson's draft of the Virginia Statute of Religious Freedom—still resting in legislative limbo—the petitioners echoed the Declaration of

A BILL *for eſtabliſhing* RELIGIOUS FREEDOM, *printed for the conſideration of the* PEOPLE.

WELL aware that the opinions and belief of men depend not on their own will, but follow involuntarily the evidence propoſed to their minds, that Almighty God hath created the mind free, and manifeſted his Supreme will that free it ſhall remain, by making it altogether infuſceptible of reſtraint: That all attempts to influence it by temporal puniſhments or burthens, or by civil incapacitations, tend only to beget habits of hypocriſy and meanneſs, and are a departure from the plan of the holy author of our religion, who being Lord both of body and mind, yet choſe not to propagate it by coercions on either, as was in his Almighty power to do, but to extend it by its influence on reaſon alone: That the impious preſumption of legiſlators and rulers, civil as well as eccleſiaſtical, who, being themſelves but fallible and uninſpired men, have aſſumed dominion over the faith of others, ſetting up their own opinions and modes of thinking, as the only true and infallible, and as ſuch, endeavouring to impoſe them on others, hath eſtabliſhed and maintained falſe religions over the greateſt part of the world, and through all time: That to compel a man to furniſh contributions of money for the propagation of opinions which he diſbelieves and abhors, is ſinful and tyrannical: That even the forcing him to ſupport this or that teacher of his own religious perſuaſion, is depriving him of the comfortable liberty of giving his contributions to the particular paſtor whoſe morals he would make his pattern, and whoſe powers he feels moſt perſuaſive to righteouſneſs, and is withdrawing from the Miniſtry thoſe temporal rewards which, proceeding from an approbation of their perſonal conduct, are an additional incitement to earneſt and unremitting labour for the inſtruction of mankind: That our civil rights have no dependance on our religious opinions, any more than on our opinions in phyſicks or geometry:

"A BILL for ESTABLISHING RELIGIOUS FREEDOM," 1779. As governor of Virginia Thomas Jefferson circulated his draft of the Bill for Establishing Religious Freedom as war raged in 1779, though James Madison could not secure its passage through the House of Burgesses until 1786. Courtesy, Trustees of the Boston Public Library.

James Madison, by Charles Willson Peale, 1783.
Courtesy, Library of Congress.

Independence by asserting that religious liberty "is in its nature an unalienable right," exempt from society's authority and from legislative control. If the state were permitted to extract taxes for Christianity, "in exclusion of all other Religions," the state could also establish a "particular sect of Christians, in exclusion of all other sects." Equality, petitioners argued, must be paramount "and ought to be the basis of every law"; the "Provision for Teachers of Religion," by contrast, "violates equality" because it taxed some citizens while exempting others (Quakers and Mennonites). History had proved that Christianity needed no state support; indeed, after almost fifteen hundred years' trial, the historical record showed the opposite; that establishments produced "pride and indolence in the Clergy, ignorance and servility in the laity, [and] in both superstition, bigotry and persecution."[22]

If Virginia now enacted this establishment law, Madison and his fellow petitioners claimed, the larger mission of the Revolution would be undermined. "Instead of holding forth an Asylum to the persecuted," Virginia law would establish the very persecution that "degrades from the equal rank of Citizens all those whose opinions in Religion do not bend to those of the Legislative authority." Though the Virginia proposal might seem distant "from the Inquisition," the petitioners declared that "it differs from it only in degree." Most fundamental of all, this "Provision for Teachers of Religion" could undo the entire rights regime of the free Republic. Equal rights in religion were inseparable from other rights because all rights were "equally the gift of nature." If the legislature could restrict religion, it could "sweep away all our fundamental rights"; freedom of the press, jury trial—even the right of suffrage might be erased.[23] This extreme rhetorical stance illustrates the profound opposition of some Virginia voters to the clergy's seeming threat to their enlightened republic.

An even more popular petition, signed by three times more voters than Madison's "Memorial and Remonstrance," focused the argument against state-supported teachers of religion on the "Spirit of the Gospel," not natural equality. For Baptists, especially, the idea that support for their faith would be compulsory, not voluntary, was anathema. Even Presbyterians who supported the bill in the early spring, and whose sect defended their state assistance in New England, turned against it in the summer of 1785. After a sermon on Matthew, "Render, therefore unto Caesar the things that be Caesar's, and unto God the things that are God's," the great Presbyterian convention of ministers and lay representatives in Augusta County voted unanimously "against the bill, for establishing a provision for teachers of the Christian religion."[24] By the time the legislature returned in October 1785, opinion had turned overwhelmingly against the teachers of religion bill. Sectarian petitions criticized it, and of the nearly fifty counties that responded to the General Assembly's request for advice, just seven favored it. In all some eleven thousand Virginians attested their opposition with signatures. Madison was triumphant. Popular opposition had killed the establishment proposal, opening the path for resurrecting Jefferson's statute of religious liberty.[25]

Madison immediately took the offensive by bringing up Jefferson's old bill, whose fundamental principles had been restated in the "Memorial and Remonstrance." On October 31, 1785, Madison proposed the Statute for Religious Freedom among a multitude of legal revisions. The text of Jefferson's bill, extensively circulated in the press since 1779, was eighteenth-century America's most dramatic statement of religious freedom and equality. Like Madison's "Memorial and Remonstrance," Jefferson's statute began with Locke's proposition that God "created the mind free." Temporal punishments had no place in the design of "the Holy author of our religion" and should not be imposed by any civil or ecclesiastical power. "Our civil rights," the law stated, "have no dependence on our religious opinions, any more than our opinions in physics or geometry." The preamble's case for unfettered religious choice closed with a prohibition against the "dangerous fallacy" of magistrates' interference in "the field of opinion"; paraphrasing John Milton, "Truth is great and will prevail if left to herself." Having stipulated these premises, the statute directed: "No man shall be compelled to frequent or support any religious worship," and "all men shall be free to profess . . . their opinion in matters of religion," without in any way affecting "their civil capacities."[26]

Six weeks later, when it seemed that the statute might be lost to delay among unrelated proposals, Madison called up the bill and the House of Delegates swiftly passed it the week before Christmas by the decisive vote of seventy-four to twenty. When delegates proposed an amendment so that "Jesus Christ" would be identified as "the Holy author of our religion," Jefferson boasted later that "a great majority" voted the change down. Jefferson believed that the "great majority" shared his intention to protect "the Jew and the Gentile, the Christian and Mahometan, the Hindoo, and infidel of every denomination." In short, the law's "protection of opinion was meant to be universal." A month later, after the senate adopted minor changes, the house voted final passage, and the Statute for Religious Freedom became law on January 19, 1786.[27]

Virginia's law, with its fully developed, unambiguous preamble setting forth the principles of religious freedom, moved decisively beyond toleration to religious equality. No religion stood above others, indeed the statute even accorded the absence of belief equal stature with formally incorporated religious societies. Though article 16 of the 1776 Declaration of Rights had suggested as much, the legislative wrangles of the ensuing decade had demonstrated that even in the minds of Revolutionaries like Patrick Henry, an Anglican who championed Baptist liberation, it was enough to tolerate religious diversity — to allow people to choose their religion without coercion. It was neither necessary nor desirable to treat all religious beliefs equally by stating explicitly that no sect ranked higher than others.

II

In Pennsylvania the 1776 declaration of rights, which preceded the state's new constitution, had assured full civil rights to everyone "who acknowledges the being of a God," a guarantee approaching complete religious freedom. Indeed, citizens embraced the state's policy generally since it gave no offense to Baptists, Catholics, Mennonites, Methodists, Presbyterians, Quakers, or any of the other Christian sects who had flocked to Pennsylvania in the century since the founder, William Penn, had proclaimed toleration in his proprietary colony. But notwithstanding the assurance of civil rights for all believers, the new constitution included a "religious test" for legislators. Each member must swear: "I do believe in one God, the creator and governor of the universe, the rewarder of the good and the punisher of the wicked. And I do acknowledge the Scriptures of the Old and New Testament to be given by Divine inspiration." In December 1783 the members of the Philadelphia Synagogue pointed out that, contrary to the declaration of rights, this tenth section of the constitution "deprives the Jews of the most eminent rights of freemen." Although Jews were not, they said, "particularly fond of being representatives of the people," they regarded their exclusion by the test oath as "a stigma upon their nation and religion." Consequently they asked the state's agency for constitutional revision—the Council of Censors—to present their "Memorial" to the state's next constitutional convention.[28] It was a matter of principle.

But for Pennsylvanians in general, and in state politics, the test oath troubling Philadelphia's Jews was scarcely an urgent problem. Like other constitutional issues, this one could wait, and after reading the Jews' memorial, the Council of Censors tabled it. But six years later, when the legislature convened a constitutional convention in 1790, the delegates enlarged Pennsylvania's boundaries of religious equality. In conformity to the 1776 declaration of rights, which had stated that no man "who acknowledges the being of a God" could be "deprived of abridged of any civil right as a citizen," the new constitution provided only a general religious test for officeholders. In place of the former requirement that officials "acknowledge" both the Old and New Testaments as divinely inspired, the 1790 constitution stated that officeholders must merely recognize "the being of a God and a future state of rewards and punishments," a test that would allow Jews and Muslims to serve in government.[29]

Though the Pennsylvania Constitution of 1790 was more restricted than the Virginia Statute of Religious Freedom, it offended no organized group and was likely to trouble only a handful of the most skeptical Deists and freethinkers. Indeed, Pennsylvania's new standard could even accommodate the beliefs of the eccentric Revolutionary War general Charles Lee, a Virginia plantation owner who scandalized two Christian sects by scoffing in his widely published last will and testament that he must "not be buried in any Church or Church yard or within a mile of any Presbyterian or Anabaptist meeting-house," because "I have kept so much bad company when living, that I do not chuse to continue it while dead." Lee had gone on to "recommend my soul to the Creator of all worlds and all creatures," an acknowledgment that, together with his ironic comments about future "bad company," made him a believer in both God and future rewards and punishments. Lee outraged many believers by declaring that the Creator "must, from his visible attributes, be indifferent to their modes of worship or creeds, whether Christians, Mahometans, or Jews; whether instilled by education, or taken up by reflection; whether more or less absurd, as a weak mortal can no more be answerable for his persuasions, notions, or even scepticism in religion, than for the colour of his skin." But this skepticism did not compromise his civil rights, including the right to hold office according to Pennsylvania's new standard of religious freedom.[30]

Elsewhere, however, such outspoken deism would disqualify even an elite gentleman like Lee. North Carolinians had modeled their December 1776 declaration of rights on Pennsylvania's, copying the first lines on religious liberty verbatim: "That all men have a natural and unalienable right to worship Almighty God according to the dictates of their own consciences." But they would not move so far as Virginia or Pennsylvania. North Carolina delegates, alienated from English-style establishment, forbade "establishment of any one religious church or denomination in this State, in preference to any other." Moreover, they prohibited compulsory church attendance or taxation; and henceforward their constitution disqualified any active "clergyman, or preacher of the gospels of any denomination" from membership in any state legislative body. But ending direct state support for religion and keeping clergymen out of politics need not, they believed, require equal status for all religions or freethinkers. Like the Pennsylvania Constitution of 1776, North Carolina prescribed a religious test, but this one excluded Catholics as well as Jews. Owing to vigorous efforts by the Reverend David Caldwell, a Presbyterian pastor in the constitution-drafting assembly, every officeholder must not only subscribe to "the being of God," as well as the "divine authority . . . of the Old and New Testaments," as in Pennsylvania, but must also avow the "truth of the Protestant religion."[31]

For a citizenry steeped in English, Scots, and Scots-Irish anti-Catholicism, and whose residual anti-Jewish sentiments had never been challenged by any active Jewish community, the fact that exclusion from public office was the only disability Catholics and Jews faced in North Carolina illustrates the breadth of the Revolutionary commitment to natural religious equality. Indeed, even the exclusionary religious tests were, initially at least, more ideology than practice. Less than five years after barring Catholics from public office, in 1781 the North Carolina Senate and House of Commons elected Thomas Burke, a thirty-four-year-old practicing Roman Catholic from Ireland, as governor. Burke's political talents, not his religion, guided the legislators, and after Burke escaped from kidnapping by Tories in 1781, he won reelection to the governorship a second and third time in 1782 and 1783—the constitutional limit on consecutive terms.[32]

Burke's case was unusual; but the reluctance to inquire into the religious faith of political leaders was not. In succeeding generations two other Catholics, William Gaston (1778–1844) and Matthias Evans Manly (1800–1881), rose to high office in North Carolina.[33] Gaston, who attended the Jesuit-run Georgetown College and graduated from Princeton in 1796, not only won election to the state senate in 1800 at the age of twenty-two years but was also elected speaker of the house in 1808. Subsequently Gaston would serve in the state senate and the United States House of Representatives as well as the North Carolina Supreme Court. The careers of Burke and Gaston, key members of all three branches of government, demonstrate that Caldwell's "Protestant" constitutional test for North Carolina office holding was more symbolic than real.[34]

This seeming indifference to the faith of officeholders suggests that North Carolinians assigned a higher priority to article 16 of their declaration of rights—"all men have a natural and unalienable right to worship Almighty God according to the dictates of their own consciences"—than to article 32 of the constitution, the Protestant test oath. That was the argument made by Jacob Henry of Beaufort County, a Jew elected to the legislature in 1809. When another delegate challenged his right to sit in the house, Henry defended his place in a widely reported speech. A North Carolina native, Henry rested his claim not only on article 16, but also on article 44 of the constitution, which stated, "the Declaration of Rights is . . . part of the Constitution of this State, and ought never to be violated on any pretense whatever." Therefore, Henry reasoned, if there was a conflict between the declaration of rights' guarantee of natural religious equality and any part of the constitution, the declaration of rights must rule; so he should take his place in the legislature.[35]

Henry's rhetorical claims, however, were broader and encompassed his understanding of North Carolina practice as well as lofty Enlightenment principles and his own declaration of personal beliefs, which he maintained were fully compatible with public service to the state. Protestants, in his reading of history, meant Anglicans, so the fact that "Presbyterians, Lutherans, Calvinists, Menonists, Baptists, Trinitarians, & Unitarians" all held office demonstrated that article 32 was not strictly followed and ought not be applied to him either. To do so, he claimed, violated the practice of equality:

> Who among us feels himself so exalted above his fellows, as to have a right to Dictate to them their mode of belief? Shall this free Country set an example of Persecution, which even the returning reason of enslaved Europe would not submit to? Will you bind the Conscience in Chains, and fasten conviction upon the mind, in spite of the conclusions of reason, and of those ties and habitudes, which are blended with every pulsation of the heart? Are you prepared to plunge at once from the sublime hieghts [sic] of moral legislation, into the dark and gloomy caverns of superstitious ignorance? Will you drive from your shores and from the shelter of your constit[ut]ions all who do not lay their oblations on the same alter [sic], observe the same ritual, and subscribe to the same dogmas [?] If so which among the various sects into which we are divided, shall be the favored one?

Henry argued that Judaism should be treated as just another sect. By denying him equal access to office, the state was coercing his conscience by prohibiting his equal right to choose his religion. "Conduct alone," he asserted, "is the subject of human laws, and . . . man ought to suffer civil disqualification for what he does and not for what he thinks." Henry's own religion, he proclaimed, "inculcates every duty which man owes to his fellow men; it enjoins upon its votaries, the practice of every virtue, and the detestation of every vice; it teaches them to hope for the favor of Heaven exactly in proportion as their lives are directed by just, honorable and beneficent maxims." Henry went on to add that he did not seek to make converts nor to exclude anyone from his friendship owing to belief, even the "officious friend" who had moved his removal from the house. Closing on an ecumenical note, Henry quoted the Golden Rule: "Whatever ye would that men should do unto [ye], do ye so even unto them, for such is the Law and the Prophets."[36]

Henry's oratory succeeded, but only in part. Supported in the house by William Gaston, the Catholic, the delegates voted to allow Henry to take his seat according to the convenient fiction that a place in the legislature was not a civil office. When Gaston, Henry, and others proposed to eliminate the Protestant test oath from the constitution, they failed. A generation later, in 1833, the legislature by a count of fifty to nine voted to end the test oath because "its spirit is in conflict with Religious freedom; it has no practical use; and it may be considered a mere badge of ancient prejudice . . . unworthy of the present age of enlightened liberty." In the following year, with the test oath still in the constitution, Matthias Manly, a Catholic, won a seat in the house; but in 1835 North Carolina modified that oath. Now, in a compromise between the friends and foes of the test oath, the constitutional convention replaced the word "Protestant" with "Christian," allowing Catholics to hold office. It was in that year that President Andrew Jackson nominated the first Roman Catholic to the U.S. Supreme Court, Roger B. Taney of Maryland. During Reconstruction, in 1868, North Carolina would enlarge its standard of religious equality once more by substituting belief in God for "Christian" faith.[37]

III

In the first decades after independence the North Carolina pattern of setting boundaries on religious freedom and withholding complete religious equality was more common among the thirteen original states than the full freedom Virginia had adopted just three years after the war ended. In most of New England, where government responsibility for promoting religion and piety had been the rule for generations, even the North Carolina approach—which supplied no tax support for clergymen and churches—seemed dangerously secular. Though majorities of voters in Connecticut, Massachusetts, and New Hampshire expressed their belief in "religious liberty," they were convinced that the kind of full-scale disestablishment being introduced in New York and to the south would invite immorality and disorder. Instead, they struggled for decades to fashion a system—somewhat resembling the rejected Virginia "Bill Establishing a Provision for Teachers of Religion"—that would calm Dissenters by assuring support for the major Protestant sects while giving preference to the Congregational churches.

In New England the Revolutionary distinction between toleration and full-fledged religious freedom, the idea that religious equality was essential for complete freedom, met prolonged, vigorous resistance based on ideology and interest. Apart from their concern about morality and social order, the clergymen whose salaries depended on compulsory tithes and the congregations that were bound by contract to support their pastors feared that a wholly voluntary approach to religion might doom their churches. Reassurances based on nearby states, whether New York and its neighbors to the south, or Rhode Island, traditionally New England's home of religious pluralism and the target of orthodox scorn, did not convince proud, insular Yankees. Moreover, during the independence movement the most vocal critics of the establishment, Baptists led by Isaac Backus, had not demanded complete separation of church and state. Sometimes they accepted the idea of compulsory church taxes if their money could go to their own preachers. Consequently, though defenders of religious freedom undermined the old religious establishments, for most of New England it took two generations to fulfill the principle of natural equality in religion.

As in Virginia, Baptist efforts to practice freely and without supporting a rival church provided the catalyst for change. During the colonial era Connecticut and Massachusetts Baptists had looked to the Crown for protection, but during the independence movement they were reluctant to call on British authorities for aid. Instead they turned to the Continental Congress as early as October 1774, when Isaac Backus led a Baptist delegation from Massachusetts to Philadelphia. As Congress would later tell petitioning New York Catholics, it had no authority to act on religion, and as with the New Yorkers later, Congress advised Massachusetts petitioners to seek redress from their legislature. At the same time, however, Congress expressed support for civil and religious liberty for every denomination.[38]

That was not much help in Connecticut and Massachusetts. Connecticut had long required churches to subscribe to the 1708 Saybrook Platform of Christian faith in order to receive tax support and refused to change during the Revolutionary crisis when the legislature made its colonial charter serve as the Connecticut constitution. A Massachusetts convention proposed a new constitution in 1777–78, promising "the Free exercise and enjoyment of religious profession and worship . . . to every denomination of Protestants"; but it failed to win ratification on other grounds. At the time Backus complained that this new constitution would have done no good because it retained the old ecclesiastical laws. Massachusetts's cautious temperament was expressed by the 1778 Election Day preacher Phillips Payson, who warned that "the restraints of religion" necessary to "support & preserve order and government" would be "broken down" if state policy on public worship was left "to the humors of the multitude."[39] The people could not be trusted with religious liberty.

Within a month of Reverend Payson's sermon his wisdom seemed borne out, though not as he anticipated. Orthodox church mobs drove Baptists out of three Massachusetts towns in June 1778. When the legislature next convened it was embarrassed by these attacks and eager to win Baptist support for the Revolutionary cause. It smarted under charges by Backus and others that in religion Massachusetts, like Britain, practiced taxation without representation. Backus argued that all Christians should enjoy identical rights. In response, the legislature voted for the first time to invite a Baptist elder, Samuel Stillman, to deliver the 1779 annual election sermon. Thereafter, Massachusetts towns elected 6 Baptist delegates (out of 293) to the state's 1779 constitutional convention.[40]

For John Adams, principal drafter of the constitution of 1780 and its declaration of rights, a stable republic depended on a virtuous citizenry, so churches were essential social institutions. His personal religion was much like Jefferson's and Madison's, and he was not a devout churchman. But like the Reverend Payson—and unlike Jefferson and Madison—Adams doubted the virtue and self-restraint of "the multitude." Massachusetts's church establishment was an important bulwark of order, so like George Washington, John Marshall, and Patrick Henry in Virginia, he accepted tax-supported churches, hoping that public support for religion and religious freedom could be compatible.

Four years after the 1776 pronouncements of Virginia, New Jersey, Pennsylvania, and North Carolina, the second article of the declaration of rights that Adams proposed recalled their promises that "no subject shall be hurt, molested, or restrained, in his person, liberty, or estate, for worshipping God in the manner and season most agreeable to the dictates of his own conscience." Even Catholics, Jews, and Muslims would enjoy freedom to practice their faith, although they would not be permitted to hold office. Because Adams's own Unitarian-tinged religious views lay outside the Massachusetts mainstream, he did not draft the third article treating public support of religion. His devout Congregational cousin Samuel Adams assumed this task at the convention as part of a seven-man committee that included one Baptist. This committee divided over the question of religious establishment. Its four leading secular members—the politicians and lawyers Samuel Adams, Robert Treat Paine, Theophilus Parsons, and Caleb Strong—favored tax-supported religion, outvoting the Congregational pastor, Baptist elder, and militia officer who believed that church support should be wholly voluntary.[41]

As a result, following John Adams's freedom-of-religion guarantee in the second article, the third article ordained a church establishment. Localities and "religious societies" must provide for "the public worship of God, and for the support and maintenance of public protestant teachers of piety, religion and morality." Further, the third article directed the legislature "to enjoin upon all the subjects" church attendance when people could "conscientiously and conveniently attend." If a taxpayer went to a Dissenting church, his taxes should go to his "own religious sect," but if he attended no church regularly, his money would support the parish clergyman where the taxes were raised.[42] Overall, the declaration of rights and the constitution tried to reconcile religious freedom with government support for the Congregational church. Many who declared in favor of equal religious rights believed that religious freedom was compatible with a privileged status for Protestantism and especially Congregationalism.

On the question of equality, the declaration of rights seemed unambiguous on the surface: "Every denomination of christians, demeaning themselves peaceably . . . shall be equally under the protection of the law." Likewise, the constitution expressed this commitment to Christian equality for oaths of office, prescribing only belief in "the christian religion." Yet church taxes supported Protestants only, not Catholic priests. Quakers, with no clergy, must contribute to Congregational salaries; and the constitution assigned governance of Harvard College to "ministers of the congregational churches" of six parishes in and around Boston as well as several state officials. Clearly the constitution represented a compromise between champions of religious equality and advocates of toleration only.

For decades the toleration side succeeded in maintaining privileges for the long-standing religious establishment. Congregational churches lost ground to Dissenters, who could withhold tax support from Congregational parishes, but almost everyone else remained obliged to support them, and Congregationalists retained control of Massachusetts's only college. The declaration of rights, moreover, assured equality of religion among Christians only, an "equality" that explicitly favored Protestants. Baptists, whose chief concern was their own faith, not defending full-scale religious equality, accepted this settlement for the time being. Since Baptists had always opposed a learned clergy, Congregational control over Harvard did not much disturb them.[43]

But administration of article 3, treating the "support and maintenance of public protestant teachers of piety, religion and morality" by towns and parishes, did bother them. The ambiguity of this and other provisions of the constitution led to five decades of controversy, litigation, statutory changes, and finally a constitutional amendment ending all church establishment. In practice, access to religious taxes, and even authority to perform marriages and collect related fees, was never straightforward for minorities. From the time the constitution went into effect in 1780, Congregational churches and clergymen tried to secure as much as they could of revenue streams that were once their monopoly.

Consequently, access to tax monies by Baptists, Methodists, and Catholics was seldom easy. Many local authorities assumed that Baptists and others used their religion to evade church taxes. So each year they required fresh certificates authenticating actual church membership. In addition, they sometimes required that the legislature formally incorporate a church within a locality. For many Baptists, whose fledgling churches were often small and poor, meeting irregularly at multiple locations, incorporation was unattainable. For Methodists, whose clergy were itinerant, and for Catholics outside Boston served by traveling missionaries, certification was also impossible.

Almost immediately courts and the legislature heard these complaints. In 1785 a jury reversed a bench ruling by awarding support to a Universalist minister though his church was not incorporated. The following year the state's highest court concurred, declaring "as the constitution was meant for a liberal purpose . . . it meant in this instance, teachers of any persuasion whatever, Jew or Mahometan," were entitled to their followers' taxes. Still, the court ruled that the Universalist was not empowered to perform marriages—a civil office. Fifteen years later, when confronted by a similar case of a Roman Catholic priest, the court reversed the liberal 1786 ruling by ordering that taxes could go only to Protestant teachers. When the attorney general, James Sullivan, a first-generation Protestant, tried in 1800 to shame Federalist officials by prosecuting a Catholic priest for performing marriages, the judges ruled against the priest, only to reverse themselves the following year by ruling that Catholic priests could execute valid marriages.[44] The high court confirmed the policy ambiguity in 1803 when it ruled that neither a Methodist nor a Catholic could claim tax support without a fixed parish.

These mixed rulings reflected uncertainties over the meaning of Massachusetts statutes as well as its constitution. They led parishes and towns to approach religious liberty creatively. One anomaly introduced by the new constitution was the choice of a clergyman, which had belonged to admitted male church members. But now all parish voters, including men who were not members, chose the pastor.[45] Normally, and in keeping with tradition, voters left choice of a pastor to the majority of church members; but when conflicts between orthodox Trinitarians and liberal Unitarians sharpened, article 3 of the constitution became problematic. Inadvertently, by adhering to Revolutionary principles the state transformed churches from faith communities to republican associations of town or parish.

Just as the parish was distinct from the church, the meetinghouse—a public building constructed by the taxpayers—could also be separate from the church. In 1803 in Fitchburg, Massachusetts, a community of fourteen hundred people where five distinct Protestant denominations competed for public support, clerical salaries were only one challenge. On the Sabbath, who should possess the meetinghouse? Building four additional church structures was impractical, so town meeting voters chose proportional access to the meetinghouse. With 46 percent of taxpayers Unitarians, they would have the building twenty-four Sundays annually. Because Trinitarian Congregationalists constituted 33 percent of taxpayers, they would have the meetinghouse on seventeen Sundays. Universalists could use it for eight Sabbath days because they composed 15 percent of taxpayers. And Baptists and Methodists, who together made up 6 percent of Fitchburg ratepayers, would share the building three Sundays each year.[46] This approach seemed fair, but because it satisfied no group entirely, like other aspects of Massachusetts religious law, it was inherently unstable. Unlike Virginia, where the alliance between Dissenters and Deists in 1785–86 enabled the state to break with its establishment past, in article 3 of the 1780 constitution a divided Massachusetts leadership tried to reconcile, not resolve, the conflict between toleration and religious equality.

Because Massachusetts courts, even the state's highest supreme judicial court, seldom provided definitive guidance, the legislature made adjustments. In 1800, An Act Providing for the Public Worship of God supplied an explicit tax exemption for Quakers, who had no clergymen to support, and authorized towns to specify further denominational exemptions. In communities where members of dissenting sects were numerous, they often won exemptions. A decade later in 1810 the supreme judicial court tried again to determine whether clergymen for unincorporated churches were entitled to the tax support of their followers and ruled to exclude most Roman Catholic and Methodist churches, as well as half the state's Baptist churches. When these groups appealed to the legislature, they invoked Madison's 1785 "Memorial and Remonstrance"; in addition, Baptists gathered fifteen thousand signatures on reform petitions. With a title modeled on the Virginia statute, reformers passed the Religious Freedom Act of 1811, which explicitly ended the incorporation requirement. Subsequent Congregational attempts to overturn this law failed, and in 1817 the highest court sustained it. By this time Baptists were so powerful and Congregational privileges so reduced that the state granted land in Maine to assist a Baptist college, the Maine Literary and Theological Institution (later Colby College), as well as two Congregational colleges, Bowdoin and Williams.[47]

But divisions among Congregationalists, Unitarians, Universalists, and various Trinitarians, as well as other sects that believed they were entitled to slices of the revenue pie, made religion perennially contentious. The constitutional convention of 1820, which might have provided full religious equality by removing the state from religion, debated whether public officials must swear a Christian oath and whether tax support must maintain a Christian state. But all that delegates could agree on, by the overwhelming majority of 296 to 29, was revocation of the unenforced and unenforceable Article 3 requirement that citizens must go to church if there was a church they could "conscientiously and conveniently attend."[48]

In the year after the constitutional convention, the Supreme Judicial Court finally dismantled the political coalitions in federalism and Congregationalism that had enabled the state's peculiar form of establishment to survive forty years beyond the declaration of religious equality. This decision in the "Dedham case" highlighted the contradictions of Massachusetts's religious settlement, wherein parish voters as taxpayers, not church members, possessed ultimate power over choosing a minister. In Dedham, parish voters selected a Unitarian by a vote of eighty-one to forty-four, whereas the church members had chosen a Trinitarian by seventeen to fifteen vote. After the parish hired the Unitarian, the Trinitarians protested, and a church council dominated by Unitarians heard their claim that they should have a "concurrent voice"—effectively a veto—in the choice of a pastor. But the council ruled that although the Trinitarians were right according to "well-known usage," the law said otherwise. In retaliation, the Trinitarians left the church, taking with them its records and property, which they claimed belonged to them as members of the church. The Unitarians of the parish then sued for recovery, and between 1818 and 1820 the Dedham case made its way through the state court system. Finally, in April 1821, the Supreme Judicial Court ruled in favor of the parish and the Unitarians because, the court said, Article 3 stated explicitly "that the several towns, parishes, precincts, and other bodies politic or religious societies, shall at all times have the exclusive right of electing their public teachers." The fact that parishes had generally allowed church members to elect pastors was, the court said, merely "by courtesy," and not binding. Moreover, all church records and properties belonged to the parish, not the "members" of the church.[49]

This ruling finally set the stage for disestablishment in two crucial ways. First, the court reversed original Puritan practice by assigning exclusive control over parishes to majorities qualified to vote only by citizenship, residence, and property—not by religious confession. Second, by deciding for the Unitarians as rulers of the established church in Dedham, the court for the first time placed orthodox Trinitarian Congregationalists in the same status as Dissenters, legally no different from Baptists and Universalists. In the succeeding decade, as parish after parish fell to the Unitarians—almost one hundred between 1820 and 1834—Trinitarians withdrew their ancient loyalty from the political champions of establishment.

A few years after the Dedham case, in 1824 the passage of yet another religious liberty act dealt further blows to the old system. This new law, introduced by a legislator who was also a Baptist elder, finally ended general religious tax assessments by allowing parishes or religious societies to tax their own members only. Further, it ended restrictions on joining and separating from churches, measures that smoothed the path for people moving from one town to another or those who, like many Trinitarians, chose to separate from a church dominated by majorities whose beliefs they did not share. Finally, analogous to the general incorporation laws that would sweep the nation in the 1830s, the act permitted any group to incorporate its own religious society merely by applying to any justice of the peace.[50] These reforms hollowed out the once-dominant Massachusetts religious establishment. Each passing year rendered surviving regulations more anachronistic.

Just how anachronistic the old Article 3 had become was suggested in 1819 when Maine, the old Eastern District, sought separation from Massachusetts and admission to the Union as a state. Maine was long a stronghold of Baptists, Universalists, and other Dissenters, and its constitutional convention rejected the old toleration plan entirely in favor of absolute religious freedom. As one delegate put it, no "pre-eminence would ever be given to any religious sect . . . whether Catholics, Jews or Mahometans." Even "Hindoos" would enjoy equal rights before the law in Maine, and no religious oath would be required to hold office.[51] In Massachusetts at the time, Federalists intertwined with the Congregational interest group could still block such an outcome there.

But a decade later, by the early 1830s, nearly everyone recognized that Article 3, so narrowly adopted by Samuel Adams's committee at the 1780 convention, should be replaced. Neither Democrats nor Whigs could support it any longer, voters in some 140 towns petitioned against compulsory religious taxes, and in 1831 the general court moved to replace the old halfway provision for religious liberty with an eleventh amendment to the state's constitution. Though the new amendment would maintain the old language of concern for "public worship of God and instructions in piety, religion and morality," instead of requiring support for religion, the amendment merely permitted friends of religion to organize and pursue their goals. Without mentioning Christianity or any other belief, and with the guarantee that "no subordination of any one sect or denomination to another shall ever be established by law," the amendment made religion wholly voluntary in Massachusetts. When this went to voters for ratification in November 1833, the vote was 32,234 in favor and 3,273 opposed—over 90 percent approved.[52]

But old prejudices did not vanish without protest. No sooner had voters overwhelmingly adopted the eleventh amendment than a Yankee mob attacked and burned the Ursuline Convent boarding school in Charlestown; and Whig leaders—seeking to rally support against such disparate opponents as Jacksonian workingmen, social reformers, and Garrisonian abolitionists—prosecuted the freethinker Abner Kneeland for blasphemy. According to the state's attorney in January 1834, Kneeland's recent publications violated the 1782 statute directing punishment for anyone who "shall willfully blaspheme the holy name of God, . . . his creation, government, or final judging of the world, . . . or by cursing or reproaching Jesus Christ or the Holy Ghost, or . . . the canonical scriptures as contained in the books of the Old and New Testaments." This 1782 law, which certainly privileged Trinitarian Christianity over other faiths, had renewed a dormant colonial

"Anti-Catholic Doings," Charlestown, Massachusetts, 1834. David
Claypool Johnston's cartoon of the arson-riot that destroyed the
Ursuline Convent. Courtesy, American Antiquarian Society.

blasphemy statute that John Adams condemned in 1814. But for the anxieties aroused by disestablishment and democratic politics, it would have remained dormant.[53]

The perpetrators of the convent arson were never prosecuted; however, the contest over Kneeland's views—he called the story of Christ's birth and mission "fable and fiction"—generated four trials in Boston in 1834 and 1835, leading to a sixty-day jail sentence. Ultimately Kneeland appealed to the Supreme Judicial Court, gaining a fifth trial in March 1836. Defending himself, Kneeland argued that he was innocent of all charges and should be acquitted on the basis of the state's guarantees of freedom of conscience and of speech and press. But in 1838 Chief Justice Lemuel Shaw, the Whigs' greatest jurist, ruled that Kneeland had spoken "evil of the Deity" in a "willful and malicious attempt to lessen men's reverence of God." Accordingly, Shaw ordered Kneeland to jail. The one supreme court justice who dissented was a Democrat, Marcus Morton. "This conviction rests very heavily upon my mind," Morton wrote, since according to the Massachusetts Declaration of Rights, if Kneeland had no malicious intent, he possessed the "constitutional right to discuss the subject of God, to affirm or deny his existence."[54]

Jailing Kneeland aroused a storm of protests and petitions from Unitarians and Baptists, including such reformers as clergymen William Ellery Channing and Theodore Parker, as well as Ralph Waldo Emerson and William Lloyd Garrison. But backed by antipardon petitions sponsored by orthodox clergy, the Whig governor Edward Everett—a friend of Justice Shaw and political rival of Justice Morton—allowed Shaw's judgment to stand.[55] Ironically, by standing firm on enforcement of the blasphemy law in 1838, Justice Shaw and Governor Everett made Kneeland a martyr to the twin causes of freedom of religion and freedom of speech. They provoked a backlash against blasphemy prosecutions, once and for all.

By this time other New England states had adopted policies that professed full Enlightenment religious liberty and did in fact provide a broad degree of toleration. In Massachusetts's southern neighbor, Connecticut, the rise of Baptist churches—there were fifty-five of them by 1795—the spread of Enlightenment liberalism, and the arguments of the Baptist elder John Leland, who declared that unless every single person was converted, "the notion of a Christian commonwealth should be exploded forever," enlarged the boundaries of religious liberty in the 1780s and 1790s. According to the new 1784 Connecticut system any church, including the Roman Catholic, could be assigned the taxes of its members. In many towns and parishes, voters opened their meetinghouses to preachers of all Protestant denominations, while in northeastern Connecticut a hopeful outpouring of Protestant ecumenism led one-time orthodox Calvinists in Pomfret and Windham to form "Independent Catholic Christian Societies." The president of Yale College, Timothy Dwight, protested that toleration was merely a mask for secularism, but by 1818, when an alliance of Dissenters won control of the state government and wrote a new constitution ending the church establishment, the Baptist, Episcopalian, Methodist, Quaker, Sandemanian, and Separatist religious societies outnumbered Dwight's Congregational churches.[56]

A year later New Hampshire's legislature followed Connecticut's lead by ending its similar church establishment. The 1819 Toleration Bill provided that henceforth "no person shall be compelled to join or support . . . any congregation, church, or religious society." As in Connecticut the previous year and in Maine two years later, the political victory of Republicans over Federalists brought this further measure of Jeffersonian religious freedom. But in New Hampshire, unlike Connecticut, the constitution still required officeholders to be Protestant, a provision retained until 1876.[57]

New Hampshire's policy of restricting office holding to Protestants was one of many state exceptions to the principle of religious equality in the early Republic and later. In Maryland, for example, after a generation-long effort begun in 1797 by a Baltimore Jew, the 1822 "Jew Bill" granted full equality. In Rhode Island such equality came only when the state enacted its first republican constitution in 1842; and in Connecticut a special legislative act in 1843 year enabled Jews to form religious societies on an equal basis with Christians.[58] The federal system, which made states chiefly responsible for upholding the ideal of religious equality, assured that neither uniformity nor complete equality could be realized until the era when constitutional amendments and Supreme Court rulings made national standards apply to states.

IV

In 1787 and thereafter American leaders recognized that Enlightenment secularism was only partly responsible for barring Congress and the national government from the promotion and supervision of religion. At the state level, where government was seen as close to the people, most states were ready to mix religion and government. But the same people who applied religious tests close to home were often suspicious of granting the same powers to a national government that might conceivably prescribe alien religious beliefs. Consequently, when the Constitutional Convention voted by a large majority that "no religious Test shall ever be required as a Qualification to any Office or public Trust under the United States," delegates' fears of sectarian abuses, not just Enlightenment secularism, were operating.[59]

The difference between religious liberty at the national and state levels is suggested by the contrast between the Enlightenment views of the first four presidents—none of whom was a converted Christian—and state religious restrictions on Catholics and Jews. Washington, Adams, Jefferson, and Madison—two of whom helped write the Constitution—all supported separation of national government from religion and all followed the Constitution's wholly secular prescribed language in taking the oath of office. Washington did indeed proclaim that "religion and morality are indispensable supports . . . to political prosperity" in his Farewell Address, but he stressed their general social value, not commitment to any particular faith. When clergymen pressed him to declare publicly his own Christian faith, Washington demurred. To his pastor's dismay, he refused to take communion as president; and when he referred to divine power in his letters, Washington never referred to "Jesus," "Christ," a "savior," or a "redeemer." Even when the elder statesman lay on his deathbed, he did not speak of heaven or allude to reunion of loved ones. Facing death, Washington never called for a minister, never asked for prayers, never expressed repentance. Nor did Washington make any donations or provisions for religious purposes in his elaborate will. Holding his own views private, during the controversies over disestablishment in Virginia he said that keeping religion separate from law and politics was "productive of more quiet to the State" than any other policy.[60]

Though his successor, John Adams, accepted his home region's tradition of public support for churches, he excluded religion from national policy. When New England clerics and Federalist politicians went into a frenzy over Jacobin attacks on Christianity, Adams did not. The Washington-Adams's administration secularism was manifest in the 1796 treaty with Tripoli. Approved unanimously by the Senate in 1797 and signed by Adams, it declared: "As the Government of the United States is not, in any sense, founded on the Christian religion; as it has in itself no character of enmity against the law, religion or tranquility of Musselmen; . . . no pretext arising from religious opinion shall ever produce an interruption of harmony existing between the two countries."[61] Though both Washington and Adams accepted Protestant chaplains to assist members of Congress, for Adams no less than for Washington, religion was separate from national government. Though Americans were mostly Christians, their government had no religion.

Jefferson and Madison, of course, were far more outspoken advocates of keeping religion out of government than their Federalist predecessors. As triumphant veterans of the Virginia disestablishment struggle they brought their mission to the national government. In 1802 President Jefferson announced in his extensively reprinted public letter to the Baptist Association of Danbury, Connecticut, that he viewed the First Amendment with "reverence" because in it "the whole American people" built a "wall of separation between church and state." Madison, who had drafted this constitutional prohibition on a national "establishment of religion" with a guarantee for the "free exercise" of religion, had also proposed, unsuccessfully, to extend First Amendment protections downward, so that "no state shall violate the equal right of conscience." Madison also repudiated chaplains for Congress, arguing that this policy was "a palpable violation of equal rights, as well as of Constitutional principles."[62] But Madison lost these battles for a strict boundary separating church and state. The United States was not a Christian nation in law, but it was a popular republic whose ruling majorities embraced various forms of Christianity and wanted Christianity to flourish. Consequently, as Madison recognized, the struggle over state support for religious privileges and incentives would be perpetual. The wall of separation would be permeable; in practice, religious equality shaded toward toleration.

Americans never resolved the status of religious equality definitively. Indeed, American religious engagement was never more dynamic and assertive than during the first half of the nineteenth century.[63] And since no one could banish religion from public debates or electoral politics, the interplay of religious interests and beliefs with law and government made contested outcomes conditional. Over time each state would negotiate an equilibrium for church-state relations that—in a generally nondiscriminatory manner—allowed more government support for religion than Virginia's standard, while stripping away most sectarian and Christian privileges that were routine before 1776 and for several decades thereafter.

The rapid influx of Roman Catholics in the 1850s did lead to a militant Protestant reaction that threatened religious equality; but with few exceptions the religious freedom regime hammered out in the early Republic remained intact. Local school authorities might choose the Protestant New Testament for classrooms, and governments would subsidize all religions, but generally on the basis of equal tax exemptions, not doctrine. Simultaneously denominational campaigns to shape public policy on such widely various subjects as regulation of the Sabbath, temperance, slavery, and pornography would become routine aspects of the cultural and political landscape of the early Republic.

No resolution, of course, could be absolutely final. But the ideal of religious equality proclaimed as a natural "unalienable" right in the Declaration came close. The Virginia Statute of Religious Liberty, though merely a statute lacking the inviolable standing of a constitution or bill of rights, acknowledges the mutable character of its guarantee. "We well know," the delegates admitted, "that this assembly . . . have no power to restrain the acts of succeeding assemblies . . . and that therefore to declare this act to be irrevocable would be of no effect in law." But they proclaimed their fundamental belief "that the rights hereby asserted are of the natural rights of mankind, and that if any act shall hereafter be passed to repeal the present, or to narrow its operation, such act will be an infringement of natural right." So long as that belief remained potent in Virginia and elsewhere in the United States, the doctrine of religious equality endured. Indeed, this became the official position of the United States in 1829, according to Secretary of State Martin Van Buren. Writing to the Vatican, Van Buren assured the Holy See that in the United States the Roman Catholic Church, with others, enjoyed freedom of worship. Ironically, Van Buren's partisan opponents would later turn this declaration of religious equality against him.[64]

THREE

Equal Justice for Irishmen and Other Foreigners

"And [God] hath made of one blood all nations of men for
to dwell on all the face of the earth."
—*Acts* 17:26, Geneva Bible, 1560

"Ye shall have one lawe: it shall be as wel for the stranger,
as for one borne in the countrey: for I am the Lord your God."
—*Leviticus* 24:22, Geneva Bible, 1560

The universalism of the idea "that all men are created equal" was au-
dacious in 1776, but it was not new. The idea of recognizing equal
rights for foreigners of all descriptions was as old as the Bible, yet for governments, whether monarchies or republics, equality was and remains a
doubtful proposition. Their first responsibility has always been protecting
their own subjects or citizens, so the ancient doctrine of Leviticus notwithstanding, the inclusion of outsiders as possessors of equal rights has never
been routine. In every original state bill of rights certain guarantees were
proclaimed universally to "every person," whereas others applied only to
"inhabitants," "the people of this state," "every member of society," or "the
people." Although women, children, free people of color, and religious minorities properly belonged within such insider categories, governments routinely denied them rights most white men could claim.

Where did this leave foreigners—the most recent arrivals in a land ruled
by immigrants and their descendants? According to the statutes of each state,

even nonresident fellow United States citizens could be disadvantaged as foreigners or "strangers." The requirements for citizenship, moreover, were defined differently among states and by the federal government. Furthermore, even when immigrants acquired U.S. citizenship, their speech and manners could still mark them as foreign. In an era when insular prejudices and ethnic stereotypes were embedded in everyday cultural and social practices, one may wonder what kinds of equality foreigners enjoyed.

I

To begin, we must recognize that national identities were often less definite in eighteenth-century America than today. Even now any nonwhite American citizen with an African or Asian name is sometimes presumed "foreign." What made American nationality especially unclear in the early Republic was the fact that at least until 1776 there were no United States citizens, no Americans in a legal sense. Instead, the differences among long-settled British, European, and African inhabitants of North America loomed large. British identity itself was only emerging in the eighteenth century.[1]

When that century began Daniel Defoe brilliantly satirized the complexities of English identity in *The True-Born Englishman.* Defoe, born the son of a Presbyterian yeoman and tallow chandler named Foe in 1660, added the prefix "De" to suggest aristocratic lineage. But however much he aspired to high rank, he reacted vehemently against John Tutchin's verse attacking Britain's new monarchs as *The Foreigners.* The English, Defoe wrote, were not only "a Race uncertain and unev'n / Deriv'd from all the Nations under Heav'n," but "a Mongrel half-bred Race . . . With neither Name nor Nation, Speech or Fame." No such thing as a pure-bred Briton existed, Defoe declared, because the country had so often been overrun by invaders: Romans, "Gauls, Greeks, and Lombards, and . . . slaves of every nation"; Saxons, Danes, Scots, Picts, Irish, Normans—"All these their barbarous offspring left behind." More recently Dutch, Walloons, Flemings, Huguenots, and other French and Italian peoples had come: "Priests, Protestants, the Devil and all together: / Of all Professions, and ev'ry trade, / All that were persecuted or afraid; / Whether for Debt or other Crimes they fled." In 1701 Defoe proclaimed an English identity that anticipated the blended identity Americans later embraced. "Thus," he declared, "from a Mixture of all Kinds began, / That Het'rogeneous Thing, An *Englishman.*"[2] The idea of a *pure-bred* Englishman was nonsense.

Defoe's relish for Englishmen's heterogeneous descent was never shared by all his compatriots; indeed, as British national identity matured the chauvinism expressed in *The Foreigners* increasingly became parliamentary policy. Britain's mercantilist empire encouraged immigration and importing people from the British Isles, Europe, Africa, and the Caribbean for its American colonies, but the reasons were economic, not cultural. Where they saw profits, London policy makers did not worry about ethnic and cultural diversity among their colonial populations. The colonies were distant from Britain and different; so although African slavery was unwelcome in the United Kingdom and legally forbidden in the 1760s, the Crown encouraged slavery in the colonies, vetoing colonial restrictions on the importation of Africans. At home a chauvinistic Parliament disallowed the naturalization of foreign Protestants, Catholics, and Jews, though from 1740 onward Parliament welcomed them to the colonies, allowing colonial legislatures to make white outsiders into naturalized subjects.[3]

Eager to seize economic advantages, American settlers generally embraced the empire's heterogeneous population policy. But by midcentury some questioned its consequences, notably Benjamin Franklin, whose *Observations Concerning the Increase of Mankind* appeared in Boston and London. Fifty years after Defoe, Franklin, the Boston-born son of an English immigrant, so fully embraced English identity that he ignored Defoe's dismissal of the mythical "true-born" Englishman. Commenting as an embattled Englishman who saw Pennsylvania being overrun by Germans, Franklin demanded to know "why should the Palatine Boors be suffered to swarm into our Settlements and by herding together establish their Language and Manners to the Exclusion of ours?" Expressing fears later labeled "nativist," he asked: "Why should Pennsylvania, founded by the English, become a Colony of *Aliens,* who will shortly be so numerous as to Germanize us instead of our Anglifying them, and will never adopt our Language or Customs, any more than they can acquire our Complexion?"[4] The powerful grip of distinct ethnic identities on colonists is striking when a cosmopolitan intellectual like Franklin, possessing more direct experience with heterogeneity in Philadelphia than most colonists, believed that these fellow northern European Protestant immigrants were so alien.

Underlying Franklin's views lay a budding racial vision of what America might become. Franklin worried that "the Number of purely white People in the World is proportionably very small." Assessing the world population continent by continent, he observed: "All Africa is black or tawny. Asia chiefly tawny. America (exclusive of the new Comers) wholly so." Even Europe was doubtful. "The Spaniards," he wrote, "Italians, French, Russians and Swedes, are generally of what we call a swarthy complexion; as are the Germans also, the Saxons only excepted." In Franklin's analysis, Saxons, "with the English, make the principal Body of White People on the Face of the Earth," and he wished "their Numbers were increased." Considering America's long-term future, he asked, "Why should we [in America] in the Sight of Superior Beings, darken its People? why increase the Sons of Africa by Planting them in America?" Much better, he argued, to embrace "so fair an Opportunity, by excluding all Blacks and Tawneys," thereby "increasing the lovely White and Red." His analysis was not objective, Franklin admitted: "Perhaps I am partial to the Complexion of my Country, for such Kind of Partiality is natural to Mankind."[5] Long before full-fledged racial ideology emerged, this prospective founding father anticipated the future thrust of United States policy.

During the Revolution, however, when Americans actively shed their English and British identities, inclusive heterogeneity—not Franklin's exclusivity—captured the emerging national idea, though with a distinctly white European connotation. In *Common Sense*, Thomas Paine declared that "Europe, and not England, is the parent country of America." The colonies became "the asylum for the persecuted lovers of civil and religious liberty from *every part* of Europe." This had been true for English settlers, too: "The same tyranny which drove the first emigrants from home," Paine declared, "pursues their descendants still." Here Paine not only asserted the colonists' heterogeneous origins but detached them from European and British identities—they had "fled, not from the tender embraces of the mother, but from the cruelty of the monster." By choosing America they rejected the old tyrannies of their national origins. "Every spot of the old world is overrun with oppression," Paine exclaimed, "Freedom hath been hunted round the globe. Asia and Africa, have long expelled her.—Europe regards her like a stranger, and England hath given her warning to depart." Ultimately Paine extended America's reach beyond Europe, proclaiming an inclusive universality; America would "receive the fugitive" without qualification "and prepare in time an asylum for mankind."[6]

The Continental Congress and the Continental Army eagerly sought the support of France, the Dutch Republic, and Continental officers like Thaddeus Kosciuszko, the Marquis de Lafayette, and Baron Friedrich Wilhelm von Steuben, in addition to experienced English, Scots, and Irish officers. So Paine's rhetoric was practical. Indeed, during the later years of the war, though slaveholders feared putting muskets in black hands, the Continental Army enlisted African Americans. With survival at stake, heterogeneity trumped exclusive nationality.

At war's end Congress and the states embraced their constituents' white preferences. One classic articulation of the European "melting pot" idea was expressed in 1782 by a French immigrant to Orange County, New York, J. Hector St. John de Crèvecoeur. Following *Common Sense*, he described "that race now called Americans" as a "promiscuous breed" of European origin: "They are a mixture of English, Scotch, Irish, French, Dutch, Germans, and Swedes." Like Paine he emphasized that Americans were European castoffs—"as so many useless plants . . . [that] were mowed down by want, hunger, and war." "Two thirds of them had no country," Crèvecoeur wrote, but "in this great American asylum, the poor of Europe have by some means met together" so that "here they rank as citizens."[7] Crèvecoeur's American recalled Defoe's heterogeneous Englishman.

But unlike Defoe's representation of English descent, which included not just Europeans but also "slaves of every nation," Crèvecoeur excluded Native Americans, African Americans, and the mixed-race people he encountered in his more than twenty years' residence in America. Though he claimed that "individuals of all nations are melted into a new race of men," when he asked, "What then is the American, this new man?" his answer was unequivocally white. "He is either an European, or the descendant of an European."[8] Crèvecoeur, a Frenchman who married a woman of British descent, was more inclusive and accepting of "foreigners" than Franklin, but like Franklin and Paine he believed that America was and should be a land of white people. The popularity and influence of such voices reflected white Americans' sentiments of racial superiority and preference on launching the United States of America.

II

Consequently, when Congress passed the first "Act to establish an uniform Rule of Naturalization" in 1790, it erected no barriers against people of European descent but made racial preference explicit. The law announced that "any alien, being a free white person," could become a citizen so long as "he is a person of good character," resident in the United States for two years. Referring to men only, the law expressed gender bias, though resident free white women of "good character" could also be admitted as citizens. Children gained citizenship with their parent(s) automatically.[9] The nation's political class embraced a white "universalism" reflecting Revolutionary ideals and existing citizenship experience.

But when a new revolution convulsed France and polarized Europe, Crèvecoeur's inclusiveness, embodied in Congress's first naturalization act, ended. Now meddling by the French Revolutionary official, Citizen Genêt, threatened American neutrality, making Frenchmen suspect—a situation reinforced by France's overthrow of Christianity and embrace of military emperor Napoleon. These developments in Revolutionary America's closest ally, in addition to revolution and rebellion in Haiti and Ireland, and the eruption of radical politics in Britain, divided Americans and shook their self-confidence. These overseas disorders also brought immigrants whose ambitions could be disturbing, unlike the "work and worship" motives of earlier generations. When radicals from Ireland joined refugees from France and Haiti on American shores, some doubted that inclusiveness was prudent. By 1795 long-standing Protestant and Anglocentric prejudices and beliefs, once mostly latent, joined with new republican principles to propel revision of the 1790 Naturalization Act.

Foreigners posed new threats. Sober, sturdy craftsmen and farmers were never the issue; but title-bearing aristocrats and masters of Haitian slaves might not support republican ideals. Moreover, "priest-ridden" Catholics who believed in keeping Latin as the language of religion and the laity ignorant, and who also swore loyalty to the avowedly antirepublican pope, could undermine a fragile republic. Radicals—unruly disturbers of public tranquillity—could also subvert governments.

When Congress began discussing a new naturalization bill in January 1795, the initial question concerned renouncing titles of nobility. But a Massachusetts representative, Samuel Dexter, expressing regional prejudices, introduced religion, entering "at some length into the ridicule of certain tenets of the Roman Catholic religion," before concluding that "priestcraft had done more mischief than aristocracy." Immediately the Virginian who drafted the Bill of Rights, James Madison, answered the Yankee with facts. He "did not approve the ridicule, attempted to be thrown out on the Roman Catholics." Having considered the subject carefully, Madison declared that "in their religion there was nothing inconsistent with the purest Republicanism." Driving the point home, he reported that "in Switzerland about one-half of the Cantons were of the Roman Catholic persuasion. Some of the most Democratical Cantons were so; Cantons where every man gave his vote for a Representative." Admonishing his Massachusetts colleague, Madison declared that "Americans had no right to ridicule Catholics. They had, many of them proved good citizens during the Revolution."[10] Madison's rejoinder ended debate on religion; thereafter, if anti-Catholicism was on the minds of delegates, they kept it to themselves; if they opposed admitting aliens, they acted on other grounds.

The question of aristocrats entering the United States was not so easily resolved. The Republic opposed hereditary titles, and the Constitution not only prohibited the United States from granting titles of nobility but also prohibited public officials from accepting a title from "any King, Prince or foreign State," without prior congressional consent. Now, some in Congress, fearing a flood of aristocratic refugees, wanted to restrict aristocrats' access to citizenship. But the Virginian Richard Bland Lee was worried by the idea that aristocrats might not be suited to citizenship because "the corrupting relation of lord and vassal . . . rendered him to be an unfit member of an equal Republican government." Lee "feared that this reasoning applied to the existing relation of master and slave in the Southern country, (rather a more degrading one than even lord and vassal) [and] would go to prove that the people of that country [the south] were not qualified to be members of our free Republican Government." Lee proclaimed that this was absolutely wrong: members of Congress held slaves, and "he was sure that their hearts glowed with a zeal as warm for the equal rights and happiness of men, as gentlemen from other parts of the Union where such degrading distinctions do not exist."[11]

Perhaps; but two Massachusetts delegates, Samuel Dexter and George Thatcher, proposed that every alien seeking citizenship must renounce "all possession of slaves" and declare "he never will possess them." Aiming primarily at French refugees from Haiti's revolution, they proposed that naturalized citizens must renounce not only titles of nobility but also slave ownership. This opened the divisive subject of slavery and was too much for southern delegates. The Virginian John Nicholas dismissed Dexter's proposal, noting that the New Englander had repeatedly "hinted his opinion that possessors of slaves were unfit to hold any Legislative trust in a Republic." Theodore Sedgwick, a leader in Massachusetts's delegation who helped end slavery in Massachusetts, tried a dose of realism to cool debate, asserting "to propose an abolition of slavery in this country would be the height of madness. Here the slaves are, and here they must remain." Sedgwick called Dexter's amendment "trifling." Southerners joined with delegates from the middle Atlantic and New England states to defeat renunciation of slavery by a wide margin.[12]

But the issue of titles still excited passionate pronouncements. Though some congressmen viewed the question as merely symbolic, the slaveholder James Madison declared that "abolition of titles was essential to a Republican revolution." When, after the daylong debate subsided and members cast their votes, Republican gentlemen declared a prohibition on hereditary aristocracy. A primarily southern majority asserted that being the master of slaves in America was not the same as being the lord of vassals. Consequently, they voted that any alien who had "borne any hereditary title, or been of any of the orders of nobility, in the kingdom or state from which he came" must "make an express renunciation of his title or order of nobility." Rejection of prior hereditary status must be recorded before granting citizenship.[13]

Once congressmen surmounted this hurdle, discussion became more temperate. During debate, Representative Thomas Fitzsimmons of Delaware and Elias Boudinot of New Jersey appealed explicitly to the Revolution's asylum tradition. Fitzsimmons declared, "Nature seems to have pointed out this country as an asylum for the people oppressed in other parts of the world"; and Boudinot, echoing his neighbor, stressed American inclusiveness for "the oppressed of all nations." Although Fisher Ames of Massachusetts was reluctant to throw the doors wide open — "It would not be safe or proper indiscriminately to admit aliens to become citizens" — neither would Ames stop naturalization. "A scrutiny into their [aliens'] political orthodoxy might be carried to a very absurd extreme," he admitted, backing a compromise increasing the probationary period for citizenship from two years to five. This extension of the residency requirement in the Naturalization Act of 1795 was the most significant substantive alteration to the 1790 act, though it now required not only that aliens be "of good moral character" and "attached to the principles of the constitution of the United States" as before, but also "well disposed to the good order and happiness" of the nation. The new statute reinforced concern for true allegiance to the United States by requiring the alien to declare in court the intent to seek citizenship three years before the actual application.[14]

During President John Adams's administration commitment to the Revolutionary asylum tradition would be severely tested. When relations with France brought warfare, when the Irish, assisted by France, rose in rebellion, and when partisan animosity between Federalists and Jeffersonians peaked, foreigners could become targets of suspicion or even political retaliation. At the beginning of July 1797, when Congress debated adding a stamp tax on certificates of naturalization, demand for this tax questioned the entire asylum idea. Again New Englanders and Federalists were the chief advocates of adding barriers to immigration and naturalization, whereas Pennsylvanians and Jeffersonians championed free access.

The immediate question was whether a twenty-dollar tax should be levied on naturalization certificates at a time when laborers earned about one dollar a day. Federalist Samuel Sewall, a wealthy Massachusetts attorney, defended the twenty-dollar tax since "every foreigner who came to this country had a full opportunity of getting a living without enjoying the rights of a citizen; and he knew not why he should become a citizen, if he did not think the privilege worth twenty dollars." Another Federalist, David Brooks, a New York attorney, added that "he would not have the rights of citizenship made too common." He saw no reason to welcome "fugitives from justice, and others, who never would be of any advantage to any country."[15]

Some doubted the whole notion of allowing foreigners to become citizens. Robert Goodloe Harper, a Federalist lawyer representing South Carolina, opposed this new tax because he wanted to end naturalization entirely. Frankly rejecting the asylum ideal, Harper doubted "the propriety of inviting immigrations from all parts of the world." He conceded that "there was a moment of enthusiasm in this country, when this was thought to be right—when we were not satisfied with giving to immigrants every blessing which we had earned with our blood and treasure." With misguided enthusiasm, Harper complained, Americans had "admitted them instantly to the rights of citizenship." But now, though he was willing to allow foreigners into the country, "no man should become a citizen of this country but by birth."[16]

Later Harper declared that strangers, "however acceptable they may be in other respects, could not have the same views and attachments with native citizens." Consequently, they should not exercise the rights of citizens such as voting. It was essential, he said "that none but persons born in the country should be permitted to take a part in the Government." Harper proposed ending America's role as the asylum of liberty.[17]

Others were more oblique. The Federalist attorney Harrison Gray Otis of Boston chose a historical perspective for viewing immigration and naturalization: "In the infancy of the country it was necessary to encourage emigration and foreigners of all countries had been wisely invited." In that earlier time British colonial policy had been suitable; but now, he judged, "the native American germ to be amply sufficient." Otis recognized that prosperity in some states resulted from "the industrious establishments formed by foreigners of various descriptions," but now immigrant radicals posed a threat. United States policy should exclude "the mass of vicious and disorganizing characters who could not live peaceably at home, and who, after unfurling the standard of rebellion in their own countries, might come hither to revolutionize ours." Otis claimed that his concerns were purely civic, not prejudiced, since he felt only respect for "those honest and industrious people, whether Germans, Irishmen, or foreigners of whatever country, who had become citizens." He was happy "to fraternize with them" so long as "they remained obedient to the laws, and faithful to their adopted country."[18]

But Otis, like the New Yorker Brooks, "did not wish to invite hordes of wild Irishmen, nor the turbulent and disorderly of all parts of the world, to come here with a view to disturb our tranquility." And like the South Carolinian Harper, Otis advocated excluding immigrants from office. In May 1798 he moved that henceforth "no alien born" be permitted to hold any office of "honor, trust, or profit, under the United States."[19] This proposal immediately met with vigorous opposition from the Virginian Abraham Bedford Venable, a 1780 Princeton graduate, who objected that such a policy would create two classes of citizens. But another Massachusetts representative, George Thatcher, suggested even a twenty-dollar tax was too permissive: "The doors of naturalization [were] too wide." He proposed doubling the tax on naturalization because "too many foreigners emigrated hither; they were out of proportion to the natives."[20] Blending reluctant acceptance of immigrants with a desire to keep them out, Federalists tended to abandon the asylum ideal.

In contrast, Jeffersonians repeatedly endorsed the belief that America should be a refuge for the oppressed of Europe. They began by arguing that any tax on citizenship must be low. John Swanwick, a 1770 English immigrant who had become a wealthy Philadelphia merchant, proposed four dollars as more suitable than twenty. Albert Gallatin, a native of Geneva who had migrated to Boston in 1780 and who now represented Pennsylvania, agreed that the proposed tax was too high. Congress should help family men and avoid creating a class of inhabitants who were not citizens.

North Carolina's Joseph McDowell agreed with the Federalist Robert Harper that "we had fought for liberty"; but unlike his South Carolina neighbor, "he trusted, we did not mean to confine it to ourselves, nor to sell it to others." Confronting the elitism voiced by Harper, Brooks, and Otis, McDowell declared that "it was not the wealthy, the high-bred, the well-born, that he wanted to emigrate to our country; it was a different class of men, viz.: mechanics, farmers, and other industrious persons." Later he remarked that many foreigners "were as good as any among us." Nathaniel Macon, McDowell's North Carolina colleague, also rejected any citizenship tax for the same reasons: it would "injure the poor and industrious part of the immigrants to this country, which he looked upon as the most valuable." David Holmes of Virginia went even further, proposing that U.S. laws be printed in German as well as English "since there were very many inhabitants of this country who could read no other [language]." One of the few congressmen who were ready to support Holmes's proposal was Matthew Lyon, a Vermont representative from Dublin, Ireland. Like McDowell, Macon, and Holmes, Lyon saw efforts to restrict immigration and citizenship as undermining the Revolution. Americans "had told the world, that there was in this country a good spring of liberty, and invited all to come and drink of it." It was wrong, Lyon argued, "to turn round to them and say, you shall not be admitted as citizens unless you pay twenty dollars."[21] For Jeffersonian Republicans laying a tax on citizenship contradicted Revolutionary principles.

But the chauvinist impulse died hard. Samuel Sewall, who defended the twenty-dollar tax, pronounced that, like the Jeffersonians, "he wished this country to be an asylum . . . yet he did not wish to see foreigners our governors." He had nothing against immigrants like Gallatin and Lyon, but he said that "it was well known that this game of citizenship had been played to the injury of the country." Coming from a seaport, Salem, he had "seen men take the oath of allegiance and becoming citizens of the United States, and the next again become citizens of the French Republic, by entering on board their privateers."[22] Such mischievous citizenship was an abuse; but it was limited to a handful of maritime locations and few people, none likely to win election.

John Swanwick, the Philadelphian, presented the most fully developed defense of asylum policy. Answering every Federalist objection, Swanwick —whose constituency included both Germans and Francophiles—reminded his colleagues of arguments in *Common Sense* that had mobilized Americans:

> It was said . . . the rights of citizenship would become too common. This was a doctrine contrary to any thing he had heard before on the subject. Since the year 1776, it had uniformly been the language of this country that we had in the Western world opened an asylum for emigrants from every country. This was our language: 'Come and join us in the blessings we enjoy, in a country large and fertile, and under a Government founded upon the principles of liberty and justice.' Were the inhabitants of this country all born in it? Certainly not—a great majority were foreigners. And should they, because they came a little sooner, or had better fortune than others, say to their less fortunate brethren, 'You shall not be admitted to the privilege of citizenship but on the payment of twenty dollars, though we received it without money and without price!'

Swanwick protested that "in doing this, gentlemen seemed desirous of having rich emigrants as citizens, whilst the poor wanderer, flying from the hearth-tax in Ireland, or from the oppressions of other countries, who would be very useful in the cultivation of our land and in every useful labor, would be in great measure excluded from his rights in society."[23] Swanwick's fellow Pennsylvanian Albert Gallatin completed the argument by reminding congressmen that one complaint against George III in the Declaration was that "he has endeavored to prevent the population of these States; for that purpose obstructing the laws for naturalization of foreigners; refusing to pass others, to encourage their migration thither." So far as Revolutionary ideas and practices were concerned, immigration and citizenship should remain accessible. But when the twenty-dollar tax came to a vote in the House, the majority favored this more restrictive policy by the narrow margin of four votes.[24] Immigrants from Europe remained welcome, but only up to a point.

The antipathy toward admitting people of color was even stronger. Though advocates of abolition and emancipation grew more active on both sides of the Atlantic during the 1790s, Congress wanted no part of such reform. When a 1797 Quaker memorial reminded the House of Representatives that the First Continental Congress had pledged to "neither import nor purchase, any slave imported" after December 1, 1774, members objected. And they refused to act on the Quakers' appeal for the liberation of 134 of their "brethren of the African race" who had been "set free by members of our religious society" and then reenslaved by North Carolina officials. Jeffersonians who earlier protested restrictions on white immigrants insisted that the House suppress the petition on behalf of blacks. Nathaniel Macon, the North Carolinian who regarded "poor and industrious . . . immigrants . . . as the most valuable," complained that Quakers aimed to provoke insurrections. Voicing his negrophobia, Macon declared that "there was not a gentleman in North Carolina who did not wish there were no blacks in the country." He regarded their presence "as a curse," regretting that "there was no way of getting rid of them."[25] Though Macon spoke more bluntly than most, many shared his views. Jeffersonians who denounced Federalist exclusivity and championed immigration were determined that the American asylum be as white as possible.

Broadly speaking, they succeeded. But when the political furor surrounding the French diplomatic insult of the XYZ Affair launched a quasi-war with France, it also brought a crackdown on immigrants who criticized Federalist policy and tighter administration of citizenship. One Connecticut congressman, a Litchfield Law School graduate, declared that the president should be empowered "to remove at any time the citizen of any foreign country." But giving the executive such arbitrary power was farther even than many Federalists would go. Samuel Sewall, great-grandson of a judge who sent convicted witches to the Salem gallows, rejoined that the United States must "not subject every foreigner who comes to this country . . . to the fear of the dungeon or removal." Sewall "did not contemplate the making of this country a wall against all aliens whatever, or that no alien should come here without being subject to an arbitrary authority." This proposed presidential power was "known only to the French Directory"; it would give the Republic "the character of the Turks or Arabs" and "could not be adopted." Immigrants could be inconvenient, but Sewall believed that greater dangers arose "from our own unnatural children, who, in the bosom of the parent, conspired her destruction." To say that "persons born in foreign countries, however regular and orderly their conduct may be, shall be liable to be imprisoned or sent out of the country" while at the same time excusing citizens would only "increase the evil." Instead of stripping immigrants' rights wholesale, Sewall offered narrow rules for deporting aliens charged with crimes and making exceptions for those who possessed licenses of residence. Still Sewall, like other Federalists, remained doubtful toward some classes of immigrants, preferring to bar naturalization for people from countries at war with the United States.[26]

The Alien and Sedition Acts of 1798 were emblematic of Federalist anxiety over subversion. The "Act concerning aliens" empowered the president to seize and deport "such *aliens* as he shall judge dangerous to the peace and safety of the United States, or shall have reasonable grounds to suspect are concerned in any treasonable or secret machinations against the government thereof." This radical expansion of presidential power at the expense of individual civil liberties, a law Madison privately called "a monster that must forever disgrace its parents," drew a clear boundary between the civil rights of citizens—which the president must not violate—and immigrants, who possessed no civil rights.[27] As Harrison Gray Otis explained, the rights of citizens belonged only to the people who made the Constitution, "the people of the United States; and that it was through mere courtesy and humanity that . . . the right to trial by jury . . . as well as other advantages, were made common to aliens." Because this statute was written to expire in 1800 and was never renewed, its consequences were limited. Yet it loudly proclaimed Federalist fears of "the turbulent and disorderly of all parts of the world," some of them immigrants who arrived "with a view to disturb our tranquility."[28]

The Sedition Act aimed to punish some of those aliens, especially British immigrant newspaper writers and printers who mounted slashing, vituperative invectives against President Adams and the Federalists. This law did not aim directly at aliens; instead contemporaries and later historians have seen its significance as decisive for partisan politics and a free press.[29] And, like the Alien Act, the Sedition Act, which expired in 1800, figured importantly in partisan conflict for years. To Jeffersonians these laws symbolized Federalist tyranny.

In 1798 Federalists folded a third law—on naturalization—in with the others; but this one had no expiration date. This naturalization law repealed the 1795 law, providing more rigorous and bureaucratic procedures for immigrants and citizenship. First, it sought to enumerate and regulate every white immigrant arriving on American shores. Within forty-eight hours of arrival all aliens "shall be reported" to the clerk of the U.S. District Court, the nearest collector of the port, or other designated official. This officer must create a book for recording "the sex, place of birth, age, nation, place of allegiance or citizenship, condition or occupation, and place of actual or intended residence" in the United States of every immigrant and immigrant family. If an alien refused or neglected to register, he or she could be fined two dollars and required to provide a guarantor of "peace and good behaviour." Without a guarantee, the immigrant could be jailed. Moreover, any employer, master, or parent who refused to register dependents properly could be fined two dollars per month for each offense until the dependents were registered. To assure enforcement, fines would be paid to those who informed officials charged with enforcement. The Naturalization Act of 1798 aimed to end the free, unregulated passage of foreigners into and within the United States.[30]

To end the political influence of recent immigrants this law tripled the residency requirement for citizenship from five to fourteen years. In addition, every applicant for citizenship must reside at least five years in the state or territory where he or she sought naturalized status. Consequently, fourteen years was the earliest an immigrant might achieve citizenship; those who moved across state lines would wait longer to qualify. Taking advantage of the 1798 climax in antiforeign sentiment, Federalists who a year earlier had claimed that "the doors of naturalization [were] too wide" and that "no man should become a citizen of this country but by birth," now enacted a naturalization law more to their liking.[31]

In 1802, a year after the Jeffersonians took control of Congress and the presidency, they repealed the 1798 law and restored most provisions of the 1795 law—especially the five-year residency requirement. President Jefferson himself called for reform of the 1798 law in his December 1801 address to Congress: "Shall oppressed humanity find no asylum on this globe?" The president argued that the fourteen-year waiting period denied to "unhappy fugitives from distress that hospitality which the savages of the wilderness extended to our fathers arriving in this land."[32] His congressional majority swiftly repealed the Federalists' naturalization act.

But significantly, Jeffersonians retained some elements of the restrictive 1798 law. Whereas the 1795 law demanded just one year's residence—a requirement the 1798 law raised to five years—now Congress stipulated three years' residence. And although the 1795 law required neither registration nor certificates of entry for immigrants, the 1802 law retained the 1798 requirement that any alien seeking citizenship must register with a court of record. The information to be recorded was identical to the 1798 law except that Jeffersonians, unlike the Federalists, chose not to record the "condition or occupation" or sex of the immigrant. But the law did require the immigrant's name and place from which "he or she migrated." On payment of a fifty-cent fee the applicant (and family) would receive a certificate to provide proof of date of arrival for future naturalization proceedings. This fee was paid not to an informer but to the official who made, signed, and sealed the certificate. All punitive measures in the 1798 law were erased. The 1802 law set no time limit for immigrants to register, required no guarantors of good behavior, and imposed no penalty for not registering.[33]

III

The Revolution of 1800, as Jeffersonians called their electoral victory, effectively restored the first principle of the original naturalization act of 1790.

The United States would be an asylum for Europeans. As in 1790, the 1802 law proclaimed that "any alien, being a free white person, may be admitted to become a citizen of the United States, or any of them." Henceforward this 1802 naturalization act would govern American policy for more than a century.[34] Yet Federalist misgivings about foreigners remained, and Jeffersonians, too, harbored prejudices. American identity was fluid, so it was no coincidence that each of the first three presidents and four of the first seven Congresses felt the need to prescribe terms for American citizenship.

In the new United States the national law of citizenship was one test of American principles, particularly the ideals of asylum and equality before the law. Daily experience provided other tests. Certainly the Declaration of Independence, like Leviticus, proclaimed equality among all men; but white foreigners, like people of color, did not necessarily receive equal treatment. Prescription did not always rule practice. The experiences of foreigners in American courts of law and in the "court of public opinion" provide case studies of how the ideal of equality actually fared.

For at least a generation following independence every adult who claimed United States nationality, native born or naturalized, also remembered possessing a different national heritage or identity. During the Republic's first decades this was inevitable because American nationality was a new creation. Often the boundary between "Americans" and "foreigners" was indistinct. Before 1776 even the longest-settled four-generation signers of the Declaration had, like their forebears, regarded themselves as English, Dutch, Swedish, Welsh, Scots, Irish, British, or some mixture. First- or second-generation signers, like many other settlers, possessed only shallow American identities, as did citizens whose mother tongues were German, Dutch, French, Spanish, or Portuguese. Descent and language ruled the old way of nationality.

After independence old and new ideas of national identity coexisted. When the New Yorker John Jay, descendant of Dutch settlers and Huguenot refugees, defended the Constitution, he proclaimed the nation's new, amalgamated identity as if it were fully established. To Jay, Americans were "one united people—a people descended from the same ancestors, speaking the same language, professing the same religion, attached to the same principles of government, [and] very similar in their manners and customs."[35] Jay exaggerated. In his own New York some churches conducted services in Dutch; and English was not the language of every hearth. Jews practiced their faith apart from many denominations of Christian neighbors, and Catholics were struggling for the religious liberty Jay publicly resisted. Yet Jay's and Crèvecoeur's fiction of the new "American" promoted and legitimated equality among those who looked beyond cultural realities and immediate experience.

During the 1780s and 1790s "foreigners" turned up in criminal courts. Though they did not appear disproportionately among felons or the drifting poor—in maritime Rhode Island less than 4 percent of "warned out transients were foreign-born"—when they found their way into court, newspapers noted their nationalities.[36] Formally, however, nationality played no part in the legal record, nor did press treatment play up foreign status.

Several examples illustrate the point. Cassumo Garcelli, a twenty-three-year-old Italian sailor, was among the first men executed after peace was concluded in 1783. Convicted at Boston for the fatal stabbing of a local white man, John Johnson, the Livorno native was not identified by nationality in most press reports, nor was his fellow defendant, a French sailor Bartholomeu Martell. The one newspaper that did refer to Garcelli's nationality mistakenly identified him as Portuguese. Lacking a full trial report one cannot say whether the two foreigners were treated differently from citizens, but the fact that the court rendered different verdicts for Garcelli and Martell—one convicted, the other acquitted—suggests that defendants' rights were protected in the usual way, as does the two-month interval between sentencing and execution, which allowed time to appeal for a pardon as well as preparation for death. Garcelli's "Life, Last Words, and Dying Speech" testify that he not only accepted Boston justice but also confessed to murder in Puerto Rico and to participation in a piracy scheme near Philadelphia in which his coconspirator committed murder.[37] Since newspaper coverage was minimal and did not sensationalize an Italian's stabbing a local man, xenophobia appeared quiescent.

Several trials in 1784 reinforce the view that though Americans drew distinctions between themselves and foreigners, in criminal courts they treated outsiders much like fellow citizens. The rape conviction and execution of Patrick O'Bryan, for example, were reported from Pennsylvania north to Massachusetts without mention of national identity. A highway robbery committed by two Irish men, piracy and murder by another Irish man, and a burglary perpetrated by a New Yorker and a Frenchman all generated the same terse, commonplace language as had the Garcelli case. When Richard Barrick and John Sullivan were convicted of highway robbery in Boston, and Alexander White was found guilty of murder and piracy, newspapers in New England and the mid-Atlantic states were silent on national identity. Only their "true and complete history," published in the sensational *American Bloody Register*, revealed their Irish origin in passing, without mentioning religion. One convict emphasized his Irish identity sarcastically, reporting that years before in London, after he was convicted of stealing, he was punished with thirteen stripes on his back, "signifying that I should be honoured in *America* with the *Hibernian* coat of arms, i.e. two sticks *rampant*, one couchant, a strong *pendant*, and an *Irishman* at the end of it." His gallows humor played to long-standing English and colonial bigotry.[38] Yet when Barrick, Sullivan, and White were executed, a Protestant clergyman counseled them as fellow Christians.[39]

The absence of full-blown xenophobia is also suggested by the treatment of American Derick Grout and Frenchman Francis Coven, executed for separate burglaries in October 1784. Grout, a bricklayer born in Schenectady, New York, in 1748, had served in the Revolutionary army before seeking work in Boston. Often unemployed, after twice being convicted of stealing chickens—and whipped—Grout began to steal in New Hampshire and nearby Boston. When finally convicted and awaiting execution he denied some crimes but acknowledged others, asking forgiveness. As in the other cases, the press—from New Hampshire and Vermont to South Carolina—made no mention of Grout's origins until his execution.[40]

It is revealing that Grout's "Life, Last Words and Dying Speech" identified him not as an American but as "a *Dutchman*, of New-York State," just as the same broadside identified Coven as "a *Frenchman*, belonging to Marseilles." Moreover, in Grout's account of his early days in Boston, he explains, "Not being acquainted in Town, I went to one of my Countrymen's

House." Though Grout's fellow New Yorker John Jay claimed that Americans were "one united people," in Massachusetts people regarded Grout as a *"Dutchman."* The way press accounts lumped together the natural-born American citizen Grout and the French subject Coven, suggests—not surprisingly—that American identity was not sufficiently developed in 1784 to differentiate strangers precisely.

Like the others, Grout and Coven accepted the justice of their sentences, though without trial reports one cannot say whether they were accorded equal rights. The fact that no stranger, whether American or foreign, was likely to possess a local support network surely put such people at a disadvantage, especially if they were poor. Grout sought help at the house of an unknown "Countryman" without much luck. When work was scarce, as it generally was in postwar American ports, those who lacked family, friends, and acquaintances were more tempted to steal chickens, or worse, than people who knew where they would sleep and find their next meal. Being transient may have mattered more than nationality.

Public opinion, however, took note of foreigners. At the end of 1784, following the executions of Grout and Coven and with the hangings of Barrick, Sullivan, and White imminent, Boston's *American Herald* commented that those convicted of capital crimes since independence were "chiefly foreigners." The short-term tabulation was arresting: "Out of 16 that have suffered, but four of them were Americans, and but two belonged to this state."[41] Belief that outsiders committed crimes disproportionately was widespread and probably accurate due to reasons connected to social marginality.

The question of equal treatment arose a few years later when the Irish Catholic John Sheehan was sentenced to die for burglary. This recent immigrant, arrested just months after arrival, had come to join his brother. He first found employment in the United States Army; then, after his unit disbanded, he worked irregularly as a laborer. Ultimately, he said, he purchased stolen silver and was arrested for burglary when he tried to resell it. Convicted in Boston, Sheehan protested that he was innocent of burglary and his former general, Henry Jackson, and other officers sought his pardon. In October 1787 the officers' efforts led the Massachusetts house to vote for commutation of Sheehan's sentence. The senate, however, doubted the constitutionality of a legislative pardon and directed the Supreme Judicial Court to rule. When the state's highest court determined that pardoning belonged exclusively to the governor "by and with advice of Council," Sheehan's plea went to Governor John Hancock and the council. They denied the appeal without explanation.[42]

If, facing death, Sheehan told the truth, Massachusetts punished him unjustly for a capital crime—burglary—when he was guilty only of knowingly receiving and selling stolen goods. But the prosecutor convinced the jury and the justices believed that the trial was fair. Sheehan's former officers believed the Irish immigrant's account and persuaded a majority of the House of Representatives that Sheehan deserved a pardon. This effort to save Sheehan's life, including action by the legislature and a constitutional test of the pardoning power, suggests that whatever prejudices Yankee officials harbored toward foreigners, especially Irish Catholics, they valued equal protection highly in a capital case. The Boston press report circulated from Vermont to Pennsylvania, matter-of-factly reporting Sheehan's Irish and Catholic identities and treating him sympathetically.[43]

IV

By the 1790s, however, debates over naturalization, citizenship, and the Alien Act of 1798 demonstrated Americans were expressing a more sharply defined national consciousness, one that affected thinking about equal rights. Because immigrants from Ireland figured largely in the controversies of the decade, the case of "the Irish" is critical for understanding white Americans' distinctions between themselves and other people of European descent. Owing to the influence of anti-Irish bigotry dating from the famine migration and the Gilded Age particularly, understanding American attitudes during the early Republic requires close attention to that era's record.[44]

One starting point is the English legacy of prejudices toward Ireland, its people, and Roman Catholicism. The English antipathy toward Catholicism dated from the Catholic uprising in the 1530s prompted by Henry VIII's break with Rome and his seizure of the monasteries. Subsequently, the martyrdom of Protestants burned at the stake during Queen Mary's reign (1553–58) and the Saint Bartholomew's Day Massacre of Protestants in France (1572) reinforced anti-Catholic sentiments. The 1605 Catholic plot to destroy the houses of Parliament made anti-Catholicism a key ingredient of emerging British nationalism, popularly remembered by burning effigies of Guy Fawkes annually. Moreover, during the sixteenth and seventeenth centuries the conquest of Ireland by English and Scots Protestants had led Parliament, for political security, to deprive Catholics of civil rights throughout England, Scotland, and Ireland. According to law, all office-holders must take Anglican Communion, and Catholics were barred from Britain's army. Though in fact Catholics served in imperial armies and even as officers after 1793, prejudice and discrimination against Catholics were widely accepted.[45]

In the American colonies only Maryland, a Catholic proprietorship, welcomed Catholics at first, and when a Protestant majority gained control of Maryland they instituted anti-Catholic policies comparable to New England and New York. Pennsylvania, nominally friendly to all Europeans and religions, laid a tax on all Irish servants in 1729, partly for religious reasons. In the same era southern colonies—welcoming African slaves—sought to limit the "importation of papists."[46] Nevertheless during the eighteenth century people from Ireland, both Catholic and Protestant, crossed the Atlantic in the tens of thousands, settling in the middle and southern colonies especially.

Anti-Catholicism was endemic in British America; but perhaps because there were few Catholic priests and fewer churches, the chief prejudices toward "Irishmen" were commonly ethnic, not religious. The "wild" Irish were more often Protestants of Scots descent, not Catholics; but in many American eyes, they were all one.[47] The Anglican preacher Charles Wood-mason described the Scots-Irish of the Carolina frontier in 1769 as "lazy, sluttish, heathenish." Their poverty, he explained, came from their "indolence."[48] In Pennsylvania Benjamin Franklin voiced similar views, and after American independence, a historian reports that travelers regarded the "boisterous, assertive, undisciplined and convivial culture of the region as similar to that of the wild Irish in Ireland."[49] Even as late as 1814 a Pittsburgh leader described everyone from Ireland, Protestant or Catholic, as "Irish."[50] In the early Republic the stereotype of hard-drinking, hard-fighting, rustic frontiersmen and laborers was well established.

But whereas some might disdain the Irish as troublesome outcasts, making them the butt of ethnic jokes, Irish immigrants were also welcomed as frontiersmen, laborers, and craftsmen.[51] Notwithstanding legal preferences for Protestantism in scattered states from North Carolina to New Hampshire, avenues for upward mobility were far more open than in the British Isles. Irish immigrants, both Protestant and Catholics, and their first-generation descendants won high offices, civil and military; they practiced law and medicine and, in some states, intermarried at the highest levels of society.[52] No less a personage than George Washington accepted membership in Philadelphia's Sons of Saint Patrick in 1781, joining them at ceremonial dinners.[53]

Nevertheless, as congressional debates over naturalization demonstrated, chauvinistic prejudices could color the views of even the most educated and cosmopolitan American leaders. And in popular culture expressions of prejudice were unself-conscious and direct. If the boundary between American and foreigner was not yet definite in the 1780s, the debates over naturalization in the succeeding decade suggest that national identity was coming into focus, becoming more important. When American authorities charged foreigners with felonies like murder and brought them before juries, they put the equal rights doctrine to the test.

In 1795 and 1796 public discussion of two little-known murders involving an Englishman and a German, as well as a strange prosecution of an Irish immigrant for sodomy, provide revealing glimpses of how aliens fared in American courts. In one, where the English-born chimney sweep, Henry Blackburn, stabbed George Wilkinson, an English mariner, nationality scarcely mattered. The press identified both murderer and victim as British natives; however, in an execution sermon Nathaniel Fisher, the Salem, Massachusetts, Episcopal priest, distinguished the victim, "the unfortunate stranger," from his long-resident killer. Though an English native, Fisher told Blackburn that he had been tried and convicted by "your country," Massachusetts. Living long enough in Salem to qualify as American, Blackburn's origin was public knowledge, as was his victim's; but neither fact appears to have influenced judgment of this 1795 case.[54]

Because the Blackburn trial was held in Massachusetts, where people of English descent predominated, the distinction between Americans and English people may have been muted. But in the case of Matthias Gotlieb of New Jersey, a one-time career soldier who fatally thrust a knife three times into his wife's abdomen, nationality also played a minor role. Gotlieb, a Prussian native who came to America with other British mercenaries, was an alcoholic fifty-year-old butcher. His wife's national identity and age were not recorded at the time of his trial. Since he married Catherine after the war, whatever her descent, it is likely she was, like their son, American born.[55]

Yet in the proceedings against Gotlieb, including his execution, though he was criticized for repeatedly deserting his company as a soldier in Europe and for drunkenness, New Jersey inhabitants did not associate Gotlieb's moral failings with being an immigrant or his German origin. Indeed, in at least two dozen newspaper reports, stretching across eleven states from New Hampshire to Georgia, "Gotlieb" became the Anglicized "Cutlip."[56] Evidently as the convict's name passed from person to person the more familiar English pronunciation and spelling erased his German identity. As in the Blackburn case, though the foreign nationality of the perpetrator was known, neither newspapers nor execution sermons stressed the convict's nationality or connected it to his vicious crime. Evidently "Englishness" in Massachusetts and "Germanness" in New Jersey did not evoke sufficient hostility to compromise the rights of these two murderers.

The simultaneous case of John Farrell in western Massachusetts is also revealing. Farrell, an eighty-five-year-old "cancer doctor," had practiced in Connecticut and in central Massachusetts for several years before moving to Leverett, a hill town, in 1796. That year he was convicted for the capital "Crime of Sodomy (not to be named among Christians) to the great displeasure of Almighty God, to the great scandal of all human kind, [and] against the . . . Statute." When a Northampton, Massachusetts, jury convicted him for sodomy with a dog, the local paper identified him as "a native of Ireland"; but a newspaper twenty miles away called him "John Farrol, a Frenchman." At Worcester, Massachusetts, he became "John Farrel, a Frenchman." The

Worcester paper sensationalized the report with the headline "*SODOMY,*" claiming that this was "the first conviction of the kind we ever recollect," without commenting on his foreign identity. Whether Farrell was Irish or French did not matter.[57]

The grassroots pardoning campaign Farrell's lawyer organized to save his client's life underscores the point. For when Caleb Strong, a former U.S. senator and future Massachusetts governor, saw Farrell's first two petitions fail, he rallied the doctor's former Worcester County neighbors and patients to testify on behalf of Farrell's character and medical competence. The response was unprecedented: 445 voters signed petitions declaring that the old man behaved morally in their communities and cured patients. Some petitioners mentioned Farrell's advanced age, but none spoke of his nationality or religion. Evidently, among a people who had grown up as British subjects, American national identity did not yet sustain vigorous xenophobia. People who came from other towns and counties, and other states and countries, were merely "strangers"; they were not yet "aliens."[58]

But the furor over aliens during the Quasi-War with France in 1798, and the passage of time after formation of the United States would put foreigners' rights at greater risk. A decade after the trials of Blackburn, Gotlieb, and Farrell, several murder trials demonstrate a sharper awareness of nationality. One, in New York City in 1806, concerned the Portuguese mariner Francisco Dos Santos. After being forbidden from calling on the daughter of the ship rigger Archibald Graham, Dos Santos stabbed Graham in revenge. According to the Portuguese vice consul, who gave Dos Santos a character reference at the trial, the thirty-year-old illiterate who spoke only "broken English" had been in the United States for over a year and "behaved remarkably well."[59] But Dos Santos confessed that though he was raised as a virtuous Catholic and was married, he had kept "bad company" with "lewd women" in New York City and was "greatly addicted to intemperance." Though evidence was circumstantial, because Dos Santos had declared "me will stab two Americans," the jury convicted him after only thirty minutes' deliberation.[60]

Dos Santos's lawyer was the prominent New Yorker and 1792 Princeton graduate George Washington Morton, son of a Scots-Irish father and a

German-born mother.[61] Morton would that argue his client, as a foreigner, could not be familiar with American law, so his culpability should be reduced. But the judge, asserting that American laws "protect a foreigner with as much scrupulousness as a citizen," dismissed Morton's argument. In "almost all civilized societies" death was the usual penalty for murder, he said, so "every man, therefore, however ignorant he may be of the local regulations of a foreign community, must be acquainted with the nature and consequences of *this crime*."[62] That Dos Santos was a foreigner must neither mitigate nor aggravate the charge against him.

So far as the newspaper and trial reports show, Dos Santos's foreign and Roman Catholic status (he was described both as "Portuguese" and "Spanish") was central to his identity. Moreover, his offense, a vengeance stabbing linked to pride and involving a woman, fulfilled common Anglo-American stereotypes of Latin criminality. Yet the fact that Dos Santos was a poor, uneducated mariner possessing no constructive ties to the community may have been more important than his nationality for the speedy judgment against him. Nevertheless, by 1806 adverse sentiments toward foreigners were ripening, though probably more in the New England interior than in a cosmopolitan, multilingual port like New York.

Soon after Dos Santos's trial a letter in the *Hampshire Federalist* of Springfield, Massachusetts, voiced rising anti-immigrant sentiments. Its author recalled the past sarcastically, "when our benevolence and universal love of mankind overflowed . . . when the rags and tatters of all nations were greedily sought for, and invited to our shores; a society was formed . . . for the express purpose of aiding and assisting foreigners coming to the United States." But times had changed; and the writer argued that it would "now be thought wise in the Legislature to grant to this society the power of expending their funds to aid the *emigration* of some thousands, from our own, to foreign countries."[63] The message: Send foreigners home. Though Hampshire County towns—80 to 130 miles distant from Boston—were not flooded with recent immigrants, "universal love of mankind" was in retreat.

At the same time that this xenophobic letter appeared, two murders in late 1805 and early 1806 came to trial in April 1806 at the Supreme Judicial Court meeting in Northampton, 105 miles west of Boston. In both cases

A FULL AND PARTICULAR A... r
OF THE TRIAL OF
FRANCISCO DOS ...
ALIAS,
FRANCISCO
FOR THE MURDER OF A... ...LD GRAHAM,
AT A COURT OF OYE... AND TERMINER,
Held in the City of N w... rk Jan. 9, 1806.
WITH THE SENTENCE,
Pronounced against him by his Honour the presiding Judge,

To which is added, a short account of his Life,
TOGETHER WITH HIS CONFESSION,
Taken in the presence of one of the Keepers; and also
his Behaviour from the time of Condemnation, till
his execution on the 28th March, 1806.

Trial of Francisco Dos Santos, New York, 1806. Conventional treatment of criminal, American or foreign. Courtesy, American Antiquarian Society.

Irish immigrants were charged with killing Yankees. In the first case James Busby, described in the press as "an Irishman," was tried for conspiring with the victim's wife to murder Northampton resident John Ellis, found hanging in his home after Busby spent the night there. Although there was sufficient evidence for a grand jury to indict Busby and Susannah Ellis, there was not enough to convict. However active the general prejudice against Irish people, even in the sensational circumstances of conspiracy to murder a husband, this jury of Yankee householders voted to acquit.[64]

But the trial of Dominic Daley and James Halligan the next day was different. Back on November 9, 1805, Marcus Lyon, a Connecticut man on horseback carrying a large sum of money, was attacked, and the next evening local men found his corpse, shot, beaten, dragged, and "buried" in the Chicopee River near the turnpike road Lyon and the two suspects had traveled in opposite directions. The next morning local men began a search for the killer or killers, and their hunt turned into pursuit of Daley and Halligan, whom they seized the next day 130 miles away in southwestern Connecticut.[65] Circumstantial evidence connected the two men to the crime, but only the testimony of a thirteen-year-old boy—identifying them as possessing Lyon's horse near the site of the victim's body—tied them to this robbery and murder.

By today's standards the evidence against Daley and Halligan was faulty, but it was no more problematic than in many capital trials of the period—and the suspects were convicted, sentenced to hang, and ordered to have their bodies given to medical students for "anatomization."[66] In contrast to the case of the Irishman John Farrell, also convicted and sentenced in Northampton, or even the case of James Busby, who was tried just one day before Daley and Halligan, in their case the defendants' status as foreigners and as Irish Catholics in particular stirred an outpouring of xenophobia and prejudice.

One example of this hostility was expressed barely a week after the murder and long before trial. It came from a local pastor on the Sabbath after the Irishmen's arrest. Like the murdered man, the Reverend Ezra Witter, a thirty-eight-year-old Yale graduate, came from eastern Connecticut; and he was no champion of the universal love of mankind.[67] He mocked "Ye champions of the Age of Reason, the perfectability and approaching innocence of man!" Though Daley and Halligan had only just been captured and questioned, Witter readily declared the "two ruffian footpads" to be the killers.[68] This murder touched off a jeremiad that not only condemned Thomas Paine and Enlightenment optimism but attacked foreigners as sources of social depravity.

Witter was blunt: "We see the evil attending a continual influx of vicious and polluted foreigners into this country. Many of the outrages we suffer, proceed from this source. Who break open our houses, in the unsuspecting hours of sleep?—Who set fire to our large cities and towns for the sake of plunder? and Who rob and commit murder on our highways?" To Witter, Daley and Halligan epitomized the crisis; after all, "a great portion of the crimes above mentioned, together with many others . . . are committed by foreigners." Immigrants, who "crowded . . . our state-prisons," polluted and burdened the country.[69] Though his parish was hardly the epicenter of immigration, Witter complained of "the rapid influx upon us, of late, of the vilest and most abandoned of the human race." Sermon listeners learned that "the prisons of Europe and the West-Indies are now disgorging themselves upon our shores; and this country is thus becoming the general asylum of convicts." Witter's only consolation was that the perpetrators were not "our neighbors and brethren." Local Yankees could take comfort because "we are so clearly exonerated from this crime, the stigma is wiped away." His people and his region "escaped reproach and disgrace."[70]

That Witter's excited sermon was published quickly nearby suggests a responsive audience for his xenophobia. Yet Witter's targets were not specifically Irish or Catholic; he complained of "Europe and the West-Indies." Indeed, anti-Irish and anti-Catholic sentiments were seldom expressed in print. Still, they were embedded in vernacular culture. At Daley and Halligan's trial their defense attorney, Francis Blake, declared even before the court opened that "the prisoners have . . . been tried, convicted, and condemned, in almost every bar-room, and barber's shop, and in every other place of public resort in the county, is a fact that will not be contested." Employing reverse psychology, he stressed anti-Irish, anti-Catholic prejudice, seeking acquittal by urging jurors to demonstrate their fairness by overruling local prejudices.[71]

Blake, a thirty-one-year-old Jeffersonian, known for "ardent temperament" and "vivid and impassioned" oratory, was a Harvard-educated Boston native. He had settled in Worcester in 1802, where he was twice elected to the state senate in 1810 and 1811.[72] Appointed by the court to defend James Halligan, Blake understood Massachusetts juries and appealed to reason, idealism, and emotion.[73] His reasoning concentrated on the merely circumstantial nature of the evidence. For example, a Boston shopkeeper sold two pistols like those found at the crime scene to a laboring "man who talked like an Irishman"; and the shopkeeper believed that his customer might have been the thirty-four-year-old Daley or the twenty-seven-year-old Halligan.[74] Moreover, when the suspects were arrested they carried banknotes that could have belonged to the victim. Because the prosecution could not positively connect the gun purchase or banknotes to the crime, Blake persuaded the court to exclude this evidence. Blake also argued that his clients' traveling pace, ordinary from Boston to Wilbraham and rapid thereafter, did not prove guilt any more than the fact that the boy witness Blake called "this lad" placed them holding Lyon's horse near the crime scene. Claiming that a conviction required jurors to conclude there was "not even a *possibility*" that someone else had committed the crime, Blake argued that the jury must acquit unless they were prejudiced.[75]

Though neither prosecution attorney, John Hooker or James Sullivan — Massachusetts' elected attorney general and son of an Irish Catholic immigrant — ever mentioned the defendants' origins, Blake repeatedly coupled their ethnicity with anti-Irish prejudice. He emphasized "the inveterate hostility against the people of that wretched country [Ireland] from which the Prisoners have emigrated, for which the people of New-England are peculiarly distinguished." As Americans, Blake admonished the jurors to set aside prejudice to provide equal justice. Daley and Halligan had

> lived under the fostering protection of our government, and are now to be tried by the beneficent provision of our laws. — Whether they have brought with them all the vices, without any of the virtues of this generous but degraded people, whether they are wandering fugitives from justice or exiled victims of oppression, — whether they have been transported for their crimes, or have been driven across the Atlantic by the storms of internal commotion, it is enough to ensure them a fair and impartial trial.[76]

Regardless of "popular fury" and claims arising from the "prolific imaginations of news-mongers," he told jurors that they had "pledged by their oaths, to guard . . . against the approach of prejudice."⁷⁷ Blake exhorted: "Do not therefore believe them guilty, because they are *Irishmen* but viewing them as your *countrymen*, remember you are sworn to believe them innocent, until every reasonable doubt of their guilt is removed from your minds."⁷⁸

Blake's histrionics testify to the conflicting sentiments in play, pitting the Enlightenment idealism of Paine's 1776 "asylum of the oppressed" and its related ideology of equality before the law against the exclusivity of the Puritan "city on the hill," now laced with Yankee xenophobia and the doctrine of republican virtue. Summing up, Blake referred to "that national prejudice" that led one witness to "pre-judge the prisoners because they are Irishmen." Passionately declaiming, "Pronounce then a verdict against them! Condemn them to the gibbet! Hold out an awful warning to the wretched fugitives from that oppressed and persecuted nation!" Blake's words placed the trial in the context of the national political debates at the time of the Alien Act:

> Tell them that though they are driven into the ocean, by the tempest which sweeps over their land, which lays waste their dwellings, and deluges their fields with blood;—though they float on its billows upon the broken fragments, of their liberty and independence;—yet our inhospitable coast presents no Ararat upon which they can rest in safety; that although we are not cannibals, and do not feast upon human flesh, yet with all our boasted philanthropy, which embraces every circle on the habitable globe, we have yet no mercy for a wandering and expatriated fugitive from Ireland. That the name of an Irishman is, among us, but another name, for a robber and an assassin; that every man's hand is lifted against him; that when a crime of unexampled atrocity is perpetrated among us, we look around for an Irishman; that because he is an outlaw, with him the benevolent maxim of our law is reversed, and that the moment he is accused, he is presumed to be guilty.⁷⁹

Blake finished by calling attention to the pathetic scene of the prisoners' families attending their trial and by quoting the Irish orator John Philpot

Curran, whose speech at a 1798 treason trial warned jurors that they would one day answer to God for their verdict.[80]

Blake's strategy won public praise but failed in the courtroom.[81] Attorney General Sullivan, himself a sometime target of anti-Irish rhetoric, summed up the prosecution. He pointed out that "the most powerful eloquence, or the highest strains of rhetoric" do not refute evidence. Compassion and mercy, while admirable, must not supplant justice. Confronting Blake's emotional appeal directly, Sullivan told the jurors, "The idea that you may be prejudiced against them because they are foreigners, can have no foundation but in a warm imagination," and it was "an ill treatment of your characters" to suppose otherwise. "The prisoners," Sullivan stated, "are as men entitled to as fair a trial as the men of the first rank and eminence can have." Neither "out-door opinion against them, or the feelings of pity and compassion for them" determined their guilt or innocence. As to Blake's assertion that any "*possibility*" of doubt should bar a guilty verdict, Sullivan declared, "There is no such legal expression in the books." In the authoritative words of the judge who charged the jury, the issue was "*reasonable doubt.*" Sullivan noted that "nothing exists beyond a possible doubt in the minds of men." Humans were fallible, and "our senses may decieve [sic] us, yet we cannot refuse their evidence." Eschewing "prejudice, . . . partiality, avarice, envy, pride, malice, ambition, self-interest, . . . fear and cowardice," Sullivan explained that the jury's duty was to act "with an upright heart, and from pure motives." At midnight, after deliberating for just an hour, the jury returned a guilty verdict.[82]

The defeated attorney, Francis Blake, made one last effort to save his clients with a pardon petition he drafted for Dominic Daley's mother, Ann, to sign. This petition to Governor Caleb Strong repeated the defense's arguments as to the circumstantial evidence but stressed that public opinion prohibited a fair trial:

> How natural to prejudge the wayfaring strangers as the perpetrators of the crime? Neither can your Excellency be unconscious of the strong prejudice prevailing among the Inhabitants of the interior against the common Irish people who have emigrated to

the United States; and in the present case the public mind had been influenced in great degree by conversations and news-paper publications which precluded the possibility of that impartiality of trial which the Law contemplates.[83]

Strong, a lifelong Northampton and popular Hampshire County resident, the attorney who defended Irish John Farrell in 1796 and then led his successful pardon campaign, now joined with the Council to deny Ann Daley's appeal for her son's life.

Almost certainly prejudice influenced the prosecution and conviction of the two men; but procedurally their trial appears like dozens of others in which American citizens stood charged with murder. The evidence was neither more nor less substantial than in other cases, gathered as it was in the customary way by a justice of the peace and local people. Court-appointed attorneys, though they might be local luminaries, routinely prepared arguments hastily, putting a premium on rhetoric, not investigation. So it is reasonable to conclude that the 1806 court that acquitted the Irishman James Busby and the next day condemned Dominic Daley and James Halligan provided these foreigners with equal justice. Yet Francis Blake's passionate condemnation of anti-Irish sentiment must be understood as more than a courtroom tactic in light of Ezra Witter's 1805 sermon at Wilbraham— exuding disdain for foreigners and particularly the "two ruffians"—in addition to the 1806 newspaper piece decrying foreigners and urging that they be sent home. For a decade the Jeffersonian Blake had been battling Federalists; so his criticism of their oft-expressed antipathy to foreigners, invoking the nation's destiny as "asylum of liberty," was idealistic, partisan, and familiar.

Two months later, when the two convicts came to the gallows, anti-Irish sentiment joined to anti-Catholicism surged again. For when, at the prisoners' request, Boston's Father John Cheverus traveled to Northampton to pray with the convicts and to preach their execution sermon, local opinion was so hostile that Cheverus chose the text "whosoever hateth his brother is a murderer."[84] Instead of the usual emphasis on the sins of the men to be hanged, imploring auditors to use their example as inspiration for personal reform, Cheverus's sermon targeted the sin of the hatred he felt in Northampton. Rather than focus on Daley and Halligan, he decried those "to whom the death of their fellow beings is a spectacle of pleasure, an object of curiosity."[85] Having himself been refused accommodations in Northampton—he found lodgings only after being first turned away—the Frenchman Cheverus, the first Catholic to speak publicly in the town, took to heart the prejudice directed at Irishmen. Ultimately, according to a local historian, residents' antagonism softened, and they invited Cheverus to preach more sermons.[86] That New Englanders were generally intolerant of Catholics cannot be doubted; but Father Cheverus's personal and pastoral skills disarmed prejudice in Northampton as in Boston during the preceding decade. Judging from newspaper reports, the Catholic religion was of less concern than Daley's and Halligan's nationality. Whereas the press never mentioned their faith, and some did not cite nationality, at least eleven newspapers pointed out that "they were both natives of Ireland."[87] A local pamphlet account of the murder emphasized: they were "Irishmen of foreign birth."[88]

<h1 style="text-align:center">V</h1>

This increased consciousness of foreigners—and concern with national origins—coincided with Americans' rising awareness of their own nationality. As time passed, popular consciousness of foreigners and prejudices against them grew. But whether such bias compromised their rights or access to equality before the law is less clear-cut. Paradoxically, one aspect of the national consciousness that heightened Americans' awareness of foreigners and sharpened prejudices against them was the national ideology of equality before the law. The same people who disparaged the vices of foreigners, decrying the costs they imposed on taxpaying citizens, could also defend providing alien immigrants with equal protection under the law.

Moreover, when ethnic rivalries came before the American legal system they confounded simplistic stereotypes. A conflict in 1816 among German Lutherans in Philadelphia over English language in religious services culminated in riotous confrontation, where one side denounced the other as

"Irishmen." This pejorative label referred to German Americans who, though they could speak German, refused to do so because they were "ashamed" of their mother tongue.[89] When the two sides confronted each other in the trial of Frederick Eberle and others in a Philadelphia courtroom, the state's attorney general, Jared Ingersoll, with two other Anglo-Americans and a German American, prosecuted Eberle for riot and conspiracy with other pro-German-language advocates. These "Germans" hired attorneys Moses Levy, his brother, Sampson Levy Jr., and William Rawle to defend them. The Levys were sons of an immigrant German Jewish convert to the Anglican Church and his formerly Presbyterian Scots-immigrant wife. Rawle, scion of a prominent English Quaker family, had served as U.S. district attorney in the Washington administration.

All sides vigorously asserted their rights, but though the jury found the "Germans" guilty of disorderly behavior, the judge only fined the offenders—whereupon Pennsylvania's first German American governor, Simon Snyder, canceled their fines. A succession of further court battles underscored themes that surfaced in the Eberle trial; the pro-German-language party were not "good Americans," but in the end they triumphed. Though English language advocates persuaded the legislature to assign one of the church's two buildings to them for services in English, Governor Snyder refused to sign the law. Frustrated, the English speakers concluded that "no law [existed] in the United States, and Pennsylvania, which can take the Germans from their rights." Ultimately the state refused to intervene in religious affairs. According to Pennsylvania's chief justice, "No power on earth can lawfully force the English language upon them. Nor can any power withhold from them the use of that language, if they choose to adopt it. . . . It is the affair of the congregation, to be decided by themselves only."[90] The doctrine of equal rights sustained ethnic and religious diversity.

Nevertheless, national stereotypes and prejudices associated with people from Ireland, Germany, and other countries and cultures were widely accepted. Yet their impact on the actual rights of foreigners was uneven and unpredictable. Ideals of fairness, justice, and the rule of law mattered and interacted significantly with other sentiments and beliefs. The operation of prejudice in conjunction with competing values was evident in the 1817 trial of Welsh mariner Henry Phillips for murdering an Italian confectioner's assistant, Gaspard Denegri, in Boston.

Following a tavern quarrel, Phillips, accompanied by another mariner, Joseph M'Cann, approached Denegri from behind and hit him over the head with an iron bar. Eight days later, on December 8, 1816, Denegri died, so the Massachusetts' solicitor general, Daniel Davis, charged Phillips with murder and M'Cann as accomplice. At the request of the defendants' attorneys, George Sullivan, son of the former attorney general and governor, and Lemuel Shaw, future chief of the state's Supreme Judicial Court, the two men were tried separately; with M'Cann, who was Irish or of Irish descent, being acquitted following Phillips's conviction.[91] When Phillips's trial began, the ambiguities of American nationality, even forty years after independence, were evident when the prosecutor mistakenly described Phillips as "a native American, but a stranger to this part of the country."[92] In fact, Henry Phillips Stonehewer Davis, known as Henry Phillips, was a twenty-five-year-old Welshman who, sent to sea as a nine-year-old, had been raised during voyages all over the Mediterranean and Atlantic, touching Europe, Africa, North and South America, and several British ports.[93] With this background it is no wonder that the exact nationality of this English-speaking stranger was not clearly apparent. But though Phillips was in fact a foreigner, the prosecutor argued that the jury should convict the "American," Phillips, for the murder of a recent Italian arrival who could not speak English.[94] The prosecution, clearly, was committed to the idea of equal justice even if it meant that an American would hang for assaulting a foreigner.

Phillips's distinguished attorneys, in contrast, attacked equal justice, justifying Phillips's actions by dwelling on the legitimacy of national stereotypes and common prejudices. After the initial fracas between Phillips and Denegri, witnesses testified, "the idea of an Italian with a concealed knife about him spread consternation and dismay throughout the house." Lemuel Shaw explained that Phillips "did fully and honestly believe, that Denegri was armed with a deadly weapon," so, given "the known ferocity and vindictive temper of the Italian character," Phillips's attack was well founded. Shaw elaborated: "So firmly is this bad reputation established, particularly among sailors, that in their intercourse with foreigners, the dread of a quarrel with a Spaniard or an Italian is habitual and almost instinctive; this is founded on an impression, that they are ready, upon slight occasions, to resort to the poignard and stiletto." Because Phillips believed that "this foreigner had a knife for mischievous purposes, and a disposition to use it," his assault "was not so criminally rash as is supposed."[95] In short, common prejudices justified killing this "foreigner."

Chief Justice Isaac Parker's summary charge to the jury explicitly rebutted this chauvinistic appeal. Noting the rumor that Denegri carried a knife, Parker agreed that "this suspicion may have arisen from the dread our people have of an Italian." But the prejudice had no merit. It arose, he said, "from stories of travellers, founded sometimes in fact, but exaggerated in the number of instances of assassinations said to have taken place in Italy and some other European countries." Turning the subject in favor of American republicanism, he suggested that assassination was "a practice which is probably owing to the nature of government in those countries, and to the lax principles and morals of the nobles and others, who give a stamp to the character of their nation." But, he boasted, there was "little reason to apprehend assassination" in the United States, "even from the subjects of a country where it is said to be practiced." To rely on the "loose and idle suspicion, therefore, that a person intended to assassinate, merely because he was an Italian, without any proof that he had the means of doing it, or any menaces indicating such intention, would not," Chief Justice Parker concluded, "be a reasonable ground of proceeding to violence." Rejecting the anti-foreigner defense, the chief justice declared: "Experience proves that, from the vigilance of our laws, or the moral influence of our government and manners those foreigners who come to reside here, are generally as harmless and inoffensive as our own people."[96] Even as Parker dismissed Shaw's appeal to prejudice, he expressed his own biases toward Italians and other foreigners overseas.

After Phillips's conviction, however, sympathy for this English-speaking foreigner mounted. Although the fullest newspaper account of the trial did not mention nationality—American, British, or Italian—the issue remained alive. An abbreviated trial report rushed out after the verdict reported "the dread our people have of an Italian . . . [as] it is well known that assassination by stabbing, is a frequent mode of revenge, both in Italy and Spain." Phillips's attorneys, Shaw and Sullivan, wrote to the governor arguing that their client deserved a pardon because like "all those about him," he believed that the "Italian, had armed himself with a knife for the purpose of doing mischief." This fact, though admittedly outside "the rules of law," diminished Phillips's "moral turpitude."[97] Additional petitions signed by 137 others, including a few prominent gentlemen, and one marked by the illiterate Phillips himself, pleaded mercy for "a stranger and a foreigner" who was "destitute of friends."[98] Nevertheless, Massachusetts hanged Phillips.

But though the equal rights of foreigners could be an active concern, sometimes the issue aroused no discussion. When a New Hampshire jury acquitted George Ryan of highway robbery in 1811, neither press coverage nor the trial report mentioned Ryan's origins. Six years later a jury did convict William M'Donnough for murdering his wife, but though a trial report noted that he was "not a native of this country," that fact was inconsequential because he had been working in Boston for twenty years. Ethnicity was not an issue; he bore an Irish surname, had come from London to Boston, and was known to play "Scotch airs." Yet the only time his origin was mentioned in the trial was when his attorney asked pity for "a foreigner, without many of the ties of consanguinity or friendship in this country"; this, even though M'Donnough, having slain his wife of over thirty years, possessed a grown son and daughter. Later, when the press reported his death awaiting execution, nationality was not mentioned.[99]

The same indifference to nationality was evident in two trials held about the same time in Dedham, just west of Boston. Here, two Irish glass factory workers, Stephen Murphy and John Doyle, accused of raping fifteen-year-old Rebecca Day Jr., won acquittals. The attorney general prosecuting the case never mentioned the defendants' nationality. Only their attorney, George Sullivan, who with Lemuel Shaw had unsuccessfully defended Henry Phillips earlier that year, raised the subject, hoping to arouse sympathy for his clients. Stephen Murphy, he told the jury, "is a foreigner . . . to our land, but he is not a foreigner to our hearts, and he will not be a stranger to your justice." Later, he characterized both prisoners as "valuable and respectable young men," and without specifying Ireland, Sullivan respectfully cited the "ardent friendship" and loyalty characteristic of Murphy's nation.[100]

To characterize defendants favorably and to discredit the accuser was, of course, standard for defending a rape case. But the fact that no one in court or in the press tried to disparage the factory hands on ethnic grounds is striking. Everyone could identify the defendants as Irish, but nationality was mentioned only to defend their characters. The same was true in the 1820 case of Michael Powers, a one-time County Wexford farmer who had come to Boston in 1802, worked as a hod carrier, and lived frugally. Powers had saved to finance the migration of three relatives, including Timothy Kennedy, who Powers claimed then refused to pay his debt. After legal remedies failed, Powers murdered Kennedy, stole his property, and fled to Philadelphia, where he was captured before sailing for Ireland. At trial, courtroom argument and press reports barely mentioned his nationality or that of his victim.[101]

In light of Powers's crime—revenge ax-murder, followed by burying the corpse in his cellar and flight for Ireland—possibilities for sensational expressions of ethnic prejudice were obvious. But instead the victim, Timothy Kennedy, received an admiring obituary as an Irish Catholic immigrant:

> The deceased was a native of Ireland; about 20 years of age, and had been nearly two years in this country—his disposition was amiable; he was industrious and faithful, and was never known to taste spirits of any kind. He was a constant attendant at the Roman Catholic Chapel, and though without money when he came to this country, he subscribed five dollars towards the Catholic Chapel at South Boston;—he was fond of reading religious books, and borrowed a book last Tuesday, which he has not returned, entitled the "Rich Cabinet, full of Heavenly Jewels.[102]

Kennedy, a pious young man displaying social virtues, was clearly worthy of possessing the full panoply of American rights.

VI

Evidently American citizens were of two minds regarding immigrants in general and the Irish in particular. Teague O'Regan, a leading character in Hugh Henry Brackenridge's satiric novel of the Pennsylvania frontier, *Modern Chivalry*, represents such ambivalence. On the one hand O'Regan was the stereotypical ridiculous Irishman, described by one scholar as "ignorant, foolish, and grasping." Yet at the same time Brackenridge has Pennsylvania citizens showering him "with undeserved honors and inappropriate responsibilities."[103] Brackenridge, a Pittsburgh Scot and Princeton graduate who served as a Federalist justice on the Pennsylvania Supreme Court, was scornful of uncouth Irishmen but also envious of their success. In New York, partisan criticism of Irish immigrants led an 1817 writer to defend both the Irish and American blacks. Their adversaries seemed to claim that Irishmen, though naturalized as citizens, should be excluded from public life because they were born abroad. And though blacks could vote because they were American-born, they should not be called "Americans, because their ancestors were from Africa." Such wrongheaded reasoning applied generally would disenfranchise "the American citizen," because he would still be "called a Dutchman, an Englishman, a Swede, a Highlander or Hessian."[104]

As to Irish immigrants, it was true that they were reduced to being "ashes gatherers and day laborers" in New York City; but before English conquest they were "proprietors of Irish soil." It was the English who reduced them to ignorance by proscribing schools and "interdicting reading." The Irish themselves were "republicans" who rose in revolt against British tyranny and who, after defeat, "became ashes-men in America—preferring liberty accompanied with labor to inglorious indulgence at home." For this writer the logic of American nationality dictated equal rights, not distinctions based on national origins. The fact that immigrants who were not naturalized could vote in many places, including the Northwest Territory, is testimony to popular support for equal rights.[105]

Nevertheless, as this vigorous defense suggests, not everyone shared these ideals. Public officials responsible for suppressing crime and caring for the poor had come to regard immigrants as social burdens. And although theirs was not an unprecedented response to new arrivals, it now possessed authoritative expression. In Boston the Massachusetts solicitor general, Daniel Davis, complained of immigrants. This official, who in prosecuting Henry Phillips, whom he mistakenly took to be American, had declared that "by the numerous provisions of our laws, every protection and assistance will be afforded him . . . for a perfectly impartial trial," and argued that "although it is possible the guilty may here escape, the innocent can never be

in danger of punishment," now used courtroom rhetoric to castigate immigrants in language resembling the rural pastor Ezra Witter at the time
of Halligan and Daley fifteen years earlier.[106] "Most of the robberies in this
part of the country, have been committed by foreigners," he asserted when
prosecuting an Irish immigrant, Michael Martin, for highway robbery in
1821. Elaborating his xenophobia, he contrasted Americans' own "peaceful
and happy state of society" and "the civil, social and religious blessings we
enjoy," with the "manners and morals" of "the countries from which these
foreigners have fled." Looking ahead, the solicitor general warned darkly,
"as the knowledge of this happy country shall be spread among the old
and corrupted countries of Europe, we shall be visited and infested by its
profligate and vicious inhabitants, who will be ready to flock in among us,
for the sole objects of rapine and plunder."[107] When a state's chief prosecutor stirred prejudice, the jury could not escape bias against the defendant.
Davis not only denied all pretense to fairness but now shed even the appearance of equal rights for the accused foreigner.

Davis's rhetorical volley expressed a growing feeling among some in
New England that foreigners were a chief source of social ills. The most
informed statement of this perception came from Redford Webster, the
Boston apothecary and overseer of the poor who reported on the city's problems in 1814. He began with an enumeration of Boston's almshouse and
workhouse populations over the past year. Among those admitted (570) over
half (291) were "foreigners." But unlike Davis, Webster's "foreigners" included persons from other states, not only people from abroad. How many
were foreign nationals was not Webster's concern. Indeed, Webster explicitly asserted that no preferences should be given to natives over foreigners,
especially because foreigners, as "stranger[s] among strangers," were at a
great disadvantage. Unlike local people, relatives, friends, and neighbors
could not help them. As to the Irish, Webster never mentioned them; but he
pointed out that "among all the religious societies in the town, the Catholic
is the most attentive to its people. . . . The children are early made accountable; and they *never* are found begging in the street."[108]

The only class toward which Webster directed particular attention was
"coloured people" who came from elsewhere. Some were East and West

Indians, who were "generally miserable a short time after landing." But the greatest numbers were "rogues and run-away slaves from southern states." Webster had no wish to return them to slavery, but he angrily declared, "There is a material difference between an asylum for liberty, and a city of refuge for rogues." Having been corrupted by slavery, these foreigners constituted "the most profligate wretches that ever disgraced society. . . . No beings among us are so bold, impudent and flatigious [sic]; they seem to be above all shame." They gambled and fought with each other in court and out; Webster was shocked by their "licentiousness."[109] But as disturbing as he found their behavior, he would not cut them off from support. "Foreigners" of all colors surely cost the taxpayers of the city and state, but for Webster and the town of Boston equality of treatment should be the rule.

FOUR

People of Color and the Promise Betrayed

The legislation and histories of the times, and the language used in
the Declaration of Independence, show, that neither . . . slaves, nor
their descendants, whether they had become free or not, were then
acknowledged as a part of the people, nor intended to be included
in the general words used in that memorable instrument.
— *Majority Opinion [Roger B. Taney]*,
U.S. *Supreme Court*, Scott v. Sandford, 1857

Our independence was a great epoch in the history of freedom, and
while I admit the Government was not made especially for the colored
race, yet many of them were citizens of the New England States, and
exercised, the rights of suffrage when the Constitution was adopted.
— *Minority Opinion [John McLean]*,
U.S. *Supreme Court*, Scott v. Sandford, 1857

It is not true . . . that the Constitution was made exclusively
by the white race. And that it was made exclusively for the
white race is . . . contradicted by its opening declaration
that it was ordained and established by the people of the
United States, for themselves and their posterity.
— *Minority Opinion [Benjamin R. Curtis]*,
U.S. *Supreme Court*, Scott v. Sandford, 1857

No question of original intent is more critical for the United States than
equal rights for people of color. Yet in 1857 when the U.S. Supreme
Court ruled that the founders never intended to include nonwhites among
the citizens of the new Republic, they updated the ideals of 1776. Three

generations of controversy and experience concerning slavery and race now brought many white Americans, especially in the South, to interpret their grandfathers' and great-grandfathers' beliefs so as to align Revolutionary ideals with their own racial convictions. Because so many midcentury whites had come to believe that all men were not created equal in any practical sense, they concluded that the founders must have meant, "All [white] men are created equal." Limiting equal rights to white people only, they reasoned, must have been so completely self-evident as to constitute their universally accepted (if unwritten) understanding. Speaking for them, Chief Justice Roger B. Taney explained that "the men who framed this declaration were great men . . . [who] perfectly understood the meaning of the language they used, . . . and they knew that it would not in any part of the civilized world be supposed to embrace the negro race." To contend otherwise, Taney declared, was absurd, because "when we look at the condition of this race in the several States at this [former] time, it is impossible to believe that these rights and privileges were intended to be extended to them." Although the Declaration of Independence was an assertion of American aspirations, because blacks in 1776 were almost all slaves and nothing in the Declaration proposed to abolish slavery, for Taney's majority the notion of a color-blind pledge of equal rights was unthinkable.[1] Confident in their own understanding of history and convinced in their prejudice, the court majority pronounced the United States a white republic.

Two generations earlier Redford Webster, Boston's overseer of the poor, had argued that republican principles of equal rights must override color prejudice because law directed authorities "'to provide for the *immediate* comfort and relief of *all* persons residing, or *found* therein, when they fall into distress.'"[2] But by the 1850s, when many white Americans viewed the poverty, humble social standing, and marginal civil rights of people of color — African Americans, Native Americans, and those of mixed lineage — they shared Taney's conclusion. Even foes of slavery who wished to halt its spread, commonly shared Abraham Lincoln's 1858 doubts that interracial "social and political equality" was possible. Like him, they were "in favor of the superior position being assigned to the white man." Among whites, such views prevailed.[3] But Taney's presumption of fixed and unchanging opinions—from the beliefs of those who first declared American independence and created the Constitution all the way to the 1850s—is problematic. Although historians of varied political orientations have agreed with the abolitionist Wendell Phillips that the Constitution was a "pro-slavery compact," there is more to the story.[4] Phillips's and Taney's understanding of the founding of the United States oversimplifies the realities of race and rights during the first decades after independence. Certainly Taney had it right for some leaders of the founding era. But for other founders the ideal of equal rights was more inclusive. In addition, the ways Americans thought and acted regarding race and rights could be ambiguous and fluid. To understand the movement in beliefs from the founding era to the 1850s we need to examine ideas more closely. We must also study the constitutions, statutes, and actual practices on the ground as they emerged in the growing number of American states. The starting point must be the years around independence.

I

During the decade preceding independence, the year 1772 was relatively quiet. Although Rhode Island colonists destroyed H.M.S. *Gaspee*, intensifying their conflict with royal government, and Bostonians created a Committee of Correspondence to launch grassroots opposition to imperial government, in most colonies an uneasy stability prevailed. Indeed 1772's most remarkable equal rights episode came in London, not America, when Lord Mansfield delivered a judgment in *Somersett's Case*. Because James Somersett, a one-time Massachusetts slave, had been brought into a jurisdiction governed by common law and parliamentary statute, Mansfield ruled that Somersett could not lawfully be held as a slave. Hitherto, censure of slavery belonged chiefly to clergymen and moralists, but the chief justice of the King's Bench shifted the debate over equal rights, empowering reformers who sought to destroy slavery's legal foundation. Mansfield's ruling treated a single case and so did not actually prohibit slavery; but Mansfield called slavery "odious," enabling reformers to proclaim a broad victory. "The air of England is too pure for a slave to breathe," they claimed in court, and in the popular mind these words were promptly elevated to the status of Mansfield's ruling. The poet William Cowper exclaimed, "Slaves cannot breathe in England; if their lungs / Receive our air, that moment they are free; / They touch our country, and their shackles fall."[5]

The impact of *Somersett* was immediate. Just nine weeks after Mansfield's ruling, the *Virginia Gazette* attributed to Mansfield the assertion that by the "Laws of Nature . . . a Negro cannot be less free than a Man of any other Complexion." Mocking the logic of color-based slavery, this newspaper account declared, "If Negroes are to be Slaves on Account of Colour, the next step will be to enslave every Mulatto in the Kingdom, then all the Portuguese, next the French, then the brown complexioned English, and so on till there be only one free Man left, which will be the Man of the palest Complexion in the three Kingdoms!"[6] So swiftly did *Somersett* capture enlightened Englishmen's imagination everywhere that barely a year after arrival of Mansfield's ruling, a Massachusetts slave won freedom not only by relying on Mansfield's technical arguments but also by appealing to popular understanding of his judgment: "Somersett case shews everyone setting his foot on English ground to be free, wherever he came from."[7] Chief Justice Mansfield had touched a responsive chord.

One reason for *Somersett's* wide influence and resounding echo was a long-standing belief that slavery and British soil were incompatible. In 1740 the patriotic poem that became Britain's military anthem had proclaimed, "Britons never, never, never shall be slaves."[8] And a decade before *Somersett*, James Otis, the Massachusetts Revolutionary, had ridiculed the idea that "'tis right to enslave a man because he is black."[9] Indeed, in 1728 the Virginia planter William Byrd had observed, "We all know that very bright talents may be lodged under a very dark skin." Expressing his fundamental belief in natural equality, Byrd claimed that "all nations of men have the same natural dignity. . . . The principal difference between one people and another proceeds only from the different opportunities of improvement."[10] In an era when social hierarchy was customary and unequal status the accepted rule, Byrd saw no contradiction between his own rank as master of several hundred slaves and the truth of natural equality. Different opportunities for improvement—social inequalities exemplified by his own great personal privilege—were ordained by God.

But in the 1760s and 1770s, when American colonists claimed to enjoy the same rights as residents of England, they were coming to assert a subversive idea about equality. Their claim to possess equal rights with United Kingdom residents undermined theoretical distinctions between natural, social, and political equality, creating contradictions that demanded resolution. Colonists admitted that for Europeans it might be acceptable to recognize natural equality while also maintaining extremes of political inequality; but among Britons this must not be the rule. To advocate otherwise, they claimed, undermined the sacred, ancient British constitution.

In the decade before the Declaration of Independence this transatlantic credo of "the rights of Englishmen" became commonplace among American patriots. Moreover, its application to people of color, though unusual, was not limited exclusively to northerners like James Otis. Virginia gentlemen whose livelihoods depended on slavery recognized perpetual bondage as a contradiction in their society. As far back as 1759 Richard Henry Lee, scion of a family that played leading roles in the Revolution, had urged the Virginia legislature to discourage slave importation because slavery was morally indefensible and an obstacle to economic advancement. His brother Arthur Lee declared in 1767 that "freedom is unquestionably the birth-right of all mankind, *Africans* as well as *Europeans*," asserting that "to keep the former in a state of slavery is a constant violation of that right."[11] Six years later, when news of *Somersett* came to Virginia, another patriot, Patrick Henry, called slavery "a species of violence and tyranny . . . destructive to liberty."[12]

Henry acknowledged responsibility for supporting the evils of slavery "at a time when the rights of humanity are defined and understood with precision." But although "every thinking, honest man rejects it [slavery] in speculation," Henry lamented "how few [do so] in practice." His own moral culpability distressed him: "Would anyone believe I am the master of slaves of my own purchase!" Henry understood his peers' predicament exactly. Like other planters, he admitted, "I am drawn along by the general inconvenience of living here without them. I will not, *I cannot justify it.*"[13]

So the closest he and his fellow planters came to taking concrete action on their ideals was voting to end importation of more Africans. And this move was not driven purely by idealistic motives because Chesapeake planters were turning from tobacco to grain production, and they worried increasingly about the growing black population. Virginia enacted a duty on the importation of slaves in the 1760s.[14] Crown disallowance of this duty led Thomas Jefferson to include an attack on the slave trade in the Declaration's diatribe against King George. Congress deleted this passage from the final draft in deference to South Carolina and Georgia and in recognition of the colonists' complicity in the trade—an engagement in slavery that British critics acidly noted.[15]

By July 1776 most colonies were on record as opposing the slave trade. During the summer of 1774 more than two dozen Virginia counties denounced it, with Fairfax County endorsing George Mason's judgment that the trade was "wicked, cruel and unnatural."[16] In October 1774, when the First Continental Congress adopted a commercial nonintercourse policy against Britain, twelve colonies (Georgia was absent) voted to "wholly discontinue the slave trade."[17] Nonintercourse was conditional, and colonists hoped that their boycott would be temporary, but by singling out the slave trade they registered disapproval. And in 1776 Virginia's draft constitution proposed, "No person hereafter coming into this country shall be held in the same in slavery under any pretext whatsoever." Two years later Virginia banned importation of slaves by sea or land, enforcing the ban by declaring any imported slave immediately free.[18]

But opposition to the slave trade, whether moral or economic, was not condemnation of slavery itself and was far from an embrace of equal rights. Initially the challenge to slavery came from the rise of humanitarian sentiments, not commitment to natural liberty or equal rights.[19] Moreover, enlightened men were often ambivalent, as in Patrick Henry's and other planters' quandary—simultaneously denouncing slavery and depending on it. The notion that blacks were entitled to the same rights as whites was not widely accepted, even by whites who believed that Africans possessed a natural right to liberty. Despite their inclusive, universal language—"all men are created equal"—Revolutionary leaders did not agree on the principle of equal rights for all.

The question came into sharp focus in Virginia because in that colony and state entrenched slavery collided head-on with the universalism of the Enlightenment and Christianity. Here, in June 1776, delegates to the Virginia convention faced the issue directly when they considered a bill of rights whose first article proclaimed "all men are born equally free and independent and have certain inherent natural rights." The words came from Colonel George Mason, the lawyer and planter who drafted the bill assisted by Thomas Ludwell Lee, eldest brother of the slavery critics, Richard Henry and Arthur. When Mason introduced this language on May 29, some delegates shuddered. Robert Carter Nicholas objected, doubting that a society resting on slavery could embrace such ideas without inviting rebellion.[20]

Four days later Edmund Pendleton, another lawyer and planter, proposed modified language to reassure slaveholders. The fact that all people possessed "certain inherent natural rights" applied only "when they enter into a state of society." Because slaves did not "enter into a state of society," Pendleton and fellow masters reasoned, they did not possess equal natural rights.[21] Calling on the distinction William Byrd had made between "natural" and "social" equality, Pendleton's amendment aimed to exclude slaves from the Bill of Rights. This reasoning would later provide support for Taney's conclusions. Yet by this reasoning all free persons, regardless of color, should be equally entitled to "inherent natural rights" as members of society. A generation later one prominent Virginian recognized the belief that Virginia's declaration of equal rights did not affect blacks was mistaken. It had been accepted "with too great an indifference to futurity, and not without inconsistency."[22]

For those who subscribed to the equal rights doctrine expressed by the Declaration of Independence, the denial of equal rights on the basis of color was even more problematic. Unlike Virginia, which qualified its call for equal rights with Pendleton's language of entry into society, the Declaration carried no prerequisite. "All men are created equal," the Declaration announced without caveat or qualification, and "they are endowed by their Creator with certain unalienable Rights, that among these are Life, Liberty and the pursuit of Happiness." Yet slaveholding members of Congress did not object. Why? It cannot be that their views differed from Pendleton's or that they were unaware of the implications of language so recently debated in Virginia. How could language too inclusive for Virginia planters in their Declaration of Rights be acceptable to them and other slaveholders? The explanation appears that in contrast to a declaration of rights that became a binding constitutional document, Congress regarded the Declaration of Independence as only a political instrument to rally Americans by appealing to their ideals and reminding them of British insults. Apart from the fact of independence, neither Congress nor any state regarded its language as binding. Indeed the authoritative study of the Declaration of Independence observes in "the first fifteen years following its adoption," the Declaration was "all but forgotten."[23]

II

Even if critics of slavery did not immediately press the Declaration into service to advance their cause contemporaries recognized the expansive potential of its language. In the 1770s and 1780s secular and religious advocates of universal rights carried the antislavery movement forward almost exclusively at the state level. Before the Constitution of 1787 the realization of individual rights—equal or unequal—could only be a matter for state legislatures and courts. And it was in the states that the long battle over equal rights for people of color—a battle of piecemeal victories and defeats—was joined. Before there was a Constitution of the United States there was a Confederation, and in the years 1778 to 1789 the states alone determined questions of equal rights and citizenship.

In the struggle over equal rights the central question was not slavery or abolition. Being free was essential to realize equal rights, but as Taney argued, freedom alone did not provide equal rights. Customary and statutory restrictions were everywhere. Many free citizens—women, insane men,

and juveniles—lacked equal rights. Similarly, property and residency requirements commonly limited voting while additional qualifications of religious profession, age, and wealth might be required for office-holding. In
Connecticut and Rhode Island old colonial charters ruled as constitutions,
so there were no new statements of rights whatever. Even ardent proponents
of equal rights agreed that individual rights could properly be limited to assure community well-being. Ultimately the question was whether among
free men, color or lineage should be restrictive.

In the first decade or so following the Declaration, although there is evidence that some believed whites alone should enjoy equal rights, the picture is mixed. In January 1778, when Congress debated the fourth article of
the Confederation—guaranteeing that every state would assure "the free
inhabitants of each of these states . . . all the privileges and immunities of
free citizens in the several states"—South Carolina delegates objected to its
inclusive language. William Henry Drayton complained that the wording
was "absolutely inadmissible" because people of color would claim equal
rights. "There ought to be no doubt," he declared, "that free inhabitants
should be white." So when voting on the final draft in June 1778 South
Carolina proposed an amendment to read "the free *white* inhabitants." But
a lopsided majority voted against this "whites only" amendment, eight states
to two, with one state divided.[24] Similarly, when Governor Thomas Jefferson asked the Virginia assembly in 1779 to ban free blacks from becoming
citizens and to require them to leave Virginia within a year of manumission,
the legislature refused.[25]

Certainly many whites believed that equal rights belonged to white
people only, whether or not they said so explicitly. But they used the restrictive term "white" sparingly and unevenly. Georgia, for example, stipulated "white male" in its constitutional suffrage provision in 1776; yet the
omission of "white" by South Carolina cannot be construed as inclusive.
States that routinely denied the franchise to men of color, like Virginia,
had used inclusive language in their constitutions, stating that "all men,
having sufficient evidence of permanent common interest with, and attachment to, the community, have the right of suffrage."[26] However, other states

employing equivalent language allowed blacks to vote, treating them as citizens when they fulfilled suffrage requirements such as holding property and paying taxes.

In North Carolina the inclusive language of the 1776 constitution allowed free people of color to enjoy a measure of equal rights. In 1838 North Carolina Supreme Court justice William Joseph Gaston made the point directly. "Free persons born within the State," he ruled, "are born citizens of the State." This was no innovation; in the 1776 constitution the state "extended the elective franchise to every freeman who had arrived at the age of twenty-one and paid a public tax," and Gaston explained, "it is a matter of universal notoriety that, under it, free persons, without regard to color, claimed and exercised the franchise." Two generations of equal suffrage, he noted, ended only when North Carolina voters amended the constitution in 1835 to exclude any "free negro, free mulatto, or free person of mixed blood."[27] That same year President Andrew Jackson appointed Taney to the Supreme Court.

What was true of North Carolina in the decades after independence was true for most northern states. The failed Massachusetts Constitution of 1778 had barred "negroes, Indians, and mulattoes" from voting, but many towns protested, explicitly defending citizenship for people of color. Consequently the 1780 Massachusetts Constitution included no racial tests. As in New Jersey, New York, and New Hampshire, men of color could vote if they met property and residency requirements.[28] But whites' conflicting views on equal rights—or not—were manifest. It was symbolic that Maryland and Pennsylvania, lying along the Mason-Dixon Line dividing north from south, were inconsistent. Pennsylvania's constitution, perhaps the most democratic because it did not limit suffrage to landowners, used inclusive language— "all free men having a sufficient evident common interest with, and attachment to the community, have a right to elect officers, or to be elected into office." But practices within the state varied. In Philadelphia, where free blacks were numerous and so might determine a close election, whites denied them the franchise, whereas in Bucks County, where people of color were scattered among a significantly Quaker population, they voted.[29] In rural Maryland blacks did not vote, although in Annapolis and Baltimore they did until "complaints that free negroes . . . controlled the elections" led to constitutional amendments in 1801 and 1809 restricting "the vote to every free *white* male citizen in elections in Baltimore and Annapolis."[30] These amendments resolved a wavering pattern within a state where as of 1776 "free blacks possessed all the basic civil rights of white persons—the right to contract, to possess property, to sue and even to vote." By 1787, however, Maryland ended suffrage for free blacks entering the state after 1783 or who gained freedom after that date. Meanwhile New England states decided to exclude blacks and Indians from their militias.[31] Just as there was no fixed national consensus on the universality of equal rights, there were divisions within states.

The Maryland pattern was emblematic. In the 1780s the extension of equal rights to people of color aroused little concern in much of the United States. Since nearly all people of color were slaves or Native Americans living at or beyond the frontier, the number of taxpaying, property-owning nonwhites qualified to vote was vanishingly small. Their threat to social and political order seemed hypothetical. Under these circumstances the ideal of enlightened universalism commanded widespread allegiance and, many whites believed, needed no qualification. Still, in the 1790s and increasingly during succeeding decades the growing presence of free people of color became a catalyst for latent white antagonisms. Indeed by 1790—even before the revolution in Haiti—when Congress enacted the nation's first naturalization act, it determined that the Continental Army would be white and citizenship restricted to white immigrants only.

Most American citizens, white Americans that is, had, like white Virginians a generation earlier, decided that their country must be a white republic. More African Americans meant trouble. With the crucial exception of abolitionists, white Americans who concerned themselves with race advocated transporting blacks out of the United States and colonizing them in Africa or the Caribbean.[32] Only people who saw a bright future for slavery continued to advocate importing more Africans, chiefly Georgia and South Carolina slave masters. Believing that white domination over slaves would endure, they defended the African slave trade. To them there was no contradiction in developing a republic of free white men ruling black slaves possessing no rights, civil or natural. So it had been in antiquity. The Dred Scott decision embraced this viewpoint, although when the Constitution was written and ratified in states from North Carolina northward, slavery seemed a curse not a blessing, ideologically and practically.

Whites generally liked the idea of a white United States though at present that was impossible for the whole nation. In one of its last acts under the Articles of Confederation the Congress closed a major portion of the nation—the Northwest Territory—to slavery, guaranteeing that white settlement would dominate the region. Next would be ending further importation of slaves, postponed until 1808 because at the Constitutional Convention South Carolinians exacted a pledge against earlier action. Still, the 1790 prohibition against naturalizing nonwhite immigrants expressed majority intentions, though the Naturalization Act's impact was minimal since few nonwhites sought entry into the United States. Thereafter Americans argued over how to treat color differences, ranging from colonization of people of color to assimilation as citizens. In the upper South, where slave agriculture was declining, white Americans' uneasiness over slavery, race, and citizenship played out in repeated legislative contests. In Virginia especially an articulate elite confronted the question of a multiracial society. Their actions, first in one direction, then in another, zigzagged across the decades.

Colonial Virginia operated a highly restrictive manumission regime where white Virginians' collective security came first. According to a 1723 law, no slave could be liberated unless the legislature and governor determined that the slave's "meritorious services" warranted a special act.[33] Planters replaced this law in 1782, giving priority to planters' individual liberty over collective security. Now a master's right to free his slaves took precedence, and the free black could remain in Virginia. A year later the state granted freedom to slaves who served as military substitutes in the Revolution, a policy matching New England, where 1,400 people of color, including Indians, had fought for independence.[34] So for a decade the numbers of free persons of color grew as Virginia masters voluntarily liberated hundreds of slaves. Quaker planters, especially Robert Pleasants, took the lead. By 1790, after about one thousand had been liberated annually, Virginia possessed 13,000 free blacks. Considering where Virginia had been in 1782, with perhaps 5,500 free people of color, the post-Revolutionary change was significant.[35]

This policy was not, finally, transformative. Fully 39 percent of all Virginians remained enslaved, and free people of color constituted just 1.7 percent of the state's 748,000 inhabitants. Moreover, after the bloody Haitian Revolution in the early 1790s, planters retreated from enlightened ideals. Manumissions slowed, and the motives propelling them shifted. Now planters often freed slaves to reward good service—an incentive that reinforced the system. Alternatively, free blacks purchased enslaved relatives to manumit them.[36] When George Washington fulfilled Revolutionary principles by manumitting his own slaves at his death in December 1799, his act represented fading aspirations. Within months Gabriel Prosser's plan for blacks to seize Richmond and violently overthrow slavery would be repressed. Once more collective security for white Virginia became paramount; so in 1806 Virginia enacted a new manumission law. Henceforth any person freed from bondage would not be a citizen or even a denizen (someone who dwells within a country) of Virginia; instead that person—though born in Virginia—became effectively an alien who must depart the state within twelve months or face reenslavement.[37] This denial of rights to persons of color meant that manumission, moving from slave to free status, would be abridged because any newfound "freedom" a court might grant would carry a Virginia expiration date.

In Virginia, home of grand schemes to end slavery gradually and to colonize exslaves in distant lands, the material interests of slave owners—Patrick Henry's dilemma—blocked movement toward equal rights. But even after the rollback of 1806, "most white Virginians did not claim slavery was desirable." In that year Jefferson's teacher, George Wythe, one of Virginia's most distinguished jurists, cited the state's 1776 Declaration of Rights to deny the legitimacy of slavery. Notwithstanding Pendleton's slavery loophole, Wythe ruled that "freedom is the birth right of every human being, which sentiment is strongly inculcated by the first article of our 'political catechism,' the bill of rights." But when the Virginia Supreme Court of Appeals reviewed Wythe's judgment, younger jurists reversed it, relying on Pendleton: "This court not approving the chancellor's principle and reasoning . . . except so far as the same relates to white persons and native Americans." Virginia's bill of rights did not apply to "native Africans and their descendants, who have been and are now held as slaves."[38]

The idea of black equality had become unthinkable for most Virginia whites, with the possible exception of Quakers and some Baptists. Though many elite Virginians lamented slavery and hoped that someday it could be eradicated, they always linked its ending with deportation of people with African lineage. Governor James Monroe revealed the trajectory of Enlightenment universalism a generation after 1776. Writing in 1802 to his old mentor Jefferson, Virginia's former governor and now president of the United States, this Revolutionary veteran explained sending blacks to Africa, "subject to temporary [lifelong] servitude, with liberty to their descendants," would be a "mild and benevolent" policy. Monroe recognized that this plan might not be "practicable;" but he wished that "we could make these people instrumental to their own emancipation by a process gradual and certain, on principles consistent with humanity, *without expense or inconvenience to ourselves.*"[39] When sentiments like these passed for benevolence in the upper South, it was clear that the prospects for equal rights—never bright— had been extinguished in the slave states.

III

In states created according to the Northwest Ordinance—where slavery was forever prohibited—a more extensive commitment to equal rights was practical precisely because the region was overwhelmingly white. Here former slaves could not possibly overwhelm white voters or visit bloody revenge against former masters. But starting with Ohio, admitted to statehood in 1803, and followed by Indiana and Illinois in the next decade, discriminatory "black laws" became the new normal in the region. When whites entered these states—though some were fugitives from the law—they brought with them the presumption of their own unencumbered free status. In contrast, statutes enacted soon after statehood—in 1804 and 1807 in Ohio— presumed people of color to be escaped slaves or vagabonds. Unlike whites, people of color were required to provide written proof of their free status; and if they wished to settle, they also had to post bond (five hundred dollars in Ohio), so as to assure their good behavior. In these new states white majorities placed people of color in a probationary status. Though their ability to enforce exclusion laws was limited, the underlying message to African Americans was "do not settle here; move on."[40]

Ohio policies substantially set the pattern for Indiana and Illinois. All of these states recruited many settlers from slave country south of the Ohio River, setting up a conflict between men who—notwithstanding the Northwest Ordinance—wanted to bring slaves in and those who wanted to keep slaves out. The latter group, southern yeomen farmers and migrants from northern states, brought varying beliefs concerning equal rights and race. The broadest degree of consensus formed around limiting civil rights for people of color. Though there were some champions of equality, like Ohio, the Indiana and Illinois legislatures enacted "black laws."

What happened in Indiana starkly reveals the differing views of the good society dividing white Americans. From 1776 onward, making policy in eastern capitals for frontier settlers and enforcing central control in a vast republic had been chronic problems for state and national governments. So it was with the prohibition of slavery when slave masters flouted the Northwest Ordinance, bringing slaves to the "free" northern side of the Ohio Valley and expecting to enforce their own brand of law. When that proved unworkable legally, they made slaves into long-term indentured servants possessing only the fiction of freedom. But after Indiana gained statehood in 1816, antislavery politics forced an end to this thinly disguised slave system. The result: henceforward no person of color, free or slave, was welcome in the state.[41]

Predictably, the same forces that nearly established slavery in Indiana operated in Illinois, where settlers, mostly from the South, not only accepted the quasi-slavery of long-term indentures but allowed this perversion of the Northwest Ordinance to survive the 1818 admission of Illinois as a state. Ironically, Illinois was the only "free" state or territory where the number of slaves was increasing, growing more than fivefold from 1810 (168 slaves) to 1818 (978 slaves). The proslavery forces dominating the legislature called for a constitutional referendum in 1824 to enshrine the indenture system and black laws in the state's constitution. That their referendum failed was due less to abolitionism than to farmers' belief that a pro-slavery victory would reduce land values and transform Illinois into a planter aristocracy threatened by "negro insurrections."[42]

Enlightenment idealism, however, was not easily pushed aside. Before the Illinois referendum a legislative committee reported, "It is very questionable whether the General Assembly have a constitutional right to discriminate in the punishment of negroes and white men committing the same offences. . . . It would no doubt violate the constitution and every principle of legislation to punish a mechanic one way and a farmer another for the same offence." Though support for white supremacy was widespread, the doctrine of equal rights regardless of color still found a voice in government. Yet almost another generation passed before the state finally ended indentures in 1840. And it would be five more years before Illinois's supreme court prohibited masters from bringing slaves into the state. Two generations after Congress enacted the Northwest Ordinance, the state's highest court had its own *Somersett Case*, ruling in 1845 that "when a master voluntarily bring[s] his slave within the state, he [the slave] becomes from that moment free, and if he escape[s] from his master while in this State, it is not an escape from slavery but it is going where a free man has a right to come."[43] Now, nearly seventy years after the Declaration of Independence's bold assertion of equality, the idea that a free person was, in fact, free needed restatement.

This assertion of Revolutionary doctrine was pertinent not only for the Old Northwest where so many southerners had settled; it was a necessary national reminder. The declining recognition of rights for people of color, first visible in the upper South and the neighboring states of Ohio, Indiana, and Illinois, had come to prevail almost everywhere. Just as the citizenship rights of people of color were rolled back in Maryland and North Carolina, deprivation of rights spread across northern states. Prejudice against people of color, seen as lazy, thieving, immoral—unlike hard-working European immigrants—came to prevail. The reversal is illustrated by increasing color restrictions on voting. Usually black rights were curtailed after a close election where the losing party laid blame on a few nonwhite voters.

Adamant that a handful of "dependent" people of color must not determine the government of white men, legislatures and state constitutional conventions enacted racial prohibitions. Responding to black voters' impact in Annapolis and Baltimore, Maryland legislators excluded them in 1801. New Jersey representatives followed in 1807, simultaneously disfranchising women. Later Connecticut and New York repudiated equal rights for citizens of color even though equal rights advocates claimed that the legislature lacked authority to infringe such constitutional rights. Accordingly, constitutional conventions in Connecticut (1818) and New York (1821) debated the issue. Connecticut ended suffrage for new nonwhite voters but compromised with equal rights advocates to maintain voting for people of color who qualified previously. New York's revision continued to allow people of color to vote but increased their residency and property requirements while reducing or eliminating them for whites.[44] Democracy meant enfranchising poor white men while denying suffrage to poor black men. Poverty must no longer disqualify a voter; instead, color should. As the historian John Wood Sweet concluded, "The North emerged in the early years of the Republic as a place where people of color would be free but not equal—and as the site of continuing struggles over the meanings of American citizenship."[45]

The compromises in Connecticut and New York reflect not only victories of democratic majorities but also conflicts over denying fellow citizens' equal rights. In Tennessee and North Carolina, states that stripped black voting rights in constitutional revisions in 1834 and 1835, defenders of equal voting rights protested that for decades black voters never caused problems. But Tennessee delegate G. W. L. Marr, anticipating the Dred Scott decision, argued that "We the People" in the Constitution meant "we the free white people and the white people only." The Tennessee convention agreed by a vote of thirty-three to twenty-three. Similarly in neighboring North Carolina many had come to believe the *status quo* dishonored whites by allowing propertied blacks to vote but not unpropertied whites. But William Gaston, a state supreme court justice and a Catholic, disagreed: free people of color had long been "part of the body politic"; therefore respectable blacks must not be "politically excommunicated." Free blacks paid taxes and like others were entitled to representation. North Carolina must not add an "additional mark of degradation . . . solely on account of color." Gaston's view commanded substantial support, but whites-only democracy won narrowly, sixty-seven votes against sixty-two for those who supported black suffrage with an increased property requirement.[46]

In Rhode Island disfranchisement came in 1832 when Jacksonian Democrats in Providence were incensed by black support for their opponents. Then, after briefly reenfranchising blacks in 1842 and 1843, "democratic" reformers excluded them in the 1844 constitution. In Pennsylvania the constitutional convention ended black voting in 1838.[47] Public figures defending these policies claimed that black disfranchisement would make a purer democracy. So while white men eliminated obstacles to their own political engagement, they erected barriers against men of color. The rowdy, liquor-soaked contests of the 1830s and 1840s were in no way cleansed by excluding blacks; but that had not been the point. Prejudice ruled. Michigan, settled chiefly by northerners and possessing scarcely four hundred free people of color in 1840, barred them from voting when it wrote its constitution in 1837. Wisconsin did the same a decade later.[48] Like earlier discriminatory state constitutions, the United States Congress endorsed privileging whites when it admitted these states to the Republic.

By 1840, and long before in many places, the ideology of inherent racial characteristics made discrimination legitimate. Whether in the deepest south or the farthest north, east or west, the idea that whites were superior to all peoples of color—becoming common throughout the Western world—took root. Americans still celebrated "the principles of 1776" year after year, but their observances veered away from enlightened universalism. When in 1852 the black abolitionist Frederick Douglass asked, "What, to the American slave, is your 4th of July?" he answered: it is "a day that reveals to him, more than all the other days in the year, the gross injustice and cruelty to which he is the constant victim." Because the presumption of white supremacy had come to prevail in sentiment and policy in the United States, the heroic achievements of "your" Revolution, Douglass admonished, now belonged to whites only.[49] From the point of view of Chief Justice Taney and the Supreme Court majority, it had always been thus. But the historical record suggests otherwise. There had been champions of white superiority and unequal rights since 1776, but at the creation of the United States and in every decade thereafter they had always been contested, vigorously.

IV

Indeed the first reality of early American ideas about physical and ethnocultural differences—commonly called "race" today—is the variety, complexity, and contradictory thoughts white colonists expressed about various "races," "tribes," and "nations." The seventeenth-century legacy classified Africans chiefly in connection with their heathen and alien (read "uncivilized") characteristics, not physical or inborn differences from Europeans. But by the early decades of the eighteenth century some colonists were vilifying African physical and behavioral traits.[50] Nevertheless in 1700 the Puritan magistrate Samuel Sewall raised the biblical banner of equality to attack slavery, declaring, "It is most certain that all Men, as they are the Sons of *Adam* . . . have equal right unto Liberty, and all other outward Comforts of Life." Physical characteristics were irrelevant: "These *Ethiopians*, as black as they are; seeing they are the Sons and Daughters of the First *Adam* . . . ; They ought to be treated with a Respect."[51] Sewall's opponent, the slave-trading Rhode Island merchant John Saffin, was having none of it. He described "The Negroes Character" with a vicious litany: "Cowardly and cruel are those *Blacks* Innate, / Prone to Revenge, Imp of inveterate hate, / He that exasperates them, soon espies / Mischief and Murder in their very eyes. / Libidinous, Deceitful, False and Rude, / The spume Issue of Ingratitude."[52] Saffin's nasty verse resonated. Even Sewall admitted that though Africans deserved equal treatment, they "seldom use their freedom well." Most telling, he acknowledged a powerful racial boundary: "There is such a disparity in their Conditions, Color & Hair, that they can never embody [unite] with us and grow up in orderly families." Sewall attacked slavery on religious grounds with an added objective, believing that "it would conduce more to the Welfare of the Province, to have White Servants."[53]

For generations these themes of one blood versus inborn difference and equal rights versus white superiority were embedded in American thinking.

After New-York's 1741 slave conspiracy, when the colony resorted to burning black convicts for treason, officials faced the same arguments Sewall had articulated. Before New-York's governor executed the grisly punishment a Massachusetts jurist reminded him that "the Negros . . . are flesh & blood as well as we are & ought to be treated with Humanity." He warned the governor, "By making Bonfires of the Negros . . . Divine Vengeance does & will pursue us."[54] Two decades later, when imperial reforms ignited colonial rights talk, similar one-blood arguments were voiced, now in the context of opposition to British rule.

The Virginia planter Arthur Lee and the Massachusetts lawyer James Otis both opposed British measures in 1764, and both brought slavery and race into their arguments, but in conflicting ways. Lee based his diatribe against slavery on Montesquieu's idea of natural equality. "Americans," he said, must not "persist in a conduct, which cannot be justified, or persevere in oppression, from which their hearts must recoil." Yet he castigated blacks as "cruel, vindictive, stubborn, base, and wicked," expressing a hostility resembling Saffin's. Black Africans, Lee declared, were "a race the most detestable and vile that the earth ever produced."[55] Wholly apart from the injustice of slavery, the colonies must end the importation of slaves because they were so vicious. Like Samuel Sewall's concern for the well-being of New England, Lee concluded that "the colonies might be more advantageously peopled from Europe."[56] Slavery was intrinsically wrong and especially pernicious because it brought Africans to replace Europeans in the colonies.

James Otis, who like Lee wrote to oppose British policy, was not aiming at slavery in his *Rights of the British Colonies Asserted and Proved*. He was incensed by violations of constitutional rights that he claimed belonged to colonists equally with Britons. Questions of race and slavery were seemingly extraneous. But Otis, like Lee, agreed with Montesquieu on natural rights theory, and he, too, was troubled by slavery. So deep in his eighty-page pamphlet Otis asserted equal rights across racial or national boundaries. "The Colonists are by the law of nations free born, as indeed all men are, white or black." There was no justification, none, "to enslave a man because he is black." Physical traits were irrelevant: "Will short curl'd hair like wool, instead of Christian hair . . . help the argument? Can any logical inference in favour of slavery, be drawn from a flat nose, a long or a short face?" These, Otis said, were the false claims of men "whose hearts are as hard as the nether millstone." In fact, Otis proclaimed, African slaves were "born with the same right to freedom, and the sweet enjoyments of liberty and life, as . . . the overseers and planters."[57] Here, a dozen years before 1776, Otis foreshadowed "all men are created equal . . . endowed by their Creator with certain unalienable Rights, that among these are Life, Liberty and the pursuit of Happiness."

Because Otis came from Massachusetts and Lee from Virginia their differences could have resulted from dwelling in societies where blacks' roles were so dissimilar. However in 1765 John Adams, like Otis a defender of colonial rights, suggested a natural connection between slavery and race. Adams's ordinary Yankee, "Humphrey Ploughjogger," declared: "We won't be their negroes. Providence never designed us for negroes, I know, for if it had it wou'd have given us black hides, and thick lips, and flat noses, and short wooly hair, which it han't done, and therefore never intended us for slaves." According to Ploughjogger, natural physical traits justified slavery; whereas "we are as handsome as old England folks and should be as free."[58]

Belief in white superiority, though not shared by everyone, was widespread. By 1750 New England meetinghouses routinely seated blacks and Indians separately from whites. Significantly the same Beverly, Massachusetts, congregation that rejected such segregated seating in 1738 adopted it in 1769. At this time two "gentlemen" in Connecticut told a prospective missionary that "they could never respect an Indian, Christian or no Christian so as to put him on a level with white people on account especially to eat at the same Table, no—not with Mr. Ocham [Reverend Sampson Occum] himself be he ever so much a Christian or ever so Learned." They joked, "powder and balls" were the best way to civilize Indians. Even Quakers, though in the vanguard in opposing slavery, excluded blacks and Indians from their meetings. People of color were not only different; most whites believed that they were inferior.[59]

Among many the Revolution left these views intact. Prejudices often remained latent, but when officials made policy on poor relief and transients —where people of color appeared overrepresented—race could become explicit. In Massachusetts, for example, a 1788 law "for suppressing and punishing Rogues, Vagabonds, common Beggars, and other idle, disorderly, and lewd Persons" applied chiefly to whites but included provisions aimed at "Africans and Negroes." In 1800 Boston magistrates did not simply "warn out" blacks who were not Massachusetts citizens but ordered them to depart or face whipping or imprisonment.[60] Such regulations were not necessarily enforced, since few whites chose to harry poor people who did them no harm; but these rules clearly retreated from equal rights.[61] In Virginia, where the 1782 manumission law had encouraged a swift increase in the number of free people of color, the 1792 legislature barred free blacks from moving into the state and introduced a requirement that free black Virginians renew their freedom certificates every three years.[62] Though irregularly enforced, this law set people of color apart, denying their equal citizenship and proclaiming their presumptive status as slaves.

Still, public discourse in the 1780s and 1790s reinforced the equal rights idea. In Virginia the planter Robert Pleasants led a Quaker movement stressing manumission and equal rights. Pleasants vigorously lobbied both Washington and Jefferson, among others, to free their slaves. With Washington he succeeded; with Jefferson he failed.[63] Washington thought about posterity even more than his Virginia colleagues, yet elite planters agreed: emancipation and equal rights were ideal but impossible, not only in their lifetime but in the future.

In Congress, where representatives debated legislation and the petitions of citizens, slavery and inequality were often challenged. In the 1780s policy for the Trans-Appalachian West led to debates where northern and border states, usually Delaware and Maryland, opposed slavery extension. This opposition was not friendly to people of color, but it was integral to the objective of making the republic a predominantly white country of equal rights where slavery would wither away. Some congressmen even sought to include people of color in their advocacy of equal rights, reminding colleagues that "all men are created equal" had been "the language of America in the day of distress."[64]

Several petitions to the House of Representatives in the 1790s prompted debates where champions of equality relied on the principles of the Declaration of Independence. When members introduced Quaker petitions against slavery and the slave trade, majorities quickly tabled them to preserve, they said, sectional peace. But a 1798 petition from four free blacks who had been manumitted and then reenslaved in North Carolina before escaping to Philadelphia prompted lengthy discussion of race and citizenship. The four petitioners sought relief from the fugitive slave law, which was, they said, "a flagrant proof how far human beings, merely on account of color and complexion, are, through prevailing prejudice, outlawed and excluded from common justice and common humanity." They spoke, they said, for "a class of that people who, distinguished by color, are therefore with a degrading partiality, considered by many, even of those in eminent stations, as unentitled to that public justice and protection which is the great object of Government."[65] When a North Carolinian objected to hearing the petition, the Philadelphia Democratic-Republican merchant John Swanwick declared that "petitioning was their sacred right" and urged consideration of the petition.[66]

Thereafter debate ensued over whether the petition warranted congressional attention. Some, like James Madison, also a Democratic-Republican, argued that the question was whether the petitioners were slaves—a matter for North Carolina courts. If North Carolina determined that "they are slaves," Madison argued, "the Constitution gives them no hopes of being heard here."[67] Though his argument was contrary to the petitioners, he implied that if the petitioners were free, then white or black, Congress was bound to recognize their right to petition. George Thatcher, a Massachusetts Federalist, challenged part of Madison's argument, because, following Madison's logic, henceforth all petitioners would have to prove their freedom before being heard. This was an entirely new "system of conduct which he never saw the House practice, and hoped he never should." Requiring proof that petitioners were free contradicted "the Constitutional freedom of every State where the Declaration of Rights had been made." All these declarations proclaimed "that every man is born equally free, and that each have an equal right to petition." Thatcher admitted that Congress "could not give freedom to slaves"; but Congress could and should always "secure freemen in their rights."[68] Thatcher, like Swanwick, rejected the presumption that "color and complexion" signified free or slave status. Joseph B. Varnum, a Massachusetts Democratic-Republican, underlined the point: "Surely it could not be said that color alone should designate them as slaves"; and a New Jersey Democratic-Republican, Aaron Kitchell, argued that it was unreasonable to ask these four men to return to North Carolina in the hope of gaining a favorable judgment. Instead, Congress should consider whether their petition meant that the Fugitive Slave law must be revised.

But the motion to refer the North Carolina men's petition to committee failed. Though thirty-three representatives supported the black petitioners' rights, fifty opposed.[69] This conflict over race, human rights, and constitutional rights was not partisan: both sides included Federalists and Democratic-Republicans. Nor did it clearly divide defenders and opponents of slavery, since the congresses in the two decades after 1790 mostly condemned slavery while acknowledging its present necessity. Instead divisions revealed contradictions and confusions embedded in Americans' effort to reconcile their heroic commitment to universal human rights with the racial prejudices their economic and social systems nurtured. Slavery, certainly, lay at the heart of the problem—the planters' dilemma so candidly expressed by Patrick Henry in 1773 and reiterated in 1802 in James Monroe's fantasy of slavery's abolition and removal of blacks "without expense or inconvenience to ourselves."[70]

Though some Americans could disentangle their feelings about race and slavery, at least partially, most could not. Whites' beliefs that people of color were lesser than whites and more sinful was bound up with perceptions of hereditary servitude, of slavery. Thomas Jefferson's *Notes on the State of Virginia* (1782) touched on the core issues. Slavery, he said, was Virginia's deepest and distinguishing flaw. This system, he explained, corrupted everyone's manners profoundly: "The whole commerce between master and slave is a perpetual exercise of the most boisterous passions, the most unremitting despotism on the one part, and degrading submissions on the other." This refined, self-disciplined, and reflective aristocrat exclaimed, "The man must be a prodigy who can retain his manners and morals undepraved by such circumstances." As to political leaders, this man who penned the words "all men are created equal" confessed, "With what execration should the statesman be loaded, who, permitting one half the citizens thus to trample on the rights of the other [black]." The first became "despots" whose morals were destroyed along with their readiness to labor; and the second became "enemies" whose love of country was erased. Prophetically, Jefferson concluded, "I tremble for my country when I reflect that God is just; that his justice cannot sleep forever." Anticipating slave rebellion, he reasoned ominously that "the Almighty has no attribute which can take side with us [whites] in such a contest."[71] Though the vast majority of whites, never having owned slaves, did not likely share Jefferson's guilty discomfort, all lived in a world—North and South—where whites were ordinarily presumed superior and people of color were subordinate.

Jefferson's observations revealed the ambiguity of citizenship for people of color. He rejected Edmund Pendleton's sophistry concerning the rights of persons who were or were not "in society." According to Jefferson's analysis, "one half of the citizens" were trampling "on the rights of the other" half—that is, on the rights of enslaved citizens. Seemingly Jefferson's unguarded observation treated all Virginians, free and slave, as citizens regardless of color or status.

Like many other whites, Jefferson found it hard to disentangle concerns for social peace from his aspirations for justice. The racial prejudices permeating white thinking made the predicament intractable. Jefferson's 1791 response to free black Benjamin Banneker's almanac betrayed the now U.S. secretary of state's skepticism toward Africans' mental abilities. "No body," Jefferson claimed, "wishes more than I do to see such proofs as you exhibit, that nature has given to our black brethren, talents equal to those of other colors of men, and that the appearance of a want of them is owing merely to the degraded condition of their existence, both in Africa & America." In the here and now, Jefferson stated what most whites believed: people of color were "degraded." Many years later, when he was leaving the White House in 1809, he remained skeptical of black ability: "No person living wishes more sincerely than I do, to see a complete refutation of the doubts I have myself entertained and expressed on the grade of understanding allotted to them [blacks] by nature and to find that in this respect they are on a par with ourselves [whites]." Later still, in 1823, Madison described free blacks

Torturing American Citizens.   Page 129.

"Torturing American Citizens" follows a Virginian's report of seeing a farmer "who had a coloured citizen tied to a large log or a tree lying on the ground. The man was lying on his face uncovered, from his neck downwards. His driver had been lacerating him mercilessly." From George Bourne's *Picture of Slavery in the United States of America* (Middletown, Conn.: Edwin Hunt, 1834). Bourne, a minister in Virginia and elsewhere, was a founder of the American Anti-Slavery Society. Also printed in Boston in 1838 by Isaac Knapp, William Lloyd Garrison's friend and cofounder of the New England Anti-Slavery Society. Courtesy, University of Connecticut Library.

as "generally idle and depraved; appearing to retain the bad qualities of the slaves with whom they continue to associate, without acquiring the good ones of the whites, from whom [they] continue separated by prejudices ag[ain]st their colour & other peculiarities." Jefferson like most other whites of his era never did experience "a complete refutation" of these doubts.[72]

But regardless of prejudices about the abilities and social character of people of color, many whites believed, with Jefferson, that "whatever be their degree of talent it is no measure of their rights." Denying equal rights to people of color might be prudent socially and politically, but that did not make it right. As Jefferson admitted, "Because Sir Isaac Newton was superior to others in understanding, he was not therefore lord of the person or property of others."[73] In short, whatever degradation blacks might display, it ought not bear on their rights. Yet especially after 1800, pragmatic considerations attuned to white prejudices increasingly ruled national politics. In 1807, when a British warship attacked the American *Chesapeake*, killing three U.S. sailors, the victims—two black—were called "citizens" in keeping with international law, which treated black Americans as citizens.[74] Five years after professing that the rights of a poor black *ought* to be equal to an Isaac Newton, Jefferson told Edward Coles, the Virginia abolitionist who freed his slaves in Illinois, that slavery could never be a nursery for citizenship. "For men probably of any color, but of this color [black] we know," Jefferson explained, "brought from their infancy without necessity for thought or forecast, are by their habits rendered as incapable as children of taking care of themselves." Releasing them freely would be disastrous: "They are pests in society by their idleness, and the depredations to which this leads them." Jefferson held their sexual activity to be even more disturbing, because "their amalgamation with the other color produces a degradation to which no lover of his country, no lover of excellence in the human character can innocently consent."[75] No one articulated more clearly that blacks should possess equal rights in principle but absolutely not in practice.

V

By the 1830s attacking "the aristocracy of color" was a losing battle. The nation's attorney general, then Roger Taney, said in 1832 that blacks could not be U.S. citizens. Arguably the Connecticut lawyers William W. Ellsworth and Calvin Goddard were correct to challenge him by claiming in 1835 "a distinction founded in *color*, in fundamental rights, is *novel*." But though the beliefs they criticized were new in some respects, they were widespread, sustained by slavery's legacies in behavior and belief. Secretary of State James Buchanan refused passports to Americans of color in the 1840s even though, as seamen, they had long possessed U.S. protection internationally as citizens. Historical argument did not overturn deeply held convictions. By the 1850s American culture had embraced racial ideology so thoroughly that equal rights historical arguments became suspect, criticized as radical abolitionist propaganda. Indeed in 1857 when Chief Justice Taney issued the United States Supreme Court ruling in *Scott v. Sandford*—stating that "a free Negro of the African race, whose ancestors were brought to this country and sold as slaves, is not a 'citizen' within the meaning of the Constitution"—only two of the court's nine justices chose to challenge Taney's now-mainstream historical arguments.[76]

Those justices, the Ohio Jacksonian John McLean and the Massachusetts Whig Benjamin R. Curtis had little in common. The seventy-two-year-old McLean had served since 1830, six years longer than Taney, whereas the forty-eight-year-old, Harvard-trained Curtis was appointed in 1850. Yet both justices called on facts that Ellsworth and Goddard presented decades earlier: men of color were among the original citizens when the Constitution was adopted, voting in many states. Both jurists rejected the racial view of citizenship endorsed by Connecticut Chief Justice David Daggett in 1835 that now provided one pillar for Taney's ruling.

McLean argued that prejudice, not law or precedent, guided Taney and the majority. Although "it was said that a colored citizen would not be an agreeable member of society," McLean found that "more a matter of taste than of law." States, he added, "have admitted persons of color to the right of suffrage"; and "on the question of citizenship, it must be admitted that we have not been very fastidious." The president and the Congress, "under the late [1848] treaty with Mexico, . . . have made citizens of all grades, combinations, and colors." South Carolina senator John C. Calhoun had protested—declaring, "Ours is a government of the white man"—but to no avail. "The same was done in the admission of Louisiana and Florida,"

McLean drily noted. Using race as a test of national citizenship was new. "No one," he asserted, "ever doubted, and no court ever held, that the people of these Territories did not become citizens." All these people of various and mixed races "exercised all the rights of citizens without being naturalized under the acts of Congress." McLean concluded that basing national citizenship on race actually reversed long-standing practice.[77]

Justice Curtis declared categorically, "It is not true . . . that the Constitution was made exclusively for the white race." Like McLean he was convinced the principles of the Declaration of Independence applied literally, though it did not confer equal political or civil rights on all citizens. No one doubted that white women, children, and persons under guardianship were denied political and civil rights, yet none denied their citizenship. According to the Constitution, states determined who could vote, and it was obvious that not every citizen could be a voter. The history was clear. When states like Connecticut, New York, New Jersey, and Pennsylvania established a color bar for voting they did not and could not erase or repeal the citizenship of nonwhites. Citizenship as such never provided the full array of civil and political rights.[78]

Taney's conflation of slaves with everyone possessing African ancestry, free or slave, was actually a nineteenth-century anachronism describing neither the beliefs nor the practices of most states before 1800. At Virginia's 1776 convention Edmund Pendleton had reasoned that slaves were excluded from the social compact and therefore from the possession of equal natural rights; but that was because of their slave status, not, as Taney claimed, their racial lineage. Yet in regard to citizenship and race, Taney's elaborate race and precedent-based historical arguments were widely accepted. Citing Connecticut Chief Justice David Daggett's 1835 rejection of United States citizenship for anyone descended from slaves—"blacks not being citizens of the United States within the meaning of the Constitution"—Taney presented a popular white viewpoint. To many whites his racist reasoning was common sense: "When we look at the condition of this race in the several States at this time, it is impossible to believe that these rights and privileges were intended to be extended to them."[79]

The majority decision in 1857 was explosive politically, but less because of its judgment on African American citizenship than its revocation of the 1820 Missouri Compromise. According to the court, Congress had no power to exclude slavery from United States territories such as Indiana, Illinois, Kansas, or Nebraska. Many in the free states believed that this meant that slavery, once seen as dying out, could become the national standard. Ultimately they feared that the court might allow masters to bring slaves into "free" states and hold them in bondage—effectively erasing long-standing state prohibitions on slavery. These Free Soil concerns—not racial equality—provided core issues for the new Republican Party. Significantly, in 1858 the Illinois Republican Abraham Lincoln targeted this part of the Dred Scott decision, not Taney's rejection of "negro" citizenship. "The new territory," Lincoln said, must be "an outlet for the free white people, for new homes in which all free white men from all the world may find place, and better their condition in life."[80] This was his chief objection to *Scott v. Sandford.*

Lincoln never endorsed the Court's denial of black citizenship; but debating Stephen Douglas he expressed common prejudices in speeches carried in newspapers nationwide. In central Illinois in September 1858 this antislavery Free Soil Republican expressed majority racial views, declaring: "I am not nor ever have been in favor of bringing about . . . the social and political equality of the white and black races, . . . I am not . . . in favor of making voters of the negroes, or jurors, or qualifying them to hold office, or having them to marry with white people, . . . There is a physical difference between the white and black races, which I suppose, will forever forbid the two races living together upon terms of social and political equality, and inasmuch, as they cannot so live . . . There must be the position of superior and inferior, that I am as much as any other man in favor of the superior position being assigned to the white man." Not only did Lincoln endorse white superiority on the stump, but he claimed this view was universal: "I have never seen, to my knowledge, a man, woman or child who was in favor of producing a perfect equality, social and political, between negroes and white men." For Lincoln and most Republicans *equal* citizenship was off the table.[81]

Like many who opposed slavery and its expansion, Lincoln saw no contradiction between defending race-based inequality and the Declaration's "all men are created equal" doctrine. He judged that "there is no reason in the world why the negro is not entitled to all the natural rights enumerated in the Declaration of Independence—the right to life, liberty, and the pursuit of happiness." These, after all, were not specific political rights. To believe that a man of color possessed "the right to eat the bread . . . which his own hand earns" in no way contradicted the emerging doctrine of white supremacy.[82] By this time hereditary race theory was supplanting Enlightenment explanations of color differences based on environment. The natural equality idea was losing ground.

Nevertheless before some audiences Lincoln employed the Declaration's equal rights dictum to challenge racial hierarchies. In Chicago he called on voters to "discard all this quibbling about this man and the other man—this race and that race, and the others being inferior, and therefore they must be placed in an inferior position." Americans, he said, should "unite as one people throughout this land until we shall once more stand up declaring that all men are created equal."[83] In the context of the Dred Scott controversy, Lincoln's emphasis on the Declaration's equal rights doctrine challenged racial hierarchy directly, anticipating his Gettysburg pronouncement that the United States was "dedicated to the proposition that all men are created equal."

Lincoln's opponent, Stephen Douglas, derided Lincoln's words. Douglas reported Lincoln as saying "The Declaration of Independence declared that the negro was the equal of the white man." Douglas quoted Lincoln: "If one man says it don't mean a negro, why not another say it doesn't mean a white man?" Douglas called this "a monstrous heresy . . . to pretend" that the Declaration "included Negroes in the clause declaring that all men were created equal." Lincoln was claiming that "there could be no such thing as distinction between the races, making one superior and the other inferior." Race, Douglas argued, was all-important: "The negro belongs to a race incapable of self-government, and for that reason ought not to be put on an equality with the white man."[84] Downplaying race distinctions was not popular in central and southern Illinois or the United States as a whole in 1858; and Lincoln explicitly rejected "political and social equality between the white and black races." Like Douglas he favored "the superior position" for whites. Like many Americans in the north and west, Lincoln was ambivalent.

But whatever his doubts and adjustments to political realities, Lincoln would not retreat from including all people in the Declaration. Repeatedly he pointed out that until recently no one had expressed that "astounding sentiment, that the term 'all men' does not include the negro." Clearly, he said, the Declaration never meant "all men equal in all respects . . . equal in color, size or intellect, moral development or social capacity." But it did proclaim that they were equal for "certain inalienable rights, among which are life, liberty, and the pursuit of happiness." Of course the Declaration did not mean "the obvious untruth that all were then actually enjoying that equality, nor yet that they were about to confer it immediately." Congress possessed no such authority. Rather, Lincoln argued, the signers intended that equality "might follow as fast as the circumstances should permit." Theirs was a declaration of aspirations: "To set up a standard maxim for free men which should be familiar to all, constantly looked to and constantly labored for, and even though never perfectly attained, constantly approximated . . . spreading and deepening its influence and augmenting the happiness and value of life to all people of all colors everywhere."[85] This was the Revolution's Enlightenment legacy that Lincoln and his supporters embraced.

But by 1858 the original 1776 division in Virginia over "all men are created equal" and its consequences could as readily be interpreted to exclude people of color as to include them. Douglas's argument followed Taney's reasoning that the signers of the Declaration, all of whom came from states that permitted slavery, could only have been thinking of white people. Taney argued that the "negro of the African race" had always been seen as "inferior" and so could "justly and lawfully be reduced to slavery for his benefit." This "axiom in morals as well as politics," Taney asserted, was beyond doubt or dispute. From this perspective Lincoln's reasoning was misguided. Though the Declaration "would seem to embrace the whole human family," in fact the "African race were not intended to be included."[86] Because the Supreme Court majority conflated slaves with all persons with African lineage, the justices could brush aside the rights of four hundred thousand free people of color. Race theory combined with prejudice to erase the distinction between them and four million slaves.

Frederick Douglass, New York, 1855. Douglass was a leading voice in the 1850s pronouncing the nation's betrayal of the Declaration's ideals. From the author's private collection.

As the Independence Day orator, abolitionist Frederick Douglass, bitterly explained to white audiences, "The rich inheritance of justice, liberty, prosperity and independence, bequeathed by your fathers, is shared by you, not by me." The bright promise of 1776, "the sunlight that brought life and healing to you, has brought stripes and death to me. The Fourth [of] July is *yours*, not *mine*." In the *Dred Scott* decision, Chief Justice Taney rewrote history, rebutting abolitionist arguments so as to enshrine racial hierarchy. By subverting the American Revolution's expansive prospect of equal rights, *Dred Scott* revoked the once self-evident truth that "all men are created equal" and helped propel the nation into civil war.[87]

FIVE

People of Color and Equal Rights

New England Cases

"A distinction based on *color*, in fundamental rights is *novel*,
inconvenient and *impracticable.* Hitherto we have seen no such
distinction; none in the ancient common law of England which
justly boasts her equal principles; none in that immortal instrument
which our republican fathers put forth as the ground-work of
all just government—the Declaration of Independence."
—*William W. Ellsworth, "Report of the Arguments . . .
in the Case of Prudence Crandall," July 1834*

"America is ours—it belongs to a race of white men, the
descendants of those who first redeemed the wilderness."
—*Andrew T. Judson, "Report of the Arguments . . .
in the Case of Prudence Crandall," July 1834*

As we have seen, white policies toward people of color were fluid and
inconsistent, varying from state to state. Restrictions on free blacks in
Georgia or South Carolina differed from those in North Carolina, Virginia,
and Maryland, just as the circumstances of free people of color differed
among Middle Atlantic, Old Northwestern, and New England states. Everywhere realities collided with elevated constitutions and declarations of
rights. In criminal courts Americans acted out the tensions between equal
rights principles and actual practices. When whites and people of color
faced accusations of crimes like murder and rape, prosecutors and defense

lawyers, together with clergymen and the press, expressed strong, often un-varnished opinions on race and equality. Examination of criminal cases can sometimes reveal how equal rights were realized or blocked.

Because more people in New England professed no attachment to slavery and serious commitment to equal rights, in all likelihood that region more than the middle Atlantic states or Old Northwest can reveal how closely the ideal of "all men are created equal" could approach actual practice.[1] In New England's criminal prosecutions the extent to which law enforce-ment provided equal treatment is visible. Violent crimes bred strong emo-tions, so strict adherence to equal justice principles were at risk. Occasions when New Englanders stood firm against prejudice are as revealing as those where their bigotry blocked equal rights.

Early American execution statistics reveal that, even allowing for dispari-ties of wealth and class, whites executed people of color more readily than fellow whites. And in New England the seventeenth-century record shows that African Americans were more than three times more likely to be ex-ecuted than whites. Native Americans faced even greater risks. During the eighteenth century, per capita, New Englanders resorted to hanging less often than other regions, but color differences became even more marked than earlier. Now African Americans charged with a capital crime were at nine times greater risk than whites, and Indians were twice as likely as Yan-kees to be hanged.[2] It is revealing that in the history of New England before 1860 just three white men were executed for murdering people of color: two in 1676 following King Philip's War and one in 1822 for killing a fel-low inmate in Massachusetts's state prison. In the middle Atlantic colonies and the South, though slave uprisings—real or imagined—multiplied the numbers of blacks executed, the racial disparity for judicial executions was less than in New England. Even though white New Englanders were not surrounded by blacks and had no reason to fear insurrections, as did South Carolina whites in 1739 or New York City whites in 1741, in courtrooms New Englanders before the Revolution were more likely to judge blacks guilty and punish them more severely.[3]

What about the decades after independence when the United States proclaimed equal rights to "life, liberty, and the pursuit of happiness"? If the commitment to equal rights was more than rhetorical it should have affected criminal defendants. Certainly the inertia of past practices operated, especially since the same people often served as magistrates, judges, and jurors. But the impact of Beccarian reforms must also be considered. Before independence no colony had broken with Britain's "bloody code"; afterward, in the 1780s and 1790s especially, states moved toward "proportional" punishments, cutting the number of capital crimes. So fewer executions of people of color did not necessarily signify recognition of equal rights. Statistics are helpful, but with small numbers their guidance is limited. To understand the conflicting impulses operating in the early Republic—the interplay of equal rights ideology with law, custom, and standing prejudices—actual cases are informative.

I

One revealing test of equal rights was the 1786 murder trial of Hannah Ocuish, a twelve-year-old mixed-race native of Groton, Connecticut. As in Britain, colonial and early national criminal law made limited provision for children. Through their sixth year they were protected from hanging; but from age seven through thirteen they could be executed if the court found "evidence of malice, revenge and cunning," since "malice supplies the want of age."[4] At age fourteen and above the law recognized no distinction. In Britain courts sent young children to the gallows, notably a seven-year-old girl in 1808 and a boy of nine in 1831. Like Hannah Ocuish these English children were poor, but they were white. Republican beliefs and Beccarian humanitarianism affected American courts earlier than in Britain, and yet New Jersey hanged a twelve-year-old black boy, James Guild, in 1828 for murdering an elderly white woman, and the black girls Jane Huff, age fifteen in 1837, and Rosanne Keen, sixteen years old in 1844.[5] Because Ocuish, Guild, Huff, and Keen were children of color, it appears that equal rights before the law was not being practiced, even in states where slavery was vestigial. Nevertheless these cases illuminate crosscurrents of values and practice.

Color surely affected Hannah Ocuish's conviction and punishment, but Puritan custom and Christian teachings may have counted more. Neither law nor custom made an exception for children of Hannah's age. A child of seven could be judged a murderer and hanged as an example to other children, and girls were deemed capable of sexual consent at age ten. So Hannah's crime might be punished either according to law and tradition or following the new humane values, which recognized that twelve-year-olds possessed less capacity for judgment than adults. Even more important than Hannah's age, some believed, was her ignorance of Christianity. Hannah had no moral instruction, being the illegitimate child of an unknown father and a mother, "one of the Pequot tribe of Indians," who was "an abandoned creature, much addicted to the vice of drunkenness." Hannah was so benighted that the Reverend Henry Channing, who visited her in jail and preached her execution sermon, reported that "she hath repeatedly declared to me, that she did not know that there was a GOD, before she was told it after her imprisonment."[6] Religious ignorance had made Hannah, though "in the beginning of life, a *murderer*." And, Channing concluded, she must be punished because God ordained in Genesis that "*whoso sheddeth Man's blood, by Man shall his blood be shed.*"[7]

Hannah's crime was horrific—beating six-year-old Eunice Bolles to death with stones to avenge the child's tattling on Hannah "for taking away her strawberries." Nor was this Hannah's first offense. At age six she had joined her eight-year-old brother in robbing and beating "a little girl," and stealing her gold necklace and clothing. Bloodied, the victim reported the Ocuish children, whom the Groton selectmen took from their mother, binding them out. By Hannah's 1786 trial, witnesses swore that "theft and lying were her common vices." Possessing "a degree of artful cunning and sagacity beyond many of her years," she acted with "a maliciousness of disposition which made the children in the neighbourhood much afraid of her."[8] No one had a good word for Hannah Ocuish.

If Hannah had been a respectable white child—not the "mulatto" daughter of an alcoholic Pequot mother and a black or mixed-race father—authorities might have found a way to mitigate her crime to avoid hanging. That said, Hannah's color notwithstanding, an experienced court-appointed attorney defended her and later appealed to the legislature for clemency, arguing that Hannah never intended to kill her victim. But the assembly accepted the jury's judgment; so the sentence stood. Procedurally, the state accorded Hannah equal rights.

In his execution sermon, the Reverend Channing explicitly admonished his audience to look past race. That Hannah was a person of color, variously described as "Indian" and "Mulatto," was so much in people's minds that he confronted race prejudice directly. The clergyman spoke plainly to youth: "Think not that crimes are peculiar to the *complexion* of the prisoner and that ours is pure from these stains." Such an "illiberal and contracted" idea was wrong. Hannah was "one of our guilty race," the human race. Channing reminded them that Hannah's body, "notwithstanding its colour, contains an immortal soul, a Jewel of inestimable value." If "polished by divine grace," Hannah's soul "would shine . . . with a glorious luster." Channing warned white listeners against false confidence based on "brighter" skin; if their own jewel was "left in its natural state, [it] would be *blackness and darkness forever.*" In 1852 the historian of New London described Hannah as "a fierce young savage," but in 1787 her sinful ignorance was more salient than race.[9]

Indeed officials, like citizens, apparently felt revulsion in 1787 even as they enforced their deadly statute. In a remarkably similar case eight years later Connecticut officials revisited strict adherence to the law. In November 1795, "Ann, a negro girl between 12 and 13 years of age," confessed to cutting the throat of her master's daughter, a five-year-old white girl. Following traditional rules, Ann was indicted and charged with murder. But when she was tried in March 1796, though there was no doubt that Ann "took a sharp knife from the buttery, and cut the child's throat" before blaming a stranger for the killing, the jury refused to send her to the gallows. Instead, contrary to her murder indictment, jurors found her guilty of manslaughter. She was punished severely with thirty-nine stripes and "burnt on the hand with the Letter M," but black though she was, she did not hang.[10] The ideas of Count Cesare di Beccaria and appreciation of the difference between children and adults prevailed.

I know of no young white child executed in the early Republic, but the case of a black twelve-year-old, James Guild, in New Jersey thirty-two years later is instructive. Guild was convicted for a crime only slightly less shocking than Ocuish's and Ann's because the victim was an elderly woman. "Little Jim" was an indentured servant age twelve years, five months in September 1827 when he attacked Catherine Beakes because she refused to lend him her fowling gun. After his first blow flattened the old woman, he bludgeoned her to death. New Jersey law was the same English law that Connecticut applied to Ocuish and Ann. As William Blackstone's *Commentaries on the Laws of England* (1770) explained, malicious children aged seven through thirteen could be guilty and sentenced to die. But in 1828 executing a child stirred greater uneasiness than in 1786. Reminiscent of Ann's case, at the urging of Guild's attorney, the judge "humanely suspended the sentence of the law," permitting review at the highest level. Yet the New Jersey Supreme Court upheld the sentence, and though New Jersey's legislature considered commuting Guild's sentence to life in prison, after extended debate it denied clemency.[11]

Similarly, nine years later in 1837, New Jersey showed no mercy for fifteen-year-old black servant Jane Huff, perhaps because her sixty-two-year-old mistress's murder seemed especially brutal: Huff knocked the old lady out with fireplace tongs before plunging her head into a kettle of boiling water. And in 1844, when Rosanne Keen, also black, murdered her employer, though her case was appealed and anti-death-penalty opponents pleaded that she was mentally incompetent, the governor declined to pardon her. Though race, as such, did not enter the legal discussion of these cases, the press mentioned it, and race likely influenced the decisions of New Jersey courts and the assembly. In the colonial era Huff's and Keen's crimes, murdering a mistress and a master, respectively, could have been prosecuted as petty treason and punished by burning at the stake, as in Boston in 1755. After the Revolution, however, no such punishment was inflicted, and Huff and Keen, like two female slaves who murdered their Virginia mistress in 1806, were hanged. Regarding the executions of Ocuish as well as Guild, the historian Holly Brewer believes that color was critical.[12]

During a period of increasing expressions of color consciousness, when whites routinely disparaged Indians, mulattoes, and blacks as more prone to laziness and vice than their white compatriots, color-blind justice was impossible.[13] Yet republican ideology and legal precepts denied that color was a legitimate consideration for determining guilt or levels of punishment—so tension between prejudice and principle was constant, playing out according to circumstances. While the nonwhite Ocuish and Guild may have been victims of unequal rights due to prejudice, in the same era other people of color charged with murder were acquitted. Press coverage surrounding acquittals was usually sparse; no sermons or broadsides sketched the crime or the defendant's life. But the rare trial report of an acquittal can be revealing. In the cases considered here, as with Ocuish, Ann, and Guild, racial sentiment affected court officials and public attitudes, but they did not necessarily trample defendants' rights.

An 1810 trial in Schenectady, New York, shows prejudice and equal rights coexisting within the justice system. Susanna, "a coloured woman" who worked her way out of slavery, was charged with murdering "her infant male bastard child." The evidence, including Susanna's confession, showed that after she delivered her child, he was found on the floor in her room, his throat cut, with Susanna lying nearby in a bloodstained bed. After concealing her pregnancy, the prosecution argued, Susanna delivered the infant secretly, murdering him to escape "the disgrace" of bearing a "bastard."[14] For generations this line of argument, accompanied by incriminating testimony, had led to infanticide convictions. But in Susanna's case, though the evidence was reinforced by the legal presumption that all killings constituted murder unless proven otherwise, the white jurymen voted "Not Guilty!"[15]

To comprehend why a white court chose to acquit a black woman when all agreed that she killed her child, we must look more closely at the case and the beliefs and of the men who held Susanna's life in their hands. The first point to recognize is the value the community placed on the life of a lowly infant with no market value. Even during the period of northern slavery the expense of raising a child to working age was so high that a Boston clergyman reported, "Negro children were reckoned an incumbrance [sic] in a family; and when weaned, were given away like puppies."[16] The death of this unnamed newborn was not a material loss in 1810, so prosecuting Susanna demonstrated the community's concern for morality and the law.

Yet infanticide prosecutions had become a rarity by 1810. In the 1760s, when Beccaria's *Essay on Crimes and Punishments* was translated into English, Voltaire's accompanying comments began by criticizing the "unjust, inhuman, and pernicious" execution of mothers for concealing the birth and abandonment of infants.[17] This crime remained law after the Revolution, but few states enforced it vigorously. During the 1780s Massachusetts executed women for infanticide, one white and one Indian, for the last time. New Englanders thereafter occasionally prosecuted the crime but ceased hanging.[18] New York was similar—by 1800, infanticide prosecutions were rare—although fifteen years *after* Susanna's trial the state executed a white woman for killing her newborn child.[19] Even as late as 1810, New Yorkers might condemn Susanna to death.

But they did not. Two arguments by Susanna's attorneys apparently influenced the judge's charge to the jury. Most important was Susanna's sanity. One who questioned Susanna when the killing was discovered reported that "she seemed greatly cast down about the child; of which she appeared to think more of than herself. She said she would give the world, or she would give a thousand worlds if she had them, or some such expression, if the child could be brought to life." In addition a "man of color" who knew Susanna for six years testified that she "sung in the night, and acted strangely," and was "supposed to be . . . insane or crazy," as demonstrated by giving "herself a wound in the breast" in an attempt "to make away with herself." Summarizing, Judge Ambrose Spencer added a defense argument, noting "the hour of travail . . . sometimes produces fitful convulsions, and sometimes delirium."[20] Susanna's conduct and history made the insanity claim plausible and perhaps decisive.

Her defense attorney, Theodore Sedgwick Jr., also used race prejudice to rebut the prosecution's standard argument for motive: escaping shame for bearing an illegitimate child. Sedgwick argued that race was crucial for shame. "Among *us*," he declared, "there can be no higher disgrace. . . . Shame, ridicule, infamy, exile, attend it." But not so for Susanna: "People of color were her society; and the licentiousness of the intercourse of those people was notorious." Though "a sense of shame" was "instinctive in the [female] sex; . . . in a person of her condition" it could never be sufficiently powerful to motivate murder. Appealing to white prejudices about black sexuality, he remarked, "Among those of her color there is a general freedom and licentiousness of connexion; illicit intercourse is no crime; no disgrace here persecutes the parent, and no inconvenience results to the child."[21] Sedgwick explicitly sought to make *inequality* before the law work to Susanna's advantage. She had no reputation to protect—no reasonable motive for murder.

But Judge Spencer, a Connecticut native and Harvard graduate, countered Sedgwick's racial assumptions. When Spencer, a former slave owner and abolition advocate, instructed the jury he acknowledged race but dismissed its importance.[22] Jurymen should treat the testimony regarding Susanna's attempted suicide as credible because the witness, "though a man of color, is to be believed, perhaps, as well as any man." Spencer dismissed Sedgwick's argument that among "people of color" illegitimacy was scarcely shameful. Certainly "in the higher walks of life" shame for this transgression was "more acutely felt," but Spencer declared that "to all, in every rank, an illegitimate conception is a source of infamy that ought, and probably does, sooner or later, fill the bosom of the wretched subject with shame." The judge believed that Susanna's "humble and degrading" station mattered, not her race. Speaking of her as a former slave, he remarked that "people under such circumstances during early life, are, for the greater part, shamefully neglected in their education, unguarded in their morals, and uncultivated in their notions of character." Among such lowly people one could not expect "the same acute sensibility to dishonor as in the superior grades of society." But Susanna certainly felt "shame arising from her pregnancy." Only "shame," Judge Spencer reasoned, explained Susanna's "continual silence and secrecy about her situation."[23] Whether she was guilty beyond reasonable doubt the jury would decide, but judgment must rest on equal justice before the law, not some specious claim that the moral indifference of people of color allowed them to answer to a different standard of justice.

In neighboring Massachusetts the acquittal of another black defendant charged with infanticide reveals more of the interplay among prejudice, principle, and procedure. Here the accused was not the mother but the father, William Hardy. The victim was a three-week-old girl. Hardy was a servant in the home of Dr. Charles Jarvis, a prominent Boston physician and political leader; and when Elizabeth Valpy, a white woman from Salem, Massachusetts, worked in the Jarvis household the two servants had sexual relations.[24] According to trial testimony, after seven months with the Jarvises and in the fifth month of pregnancy, Valpy went back to Salem in June 1806. Yet Valpy returned to South Boston after Hardy sent a note explaining that he had found a place for her to stay with a widow named Bridget Daley. There, in the ten-by-fifteen-foot "apartment" the two shared, Daley helped the thirty-eight-year-old deliver a healthy girl on November 6, 1806. Three weeks later, however, the baby, called "it" by her mother, was found in tidal mud near the South Boston bridge. A chain attached to a lead weight was fastened around the infant's neck.[25]

Valpy and Daley swore that they had given Hardy the child the night before to place in a woman's care. The testimony of these two white women, that Hardy was the last person with the living child, convicted him.[26] No trial report permits closer analysis, but white prejudice apparently played a role in his conviction. As the Salem clergyman William Bentley noted, "a negro for murdering a child finds no difficulty in his way to the gallows."[27] Yet although prejudice helped convict Hardy, judicial commitment to equal procedural rights rescued him. An error in the black convict's arraignment enabled his attorneys, George Blake and Peter Thacher, to gain a new trial.

This time they won an acquittal. Blake, a Harvard graduate who studied in Attorney General James Sullivan's office, had been practicing in Boston for fifteen years. President Jefferson had appointed him in 1801 as U.S. attorney for Massachusetts, and in 1802 he led a successful effort to pardon and deport a dark-skinned native of India sentenced to hang for rape.[28] Thacher, like Blake a Harvard graduate, had three years of practice and was a grandson of Patriot lawyer Oxenbridge Thacher. They defended Hardy by attacking his accusers and supplying testimonials to his character from Doctor Jarvis and his family.

Assailing the character of Elizabeth Valpy and Bridget Daley was easy. Neither was defended by a husband or father, and neither held a respectable job. Daley was the widow of Dominic Daley, the recently hanged highway robber and murderer. A neighbor, Sally Talbot, using the common term for brothel, swore that "Mrs. Daley's house is very disorderly. I have often seen people, black and white, and of both sexes, *as low as the lowest regions,* going there, and coming away, at all times, by night and by day." Talbot elaborated: "I have seen them drunk and staggering and tumbling down before her door; and her house is a dreadful nuisance to the whole neighborhood." Talbot swore that Daley's accusation against Hardy was worthless, since "with regard to truth . . . her character in all respects is as bad as bad can be." She concluded: "The life of a dog ought not to be taken *away*, upon the evidence of such a woman as she is."[29]

Valpy's character was equally vulnerable. She faced the white male jury as a white woman making accusations based on her illicit sexual relations with a black man. Valpy acknowledged that she "was *once* or *twice* . . . criminally connected with the prisoner" and that "I found myself with child by him."[30] Hardy took responsibility for her and the baby, she explained, until she gave him the child the night before discovery of the tiny corpse. Her story, corroborated by Daley, made William Hardy the presumptive murderer.

When Valpy finished testifying, Hardy's attorneys attacked her credibility, first calling on Salem selectman Benjamin Ward, Esquire. When the judges asked, "What was her general character . . . with regard to veracity?" Ward testified, "As bad as can be; and I remember about ten years ago, when I was conversing with her mother about sending her daughter to the poor house, her mother observed, that '*She was such a lying mischievous plague*' that she did not *dare to trust* her in a private family." Another witness, James Cheever, had "known her for ten or fifteen years," swearing, "She was always considered as a loose woman." There was more. Dr. Charles Jarvis and his wife each contradicted Valpy's sworn testimony. Valpy had testified that after her employers suspected her pregnancy, they "often questioned her about being pregnant," going on to swear that she had "neither confessed nor denied the fact." She further claimed that Jarvis "*gave her medicines without being asked for them*," abortifacients, which she said "she never used but threw them aside." But on oath Jarvis contradicted her. He had "often questioned her about being pregnant," but her answers were "sometimes peremptory and sometimes evasive." Moreover, contrary to Valpy's court admission to a liaison with Hardy, Jarvis testified that Valpy "most strenuously denied that Hardy was the father of her child: and that she never had any connection with him; and said that she was courted by a man who was gone to sea." As to abortifacients, Jarvis swore that Valpy "often" asked him for "strong medicines." Jarvis's wife reinforced Valpy's reputation as a liar, testifying that when she "accused" Valpy of being pregnant, "*she denied* [*it*] *in the most positive and peremptory terms*, and persisted in the same denial." After Mrs. Jarvis's cousin reported overhearing Valpy "in the kitchen" telling another woman that "*she had always understood that when a woman had provided baby linen, she could not be condemned if the child were afterwards found dead*," jurymen could conclude that Valpy was a liar who had contemplated infanticide long before the baby's birth. The "benefit-of-linens" or "preparation defense" was traditionally used to deny premeditation, because a woman who prepared baby clothing supposedly intended to care for the child.[31]

With Hardy's life at stake, Blake's closing assaulted the character and credibility of his accusers. Blake buttressed reasoned argument with blatant appeals to prejudices concerning women, interracial sex, and Irish immigrants. Valpy was a "flippant harlot," not "the mute, passive creature" she appeared to be in court. "What," he asked jurors, "will you say of a woman in a christian country, who will not only receive, but will invite to her arms a negro?" He continued: "Lewdness of this sort in a woman, even with a person of her own complexion, is shameful enough, but when the complexions are mingled it becomes most shocking! Abominable!" Blake claimed, "from this single specimen of her amours," that Valpy's "libidinous intercourse with others of all characters and complexions, has for a long time been indiscriminate and promiscuous." Vicious sexually, she gave worthless testimony. "Was there ever," Blake asked, "a common prostitute who was not also a common liar?" Moreover Valpy and Daley were, he said, "*deeply interested*" in convicting Hardy, because otherwise they would be suspected for the infant's death. By blaming "a defenceless negro," a man who was merely "an unheeded African," they saved their own necks.[32]

With this "lowly negro" argument Blake adroitly summoned antiblack prejudice to Hardy's advantage—as Sedgwick did for Susanna. Hardy was a "simple man" and, if involved at all in the crime, was merely "an instrument in the hands of superior agents." The technique of diminishing a client's responsibility was familiar, but often it defended women, minors, and the mentally ill. Blake's argument was imaginative and subtle; he linked his characterization of Hardy as being insufficiently clever or hardened to commit murder with a standard defense describing Hardy's innocent behavior in the days following the crime. Blake coupled Hardy's guiltless conduct with character references from Jarvis, who had known Hardy for eighteen months and "always found him punctual, methodical and faithful," as well as temperamentally "remarkably tender, gentle and humane." Jarvis's wife reinforced her husband's judgment, saying that she "always found him [Hardy] mild to a high degree, never rough, and I never knew him to utter an unseemly expression." He was "remarkably gentle in his manners," a view her cousin echoed, testifying that she "always thought him an honest, excellent servant."[33]

In Hardy's first trial the accusers' testimony outweighed his character references. This could explain the intensity of Blake's repeated attacks on the morality and truthfulness of Valpy and Daley, who, he reminded jurors, could themselves be charged with murder if they could not transfer their guilt onto his "*poor, humble, solitary* domestic" client, "the simple man whom you see at the bar." Again and again Blake's language—"degraded harlot," "miserable harlot," "abandoned libertine," "foul degraded loathsome prostitute," "beastly strumpet," "flippant harlot," "vile associate," "miserable wretches"—characterized the women. Valpy, "poor and destitute," was the key target. Enlisting racial prejudice in the cause of his client, Blake played on the fact that Valpy chose to lie with a "Blackman," and he reminded jurors that she was "the mother of a black bastard."[34]

Having exploited race to Hardy's advantage, Blake aroused ethnic, class, and gender prejudices to destroy Bridget Daley's credibility. After pointing out her "outlandish brogue," Blake claimed that he had no "intention to attempt to excite a prejudice against this woman by any invidious allusion to the nation in which she was born." With Attorney General James Sullivan, a son of Irish immigrants, in the courtroom Blake declared, "No man thinks more highly of that people than I do." The Irish were distinguished "by the best or the very worst properties which belong to human nature." Indeed, from the mouths of the "brightest and most exalted" Irishmen we learn of "the shocking depravities, which prevail and abound" among the degraded Irish, such as "*murders, assassinations and perjuries.*" Blake did not specify, but many remembered how only months earlier James Sullivan had won the murder conviction of Bridget Daley's husband. Exploiting this connection, during Hardy's trial a Boston newspaper advertised Daley's trial report pamphlet. Blake claimed to shun prejudice, but he used it to discredit Daley. Bridget was not among Ireland's "brightest and most exalted"; she was among the recent immigrants who were drawn from "degenerate classes of society." Righteously Blake observed, "If we look into the cells of our prisons, or consult the register of our gibbets, we shall discover that the sentiment which almost universally prevails in this country against this description of people," the degenerate Irish, "has its basis in something more substantial than prejudice."[35]

Blake tied Widow Daley to "the names inscribed on the hangman's calendar." After Sally Talbot's testimony he need not speak of the hanging of "the dear companion of her youth and bosom," he said, "to blacken her character." Sarcastically Blake reported that following Daley's "*sad bereavement*" she had made her home "the very nursury [sic] of crimes, the receptacle [sic] of everything filthy and abominable." Here "fornication and drunkenness, perhaps murder and rapine, . . . mingle and revel together." Blake quoted Daley mockingly on the "'*genteel, honest, well bred company*'" that she swore "were permitted to sojourn in her hospitable mansion." Daley should be judged by the company she kept, "the lewd and drunken rabble." Because Valpy and Daley were vicious and self-interested in the verdict, they were "unfit" to determine the life of "the miserable man at the bar."[36]

When Chief Justice Theophilus Parsons charged the jury, he passed over Blake's appeals to prejudice based on race, ethnicity, class, and gender. Indeed, in Judge Parsons's view, the two lowly women, "whatever might appear to be their character," were more credible than not, because they corroborated each other's testimony. Parsons argued that the only reason to acquit Hardy was the belief that Valpy and Daley killed the child or were Hardy's accomplices and conspired to frame him. Otherwise, Parsons said, a guilty verdict was justified. At 10:00 p.m. he sent the jury to deliberate.[37]

As in other cases, there is no record of the jurors' deliberations, but they must have been divided. By law jurors were deprived of refreshments until they reached a verdict, and they argued over Hardy's fate all night and into the morning before finally concluding at noon the next day. Their decision—"NOT GUILTY!"—was remarkable.[38] In this second trial before the Massachusetts Supreme Judicial Court, conducted only because of a technical error preceding the first trial, a white jury disregarded the chief justice's advice and acquitted a black convict.

It is tempting to conclude that Massachusetts incurred the trouble and expense of an additional trial to secure equal rights for lowly William Hardy. Yet other factors were in play. Hardy was servant to a distinguished and powerful patron, Charles Jarvis, whom Boston voters chose for the 1780 Massachusetts Constitutional Convention and elected as their state representative for a decade, usually as the top vote-getter. Though Jarvis was a Jeffersonian allied to former governor Samuel Adams, as a founder of the American Academy of Arts and Sciences and the Massachusetts Medical Society, his voice was respected across political boundaries. That Jarvis stood up for Hardy counted; when a prominent white argued a black man or woman's cause, courts everywhere paid attention.[39]

Yet something else, perhaps, tipped the scales in favor of a new trial. The murder of the mixed-race infant occurred during the year's most sensational criminal trial, the manslaughter trial of Federalist Thomas O. Selfridge for killing Jeffersonian Charles Austin on Boston's State Street. Hardy's first trial, held a week after Selfridge's indictment, thus seemed commonplace because the parties involved came from the lowest classes. Perhaps this explains why, when Supreme Court Justice Theodore Sedgwick presided at Hardy's indictment, everyone overlooked the fact that Sedgwick was alone on the bench—even though the previous year the legislature stipulated that indictments for "any capital offence" required "three or more" justices.[40] After Hardy was found guilty, his attorneys—perhaps alerted by the debate over one judge or three judges for Selfridge's trial—sought and won his new trial.[41] At this moment of heightened scrutiny of defendants' rights, consciousness of fair and equal procedures was conspicuous. Because three judges had presided at Hardy's first trial (as opposed to his indictment), Selfridge's friends now "hoped (if agreeable to law) that as many Judges would decide on this question [Selfridge's trial] as on the case of Hardy, the black man."[42] Certainly the elite white Federalist, Selfridge, possessed equal rights with the lowly black. Ironically, at least one Boston black woman viewed Hardy's conviction as unfair. Comparing both cases, she reportedly said: "Ha, you Hardy, you no lawyer—you fool! Why you no take 'em down '[S]tate '[S]treet and shoot 'em—den you be clear?"[43]

In the end, Hardy had three judges at both his first and second trials, and Selfridge only one. Justice Isaac Parker apologized, explaining to Selfridge's jury that "all criminal cases, other than capital, are triable before one judge," an arrangement "calculated for the dispatch of business." If available, more judges could participate, but, Parker advised, "at this time, the court being in session in three if not four several counties, it was impracticable" and would have meant "great delay." At Hardy's indictment this scarcity of judges, coupled with the desire to act promptly, led Sedgwick to overlook the new requirements. In contrast, because Selfridge's indictment was for the noncapital crime of manslaughter, though the coroner's jury had found "willful murder" and many clamored for a three-judge bench, as Parker explained, a single judge met the legal standard.[44]

Jeffersonians were not mollified. Boston's Jeffersonian newspaper asked, "If a *black man* was tried a second time for MURDER, merely from the punctilio that he was arraigned before one *Judge*, ought not a *white man* to be tried a second time for MANSLAUGHTER," when the jury that judged him was biased in his favor? To Jeffersonians Selfridge's acquittal was so outrageous that the ancient British rule against double jeopardy—guaranteed in the U.S. Bill of Rights—should be waived. Selfridge should be tried again for, "if the *black man* was *acquitted* on the first [trial], might not the *white man* be *condemned* on the second trial, though *acquitted* on the first, and the decision be equally as *legal?*" As the Reverend Bentley remarked, "many insinuations respecting this affair" compared the two cases.[45]

Courtroom rhetoric and newspaper commentary demonstrate that race was central to the Hardy trial and that condescension and contempt toward blacks were pervasive. Yet a comparison of the Hardy and Selfridge trials suggests that insofar as law enforcement and court rules provided for equal rights, those rules restrained the role of prejudice, giving in at least one case apparently equal justice. In Boston in 1806 and 1807 Selfridge's and Hardy's acquittals illustrate the legal system's ability to command deference, whether by providing a second trial for a black servant or enabling a well-connected white man to avoid a capital trial and then go free.

Detailed records of acquittals—whether defendants were white or people of color—are scarce.[46] But cases leading to guilty verdicts are also instructive. Two cases in 1804 and 1805 reveal the extent to which New Englanders resisted the impulse to prejudge people of color and resort to vigilante justice. In one shocking Massachusetts case, where a nineteen-year-old mulatto, John Battus, raped his white, thirteen-year-old victim and then killed her, hoping to conceal the crime, the Supreme Judicial Court made it hard to plead guilty, first rejecting Battus's guilty plea. When justices accepted his second guilty plea, they did so only after the sheriff, jailer, and arresting justice of the peace testified to Battus's sanity; he had reflected on his decision and was not hoping to trade a guilty plea for leniency or a pardon. Historically, in Britain and the colonies these procedural hurdles guarded against guilty pleas, since hasty or insincere pleas could hide the truth and lead straight to hanging.[47] Justice and order must not rest on concealment or falsehood.

Attention to legal process and the measure of equal rights it provided is evident in the prosecution of a man of color for an Indian woman's 1805 killing in eastern Connecticut's hill country. Here Samuel Freeman, the twenty-five-year-old son of an African American father and a Native American mother—a "mustee," though often labeled "mulatto"—was charged with murdering his companion Hannah Simons. Unlike Hardy's Boston murder trial, Freeman's case unfolded far from high politics in rural Windham County. Here, a printer published sermons but no trial report. So, like most poor people's trials, Freeman's case is known only from brief court records and his execution sermon.[48] Consequently, evidence of race or class arguments is lost.

But the crime and prosecution are clear. Freeman, a Rhode Island native, and Simons, born in Rhode Island or Cape Cod, probably of Wampanoag descent, were transients. They first met in 1802 in Massachusetts, but after a chance meeting in Connecticut in April 1805 Simons decided to leave her male companion to join Freeman. During April and May they worked in and around Ashford, a town of 2,371 whites and 37 nonwhites in

THE
CONFESSION
OF
JOHN BATTUS,

A Mulatto, aged 19 Years and 7 Months;—

Who was Executed at Dedham,
NOVEMBER 8, 1804,
For the CRIMES of a moſt cruel
RAPE and MURDER
on the Body of
SALOME TALBOT,
of Canton, in the 14th Year of her age.
To which is added his WRITINGS, during
his imprisonment.

Confession of John Battus, Dedham, Massachusetts, 1804.
While this execution broadside was conventional in some
respects, Battus's racialized silhouette connected blacks
and crime. Courtesy, American Antiquarian Society.

1800, including two slaves.[49] It was in Ashford, on May 24, 1805, near their
dwelling hut, that Hannah Simons was last seen alive. Later that day Freeman, "traveling fast about the neighborhood," set off the alarm, exclaiming
that Hannah had "gone off and he could not find her." Thereafter, though
Simons remained missing, Freeman stopped looking for her. When an un-

known woman in the next town casually asked Freeman about Hannah the day after the disappearance, he answered that she was *"at work."* Soon after, in response to the suggestion that Simons might be dead, Freeman showed no concern: *"If she is dead, I am glad of it, for she has been a plague to me, and everybody else that had anything to do with her."* Now neighbors grew suspicious, so when searchers found her body near their hut in a thicket that Freeman claimed to have searched, and with fatal stab wounds under her ears, the justice of the peace ordered Freeman's arrest. After Freeman's initial agitation, when he claimed that she had "gone off," he showed no interest in finding Hannah during the week between her disappearance and discovery of her corpse. Yet he had begged soap from a neighbor so that an Indian woman from a neighboring town could wash his shirt.[50]

When the superior court tried Freeman ten weeks later, two respected attorneys defended him; one, Calvin Goddard, was a Dartmouth College graduate, a Federalist who had just served two terms in Congress and who would in 1807 be chosen to lead the Connecticut House of Representatives as Speaker.[51] No record of the defense survives, but if it followed Freeman's account, an unknown assailant murdered Simons in the thicket sometime after she left their hut and before Freeman went looking for her. This explanation, when weighed against evidence of Freeman's connection to Simons, his admitted assaults on her, and his words and behavior after her disappearance, did not persuade the jury. Still, after the verdict Goddard and his junior counsel made one last effort to defend their client by seeking to set aside the guilty judgment due to procedural errors. But the superior court denied their motion, so the verdict stood. On October 4 the court ordered Samuel Freeman to hang at Windham on November 6, 1805.[52]

During the next month the Reverend Moses C. Welch, who lived nearby, visited Freeman, seeking his conversion, confession, and repentance. Welch succeeded in part, because as "execution drew near . . . he manifested an overwhelming sense of his danger as a great sinner" and confessed a catalog of sins. Not only had Freeman sinned by lying, swearing, and Sabbath-breaking, but he had abused his former wife and had engaged in fornication and adultery, as well as "repeated attempts to commit filthiness with beasts." Yet Freeman did not confess to murdering Hannah Simons, who he claimed could not have died by his hand, though he admitted that he "struck her twice with his fist," "knocked her down," gave her "a severe stroke in the stomach," and "pulled her off the bed and drew her about the floor." This, he insisted, was not *"enough to kill her."*[53]

Samuel Freeman was hanged after religious exercises and with "an escort of infantry and cavalry." Ashford's pastor, the Reverend Enoch Pond, "made an excellent, suitable prayer," Welch delivered his execution sermon, and Freeman made a "humble confession of the many crimes he had committed," exhorting the crowd "to avoid the evil practices" that brought him to this end. After another prayer Freeman "was launched into the eternal world." The state had meted out justice while teaching "a vast assemblage" lessons in state power and orthodox Christianity.[54]

But was this equal justice? Perhaps Freeman's trial and execution was another example of the white majority's readiness to execute people of color in the early Republic. Yet the attention to procedure, which included the formal hearing of evidence before a justice's court on May 31, 1805, the presentation of evidence to the grand jury when the superior court convened in September, and Freeman's jury trial, where he was defended by the prominent attorney Calvin Goddard and an associate, all testify to maintaining the forms of fairness. That Freeman's lawyers went on to challenge the verdict's legitimacy on procedural grounds recalls the Hardy case and underscores the commitment to correct professional standards—standards that supplied a measure of fairness. Never was there any hint of a movement to lynch the mustee outsider. Instead Freeman was subject to regular court procedures in which Connecticut taxpayers spent $240.19 on incarceration and trial and an additional $243.59 for execution, a total of $483.78—at a time when a day's work brought the average laborer $1.00. To ordinary Yankees this was a large expenditure to provide justice for a recent sojourner from another state, described in their press as a "mulatto fellow."

It is notable, too, that no one challenged spending nearly five hundred dollars of public funds to prosecute the killer of "a transient person," a Native American woman. It may be significant that the language of court records omits racial identifications, even though in newspaper reports and the Reverend Welch's published sketch local people routinely identified Simons and Freeman racially. Prejudice operated actively, if silently, in the fact that no nonwhite witnesses were called to testify. The Indian couple with whom Freeman said "he had been intimate . . . the Indian woman washed a shirt for him," were never called to testify, perhaps because they were deemed unreliable a priori or, unlike Susanna's trial in Schenectady, their testimony would not be credited. Neither did anyone, white or nonwhite, stand up to support the transient Freeman. Welch stressed that Freeman was given a proper hearing before the grand jury, that he was defended "by able and learned counsel" and judged by "twelve sober, judicious, disinterested jurors," yet it is hard to imagine that though he was probably guilty, prejudice was absent from the proceedings. The cultures of law and of Christianity could not erase common prejudices, but they could restrain them to channel behavior toward the ideal "that all men are created equal."[55]

II

In contrast, the political arena could inflame popular prejudice. In Connecticut a private girls' school set off a firestorm that led all the way to the legislature and the state's highest court. The conflict was accidental. In 1831 Prudence Crandall, a Quaker teacher, purchased a mansion opposite the Congregational meetinghouse in the center of Canterbury, Connecticut, proposing a day and boarding school to teach "several higher branches of education not taught in the public district schools." With enthusiastic patronage from aspiring gentry, Crandall's school flourished for a year until she admitted Sarah Harris, daughter of a local black farm family, who had attended district school with white neighbors without protest. When Crandall refused to dismiss the black girl from her academy, white parents rebelled. Withdrawing their daughters, they closed the school. Crandall might have sold the mansion on which she owed hundreds of dollars, but with support from local abolitionists with Boston and Providence connections, she determined to reopen her school—now for girls of color. Responding to advertisements in abolitionist papers, more than twenty girls enrolled in April 1833 from Boston, Providence, New York, and Philadelphia.[56] Canterbury, once the proud home of a white academy, became home to a black academy.

Canterbury, Connecticut, c. 1838. John Warner Barber's engraving of
Canterbury shows the meetinghouse where townspeople met to condemn
Prudence Crandall's school, which was located in shadow at the left,
facing the meetinghouse. The genteel scene Barber depicts belies the
violence a few years before. From the author's private collection.

Local officials who originally sponsored the school were outraged. They
called a town meeting at the meetinghouse where an excited voice vote
directed them to tell Crandall "the incalculable evils" of her plan and "persuade her . . . to abandon the project." Crandall's next-door neighbor, the
prominent Jacksonian and colonizationist, state senator Andrew T. Judson—
a clergyman's son who supported the original school—led the attack. "A
school for nigger girls," he told the meeting, "was insupportable"; it would
damage real estate values and destroy Canterbury's prosperity. Later, when
Crandall volunteered to move her school to "some more retired part of the
town or vicinity," Judson declared, "There shall not be such a school set
up anywhere in our State." He was implacable: "Let the niggers and their

descendants be sent back to their fatherland; and there improve themselves as much as they may." Thus spoke Canterbury's leading official.[57]

Judson's proclamation that Connecticut would not have a school like Crandall's was no idle threat. Several years earlier in Cornwall, Connecticut, local outrage forced the closing of the Foreign Mission School for *the education of heathen youth*" after two Indian students engaged to marry local white women.[58] Then, in 1831 fears of pauperism, falling real estate values, and intermarriage fed New Haven prejudices so that town and Yale College leaders rallied townspeople to block the opening of a college for men of color.[59] The next year, when a black student enrolled at the new Wesleyan University in Middletown, white students successfully demanded his withdrawal.[60] Crandall's school battle was emblematic. Two years later, men in Canaan, New Hampshire, closed the racially integrated Noyes Academy by using nearly one hundred teams of oxen to haul the two-story academy into a swamp, where they burned it. Rural Yankee yeomen could populate antiblack crowds—or mobs—as well as urban laborers; this in communities without competition for jobs and housing among blacks, whites, and immigrants.[61]

Connecticut legislators promptly endorsed Judson's ultimatum while simultaneously professing concern for the equal rights of Connecticut blacks. The committee reporting the bill outlawing schools like Crandall's announced that so far as the "population of color" was concerned, "the constitution and laws of the State have secured to them all the rights and privileges of other citizens, except that of the elective franchise." Righteously they declared, "In every other point the white and colored population of *this State* are entitled by law to equal privileges." Connecticut people of color even enjoyed special privileges: "exemption from the poll tax and military duty." But out-of-state colored persons warranted no such protections; indeed, providing a haven for "colored emigrants" would lead to "incalculable evils," because they would prove "an appalling source of crime and pauperism." They might come for education, but afterward "a great portion of the whole number would make this State their permanent residence." It was therefore vital "to protect *our own citizens*, against that host of colored emigrants, which would rush in from every quarter, when invited to our colleges and schools." So on May 24, 1833, Connecticut enacted a law bluntly stating that towns could bar any "school, academy, or literary institution for the instruction or education of colored persons who are not inhabitants of this state." Such schools "would tend to the great increase of the colored population of the State, and thereby to the injury of the people."[62] Now Crandall and her abolitionist allies were not only defying her neighbors but breaking state law.

Crandall was arrested, and because she declined bail, she was—to the embarrassment of local officials—briefly jailed. When she came to trial in August 1833, the presiding judge instructed the jury that if they believed Crandall "committed the acts charged"—acts she freely admitted—they must find her guilty, unless they believed that "the law was void for unconstitutionality." After hearing the case the jury divided so completely that within several hours they were deadlocked. Accordingly, the judge ordered them to deliberate again. Quickly returning, they reported that "there was no probability they should ever agree." With seven votes to convict and five to acquit, only a bare majority supported Connecticut's Black Law.

Frustrated, Connecticut authorities acted swiftly to empanel a new jury to retry Crandall. The arguments were repeated at greater length in October 1833. Four judges of the state's Supreme Court of Errors heard the case, with Chief Justice David Daggett—a leader in blocking New Haven's college for men of color—presiding. Prosecuting Crandall would be her neighbor, Senator Judson, joined by Canterbury native Chauncey F. Cleveland, soon to be Speaker of the Connecticut House of Representatives and then governor. Asserting a states' rights interpretation of article 4 of the Constitution—claiming that states could recognize the rights of citizens of other states selectively—they argued that Connecticut could vest supervision of educational institutions in towns. But that was not all. Judson presented a full-blown race argument: a judgment against the Connecticut law would "inevitably destroy the government itself, and the *American Nation*—this nation of white men, may be taken from us and given to the African race." Sounding more like a politician on the stump than an attorney at the bar, he trumpeted: "America is ours—it belongs to a race of white men, the descendants of those who first redeemed it from the wilderness." More pointed, his colleague Cleveland reminded the court of accepted color distinctions: "I address four Judges who are white men. No black man can take the seat occupied by your Honors." In a moral view, he admitted, "there is no difference as to the color of the skin," but to overturn the Connecticut law would "destroy a nation of free white Americans."[63]

Compared to South Carolina's assertion of states' rights, which had just created the Nullification Crisis, threatening the nation's survival, Judson's and Cleveland's claims were modest. But on the question of race they excluded all ambiguities, contradictions, or middle ground. Judson: "What was the *intention* of those who framed the constitution? Did they mean to place persons of color on the footing of equality with themselves, and did they make them citizens?" Certainly not, regardless of the "opinion of a few madmen or enthusiasts now." The race categories, he claimed, were absolute and encompassing: "Can it be entertained for one moment, that those who framed the constitution should hold one portion of *a race of men* in bondage, while the other portion were made *citizens!* This would be strange inconsistency."[64] Judson even questioned Connecticut's own constitution because, he said, the notion of equal rights for people of color was neither logical nor historically grounded.

Crandall's attorneys, hired with the support of New York abolitionist Arthur Tappan, thought otherwise.[65] One was Calvin Goddard, a Federalist congressman during Jefferson's presidency, a former Speaker of the Connecticut House of Representatives, and the attorney who long before defended the murderer Samuel Freeman. Crandall's other lawyer, William W. Ellsworth, was a generation younger than Goddard and so could not personally recollect original meanings of the Constitution. But he was a congressman whose father attended the Constitutional Convention and served as U.S. Supreme Court chief justice. Attorney Ellsworth—later a governor and Connecticut Supreme Court justice—could speak with assurance. Together they argued that girls who came to Crandall's school were indeed citizens of their respective states—Pennsylvania, New York, Massachusetts, and Rhode Island—and were therefore free to reside in any state. Judson and Cleveland were flat wrong: "A distinction founded in *color*, in fundamental rights, is *novel, inconvenient* and *impracticable*."[66]

Recalling the 1772 Somersett decision, Ellsworth explained, "hitherto we have seen no such distinction; none in the ancient common law of England which justly boasts her equal principles." He went on to cite the Declaration of Independence—"that immortal instrument which our republican fathers put forth as the ground-work of all just government"—and its assertion "that all men are created *equal*." The Connecticut constitution provided further support, and he invoked the idea that Pendleton had employed in 1776 in Virginia: "*All* men when they enter into the social compact are equal in rights." Those words had excluded slaves in both Virginia and Connecticut in 1776, but not free blacks, who, Ellsworth argued, were certainly part of the social compact, as demonstrated by their military service in the Revolution and their inclusion on the nation's pension list.[67]

History provided further proofs. When South Carolina had sought to amend article 4 of the Confederation to specify "white" citizens, that vote failed: eight to two. When article 4 was brought into the Constitution, no stipulation of color was added. Indeed the Constitution never prohibited naturalization of citizens by color; that rule came afterward from Congress. Instead, when the Constitution prescribed the rules for apportioning representation, it specified numbers of "free persons," not "white persons." Because the nation's militia law limited membership to white male citizens, it implicitly recognized other classes of citizens, nonwhite and nonmale. Ellsworth added that colored citizens held patents and copyrights and, as citizens, could sue in U.S. courts. Moreover, the 1792 law that required U.S. ships to be commanded by American citizens had included black mariners, and the 1796 law protecting seamen enabled colored sailors to obtain U.S. certificates of citizenship. Using irony, Ellsworth pointed out that no one supposed that the 1820 law forbidding American citizens from engaging in the slave trade intended an exception allowing black Americans to import slaves.[68]

Calvin Goddard closed against Connecticut's Black Law. He dismissed Judson's straw man claim that he and Ellsworth were asserting that *slaves* were citizens. Judson's suggestion that recognizing *any* person of color as a citizen meant citizenship for *all* people of color was groundless. Goddard argued for the nation's 350,000 free people of color, including the 8,000 who were citizens of Connecticut. Judson's arguments tying citizenship to suffrage were misguided since voters in 1776 and 1789 were a limited class — adult male property holders — whereas the class of citizens was far more inclusive and race was never specified by the national government and by only a few state governments. Indeed, when the race qualification was raised, as on October 30, 1777, Congress refused to exclude "Indians" and "negroes" from voting on ratification of the Articles of Confederation; and on June 25, 1788, when South Carolina sought to exclude them from citizenship, Congress voted down the exclusion. Similarly, on April 26, 1783, when Alexander Hamilton wanted to amend the articles with the language "white and other free citizens," William Ellsworth's father, Oliver, succeeded in revising the amendment to read simply "free inhabitants, and all other inhabitants." The Constitution spoke of free and unfree, not white and black. More recently, the 1818 Revolutionary War pension law included blacks. Goddard himself, as a reviewer of pension applications, had read the honorable discharge of Primus Babcock, "wholly in the hand writing of George Washington." And in 1820 the law admitting the new slave state of Missouri had specified that the state's constitution must never "be construed so as to deprive any citizen of any state, of the privileges or immunities to which he is entitled as a citizen of the United States." If this was true for Missouri in 1820, it was surely true for Connecticut in 1833. The sixty-five-year-old Goddard concluded by declaring the idea "that colored persons are not citizens is a doctrine of modern origin."[69]

Whatever their historical merits, Ellsworth's and Goddard's arguments did not persuade the court. Indeed Chief Justice David Daggett, a Yale graduate and advocate for the colonization of blacks, would not be instructed on the law by a Dartmouth graduate four years his junior. When Daggett charged the jury he told them positively that the Connecticut statute was entirely constitutional, "blacks not being citizens of the United States within the meaning of the Constitution." This time the jury united to declare Prudence Crandall guilty.[70]

Crandall's attorneys fought back. They filed a motion of error, claiming that the information filed by the state's attorney was faulty. So the case was heard a third time and the arguments repeated in July 1834 before judges of the state's court of errors. This time the court delayed, reserving judgment; and when the justices finally issued their ruling, they decided that Crandall's attorneys were correct, not that the law was unconstitutional, but that the proceeding was flawed. So instead of settling the law's constitutionality, they decided that it was unnecessary to make a judgment. For the moment Crandall's school could continue.[71]

Vigilante violence triumphed where the law failed. Two attempts to burn Crandall's building and a midnight attack by men armed with "heavy clubs and iron bars" convinced Crandall and her advisers that the girls were in danger. So on September 10, 1834—after seventeen months of battling local and state opinion and authorities—Crandall sent her pupils home. Bigotry won, although some Connecticut opinion favored equal rights. This explains why Ellsworth and Goddard could argue for equal rights for people of color; and it also explains the clumsy and finally indecisive legal moves to close the school. Indeed four years after passage of the Black Law, one of its authors disowned it: "I could weep tears of blood for the part I took in that matter—I now regard that law as utterly abominable." Now he recognized "my prejudices against that poor persecuted class of people were so violent as to blind me to the dictates of common humanity and justice." Propelled by these sentiments, he led a petition drive to repeal the law.[72] And in 1838 Connecticut erased its Black Law. Yet no town stepped forward to welcome a school for blacks. Crandall's ally, the Reverend Samuel J. May, of neighboring Brooklyn, Connecticut, had been ousted from his Unitarian church in 1836 after he abolished its segregated "nigger pew." As May explained: "The prejudices of the whites against those of African descent . . . [are] deep and inveterate." Indeed almost fifty years before, in 1787, the abolitionist Reverend Samuel Hopkins had argued that blacks would always be "unhappy, while they live here among the whites." Like Judson and Daggett, Hopkins advocated colonization. Americans were republicans, but on color they were also habitually intolerant and biased. People who aligned themselves with Crandall were seeking to overturn "that aristocracy of color which," May recognized, "has become hereditary among us." Twenty years later the Know-Nothing Massachusetts legislature of 1855 would revive May's agenda by enacting a law stating: "In determining the qualifications of scholars to be admitted into any Public School or District School in this Commonwealth, no distinction shall be made on account of the race, color, or religious opinions of the applicant or scholar." But in this Massachusetts was alone.[73]

By the 1830s, whether states were free or slave, except for Massachusetts, in New England as elsewhere, attacking "the aristocracy of color" was a losing battle. Evidence supported attorneys like Ellsworth and Goddard who claimed that "a distinction founded in *color*, in fundamental rights, is *novel*." Even the great New York jurist Chancellor James Kent came to agree; for when he revised his *Commentaries* at the end of his life he declared that free blacks were citizens. "The privilege of voting and the legal capacity for office," he stated, "are not essential to the character of a citizen, for women are citizens without either, and free people of color may enjoy the one, and may acquire . . . and transmit . . . real and personal estates." But though the beliefs Ellsworth, Goddard, and Kent criticized were new in some respects, they were widespread—sustained by slavery's legacies in custom and belief throughout the United States. Neither logic nor historical argument could overturn deeply held convictions. A generation later, when American culture had assimilated racial ideology and beliefs even more thoroughly, such historical arguments became suspect, often characterized as radical abolitionist special pleading—merely the "opinion of a few madmen or enthusiasts." Indeed by 1857, when Chief Justice Taney issued the U.S. Supreme Court ruling in *Scott v. Sandford*, only two of the Court's nine justices, from Massachusetts and Pennsylvania, chose to challenge Taney's different, now-mainstream historical arguments.[74]

SIX

Subordinate Citizens

Women and Children

Remember the Ladies, and be more generous and favourable
to them than your ancestors. Do not put such unlimited power in
the hands of the Husbands. Remember all Men would be tyrants if
they could. If perticuliar care and attention is not paid to the Laidies we
are determined to foment a Rebelion, and will not hold ourselves bound
by any Laws in which we have no voice, or Representation.
—*Abigail Adams to John Adams, Braintree, Massachusetts, March 31, 1776*

"Chapter I.—the Right which the Husband acquires
to the Personal Property of the Wife"
—*Tapping Reeve,* The Law of Baron [Husband]
and Femme [Wife]; of Parent and Child; of Guardian
and Ward; of Master and Servant . . . , *1816*

The civil law, as well as nature herself, has always recognized a
wide difference in the respective spheres and destinies of man and
woman. Man is, or should be, woman's protector and defender.
The natural and proper timidity and delicacy which belongs to the female
sex evidently unfits it for many of the occupations of civil life. . . . In
view of the peculiar characteristics, destiny, and mission of woman, it is
within the province of the legislature to ordain what offices, positions,
and callings shall be filled and discharged by men, and shall receive
the benefit of those energies and responsibilities, and that decision and
firmness which are presumed to predominate in the sterner sex.
—*Justice Joseph Bradley, for the eight-to-one majority,*
U.S. *Supreme Court,* Bradwell v. Illinois, *1873*

Today we commonly assume that all citizens possess equal rights because we claim that the United States is no place for second-class citizens. But that is a fiction that has never been true. Considerations of race and color, of gender and age, as well as of mental capacity and criminal record have justified subordination of some citizens to first-class citizens. Although some Patriots contended that the phrase "all men are created equal" included men of color in 1776—witness Virginians' debate over the opening words of their similar Declaration of Rights—the same was not true for women. That year, when Abigail Adams privately admonished her husband to "Remember the Ladies," though they practiced companionate marriage, he flatly rejected her call for equal rights.[1] No one doubted that women, like children, were citizens of the new United States, but John Adams and his peers prescribed women's role as subordinate; women were, like children,

John Adams, 1784. From the author's private collection.

subordinate citizens properly ruled by their fathers or their husbands. The condition of a woman was, by default, daughter or wife. To live as a single woman or widow was understood as anomalous, a temporary status soon ended by marriage or death.

Abigail Adams's call for equal rights was virtually unique in 1776 and for nearly a generation thereafter. Though a few women, chiefly, called for equal rights for their sex, including political enfranchisement, the obstacles were formidable. Learned authorities claimed that each sex was so fundamentally different that natural law dictated men's mastery over women. Accordingly, women's legal status was justified by centuries-old social custom and family law. No wonder the thought of elevating women to equal citizenship challenged the natural and customary social order. Though law often lags behind social practice, asserting equal rights for women, many believed, introduced an extreme and irrational dimension to American independence.

Theories of women's *nature* supplied legitimacy for their exclusion from public life. However, women's natural subordination was understood to be so comprehensive as to govern private as well as public life. The English law of coverture with closely related family law provided the legal bedrock for subordination, which, practically speaking, canceled a woman's legal personhood at marriage. Husbands stood as rulers and custodians of the nuclear family, servants, and, with limited exceptions, the owner of family property. Patriarchy—rule by fathers—was a core principle of America's social order before and after independence. The fact that patriarchy was the pillar of monarchy, mocked exuberantly by Thomas Paine's *Common Sense* before Revolutionaries created republics, did not erase patriarchy from their hearts and minds. Although the logic of the Declaration of Independence undercut the hierarchical foundations of patriarchy and it was often compromised in companionate marriages, the idea was so pervasive that even the boldest Revolutionaries refused to admit that their pursuit of republicanism contradicted their support for domestic patriarchy. In the 1790s the same men who proudly embraced the Democratic-Republican label dismissed advocates for women's rights.

So the need to defend patriarchy in the 1790s was itself truly revolutionary. Even before the 1792 London publication of Mary Wollstonecraft's *Vin-*

dication of the Rights of Women, a few American women publicly called for women's recognition in the republic of letters and actual public affairs. In one state, New Jersey, a 1790 law covering more than half the state's counties enfranchised women qualified by age, residency, and property. Three years later a New Jersey congressman boasted on Independence Day that "the Rights of Women are no longer strange sounds to an American ear"; and in 1797, New Jersey extended women's suffrage to the entire state. When the assembly considered further revision in 1800, a newspaper explained, "Our constitution gives this right to maids or widows, black or white." Evidently New Jersey chose to recognize the Revolutionary ideal of equal rights, as a Trenton paper explained, to fulfill "a principle of justice"; it was only "right that every free person who pays a tax should have a vote." Quakers, influential in the counties that first allowed women's suffrage, may also have acted from religious principles, while propertied Federalists who expected wealthy women's votes may have seen political advantage in this aspect of equal rights. Just a few hundred widows actually voted in any election, but their ballots could decide a tight partisan race.[2]

Women's exercise of voting rights was short-lived. Revocation in 1807 was emblematic of a widespread assertion of white men's prerogatives. Although few New Jersey voters doubted the principle of linking taxation and representation, when it came to women more deeply rooted beliefs prevailed. Year after year critics claimed that including women in politics would corrupt government and subvert patriarchal authority. And when irregularities in a local election pointed to fraudulent voters, Federalists and Republicans agreed to defend electoral integrity by ending voting by women and blacks. For a generation thereafter Americans chiefly sought equal rights for men, white men. As for women, few questioned women's subordinate status until a new generation of reformers vigorously restated and expanded the case for women's equality in the 1830s. Though New Jersey officials were willing to extend equal voting rights to women in 1790 and 1797, when the legislature reversed itself in 1807, denying the franchise to women and people of color, there was no public protest.[3]

American adaptations of English law provided the bedrock supporting men's mastery over women, children, and servants. Here the key American legal text came from the scholarly jurist Tapping Reeve in 1816. His

The Law of Baron [Husband] and Femme [Wife]; Of Parent and Child; of Guardian and Ward; of Master and Servant . . . would become standard for generations, reprinted six times before 1880. Reeve had founded the nation's leading law school in 1784 at his home in Litchfield, Connecticut. Drawing students nationwide—including two future vice presidents, Aaron Burr of New Jersey and New York, and John C. Calhoun of South Carolina—Reeve, later the chief justice of the Connecticut Superior Court, was a moderately reform-minded nationalist who challenged some of the most absolute denials of women's rights derived from Blackstone's influential *Commentaries on the Laws of England*. Nevertheless between Blackstone and Reeve, women's subordination reigned.

Consequently, obstacles to realization of equal rights for women were many and formidable. Beginning with legal disabilities such as near-permanent marital bondage, denial of parental rights, and abridged recognition of women's personhood and responsibilities, customs reinforced subordination. And while behavior often rested on tradition, new romantic ideas concerning men's and women's fundamental nature gave fresh impetus to different roles, responsibilities, and rights for women and men. In the new Republic ideals of equality were limited not only by racial prejudice but by gender and social class. But unlike class and juvenile status, race and gender were permanent, lifetime conditions. Women, chiefly, would challenge the paradox of their denial of equal rights in the Revolutionary Republic. In opposition an ideology of inherent female difference would, like racial ideology, provide justification for blocking the recognition of equal rights for generations.

I

Abigail Adams's 1776 declaration of women's rights has sometimes been treated as a curiosity—a private expression that went nowhere. But her argument was fundamental. A decade earlier the polemical theorist James Otis suggested it in his 1764 tract on colonial rights. Alone among Revolutionary pamphleteers, Otis touched on women's rights as well as "negro rights." Reasoning from Lockean theory, he asked rhetorically: "Are not women born as free as men? Would it not be infamous to assert that the ladies are all slaves by nature?" This brother of Mary Otis Warren argued that "every man and woman . . . has, and will have, a right to be consulted, and must accede to the original compact before they can with any kind of justice be said to be bound by it." In the state of nature "every man and woman

Abigail Adams, 1767. From *Familiar Letters of John Adams and His Wife Abigail during the Revolution*, ed. Charles Francis Adams (New York: Hurd and Houghton, 1876). Courtesy, University of Connecticut Library.

were . . . equal." Consequently, "every one of them [possessed] a natural and equitable right to be consulted." In short, women enjoyed "as good a right to give their respectable suffrages . . . as the philosopher, courtier, petit maitre and politician."[4] These pronouncements were too bold, too unsettling for Otis's male peers. But John Adams confronted the radical implications of this logic when he answered his wife.

John's direct response to Abigail was flippant. "I cannot but laugh," he said, "you are so saucy." Men's power, he claimed, was merely theoretical. Though men carried "the Name of Masters . . . in Practice you know We are subjects." But he quickly added, "We know better than to repeal our Masculine systems." Real worries lay beneath his jocular tone. Sarcastically he claimed that America's political enemies in the British ministry, "after stirring up Tories, Landjobbers, Trimmers, Bigots, Canadians, Indians, Negroes, Hanoverians, Hessians, Russians, Irish Roman Catholicks, [and] Scotch Renegadoes," had at last "stimulated . . . another Tribe more numerous and powerfull than all the rest . . . to demand new Priviledges and threaten to rebel."[5] Any threat from women was imaginary, but John Adams's rejoinder underscored the implications of Abigail's challenge. Six weeks later he elaborated in 1,352 carefully argued words to Patriot James Sullivan.

Sullivan, then engaged in reconsidering Massachusetts government, had concluded that because the colony's property requirements for voting contradicted natural law, they should be revised. Adams, however, tried to persuade Sullivan to leave well enough alone. "In Theory," Adams agreed, "the only moral Foundation of Government is the Consent of the People." But in practice, he asked, "To what Extent Shall We carry this Principle?" Certainly Sullivan would agree that it was "impossible" to include "every Individual of the Community, old and young, male and female, as well as rich and poor." Returning to Abigail's issue, Adams asked: "Whence arises the Right of the Men to govern Women, without their Consent? Or, for that matter, the majority to govern the minority, or the old to rule the young without consent?" Adams presumed that all Patriots would justify such rule as "Necessity, . . . because there can be no other Rule." Then Adams challenged conventional political reasoning:

But why exclude Women? You will Say, because their Delicacy renders them unfit for Practice and Experience in the great Business of Life, and the hardy Enterprizes of War, as well as the arduous Cares of State. Besides, their attention is So much engaged with the necessary Nurture of their Children, that Nature has made them fittest for domestic Cares. And Children have not Judgment or Will of their own. True. But will not these Reasons apply to others? Is it not equally true, that Men in general in every Society, who are wholly destitute of Property, are also too little acquainted with public Affairs to form a Right Judgment, and too dependent upon other Men to have a Will of their own? . . . The Same Reasoning, which will induce you to admit all Men, who have no Property, to vote, with those who have . . . will prove that you ought to admit Women and Children: for generally Speaking, Women and Children, have as good Judgment, and as independent Minds as those Men who are wholly destitute of Property: these last being to all Intents and Purposes as much dependent upon others, who will please to feed, cloath, and employ them, as Women are upon their Husbands, or Children upon their Parents.

Adams shuddered at the implications of Sullivan's egalitarian thinking on suffrage. Finally Adams was pragmatic: "It is dangerous to open So fruitfull a Source of Controversy and Altercation, as would be opened by attempting to alter the Qualification of Voters. There will be no End of it. New Claims will arise. Women will demand a Vote. Lads from 12 to 21 will think their Rights not enough attended to, and every Man, who has not a Farthing, will demand an equal Voice with any other in all Acts of State." Coupled with the influential James Sullivan's consideration of equal voting rights for men, Abigail's admonition to "Remember the Ladies" threatened to unravel social and political order. "All Distinctions," Adams warned would fall, so as to "prostrate all Ranks, to one common Levell."[6] Adams admitted that Revolutionary theory pointed that way, but Patriots must not go there.

Americans generally agreed. Neither public officials nor political writers, male or female, joined Abigail Adams to advocate equal rights for women.

Yet the Philadelphia Quaker novelist Charles Brockden Brown declared that on equal rights, the American republic was an emperor with no clothes. Brown created a fictional widow who complained that she was equally subject to the law with men: "I cannot perceive the justice of your pretentions to equality and liberty, when those principles are thus openly and grossly violated. . . . I am a woman. As such, I cannot celebrate the equity of that scheme of government which classes me with dogs and swine." Citing the Declaration, she remarked: "'All,' says the code, 'are free.' Liberty is the immediate gift of the Creator to all mankind, and is unalienable." These, she said, were "plausible and specious maxims! But fallacious." In fact suffrage was denied all who did not meet age, residency, taxpaying, race, or gender requirements. Brown emphasized the gender barrier since age, residency, taxpaying, and race requirements might be plausible. From the standpoint of the Revolution's logic, Brown's widow, like Abigail Adams, won the argument. But Brown's male character closes the discussion by declaring, "You, Madam, are singular. Women in general do not reason in this manner. They are contented with the post assigned them." Like John Adams, he scoffed, "It would be hard to restrain a smile to see her [a woman] rise in a popular assembly to discuss some mighty topic."[7]

Judith Sargent Murray's 1790 magazine essay "On the Equality of the Sexes" supported the male character's judgment. Murray asserted equal intellectual capacity—as John Adams had admitted—but Murray made no political demands. Instead, her assertion of equality called only for improvements in women's education.[8] Murray's voice was significant for opening America's "republic of letters" to women, but from the outset essentialist ideas about women's nature shaped enhancement of their educational opportunities.

Dr. Benjamin Rush of Philadelphia was an especially influential national advocate. This signer of the Declaration wrote on many subjects— politics, medicine, race, and education especially. Though a promoter of "the elevation of the female mind," Rush grounded his arguments on their properly subordinate role. Though an ardent believer in "equality," his condescension was palpable: "The equal share that every citizen has in the liberty, and the possible share *he* may have in the government of our country, make it necessary that *our ladies* should be qualified *to a certain degree* by a peculiar and suitable education to concur in instructing their *sons* in the principles of liberty and government." No need for women to master Latin or foreign languages. Women's instruction should include: handwriting, arithmetic and bookkeeping, geography, history, travels, astronomy, chemistry, vocal music, and dancing. This learning would "prevent superstition," common among women, and prepare "not only for a general intercourse with the world, but to be an agreeable companion for a sensible man. Religious instruction was fundamental, made easier because "the female breast is the natural soil of christianity."[9]

While Rush delivered this wisdom, Matthew Carey's new national magazine the *American Museum* presented an English essayist who, though straining to preserve the idea of equal sexes, defended natural male superiority. "The author of nature" made man more powerful "by giving him not only a body more large and robust, but [also] a mind endowed with greater resolution, and a more extensive reach." Providence balanced "superiority in our [male] nature" by giving females "different qualifications"; so with proper cultivation and exertion "men and women [were] *nearly* on an equal footing with each other." Rush elaborated: "A natural and original difference between the mind of a woman and a man, as certainly as there is between their bodies." Women possessed a more developed "sensibility," but men enjoyed superior reason. Consequently, whatever "all men are created equal" might mean, Rush—like Americans generally—was convinced that in matters of intellect, understanding, and judgment, women's natural inequality was self-evident. As historians Linda Kerber and Jan Lewis long ago explained, Revolutionaries created a new role for women as republican wives and mothers. Patriot wives must prepare sons for active citizenship and train daughters as republican wives.[10]

Women from all social classes accepted the conventional wisdom of natural difference and that subordination to men was proper. Nevertheless the new emphasis on women's education, if not yet for equal rights, led men and women to promote girls' education in common schools and academies. They did not intend to challenge the gendered status quo by overturning legal and social conventions, but in time more women, especially, would challenge the founding generation's assumption that women were intrinsically unsuited to full citizenship rights, including suffrage. Once educated, graduates used experiences at female academies to redefine their social roles.[11]

Miss Pierce's Female Academy at Litchfield, Connecticut, was among the most influential. Started in 1792, its curriculum featured embroidery, music, arithmetic, and composition—instruction for genteel wives. But after 1814 elite women at Miss Pierce's began to study according to standards at men's colleges. That year the twenty-one-year-old Williams College graduate John Pierce Brace, Miss Pierce's nephew, taught students from his college texts. Pierce decided that hitherto "male" subjects—Latin, moral and natural philosophy, logic, and rhetoric—were necessary for her students, and her academy flourished. In the decades that followed these innovations spread throughout the United States as dozens of Pierce's graduates left to teach in other academies or found schools of their own.[12]

Women did not reject "republican motherhood," but their actions demonstrated its inadequacy. A Philadelphia academy student who noted that the ministry, law, and politics barred her sex, called for change in 1793. Urging her peers to "qualify for those high departments" by education, she predicted that "they will open before us." Learning would proclaim women's mental capacities. Hannah Mather Crocker, the seventy-year-old granddaughter of Cotton Mather and an avid reader of Mary Wollstonecraft, declared in *Observations on the Real Rights of Women* (1818) that with "the same mode of education, their [women's] improvement would be fully equal [to men]." Men, especially, doubted her judgment, but as education expanded across the century women became predominant among teachers. Earlier women only taught basic literacy in "dame schools" for small children; but by the Civil War over two-thirds of America's teachers were women.[13] If republican mothers could educate their own children, women were equipped to teach the entire nation.

Female learning undermined old assumptions. During the eighteenth century women's literacy and writing skills trailed behind men. But female academies for elite women and common schools for middling and working people changed understanding of women's roles. In the eighteenth century there were few women writers in Britain and America; but now their numbers increased geometrically. In the generations from 1800 to 1860 thousands of American women published books, magazines, and newspaper commentary. Few wrote about science, but women were prolific authors of novels and poetry, as well as nonfiction—history, biography, and travel. America's most influential novelist, Harriet Beecher Stowe, was shaped by Miss Pierce's. Her sister Catharine was a graduate, and Harriet briefly attended before completing her education following a male curriculum at Catharine's Hartford Female Academy, one of Miss Pierce's many offshoots. Men still dominated the world of print—especially public affairs—but their domination of the whole world of print was finished. In 1855, three years after the astonishing popularity of *Uncle Tom's Cabin*, Nathaniel Hawthorne complained, "America is now wholly given over to a damned mob of scribbling women."[14]

Hawthorne's lament reveals his failure to understand how gender roles had changed since his college graduation in 1825. Stowe's novel, America's most influential antislavery text, was a woman's powerful foray into the nation's most central political contest—an intervention prepared by decades of women's engagement in the republic of letters and more than a generation of organized political action. Being barred from voting, women showed, had not barred them from political life.

As early as the 1760s, when colonists protested parliamentary taxation by signing boycott pledges, women had joined the fray. A 1767 Boston protest included nearly fifty women among its 660 signatories. They could not vote, but they joined the political dispute. Self-conscious women's protest came in 1774 when forty-seven women in Edenton, North Carolina, signed a pact to boycott all imports from Britain. From the beginning of the Revolution women tacitly challenged political patriarchy by repeatedly expressing their views individually and collectively.[15]

This was the context for Abigail Adams's "impertinent" demand for women's suffrage, a proposal that ran into a stone wall. But as women gained education and participated in the republic of letters they also organized voluntary associations. They created, first, charitable societies within churches and, later, groups with broader philanthropic aims. They won acceptance, north and south—including the corporate right to collect and disburse money.[16] Because they aimed to advance Christianity and ameliorate the lives of the poor, orphans, disabled mariners, fallen women, and prison inmates, they posed no direct threat to the political status quo. Displaying their nurturing character, women's charitable services fulfilled their natural role. Though mobilization of elite and middle-class women's energies outside the home was subversive, men did not object.

II

Why would they? Public office was their monopoly. Acquisition and manipulation of property was most men's central activity, and women provided opportunities to acquire and accumulate property. On the few occasions when women contested their subordinate domestic status, male advantage was established. Custom as well as statute law and legal precedent defended male prerogatives.

Masculine power over women extended from male ownership of their clothing and furnishings to a woman's earnings and inherited real estate. A husband was entitled to control of his (not their) children, and his wife's labor as well as sexual access. Abigail Adams's warning, "Do not put such unlimited power in the hands of the Husbands. Remember all Men would be tyrants if they could," was not a rhetorical flourish; she was confronting the reality that "even in the freeest countrys our property is subject to the controul and disposal of our partners, to whom the Laws have given a soverign Authority." Women's subordination was established by the common law of coverture. That law derived from the basic feudal protection covenant between lords and their inferiors. In exchange for protection, subjects owed their lord allegiance and submission. By the eighteenth century this code had been modified, but its core remained intact. As Blackstone explained in 1765, "By marriage, the husband and wife are one person in law: that is, the very being or legal existence of the woman is suspended during the marriage." She was "incorporated" into her husband so that "every thing" she did was under his "protection and influence." Whether nobleman or day laborer—to his wife a husband was "her *baron*, or lord."[17]

In light of this patriarchal model where generations of husbands and fathers ruled their domestic baronies, Abigail's bold assertion of women's share in ruling the state was an outlier. Wives, like children and apprentices, knew only a world where coverture was the law and they were subjects of masculine discipline. According to Blackstone this power of correction must be confined within "reasonable bounds," and husbands ought not to resort to "violence." But as to "the lower rank of people, who were always fond of the old common law," Lord Mansfield acknowledged that older ways persisted: "Courts of law will still permit a husband to restrain a wife of her liberty." American courts accepted this practice through the 1850s at least. Similarly, though no statute authorized husbands to beat wives—and few judges would defend such violence—the "rule of thumb" permitted a man to beat his wife, his child, or his apprentice with a rod no thicker than his thumb. This custom was so widely accepted that well into the nineteenth century juries used it to acquit husbands and fathers of abuse. For school teachers the birch rod was basic equipment.[18]

Resort to a whip or a rod had always been part of Britain's penal code as well as a common domestic practice. No one, young or old, male or female, had been immune. But after the Enlightenment ideas of Beccaria's *Essay on Crimes and Punishments* swept across the United States, reformers sought to end court-ordered whipping, branding, ear cropping, and finger amputating. Yet such reforms did not entirely permeate American society. The U.S. Army whipped misbehaving soldiers until 1807, and because naval officers regarded flogging as essential, the U.S. Navy flogged sailors until 1850 at least.[19] National policy could be reformed only after eleven slave states seceded. In slave states, whipping remained an accepted punishment.

Consequently, though Reeve's *Law of Baron and Femme* reinforced women's, children's, and servants' subordination, it could be seen as reformist. As early as 1795 the thirty-six-year-old Windham, Connecticut, lawyer and congressman Zephaniah Swift rejected "the power of the husband to chastise his wife." In his treatise on Connecticut law Swift discarded "the savage doctrine of the common law," believing that a husband should be "punishable for the unmanly act of chastising his wife." Swift argued that "tenderness and delicacy" were keys to "happiness in the conjugal state."

Here the United States led the world: "No country has a better right to boast of this state of manners, than America." Swift was more critical of the masculine system than most, arguing that husbands should never employ even "moderate chastisement" because it destroyed "all prospects of pleasure and felicity" in marriage.[20] Yet he was so well regarded that Federalists appointed him to the state's highest court in 1801.

Admittedly, Connecticut had never been as friendly to full-blown patriarchy as jurisdictions where British law was more thoroughly adopted.[21] But Connecticut jurists were respected, and though Tapping Reeve was not located in Philadelphia, New York, or Boston, before his death in 1831 his Litchfield law school was the most influential in the nation. Consequently, his textbook on coverture and the rights of women and children is especially significant. Reeve's *Law of Baron and Femme* challenged Blackstone's assertion of husbands' prerogatives, but only at the edges. Neither Reeve nor the American court system was ready to undo centuries of law and custom.

Reeve's treatise began by declaring legal fact: "The husband, by marriage, acquires an absolute title to all the personal property of the wife, which she had in possession at the time of the marriage; such as money, goods or chattels personal of any kind." It was, Reeve pronounced, as if he had purchased her property with his own money, and it could "never again belong to the wife." When a husband died this property did not return to the wife but was governed by his executors according to his will. If women owned real estate before marriage, ownership ceased the moment the knot was tied, since a husband possessed his wife's "Real Property during Coverture and also after her Death." The fact that some wives like Abigail Adams in fact managed family property, serving as "deputy husbands," did not alter legal prescription.[22] In a social and political system where property ownership was the prerequisite for personal autonomy and political enfranchisement, terminating a wife's property assured her dependence and subordination.

So long as the marriage lasted dependence was fixed, because her propertyless status was permanent. Any personal or real property given the wife during marriage became her husband's unless, as in some elite families, property was given with a proviso for her separate use. But any money a wife earned belonged to her husband because all her service belonged to him.

She was her husband's worker in a condition analogous to a slave; thus if someone injured her, like a slave owner her husband could sue to recover damages for lost labor. As with a slave master, if a wife ran away her husband had the right "to seize upon her person and bring her home." He might even "imprison her" if she tried to elope with another man or squander or damage his property.[23] For free women the transition from daughter to wife generally provided continuous subordination, with fathers handing off control to husbands.

Reeve explained the legal similarities between wives and children. The protection covenant meant that a husband must provide food, clothing, and shelter for wife as for children. Moreover, if she lived with him he was responsible to pay debts she incurred, both before and after marriage. In addition, a husband was responsible for his wife's misdeeds, civil or criminal, if he appeared to approve or tolerate them. Here English law reduced wives below their sons since, Blackstone wrote, "neither a son nor a servant are excused . . . of any crime" because they acted "by the command or coercion of a parent or master," whereas a wife committing the same act "is not guilty of any crime," excepting only murder and treason. When a wife participated with her husband in a crime such as stealing, or when a wife harbored her criminal husband, she faced no penalty because she was presumed to be acting in obedience to her husband's will. This mantle of protection, however, was limited. As Reeve explained, "Where she commits offences, not being under the coercion of her husband, she is as liable to punishment as any other person." He further argued that presuming coercion if the husband was simply present, the old English and colonial practice, was wrongheaded. A husband might show that "the offense was committed against his will," in which case "it surely would be absurd to punish the husband."[24] Inasmuch as children aged eight could be held accountable for crimes, treating wives as punishable was consistent with their subordination.

Of course children's subordinate status was temporary; they would grow up. But women's subordination was all but permanent because after completing childhood they entered matrimony. And from marriage there were few escapes. Death in childbirth was the most common release. A husband's death was next most frequent. Widowhood could mean either poverty and dependence on children or a kind of liberation. Because most widows, like most widowers, remarried, freedom from coverture was often short-lived. But for those widows who inherited substantial property, either through the legally stipulated "widow's third" of a husband's estate or from their family of origin, they might live as widows for decades. That was Hannah Mather Crocker's choice and the choice made by Charles Brockden Brown's politically astute fictive widow.[25]

Divorce was the other means of escape from married coverture—either by illegal desertion or by termination of marriage through law. For women who were concerned with property or respectability so as to remarry, lawful divorce was a difficult path but the only one. Because each state enacted its own divorce rules, it was not even a single path. In Britain divorce required a private bill by Parliament, and divorce was highly restricted because Anglican doctrine was rooted in the Roman Catholic belief that marriage was a permanent, irreversible sacrament. In states like Virginia, founded on English law, divorce similarly required a private legislative act, and Virginia usually denied divorce petitions. In the sixty-five years from 1786 to 1851, on average Virginia granted just 2.4 divorces annually. In New England, where the Dissenting heritage made marriage a civil contract, divorce was vested in the courts, where, though marriage was also deemed permanent, like other contracts it might be voided by violation of its terms. In Connecticut, for example, if husband or wife willfully deserted for three years "in total neglect of all conjugal duties," the marriage ended, and if either was "unheard of" and gone for seven years, that person was presumed dead, ending the marriage. In either case remarriage was permitted.[26]

But often legislatures or courts might grant separations instead of a divorce, in which case the parties could live apart but could not remarry, and coverture—the husband's control of what had been the wife's property and earnings—remained intact. In New York the state would grant a full divorce only if husband or wife was found guilty of a moral crime such as adultery or bigamy. Because every state regarded matrimony as permanent, none would grant a divorce just because husband and wife agreed that their marriage was intolerable. The closest courts came to no-fault divorce was when one party, usually a deserting husband, failed to contest his wife's divorce petition, enabling courts to rule that he was at fault for desertion.[27]

Such cases where women gained divorces with seeming ease are misleading, because normally when property was involved husbands defended their rights aggressively—making the stark disparity between male and female rights conspicuous. One might have expected Zephaniah Swift, the jurist who championed companionate marriage, to defend even-handed justice. But for adultery Swift proclaimed the double standard in his 1795 treatise: "The common opinion of mankind declares, that it is a very different and much more heinous crime for a woman that is married, to have criminal conversation with a single man, than for a married man with a single woman." Common opinion must rule because "a married woman that submits to the embraces of any man but her husband, does by that act, alienate her affections, deprave her sentiments, and expose him to the greatest of all misfortunes, an uncertainty with respect to his offspring." In contrast, when a man strayed it was different: "A married man may be concerned in an intrigue with a girl, without impairing his conjugal affection, . . . nor does that act produce such total depravity of moral character in a man, as in a woman: for when a female once breaks over the bounds of decency and virtue, and become abandoned, she is capable of going all lengths in iniquity." In contrast, the male adulterer—while punishable—was not necessarily wicked. Swift concluded, "There are frequent instances of men, who disregard the principles of chastity, but in other respects conduct with propriety."[28] Society forgave an adulterous man, not so a woman. Nevertheless a husband's adultery, like a wife's, provided grounds for divorce. But short of abandonment and bigamy, there were few others.

For today's social ethics and sensibilities the freedom of husbands to treat wives abusively was the most disturbing aspect of the marriage bond's permanency. The concept of marital rape came to be treated as a crime only in the second half of the twentieth century. But no court in the early Republic recognized that offense. Nevertheless courts and legislatures in the North and South acknowledged other kinds of abuse. In Virginia among the 204 cases where women's divorce complaints were recorded between 1786 and 1851, battery—42 percent of cases—was second only to adultery. Wives who charged husbands with battery succeeded more often than with any other complaint. Still, whatever claims wives brought to the legislature, and whatever their social class, the state rejected their complaints over 60 percent of the time.[29]

Though husbands did not possess complete control over their wives in law, in every social class the allocation of rights was wildly unbalanced. Two divorce cases—an early nineteenth-century elite Virginia marriage and a second from the 1840s involving a Connecticut couple with scant property—are illustrative. Wealthy fathers could only try to protect daughters from avaricious and abusive husbands. And when widows remarried hoping for protection and security, misery could be their reward. In most marriages mutual love and respect might override the legal inequalities between husband and wife, as with Abigail Adams and John, enabling husbands like John to joke that his sex merely carried "the Name of Masters." But neither John Adams nor any other husband could deny that law and custom dealt them winning cards they could play at will. No woman, not even John's beloved Abigail, could ignore the reality of men's customary and legal advantage. Rejecting the sentimental rhetoric of the era, she admonished Congressman Adams: "Do not put such unlimited power in the hands of the Husbands."[30]

This reform demand would have been eagerly embraced by Ann Pierce Parker, the twenty-seven-year-old Virginia gentlewoman who in 1802 married William Cowper, five years her senior. Ann Parker had already borne Cowper a son two years earlier, and in their marriage year she would bear him a second son. Her husband, a former U.S. Navy captain with a seafaring and merchant background, descended from a long-established Virginia family. After marriage he joined his brothers' mercantile business. But when it failed William Cowper returned to sea in 1803 and Ann Parker Cowper went to her father's plantation with her two sons. Though Cowper was mostly away, Ann delivered a third son, William Junior, in 1804. Two years later, in 1806, Cowper returned to Virginia, bringing with him five thousand dollars to start a new firm. His father-in-law, the Revolutionary soldier and statesman Josiah Parker, provided additional capital, but Cowper's business languished almost immediately. As early as 1806 William Cowper's "temper" became public with an assault and battery charge. Privately, he began abusing his wife. That year she fled to her father's house, where she gave birth to their fourth son.[31]

Josiah Parker, witnessing his daughter's suffering, urged divorce. Because he still commanded influence in Virginia's legislature, her petition might succeed. But she hesitated, and when Cowper begged her forgiveness, Ann rejected her father's advice and tried to restore her marriage. Five years later she would appreciate her father's wisdom, though it was too late. Parker died in 1810, and the legal instruments he provided to guard his only daughter proved inadequate compared to Cowper's power to keep her in thrall and in danger. Ann inherited an annuity, seven slaves, and, if she wished, lifetime residence at the home plantation — all under the supervision of his executor. But Cowper subverted his father-in-law's will. The estate would go mostly to Cowper's eldest son if the ten-year-old adopted the Parker surname, so Cowper tried to make the change hastily so that, as his son's guardian, he could control the property. And, should the boy die, as his son's heir he would gain full ownership. What Cowper felt about his son is conjecture, but Ann Cowper testified that her husband threatened to "cut his throat from ear to ear" if the boy resisted changing his name. Soon after, during her pregnancy in early 1811, Cowper beat Ann severely and threatened to kill her if she refused to abort her pregnancy. This repeatedly "repentant" husband even tried to starve his wife before his attack produced a miscarriage.[32]

Ann Cowper's feelings are unclear. The couple's pattern of separation and reunion continued until April 1811, when even after violence and murderous threats she accepted his apology, "guaranteed" by written promises of reformation and restoration of her property. Evidently she hoped to preserve her family and access to her children. But William Cowper was erratic: in summer 1811 he ordered Ann out of her family's plantation, threatening to kill her if she did not destroy his written promises. Now she began to seek divorce. William responded by again swearing to reform and signing another promise to behave. So in December 1811, Ann withdrew her divorce petition. But in early 1812 his abuse resumed, so Ann, hoping to curb her husband's rages, brought a female relative to live with the family. William, however, would not be restrained. When he whipped Ann, her relative intervened—so he whipped her, too. This marked the turning point. Ann Cowper brought William before the county court, where the justices of the peace ordered him to desist. To no avail. Afterward, when he attacked Ann with a knife, she locked herself in a bedroom. She threatened him with a pistol; he went to buy guns. Thoroughly frightened, Ann fled with her youngest child to her maternal uncle. Now Ann asked the county superior court for protection and the return of her property. The justices decided in her favor, declaring Cowper without "honor." But the court possessed scant enforcement powers, so William ignored the judgment. Possession seemed to be nine-tenths of the law when the rights of husbands were concerned.

Thereafter Ann never again lived with William. Ann's father had tried to protect his daughter, but coverture was so powerful in Virginia that his detested son-in-law now controlled his plantation, his slaves, and his three eldest grandsons. For five years Ann lived with her youngest at the homes of relatives while William managed the Parker estate into decline. Once William tried to shoot Ann's protective uncle, but he was never prosecuted. The only legal hurdle frustrating William was the legislature's resistance to changing his eldest son's name to Parker. Finally, in November 1816, Ann Cowper—advised by lawyers—petitioned the legislature for a limited (separation only) divorce. If granted, neither she nor William Cowper could remarry.

When the divorce came before the Virginia General Assembly it was not a confusing question of "he said, she said." Ann Parker Cowper's lengthy petition was supported by eleven affidavits attesting to her account of William's bad behavior. So in January 1817, a decade after Josiah Parker urged Ann to seek a divorce from her abusive and rapacious husband, she won freedom from him and restoration of part of the property her father stipulated for her. William Cowper was, to be sure, among the worst of husbands—devious, manipulating, perhaps unbalanced—but the fact that an elite woman, nominally protected by her father and his legal provisions, could be so abused year after year demonstrates the power of coverture. Had Cowper assaulted any other woman, justices would have prosecuted him for felony and his victim could have testified against him as wives could not. But the best Ann Cowper could gain was legal separation. William Cowper's sole penalty was loss of coverture rights to her property. Though the gentlemen of the county and legislature showed concern regarding his abuses of coverture, they did not tamper with a husband's patriarchal rule, including control of a wife's property.

Scholars of slavery have argued persuasively that when a master whipped any slave that example could intimidate many others, and for a lifetime. So it was with William Cowper's notorious abuses stretching across a decade and becoming gossip among families in Southside Virginia. We cannot know why Ann Parker Cowper accepted her suffering; but her acquiescence concurred with respected social prescriptions. In 1811, when William Cowper battered Ann severely, the Episcopal bishop of Virginia admonished his soon-to-be-married daughter, "Never attempt to controul your husband by opposition of any kind." A wife should never "take from him the freedom of acting as his own judgment shall direct; but [instead] . . . place such confidence in him, as to believe that his prudence is his best guide." Ann had not, certainly, consulted the bishop, but her conduct suggests that she shared his belief that "a difference with your husband ought to be the most studiously guarded against." The bishop expressed dominant beliefs, and his 1811 advice would be published in newspapers and magazines repeatedly between 1818 and 1839.[33] The bishop ordained Ann Cowper's submission.

John Adams's claim that husbands were really "subjects" of their wives rang hollow, especially when husbands asserted authority. Feminine "wiles" might sometimes succeed with some men, but they were no match for the combined power of law and custom. The romantic trope of women's psychological mastery of men through artful manners and feminine sexuality was fantasy in actual tests of will. In Connecticut women gained divorces more readily because it required a court judgment only, not a legislative act. Nevertheless, as the jurists Swift and Reeve explained, in Connecticut as elsewhere, marriage contracts and coverture were expected to be lifelong.

Critics of Connecticut law—which permitted divorce and remarriage after three years' willful desertion or seven years' absence—claimed that the statute was truly lax. In a 1788 sermon Benjamin Trumbull, cousin to a longtime governor, complained judges "have been grossly imposed on" and too often gave women divorces without first hearing from their husbands. Consequently women had "put away their husbands" and "gone into second marriages." Such "abominations," Trumbull protested, "are the unhappy fruits of the laws and customs of Connecticut." No matter that absent husbands often failed to present their side of the story. In fact during the eighteenth century Connecticut granted 9.3 divorces per year (nearly 1,000), whereas Virginia, home to twice as many white people, saw just 2.4 divorces (153 total) granted annually from 1786 to 1851. In Trumbull's view a divorce was justified only if one party was "guilty of a high misdemeanor," as in New York State.[34]

Connecticut was more willing to grant divorces than other states. But as to abuse and cruelty Connecticut was not so different. Early in the nineteenth century Connecticut's Zephaniah Swift and Tapping Reeve had questioned husbands' right to discipline wives as parents would correct children or masters punish servants. Yet juries accepted "the rule of thumb" and acquitted abusers. In 1795 Swift rejected this "savage doctrine of the common law," arguing that a husband could be punished for "the unmanly act of chastising his wife." Reeve reinforced Swift's pronouncement twenty years later, declaring Connecticut law did not recognize any right of a husband to "chastise" his wife. Yet in practice, even where property was scarcely at stake, statutes and courts supported coverture. Subordination of some wives may have eased in New England in the generation after 1790, but only temporarily. The case of Emeline Shaw, who sued Daniel T. Shaw for divorce in August 1845, illustrates how, even as northern critics of coverture gained ground, the system remained powerful.[35] One consequence of coverture—that a husband subsumed his wife's legal identity so that neither spouse could testify against the other—effectively barred wives like Ann Cowper and Emeline Shaw, victims of assault and battery, from charging husbands with felonies. Wives could make accusations, but only in divorce petitions.

In contrast to Ann Parker, Emeline Hunt came from an obscure farming family in Sharon, in northwest Connecticut. In 1826, at age twenty-one, Emeline married a neighbor, twenty-three-year-old Charles E. Berry, in the Episcopal church and started a family. But one infant daughter died in 1830, and in 1832 Charles Berry died, leaving Emeline with a son and two daughters. She inherited a house and land valued at $1,200 with $600 in household furnishings. Widow Berry struggled for nine years to raise her children, assisted by her mother and mother-in-law, who also dwelled in Sharon. But for a single mother near poverty, the path was hard, and in October 1841, the nine-year anniversary of her widowhood, Emeline Hunt Berry married again in Sharon's Episcopal church. Her new husband was Daniel T. Shaw from a neighboring town. Shaw was able-bodied and brought $150 into the marriage, which he invested in improvements to the house.[36] Now age thirty-six, Emeline Shaw hoped for a better life.

But after two years and eight months of cohabitation, Emeline left Daniel Shaw and went to live with her mother. Daniel's "cruel and abusive treatment," Emeline said, began just months after their marriage when Daniel "with great force and violence" first threw her "down on the floor." Though Emeline was in the seventh month of a pregnancy conceived soon after marriage, such abuse, "whereby her life and health were greatly endangered," became his practice "repeatedly thereafter." Emeline tolerated his mistreatment, she said, for nearly two years "in the due performance of all the duties of the marriage covenant."[37]

Daniel Shaw could be kind, especially if Emeline was ailing, but he was unreasonably controlling. He complained that she possessed "an irritable temperament," but her description of the episode that drove her to leave "his bed and board" suggests that he gave her good cause for irritation. The superior court's record states:

> He often spoke to her in an intemperate and abusive manner; and on several occasions, in the presence of her children by her former husband, he made use of abusive and obscene language to her. He called her "an old hypocrite"; . . . "an ugly devil"; . . . "an old imp of hell"; on another, he said "she was worse than the women at Five Points in New-York [prostitutes]"; and on another he charged her with having been to New-York, to have illicit intercourse with other men. At times when her health was such as to make it improper that she would have sexual intercourse with her husband, he unreasonably objected, and refused to suffer her to

occupy a separate bed; and on two such occasions, he took her, by force, from the bed of her daughter to which she had retired, and compelled her to occupy a bed with himself. On other occasions, he compelled her to remain with him in bed against her wishes and remonstrances, when, in consequence of her ill health, it was improper, unreasonable and injurious to her health.[38]

According to law a husband possessed the right to sexual intercourse with his wife, so whatever pain—psychological and physical—Emeline might suffer, consensual sex was not her choice; like every woman she lost that right the moment she married.

At marriage, Widow Berry also lost the right to visit as she pleased and to invite her relatives into "her" home. Daniel Shaw was "jealous of his wife, and unwilling that she should visit her friends or have any intercourse with them"—especially Emeline's mother and former mother-in-law Berry, grandmothers of her three children. According to court records, when old Mrs. Berry visited Emeline "in consequence of ill health, he [Daniel] unreasonably turned her out of his house, and forbade her to come there again," and when Emeline sought to sleep at Mrs. Berry's house because "her health was such as to make it improper that she should occupy the same bed with him, which he well knew, he forbade her to leave his house, and endeavoured to confine her." On that occasion Emeline "escaped from the house by getting out of the window."[39]

But could she escape from her marriage? Emeline's attorneys claimed that Shaw was guilty of "barbarous and disgusting abuse of his marital rights," endangering his wife's health. Daniel's lawyers argued that the law stipulated that a husband's cruelty must be "intolerable" to justify divorce, meaning that it "cannot be endured, without perishing, or extreme suffering." It must at least "endanger the life" of the victim. Nothing Daniel had done could lead to criminal prosecution, they said, because his conduct did not even approach the legal boundary: "Words, however abusive or offensive, do not amount to such cruelty; nor does violence, not endangering life, or injuring the person, or constituting a breach of the peace." Daniel's "harsh and improper language" must have been provoked by "this 'irritable' woman." In reality, his "jealousy" was evidence of attachment to Emeline; rough treatment was irrelevant since "the mere want of consideration and a delicate regard for her health, in the exercise of his marital rights, is surely not a ground of separation—much less divorce." As to "his interference in her intercourse with her relatives and friends, . . . that was within his legitimate province." If law, not sentiment, ruled, the judges must deny the divorce.[40]

The five justices did not condone Daniel Shaw's behavior toward Emeline, but they denied a divorce. "Certainly" his treatment was "harsh," but it was not intolerably cruel. Daniel's treatment must not have been intolerable because Emeline had negotiated with him "for the purpose of again cohabiting together" if only "he would return the furniture he had taken from their former dwelling house." In their agreement Daniel had also promised that "if he again abused or ill treated" Emeline he would accept divorce. But since he did not return the furniture, they had not restored their marriage. Still, the court found that when Emeline "was sick, her husband was kind to her; nor had she any just reason to fear other personal abuse" beyond his forcing her "to occupy the same bed with him, regardless of the consequences to her health." Daniel was not praiseworthy, but he had not tried to injure her when he forced sexual relations. And Emeline had conditionally agreed to live with him again. The judges sympathized with the husband: "Are we to allow nothing to the innocent opinions of a man mad with jealousy? Are we to allow nothing to the frailty of human nature, excited by passion?" Yes, Daniel Shaw had behaved improperly, "but the unreasonable exercise of the authority of a husband, in such case, has never been held to be that [intolerable] kind of cruelty" sufficient for legal separation. Chief Justice Thomas Scott Williams and three of his colleagues ruled that although Shaw displayed cruelty, his treatment of Emeline fell short of the newly reformed standard of "habitual intemperance and intolerable cruelty." One judge, Samuel Church, dissented.[41]

Normally the case was closed. But because one high court justice believed that Emeline's abuse did warrant divorce, Emeline's attorneys, Charles Frederick Sedgwick and Origen Storrs Seymour, were encouraged to appeal.[42] Whether or not the court ruling matched the letter of the law, they believed that the decision was scandalous, so they took it to the only body above the Supreme Court of Errors—the Connecticut General Assembly. There, in May 1846, the unhappy history of the Shaws' marriage was laid out before the assembly's Joint Standing Committee on Divorce. Once more Daniel Shaw's lawyers presented their rebuttal.

Emeline's petition elaborated on her courtroom complaints. She now swore that Daniel Shaw possessed "no property whatever" at marriage, whereas she not only possessed a life estate in real estate valued at $1,200 from her late husband but also an additional $600 in "notes of hand" as well as nearly $600 in furniture. Because he controlled all "her" property, Daniel Shaw was depriving Emeline of "any means of support." She also stated that Shaw's abuse had begun at "nearly the time" of their marriage and continued, "while she was in feeble health, induced by the ill treatment . . . whereby her life was greatly endangered." The fact that Shaw had "repeatedly locked her up in her own home" and attacked her with "the most foul and filthy epithets," calling her "a strumpet," and accusing her of "the crime of adultery and of keeping a house of ill fame," was further proof of his cruelty.[43]

In June 1846 the Committee on Divorce reported to the 220 elected representatives of the state. The committee stated that it had "fully heard" the two parties and judged "the facts stated in the said [Emeline's] petition to be fully proved and true." Accordingly, the committee recommended a full divorce, ending her coverture. The assembly voted in Emeline's favor, discharging her from all obligations to Daniel Shaw, making her "sole, single, and unmarried." Once more the home in Sharon and her furnishings were hers.[44]

The property Emeline recovered along with her independence suggests that hers was a middling farm family on a downward trajectory. An expert on the material culture of the era reports that Emeline possessed a few inexpensive "trappings of higher status," such as Venetian blinds and a clock, as well as a washstand and bowl for private bathing and "2 common looking glasses." Yet she owned no lamp and had but four candlesticks, only two books (both Bibles), few ceramics, and minimal kitchen utensils. Her bedding and furniture were shabby. Evidently her aspirations for respectability suffered during her widowhood, and her second marriage did not help. Emeline never remarried, though she lived more than forty years after the divorce. Her six-year-old daughter by Daniel Shaw died two years after the divorce. Her three children by Charles Berry, now fifteen to twenty years old, could not be located in the 1850 census.[45]

Compared to Virginia, Connecticut, by expanding the grounds for divorce, was becoming "the nation's first divorce factory." But if Emeline Shaw's experience in the 1840s was representative, Connecticut divorces were certainly not mass-produced. According to the 1843 "liberalization" of the law, courts were empowered to grant divorces in cases of "habitual intemperance and intolerable cruelty"—the standard the judges had applied to the Shaws.[46] In order to void the marriage contract and overturn coverture a wife had to supply evidence of repeated acts of violence and hostility and testify to them publicly. Emeline Shaw was willing to do that if, like Ann Parker Cowper, her husband would not stop his abuse. Both women pursued divorces not only because living with their husbands was painful and frightening but also because they could count on support from relatives. And most important, divorce would restore property so that they could support themselves. For women without property and family resources, the alternative to marriage was penury.

Because the legislature's Joint Committee on Divorce recommended reversal of the supreme court's denial of Emeline Shaw's divorce petition, and the assembly granted a full divorce with the right to marry, it is clear that by 1846 a majority in the legislature regarded the 1843 expansion of the divorce statute as too limited. Consequently in 1849 the assembly further enlarged the grounds for divorce. Whereas most states stipulated that the sole legitimate basis for a full divorce (not just separation) was adultery, Connecticut added serious criminal convictions to "intolerable cruelty" and "habitual intemperance" as grounds for divorce. Thus divorce could be granted if husband or wife was sentenced to life imprisonment or convicted of "bestiality, or any other infamous crime [leading to state prison] involving a violation of conjugal duty." More remarkable, the law enabled courts to grant divorce for "any such misconduct of the other party as permanently destroys the happiness of the petitioner, and defeats the purposes of the marriage relation." This remarkably sweeping and subjective statement, deeming happiness essential to marriage, perhaps derived from Swift's 1795 treatise. It would generate controversy for years because it made Connecticut's law so friendly to divorce that by 1865 its courts seldom rejected divorce petitions.[47]

III

By the 1860s coverture had begun to unravel, in northern and western states especially, yet it persisted everywhere. Much earlier Tapping Reeve challenged the notion "that a wife has no will" and was merely her husband's possession; that idea, he said, "has not the least foundation in common sense." But Reeve acknowledged that Connecticut law was in this respect "very different" from the English law that provided the foundation for governing domestic relations in most states. Indeed as scholars have shown, when it came to property or abuse within marriage, a stark inequality prevailed between the rights of husbands and wives. In addition, the power of coverture limited wives' religious rights, though this restriction has seldom been recognized because it was rarely tested before courts and legislatures. Many, perhaps most, marriages connected people who shared sectarian loyalties, and when they did not, one party was sufficiently indifferent or accommodating regarding worship that religious coercion was infrequent. In 1818 Hannah Mather Crocker declared that "women have an undoubted right, agreeable to scripture, to think, reason and determine on all points relating to religious principle," but even in a nation where religious liberty was a highly prized emblem of liberty, wives were not free to practice their own religion.[48] Patriarchy possessed a broad reach.

The story of the abolitionist and women's rights reformer Jane Grey Cannon, better known by her married name of Jane Swisshelm, is revealing. Jane Cannon came from a Pennsylvania Scots family and at age fifteen converted to predestinarian Calvinism in 1830. Before marriage to the evangelical Methodist James Swisshelm in 1836 the couple acknowledged their religious differences. Jane said that James promised he "would never interfere with my rights of conscience" and "would take or send me to my meeting when possible," though he would "expect me to go sometimes with him."

But after marriage coverture took over, erasing his promise. "Marriage," he claimed, "annuls all previous contracts" between husband and wife. Jane complained that "by further change of plan, I was to get [Methodist] religion and preach," since now he "was quite zealous." They argued, and Jane, quoting Scripture, not the First Amendment or Pennsylvania's Bill of Rights, rejected his dictate with irony: "'Let women keep silent in churches, and learn of their husbands at home.'" He rejoined with Saint Paul's command, "'Wives, obey your husbands.'" His family joined his attempt to make Jane a Methodist exhorter. But she was firm, so the two lived separate lives before Pennsylvania granted James Swisshelm a divorce in 1861 on the grounds of abandonment.[49] Jane Cannon Swisshelm never tested coverture against Pennsylvania's guarantee of religious freedom, so it never became a public controversy. Jane was ready to fight slavery, but though coverture threatened her religious freedom, like most women she acquiesced.

Not so for Eunice Hawley Chapman. She battled coverture mightily when her husband demanded that she and their children follow him into the Shaker faith. The forty-one-year-old James Chapman had married Eunice, fifteen years his junior, in Brooklyn, New York, in 1804. Connecticut natives, they met in Durham, near Albany, New York, where he prospered as a merchant and Eunice's family, also merchants, was sinking into poverty. For James, a decade-long widower with a young daughter, Eunice was a catch, whereas the match appeared prudential for Eunice and ended badly. James, she gradually learned, was alcoholic and sometimes abusive. Yet she remained dutiful, bearing a boy and two girls over a five-year period. In contrast, after seven years of marriage James Chapman opened a store twenty miles away where he could freely drink, gamble, and fornicate. Then, selling his Durham property in 1811, he pocketed $1,600, leaving his wife and children to fend for themselves.[50]

New York would not grant a full divorce since Chapman's fornication with unmarried women was not adultery, but Eunice might have sought formal separation with support for herself and their children. Lacking legal help, she worked to keep her family—George (age six), Susan (age five), and Julia (age three)—together. The next year, 1812, when her absent husband's business failed, he experienced religious conversion. Once before, in 1784, a religious awakening led him into the Congregational church. Now, twenty-eight years later, he swore off drinking and fornicating by joining the Watervliet community of the celibate Shaker sect. To Eunice and the children this became a crisis when he visited Durham two years later and, as was his right, took the children to live among the Shakers. There the two older children, George (aged nine) and Susan (aged eight), signed Shaker indentures binding them to the community. When Eunice protested, Shaker elders gave her temporary visiting rights. In January 1815 she agreed to follow her husband, dwelling with the Shaker women and he with the Shaker men. But she refused to convert. The Shakers believed that her refusal contradicted their community and rejected her "compromise" offer to live among the women. So an enraged Eunice threatened that a mob would burn the Shaker village. Soon after, in February 1815, James Chapman notified Eunice that "the marriage contract between them was dissolved, it being sinful, and at variance with the principles of the *believers*." Independently James proclaimed divorce, announcing no "legal and moral obligations resulting from the relationship of husband . . . and declaring that he would not be responsible for her support."[51]

If James Chapman had not seized their children to live among the Shakers, it is unlikely that Eunice would have challenged her husband. But because existing law was against her, she sought relief by lobbying New York assemblymen, using a self-published pamphlet to plead her victimization. Her husband had seized the children and the Shakers were protecting him. The only remedy they offered was religious conversion, making Eunice join their community as a sister. Ironically, having declared their divorce, James was seeking—through his control of the children—to compel his wife to follow his religion. This issue affected family law and coverture everywhere Shakers operated.

A few years earlier the Ohio legislature had confronted the Chapmans' issue, deciding in 1810 to confiscate the property of any married man who, like Chapman, left his wife and brought his children into a celibate sect. That year a Kentucky mob had "rescued" the children of Polly Smith from an Ohio Shaker community. In 1812 Kentucky determined that any husband or wife could divorce if his or her spouse joined the Shakers. Going beyond

Ohio, Kentucky gave both the property and child custody to the deserted wife of a Shaker. This solution would have suited Eunice Chapman, but according to New York law their marriage remained valid. James was not only the sole owner of the family property; he could control the religious affiliation of his wife and children.[52]

These controversial principles—echoing conflicts in other states—enabled Eunice to win pro bono support from important lawyers and politicians in New York's assembly, where two additional mothers sought return of their Shaker-indentured children. To many, James Chapman's collusion with Shakers to deny a mother access to her children unless she would—in the words of a New York Senate committee—convert to their "peculiar and fanatical principles," appeared unwarranted, notwithstanding "the importance of preserving to every one the free and undisturbed exercise of their religious principles." But revising New York family law was difficult. A March 1815 bill that would have enabled a court to grant Eunice a divorce with child custody failed, though in April the state enacted a law allowing mothers to seek custody in court.[53] Divorce, however, remained stalled.

Some New York legislators found that the Shaker belief that "the marriage contract" was "unlawful and immoral" was truly dangerous—since it absolved Shakers from "the legal, moral and religious ties and duties which have always been considered of the utmost importance to the peace and welfare of society." If fathers could escape responsibilities by joining the Shakers, then any family could, like Eunice and her children, suffer "distress and misery." The simple act of joining the Shakers would allow "the dissolute and unprincipled" to bypass New York marriage and divorce law. A state senate committee declared that "religious toleration" was "the brightest gem in the political institutions" of New York, but though they wanted to protect Shakers and tried "to preserve the most scrupulous regard to the rights of conscience," they rejected James Chapman's actions and Shaker doctrine that marriage was sinful. If Shakers like Chapman denied the laws of the state, then Shaker men should be declared "civilly dead" and "instantly divorced," just as a married person sentenced to life in prison became civilly dead. And as with civil death, their property should be dispersed. This, a New York Senate committee reported, was the only

No. 2,

BEING

AN ADDITIONAL ACCOUNT OF THE CONDUCT OF THE

SHAKERS,

IN THE CASE OF

EUNICE CHAPMAN AND HER CHILDREN

WITH THEIR RELIGIOUS CREED.

WRITTEN BY HERSELF.

ALSO,

A REFUTATION OF THE SHAKERS REMONSTRANCE TO THE
PROCEEDINGS OF THE LEGISLATURE OF 1817.
BY THOMAS BROWN.

ALSO,

THE DEPOSITION OF MARY DYER,

WHO PETITIONED THE LEGISLATURE OF THE STATE OF NEW-
HAMPSHIRE FOR RELIEF IN A SIMILAR CASE. ALSO, AFFI-
DAVITS FROM DIFFERENT PERSONS WHO HAVE BEEN
MEMBERS OF THE SHAKER SOCIETY.

ALSO,

COMMUNICATIONS FROM THE STATE OF OHIO, RESPECTING THE
SHAKERS IN THAT STATE, AND OTHERS. ALSO, THE PRO-
CEEDINGS OF THE LEGISLATURE OF THE STATE OF
NEW-YORK, IN THIS CASE FOR THREE YEARS.

"How sweetly roll'd over the morning of life,
How free from vexation. from sorrow and strife,
But soon was the morning of life clouded o'er,
And its charming serenity lost ;
Too soon was I forced to abandon the shore,
And, on ocean's rude billows, be tos'd."

ALBANY:
PRINTED BY I. W. CLARK,
FOR THE AUTHORESS.
1818.

Eunice Chapman's pamphlet account of her experience with
Shakers was augmented with additional criticisms, as well as
newspaper reports. Courtesy, American Antiquarian Society.

way to provide for "the welfare and maintenance" of wives and children—
dependents—who did not convert. This would also remove any financial incentive for divorce by converting. As death ended coverture, so, too, would a
husband's joining the Shakers, and neither his wife nor his children would
be compelled to join him.[54] Still, the New York Senate refused to act.

The proposed law was too broad to pass, so in 1817 the New York Senate voted to grant Eunice a divorce with the right to remarry while denying re-marriage rights to her ex-husband. As in Ohio, anyone whose spouse joined the Shakers would be entitled to seek divorce in the courts. This law passed narrowly before going on to the Council of Revision for final approval. This council, composed of the governor, chancellor, and supreme court justices, and operating from 1777 to 1821, rejected the law, deciding that it would un-fairly deny ex-Shakers the right to remarry. Yet when the New York Assem-bly accommodated this objection, the council vetoed the revised statute, ar-guing that it would allow divorce without proof of adultery and without jury trial. Opponents claimed that loosening divorce law meant "mob rule" and undermined marriage. Nevertheless in March 1818, the legislature overrode the veto by a wide margin and the Act for the Relief of Eunice Chapman finally became law. Still, New York's general laws remained in place. In 1832, after a husband denied his wife the right to choose her church, a New York court rejected the wife's petition for a separation. And in 1860 Illinois permitted a Presbyterian clergyman to send his wife to the insane asylum because he complained that she was a freethinker. Freedom of religion did not fully belong to wives.[55]

Because of challenges to Shakers in New York, Ohio, and Kentucky, the coverture requirement that a wife follow her husband's religious dic-tates was breached, but only narrowly. Because Shakers opposed America's ruling system of domestic relations—monogamous, procreative marriage and family—these states and perhaps others denied Shaker husbands full coverture rights. Yet even this narrow crack in the system aroused vigorous defense of the patriarchal way. One revealing irony is that opponents of Eunice's religious liberty viewed James Chapman, not her, as the victim of religious oppression. A Democratic-Republican in the New York assembly asked: "Shall we say, that because one party has joined the Shakers, the marriage contract shall be annulled? The principle would apply equally well to a Jew."[56] This defender of husbands' prerogatives in marriage ig-nored the fact that, unlike Jews, those who entered Shaker communities re-nounced two central obligations of the marriage contract they had pledged to uphold when they married: family support and sexual relations. In most states refusal to fulfill these obligations provided grounds for legal separation (not full divorce). The legitimacy of coverture, after all, was grounded in the protection covenant to provide support, however incomplete.

IV

Wives' dependent status as citizens was consistent with their subordination flowing from the protection covenant. This dependency justified a different standard of responsibility for all women and wives especially. Regarding sexual chastity and marital fidelity, law and custom had long assigned women greater responsibility than men, so they bore the greater stigma if they appeared guilty of adultery or fornication. But when it came to criminal felonies, jurymen and the judges who assigned punishment believed that women deserved compassion more often than men. Just as age and dependent status limited children's responsibility, so gender affected women. Certainly they committed violent acts like assaults and felonies like fraud or counterfeiting less frequently than men; but whenever they did face criminal charges their female status implied diminished responsibility and capacity for judgment.

For those crimes where a woman participated with a husband or father, ruling presumptions and *The Law of Baron and Femme* assigned him positive culpability, whereas she could be seen as properly obedient. For common crimes like theft or burglary, courts normally found women guilty only when acting alone. And even when prosecutors charged women with a hanging crime like murder, by the early nineteenth century juries and judges commonly found ways around the gallows. It had not always been so. Though women committed far fewer capital crimes, in the eighteenth century they were punished with a severity comparable to men, including whipping, branding, and hanging. Records from New Jersey north through New York and New England show executions for at least 55 women (compared with 637 men). Usually the hanging crime was murder—39 cases, 71 percent of the whole. Arson and property crimes (grand larceny, highway robbery) each accounted for 13 percent. Most telling was the fact that of the 39 women convicted of murder, two-thirds (25) had killed their infants. Almost invariably this woman's crime sought to conceal illegitimate pregnancy. Among the remaining 14 executions for murder, most often (10 cases) black or Indian slaves and servants killed white masters or their children. Murdering a husband was rare: authorities executed women (2 white, 1 Indian) for this crime only three times, in 1708, 1711, and 1778.[57]

The actual number of executions was trending down across the century, from 14 in the decades 1700 through 1719, to 9 from 1780 through 1799. In the first half of the century, 33 women were executed (60 percent of all executions), whereas the number fell to 22 in the second half. This decline in female executions coincided with the region's dramatic population growth—a fifteenfold increase from about 126,000 residents in 1700 to 1.9 million in the region in 1800.[58] Per capita all executions were declining, but for women the drop-off was so precipitous that in the 1790s, when the entire population had risen to 2 million, from New Jersey north just three women were hanged, all black, and all for arson, a crime that threatened whole communities. By the 1790s execution of white women had virtually ceased—the last case of any woman in New England—of any color—coming in 1789. In New York and New Jersey the execution of women became exceedingly rare and no longer included infanticide. After an interval of forty-six years New Jersey executed white, twenty-one-year-old Mary Cole in 1812 for murdering her mother, and after a thirty-three-year hiatus New York executed white Margaret Houghtaling in 1817 for murdering her mulatto toddler.[59]

The importance of race in the 1790s was nothing new. Throughout the eighteenth century people of color, both women and men, suffered execution disproportionate to their numbers. During that century authorities executed 25 white women, 5 fewer than the 30 women of color they executed—a dramatically lower rate per capita. After 1780 the imbalance became even more marked. No single factor explains this change, but the sharp decline in death sentences for infanticide—the sole crime for which more white women suffered death than women of color—was important. Among the 23 white women hanged before 1780, 15 were convicted of murdering or concealing the death of bastard infants, and all these executions came before 1770 in New England and New Jersey. After that date, the only infanticide hangings—1 white, 1 Indian—were in Massachusetts in the 1780s.[60] Pennsylvania, where prosecutions for this crime increased during the century, nevertheless followed the same trajectory for executions. Never common in the originally Quaker colony—there were 8 such executions in the eighteenth century—hanging women for infanticide virtually ceased after 1767. The last Pennsylvania woman hanged for this crime was executed by mischance in 1785 because her reprieve arrived late.[61]

Three cultural forces worked against executing women during the last third of the century, especially if they were white. The most important influence was declining public support for harsh penalties to punish fornication by unwed mothers. For even as the population was growing and premarital pregnancies were rising sharply, prosecutions for chastity violations and adultery declined. New York had never punished such misbehavior systematically, and in New England, site of 68 percent (17 of 25) of these hangings, using the death penalty for infanticide was ending. Massachusetts's last criminal prosecution of fornication was in 1784, when a young white woman was convicted of "negro fornication" and punished with an hour on the gallows and a whipping and was required to "forever hereafter to wear a capital A . . . cut out in Cloth of a contrary colour, to her cloaths and sewed upon her upper garment on her back in open view." This Puritan-style punishment was seen as unduly harsh, so the legislature revised the law in 1786 so that women convicted of fornication were fined, not prosecuted criminally. In Connecticut the law remained in place, but fornication prosecutions dropped off after 1770 and virtually ceased after 1780. Farther south, adultery and fornication were rarely prosecuted, and in South Carolina bills to punish these moral breaches failed.[62]

This greater leniency was inspired in part by Beccaria's *Essay on Crimes and Punishments*, which, with Voltaire's commentary, circulated widely in British and American editions and in American newspapers and was cited in American courtrooms.[63] Voltaire introduced Beccaria's essay by making execution for infanticide the prime example of ancient cruelty:

Within a few miles of my abode, they had just hanged a girl of eighteen, beautiful, well made, accomplished, and of a very reputable family. She was culpable of having suffered herself to be got with child, and also, of having abandoned her infant. This unfortunate girl, flying from her father's house, is taken in labour, and, without assistance, is delivered of her burden by the side of a wood. Shame, which in the sex is a powerful passion, gave her strength to return home, and to conceal her situation. She left her child exposed; it is found the next morning; the mother is discovered, condemned and executed.[64]

Voltaire believed that men's response should be protective, so he presented the female, though above the age of consent, as an "unfortunate girl" who should escape legal punishment because her gender-based disgrace drove her irresponsible action. When Voltaire expressed this judgment in 1766 few others were equally outspoken, but the sentiment appeared widespread. After that year from New Jersey north through New England, authorities executed only one girl or woman for infanticide who was "accomplished, and of a very reputable family." In Connecticut the gallows was deterring infanticide accusations and convictions.[65]

The growing reluctance to hang women went beyond sex violations. Reformers had sent executions into retreat because many believed that the spectacle of humans, especially women, struggling at the end of a rope, urinating and defecating as strangulation took hold, was barbaric. Consequently by the Revolution executions of white women had all but ceased, and the aversion to executing females, no matter their color or class, was growing.[66] In the 1780s there were only a few exceptions: chiefly repeat offenders and convicts whose crimes juries and judges regarded as especially aggravated.

There were, however, two last New England executions for infanticide, in 1785 and 1788, where the only aggravating circumstance was evidence that the unmarried mothers, Hannah Pegin (or Peggin) and Abiah Converse, had borne live infants, strangled them, and hidden the corpses. Both Pegin, an Indian of unknown age, and Converse, a respectable, white twenty-three-year-old, came from small, upland western Massachusetts towns where old ways persisted into the 1790s, including prosecution for sexual misbehavior: adultery, lewd and lascivious conduct, cohabitation, incest, and sodomy.[67] This backwater region provided New England's belated hangings for infanticide.

By 1790 the aversion to executing young, vulnerable women for this crime applied to women of color as well as whites. In Pennsylvania the 1785 execution of white twenty-six-year-old Elizabeth Wilson led to what many saw as a horrific injustice.

Only after Wilson's conviction did officials recognize that the father of Wilson's twin infants probably killed them, hid their corpses, and forced Wilson to keep the secret. But official reconsideration failed. Pennsylvania hanged Wilson twenty-three minutes before her brother arrived at the gallows carrying her reprieve. Wilson's "doubtful" execution, widely reported in the press, helps explain the 1787 pardon of a sixteen-year-old slave, Alice Clifton, "a mulatto girl," sentenced to hang for concealing her bastard infant after cutting its throat.[68] Wilson's execution and Clifton's pardon propelled revision of Pennsylvania's 1718 statute based on a 1624 English law treating concealment of a newborn's death as equivalent to murder. After the 1794 revision, concealment of a bastard's death became a separate crime with maximum punishment of five years in prison. Now only especially vicious first-degree murder could lead to execution.[69] In actuality in Pennsylvania and other states, women who killed their illegitimate offspring were no longer executed. Americans believed with Beccaria and Voltaire that the best way to prevent this crime was "to protect the weak woman."[70]

In New England reform of old infanticide laws took longer. But it is significant that, as in Pennsylvania, the desperate plight of a young woman of color finally prompted legislative action. By the 1790s it appears that whites who found themselves in similar trouble found ways around the law, pathways not always available to mixed-race servant girls dwelling in white households. Twenty years after Alice Clifton's trial in Pennsylvania, in 1808 the Norwich, Connecticut, *Courier* announced the case of Clarissa Ockry: "The trial of the black girl confined for the murder of her child, will

A

FAITHFUL NARRATIVE

OF

Elizabeth Wilson ;

Who was executed at Chester, Jan. 3, 1786,

Charged with the M U R D E R

OF HER

T W I N   I N F A N T S.

Containing some account of her

D Y I N G   S A Y I N G S;

With some serious reflections.

Drawn up at the request of a friend uncon-
nected with the deceased.

PRINTED IN HUDSON, BY ASHBEL STODDARD,
M.DCC.XXXVI.

Faithful Narrative of Elizabeth Wilson (Hudson, N.Y.,
1786). This poignant story was reprinted as a pamphlet
at least three times, with newspaper versions published
in nine states from South Carolina to Vermont.
Courtesy, American Antiquarian Society.

commence in this city on Thursday next." The vulnerable Ockry, whose surname reflects Indian heritage, had confessed to concealing her dead infant, a child that may have barely survived its birth.[71] With no defense witnesses—they arrived at court too late—the jury found Ockry guilty, and Judge Swift, the same Zephaniah Swift who advocated companionate marriages where husbands must not strike their wives, sentenced her to hang according to statute.

A few days earlier, anticipating jurors' doubts, Swift had defended Connecticut's law on "murdering Bastard Children." Addressing the Norwich grand jury, he instructed them that although the 1699 statute prescribed a verdict of murder for concealment "whether it [the child] was born alive or not," Connecticut courts now followed "a milder construction," requiring "some kind of presumptive evidence that the Child was born alive." Concealment alone could not be "deemed sufficient to convict the mother." Everyone should understand that "this mild, humane, and benevolent construction of the Statute has removed all grounds of complaint." As to sexual morality, Swift defended Connecticut's old laws, which "wisely prohibited, and punished under severe penalties, all criminal connection from the highest to the lowest stages of familiarity:—from adultery, to lascivious carriage and behavior." The grand jury approved Swift's sentiments, calling unanimously for their publication.[72]

But one of Clarissa's attorneys complained. Convinced that her sentence was wrong, he hoped to overturn this miscarriage of justice and told his penniless client that he would help draft a clemency petition to the legislature. This experienced Norwich attorney, who had defended the mustee Samuel Freeman and later Prudence Crandall against Connecticut's Black Law, was Calvin Goddard, a forty-year-old Massachusetts native and Dartmouth College graduate. In the 1790s he had often represented Norwich in the Connecticut House of Representatives, rising to Speaker in 1800. Then, following two terms in the U.S. Congress as a Federalist, in 1807 he was again elected Speaker.[73] Goddard believed that his client could win relief and that her case could provide leverage to reform Connecticut law.

The four-page petition he drafted for Ockry sought a pardon, new trial, commutation of the death sentence to a lighter punishment, or complete reprieve. Goddard's arguments were based on more thorough conversation with Ockry than had been possible before trial. She now explained how pious citizens had pressured her into confessing "facts" that were not accurate. It was true that the infant boy was born alive, but "it was very feeble and died [after] a few moments." She never tried to "stifle, smother & suffocate" the child. Nor had she concealed her pregnancy, as three women and two men would attest. The jury, she said, had not had all the facts. After she signed "Clarissa Ockry," Goddard brought her petition to his old colleagues in the Connecticut Assembly.[74]

Would both houses vote to reduce her penalty? Representatives endorsed Swift's argument that "severe penalties" should follow sexual misconduct; moreover, the convict had been tried fairly and convicted. Still, Ockry's defender, Goddard, was no radical but a respected Federalist, and his role in the state assembly magnified his voice. So on June 8, two days before her scheduled hanging, poor, mixed-race Clarissa—ironically linked by her name to the novelist Samuel Richardson's virtuous rape victim—won commutation. A divided legislature concluded that six months in jail was sufficient punishment. Alas, Ockry could not complete her sentence; she died a week later in jail.[75]

Goddard had done what he could for his piteous client, but now he attacked the supposedly "mild, humane, and benevolent" law itself, particularly its presumption that a mother who hid a bastard's death must have murdered it. And like Pennsylvania in 1794, the legislature acted. Connecticut's new law of 1808 stipulated that hiding an illegitimate birth would bring a fine of $150 for women whose families could pay or three months in jail for those who could not. Concealing a bastard infant's death would be punished by an hour on the gallows with a rope around the disgraced woman's neck. Anyone, including a mother, who willfully killed an infant, would be prosecuted for homicide and subject to hanging. In practice, as in Pennsylvania, the reform effectively ended the death penalty for infanticide.[76]

A century earlier the law, whether in Pennsylvania or Connecticut, expressed no qualms about holding women responsible and executing them, and women of color had been sent to the gallows as a matter of course. But now hanging women, who were by nature irresponsible, especially poor

black women—presumed the least prudent of all—had led to reform. Punishments meted out to women became milder, but not because their rights
as citizens were gaining greater recognition. Ironically, it was the reverse.
States treated them indulgently because they regarded them as resembling
children, not men. From the time of the Revolution onward the appeal of
Beccaria's criticisms of capital punishment grew; so a woman or a child
could be hanged only if their crime appeared especially atrocious.

The 1786 execution of twelve-year-old Hannah Ocuish in Connecticut,
treated in Chapter 4, is illustrative. When she went to the gallows for beating a six-year-old girl to death with stones she was already known as a thief
and a liar who had been tried and convicted of beating another "little girl"
and stealing her necklace and clothes. Because Hannah was said to possess "a maliciousness of disposition which made the children in the neighbourhood much afraid of her," she seemed incorrigible. The judge who
sentenced her acknowledged that her youth entitled her to special consideration, but he concluded that Hannah's attempt to disguise the murder as
an accident erased any indulgence. In ordering her to hang he noted "circumstances have supplied the want of age," and so, in 1786, Connecticut
executed her as it would execute a man.[77] Yet the severity of her punishment
raised qualms, and when Ann, a black girl Hannah's age, cut the throat of
a five-year-old girl in a neighboring county in 1795, the jury did not send
Ann to hang. After a day-long trial in March 1796 the jury stayed up all
night before finding Ann "not guilty of murder, but guilty of manslaughter."
The same newspaper report informed readers that the effort in New York
"to abolish all capital punishment, except in case of murder and treason,"
passed the state senate.[78] Later in 1796 New York, New Jersey, and Virginia
enacted this reform, as would Kentucky in 1798.[79] Beccarian ideas joined to
protective sentiments toward women and children led these states to reserve
their harshest penalties for men.

Two final examples of the waning power of the idea of equal severity
toward women and children come from Massachusetts, where the state executed a white woman for a violent property crime—highway robbery—in
1789 and a white youth for arson in 1821. Though no one was killed, the
convicts' circumstances and crimes help explain why authorities adhered,

reluctantly, to old punishment standards instead of following recent, more popular precedents. Both executions were the last of their kind from New Jersey north through New England.

The final female executed in New England—white, black, mulatto, or Indian—was Rachel Wall, a twenty-nine-year-old white woman from Carlisle, Pennsylvania. By age twelve Rachel rebelled against family prayers, Sunday catechism, and lessons in "the holy scriptures." When the Revolution began she ran away from her respectable Presbyterian parents with George Wall to Philadelphia, New York, and Boston, where her husband, George, abandoned her in the 1780s. She found domestic work, including at a brothel, where she may have been a prostitute. For a time Rachel Wall worked in the home of the attorney Perez Morton, future Speaker of the Massachusetts House of Representatives and attorney general. But she was convicted and sentenced to fifteen lashes and three years' indentured labor for stealing from Morton's household. While indentured she stole again, boarding ships while their crews slept and taking such valuables as a "handkerchief containing upwards of thirty pounds in gold crowns," "a silver watch . . . a pair of silver buckles . . . [and] a parcel of small change." Usually a successful thief, in September 1788 she was convicted for "breaking up and entering . . . and carrying away . . . goods and chattels." Again punished with fifteen stripes, as a second offender the judge gave her a grave warning: she must sit an hour on the gallows. But Wall was defiant and returned to stealing. Within six months, in March 1789, she was arrested for knocking a woman down, silencing her by stuffing a cloth in her mouth, and taking her victim's purse, shoes with buckles, and hat. Passersby quickly captured Wall with her seven shillings' worth of loot.

At trial before the Supreme Judicial Court in September 1789, Massachusetts's attorney general and signer of the Declaration Robert Treat Paine, charged her with highway robbery, a capital crime. Defended by a young attorney, Christopher Gore (a future governor), Wall was nonetheless convicted, and the court ordered her execution. Wall, probably with Gore's assistance, petitioned for pardon, denying the facts in the trial. But Governor John Hancock and the Governor's Council rejected her plea. So on October 8, 1789, Rachel Wall swung from the gallows with two other highway robbers—white men who stole clothing and silver shoe buckles at knife-point from three separate victims. This execution of these highway robbers in 1789 marked the last time a woman was punished equally with men for a capital crime in New England. Thereafter though penal statutes made no gender distinctions, juries, judges, and executive officials found ways around the most severe punishments.[80]

The murder trial of Deborah Stevens, an illiterate Boston mulatto who drowned her three-year-old bastard daughter in 1803, is illustrative. Because Stevens's victim was a toddler, this was not infanticide. After her conviction for murder the Massachusetts Supreme Judicial Court delayed sentencing and after six months recommended a pardon, explaining that the court's call for mercy came from "consideration of all the circumstances of her case." Officials believed that Stevens deserved further punishment, so they kept her imprisoned until 1806 before granting a pardon.[81] Significantly, they never tried to enforce the statutory punishment of hanging.

Even when officials believed in women's guilt, jurors did not convict, as in the cases of the white defendants Elsie Whipple in New York in 1827, Lucretia Chapman in Pennsylvania in 1831, Hannah Kinney in Massachusetts in 1840, and Margaret Howard in Ohio in 1849. In Connecticut, where Thirza Mansfield was convicted for murdering her husband in 1824, the legislature commuted her death sentence. Overall, execution rates for women in New York, New Jersey, and New England plunged between 1800 and 1850. While population was five times larger than the preceding half century, women's executions dropped from fifteen to thirteen. Juries, judges, and legislatures recoiled at executing women because women were not fully responsible. Such sentiments prevailed widely, and when women were tried for lesser crimes, more often than men they won lighter punishments or acquittal. Studies of Massachusetts, New York, Pennsylvania, Ohio, and England all display this pattern.[82]

V

The same sentiments—humane Enlightenment sensibility against capital punishment and protective paternalism—shaped punishment of children and youth convicted of serious crimes. As with women, this gentler treatment marked a new departure. In English law a person's rank had long mattered more than their age. Though courts recognized the incapacity of babbling babies, by age seven children could exercise judgment and were treated accordingly in law. Belief in children's moral capacity was evident in evangelical efforts to bring young children to "own" Jesus. Because evangelicals doubted infant baptism, they celebrated conversions of three- and four-year-olds. Sometimes belief in children's judgment was fictive, as when jurists Matthew Hale and William Blackstone explained that from birth a king was of full age in his political capacity. Actually, Elizabethan courts allowed children at any age to bind themselves as apprentices, to make wills at four years, and to marry at age seven.[83]

In Britain and America children from seven to thirteen years were occasionally hanged if their crimes were especially vicious. The historian Holly Brewer reports that some American colonies departed from English laws and recognized children's incapacity; nevertheless a two-year-old Pennsylvania girl marked her consent on an apprenticeship as late as 1811. In seventeenth- and eighteenth-century England and colonial Virginia, Brewer discovered a four-year-old who signed a will, a five-year-old who bound himself to labor, an eight-year-old who married, and another the same age who was hanged for committing arson. In addition a thirteen-year-old won election to Parliament and spoke on legislation. Brewer also reports a juror aged fourteen years.[84]

These examples were not routine. As Brewer explains, the Reformation taught that reason and experience should matter more than inherited status for exercising consent. In America, Revolutionaries elevated the idea of consent to the highest level, implementing it with age barriers for public service. In the Constitution they set age requirements for Congress and the presidency. Still, in the colonies and states old and new ideas and practices overlapped. For girls the age of sexual consent generally remained at the medieval ten years; and the age for children's testimony in court stayed at eight years, providing the child understood the meaning of an oath and believed in divine rewards and punishments.[85] Criminal codes made few allowances for youth.

Statutes were generally silent regarding age, but enforcement allowed discretion. Lawyers defending youthful defendants routinely argued that age was exculpatory. Convicts seeking pardons claimed youth as a mitigating factor, even in their twenties or thirties. Judging from Massachusetts's pardoning record from 1780 through 1819, such arguments seldom succeeded. Still, a defendant's age was considered in court.[86] In 1785, when Thomas Mount and Jack Miller were convicted of breaking and entering and stealing, both were sentenced to "one hour on the gallows with a rope round their necks," but whereas the adult, Mount, was also given thirty stripes and three years' hard labor, Miller, "a youth, received 10 stripes" and just one year at hard labor. Like Mount, Miller was guilty and deserved punishment, but his age reduced his sentence by twenty stripes and two years.[87] A generation later, in 1813, when a Boston court convicted "three boys" aged thirteen to sixteen for committing these crimes at night, their penalty was five days' "solitary imprisonment followed by five years' hard labor in the State Prison." The boys had broken into a store and, after dividing "their plunder," fled toward Rhode Island like professional burglars. Judge Thomas Dawes postponed issuing sentence until "after school," so that "boys from all parts of the town could hear" his admonition to the young convicts.[88]

Dawes's warning to the prisoners clearly aimed to teach every young Bostonian a lesson. In pamphlet form *Juvenile Vice and Piety Contrasted: Being the Address of Judge Dawes to Three Boys Convicted of Stealing* went through two editions selling at $3.50 per hundred. Here Dawes recalled that in the past thirty years he had witnessed "middle aged men scourged at the whipping post, set in pillories and upon the gallows, their faces branded with hot irons, or their ears cut off for crimes not more aggravated than yours." But the convicted boys would not suffer equally because the state's "later and milder laws" allowed him to prescribe five years in state prison, not the fifteen years routinely given adults. He scolded, "Had you been convicted of a similar offence in almost any other part of the known world, you might have been 'hung up between heaven and earth as unworthy of both.'" The boys had acted with the "adroitness" of "old offenders," yet Dawes treated them as less than fully responsible. "Compassion for boyhood" and a belief that "some of the parents" were "too much to blame" prompted his "lenity." He hoped to prompt remorse and reformation so that the boys might someday be pardoned. Prison would teach them to work and, he hoped, to read the Bible and repent. Dawes concluded by warning "children and young lads" to take heed. Teaching the lesson of execution sermons, Dawes explained that the convicted boys had begun "by lying and swearing, then cheating their playmates in little matters, next by pilfering small articles from older neighbors; and on Sundays . . . ripping off the lead from gates and fences, when the owners were in Church." The boys were guilty, but not fully responsible for their actions, so they deserved shielding from the penal code. Children, like women, received preferred treatment in criminal cases: fewer indictments and, if indicted, usually for reduced crimes. When convicted, as with the murderer Deborah Stevens or the boys imprisoned for breaking and entering, judges tempered justice with mercy.[89]

Yet in 1821 a youth from a poor but respectable white family became, like Hannah Ocuish in Connecticut and Rachel Wall in Massachusetts, a monument to the more nearly equal standard of punishment for men, women, and children. Like Ocuish and Wall, Stephen Clark, born in 1804 in Newburyport, Massachusetts, had earned a reputation for bad behavior. Adults recognized Stephen's *"propensity to mischief"* early. They reported that "falsehood and profanity became so habitual to him, that a lie, or an oath to attest to a lie, were usually on his tongue." Known for "the most vulgar insolence and abuse to his superiors" and frequently caught stealing, "he often showed sums of money to an amount far beyond any honest means." Around 1816 Stephen's sixty-two-year-old father, Moses Clark, apprenticed the twelve-year-old to tradesmen—first to an older brother, then to a baker, and finally to a cooper. But "after three weeks' gross misconduct and several thefts from his master," Stephen quit his brother's shop. An idler, he passed time with "vile company." Soon Stephen came to possess a record, having been fined in 1818 for *"assault and battery committed upon an old man!"* His waywardness brought his father to his wit's end. Believing that his son was "fatally bent on mischief," in August 1820 Moses Clark asked Newburyport selectmen to confine the youth. When they declined, Moses brought his son before a justice of the peace with a formal complaint. But when Stephen promised good behavior, the magistrate withheld the arrest warrant, holding it as security for compliance.[90]

A few days later, on the night of August 16, 1820, Stephen set fire to a barn, and the following night he torched a stable. Newburyport panicked. Nine years earlier a nighttime fire, believed "the work of an incendiary," had destroyed most of the town—stables, barns, dwellings, public build-ings—250 structures in all.[91] Now, Clark's second fire, "in a compact neighborhood of wooden buildings which were extremely dry," spread to six other structures, including a "mansion-house" and a dwelling where girls of Newburyport's "Female Asylum" slept. Two horses were killed, and "the loss of property," though modest, was "mostly . . . sustained by those who could but ill afford it." Residents concluded that the fires "must have originated with the midnight incendiary."[92]

When people in the maritime town of 6,800 inhabitants asked them-selves who might be guilty, suspicions fixed on Stephen Clark, so he was arrested and questioned. But officials lacked proof. Stephen denied guilt, and "bad as he was," his father testified that "he thought he was innocent," explaining that he had shared a bed with his son the night of the second fire. The justices released Stephen from custody, "though not from *suspicion*."[93] Moses, anxious about Stephen's situation, sent him to a brother in Maine to seek work. Stephen departed but, finding no work, came home. By now a female friend of Stephen's reported that he had ignited the fires, so he was jailed. Under questioning, Stephen confessed.

Based on this confession, the grand jury at Salem indicted Clark, "a mi-nor under the age of twenty-one years," in October 1820.[94] He was tried in February 1821, six months after the fires, but neighbors' anger remained intense, so no Newburyport resident was seated on the jury. Clark was for-tunate in his court-appointed defense attorneys, John Pickering and John Glen King, Harvard graduates who had practiced locally for years. Together they challenged twenty-one potential jurors, one because he declared that Clark should hang.[95] King opened the defense by stressing the prisoner's juvenile status. Stephen was "scarcely beyond the period of childhood," and he was being tried for "his folly . . . the weakness of his youth." Be-cause the prosecution rested on Clark's confession, King aimed to under-mine it. Young Clark, he said, confessed owing to "the ignorance of his own rights," not because of "any violation of the rights of others." To close Clark's defense, Pickering hammered these themes. Clark is "a *youth* of sixteen, who . . . is not of sufficient capacity to make choice of counsel, and is of too tender an age even to know that he has a right." He was a "defenceless youth," "a humble youth," "the unwary youth." Pickering's only terms for Clark were "boy" or "youth," one who "passed the whole night in bed with his father" while the fire burned.[96]

Because of a reluctance to punish youths as adults, this "youth defense" was his attorneys' best argument. No character witnesses among Stephen's neighbors and employers came forward, and gossip of "his intimacy with certain profligate females" augmented his boyhood reputation for lying, stealing, and insolence.[97] One special friend, Hannah Downes, perhaps fearing that she would be implicated and punished, testified that Stephen told her how he set the fires. And their friend Sally Chase reported Stephen saying "he would have his revenge on Newburyport, he would have his revenge on his brother for opposing his going with Hannah Downs."[98] This testimony reinforced Stephen's own confession to the magistrates.

That confession was so detailed and damning that Stephen's defenders argued strenuously it should not be accepted. He had, Pickering claimed, confessed without knowing his rights and without benefit of counsel. Confessions must be strictly "*voluntary*," without threat or promise, based only on "a sense of guilt." This was the law for "persons of *mature years* . . . who . . . have a full knowledge of their rights." The argument was more powerful for "a youth of the tender age of the prisoner—who is so far from having a knowledge of all his rights, that he is hardly conscious that he has any; who cannot weigh the consequences of his acts." Pickering asserted that Clark's confession was involuntary and so must be ignored. His jail-house confession to the Reverend Daniel Dana should be discounted because "the presence and conversation of a clergyman" surely exerted undue "influence" on a prisoner threatened with doom.[99]

Pickering further argued that Stephen's confession reported by Hannah Downes was "not entitled to belief" because she was "a woman of loose and infamous character." She and Sally Chase had been "sentenced to confinement" as "night-walkers" and "women given to lascivious conduct." Regarding Downes's veracity, one witness swore that "he would as soon believe the devil as her." Pickering declared that Downes had "the character of not being a woman of truth." And her testimony was self-interested: witnesses reported that she sought revenge on the Clarks. Pickering summed up:

"When the father of the prisoner discovered that the *unfortunate boy* had fallen into the hands of this dissolute woman and her polluted confederates, he endeavoured to extricate his child—he expostulated with her, telling her . . . that she 'would undo his son'—upon which this woman, with the spirit of a fury, maliciously replied, that she *meant to undo him*." Although the confession Downes reported matched Clark's other confessions, Pickering declared that this eighteen-year-old female was so corrupt that her words must not be believed. Lacking other exculpatory evidence than the alibi given by Clark's father, Pickering called on the ancient fable of the designing woman destroying the innocent boy. Later, a Salem paper reported that it was "generally supposed" that Clark's fate was "to be attributed to those abandoned females with whom he associated." It was the women, the press opined, who "ensnared him in the paths of vice, and instigated him to commit the crime."[100]

King and Pickering were eloquent, but officials who heard Clark's confessions swore that they first "told him . . . he was not bound to criminate himself; that if he did, it would be given in evidence against him." Indeed Stephen had initially denied the crime. Only when the justice asked how officials knew "he had taken a candle from his father's cellar-way, and broken it, and then taken another, and carried it to the stable &c.; he started from his chair apparently agitated, and said, if you will tell me how you got that information, I will tell you all about it." After Clark was told that it came from Hannah Downes, Sally Chase, Eliza Manly, and two others, Stephen "immediately said, *I done it*."[101] During the following weeks Clark recounted versions of this confession repeatedly.

For the prosecutor, Solicitor General Daniel Davis, it was critical to defend the legitimacy of Clark's first confession. After explaining when and how Clark confessed and noting the consistency of Clark's six separate confessions, Davis defended Hannah Downes's testimony, noting that "this *girl* . . . has been much abused" by "violent and persevering" attacks, all irrelevant to her competence as a witness. The prisoner's attorneys portrayed Hannah as vicious, with Stephen merely her instrument. But Davis argued that Stephen himself was deeply vicious and that his actions must not be excused as youthful errors. Clark undermined the ordinary presumption of

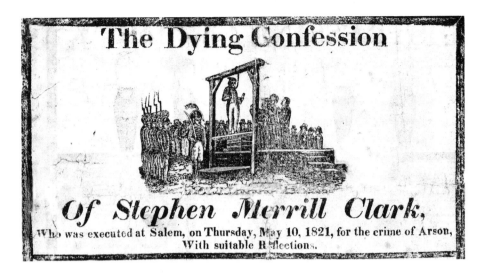

Stephen Merrill Clark's *Dying Confession* broadside was augmented by
another at his execution, in addition to a trial report, a biography, and
extensive newspaper coverage. Courtesy, American Antiquarian Society.

innocence "by the profligacy of his habits and manners, and the apparent
and unheard of obduracy of his mind." Who could presume innocence in
light of "his wanton and ferocious disposition for mischief—his diabolical
spirit of revenge?" Just because Clark was a minor, jurors must not flinch
from justice: "Though young in years he is old in depravity," dangerous
because "his understanding and intellect are unusually strong and clear."
Davis noted Clark's attorneys' appeal to the jurors' mercy, but he countered
that "mercy to the prisoner, is death to the devoted inhabitants of the town"
Clark set ablaze. Jurors must show mercy to "the parents and children, the
wives and husbands, of this peaceful and moral community" by a guilty
verdict.[102]

When Chief Justice Isaac Parker charged the jury, summarizing the case,
he reminded them that the court had ruled that Clark's confessions were
legal. But if the evidence "should excite in you a reasonable doubt as to
his guilt," acquittal it must be. However, if "no such doubt remains," jurors
must find him guilty. Clark was young, but Parker admonished, "His youth

alone is not to excuse him." All must be held responsible, an idea that animated justice for centuries, so "if he escape because he is young, then the young will be released from one of the strongest restraints from vice, the fear of punishment."[103]

Five hours later jurors declared Clark guilty. The next morning Solicitor General Davis, following the statute, called for the death penalty. Judge Parker then asked Clark if there was a reason the court should not pass sentence; Clark replied that "he was innocent of the offense." Parker responded with a lecture emphasizing the convict's "indifference to the consequences" of the fires. "Young as you are," Parker told Clark, you have "prepared the community to see" your execution "with melancholy acquiescence." Clark's "diabolical spirit" set fires that could destroy lives as well as property. "How hard must be that heart! How desperate, how worse than savage" the person who can plan, execute, and even contemplate "with delight, the terror, the cries, the slow and painful death of the aged, the sick, the tender infants," all vulnerable to the "ferocious incendiary." Clark's arson made him "an enemy of the human race"; because fire was "boundless in its consequences," it was worse than murder, robbery, or piracy.[104] Whatever doubts some might feel about capital punishment or executing a youth, Parker's exhortation justified hanging Clark.

Last, Parker addressed Stephen Clark and every child. "Young man!" he began, "you," like many other youths, stand "at the threshold of life in full health and vigor, with powers of mind and body fit for a long season of useful and active exertions." But Clark had squandered his advantages and opportunities. Foolishly he had tried to escape the law; now he must suffer. "Alas! That a youth of seventeen should be the subject of these painful remarks." Parker urged every young person to "take warning," to avoid temptation, fear God, and accept their parents' "wholesome discipline."[105] Like execution sermons of past generations, and like Judge Dawes's speech to the young nighttime burglars, Parker stressed the lessons of the criminal's sinful path in contrast to the path of righteousness.

Parker's stern warnings and vigorous advocacy for Stephen Clark's execution reflected the judge's recognition of shifting public expectations toward both the death penalty and youthful offenders. Though many in Newburyport supported Clark's hanging, many others in Essex County did not. The Salem press reported that "a strenuous effort [was] made to procure a commutation of Clark's punishment from death to perpetual imprisonment." Governor John Brooks, a sixty-eight-year-old Federalist, received one mercy petition "signed by many of the most respectable people in the county" and another actually signed "by the jury who convicted him."[106]

Brooks and the Governor's Council reexamined the facts and the arguments for and against Clark's hanging at least twice. Even before receiving any petition to save the youth Brooks appointed a three-man committee on March 7, 1821, to consider when "it would be expedient" to carry out the execution. The committee recommended a date six weeks later, April 26. But just six days before the scheduled hanging, on April 20, Brooks appointed another committee to weigh a petition from Moses Clark, Stephen's father. This committee, after hearing Moses "and his wife" plead for their son, and "having fully examined the documents accompanying" the petition, which called for "imprisonment to hard labor for a term of years or for life," recommended that it was "not expedient" to commute Clark's sentence. Nevertheless, since the "convict and his friends" had "indulged" hopes of a commutation, the committee urged a two-week postponement to allow Clark the "opportunity to prepare himself for eternity." The governor and council decided unanimously that "there was no sufficient cause to interrupt the course of justice." Their knowledge that Clark repeatedly tried to escape from jail and that "perpetual imprisonment" was seldom actually sustained may have influenced them.[107] They recognized that governors commonly gave pardons to well-behaved long-term prisoners. But releasing Clark could be dangerous; he reportedly said that if he was sent "to the State Prison, he would have his revenge, if he ever got out, if it were 20 years afterwards," that he would "in the night . . . set fire to the town in several places, so as that it could not be extinguished."[108] Despite his youth, Clark's remorseless, unrepentant attitude discouraged mercy.[109]

Clark used his postponement time to try once more to escape. First he wrote to his guard, as "but a boy," pathetically begging the jailer to unlock him "as you are the only one who can save my life." In exchange he promised a bribe of "one hundred dollars cash, some time next week." The jailer rejected his offer so Clark tried a jailbreak. Friends supplied "drilling irons" and "a large hammer" to drill holes in the stone wall. By filling them with gunpowder he would blow open an exit. But before delivery of the explosive, this scheme was discovered.[110]

Only now, a week before he would hang, Stephen Clark realized he had no way out. For the first time he turned repentant, apologizing to those whose property he destroyed; and he exonerated the twenty-year-old he once claimed as a coconspirator. Instead his former girlfriend, Hannah Downes, became his scapegoat. She had proposed setting fire to the town to avenge gossip about their "being together." Arson was not even his idea: Hannah "urged me to do it."[111] Like many convicts, even while repenting his crimes he claimed to be the victim.

From today's perspective Stephen Clark can seem a victim: first, of his own psychopathology; but also victim of a social and legal order that prized exemplary punishment. Thomas Croade Cushing, the Salem journalist who wrote the *Short Life and Ignominious Death of Stephen Merrill Clark*, was a fifty-seven-year-old Federalist shocked by Clark's crime and punishment. Stephen was "an unfortunate youth" whose "tender age" of sixteen years and nine months he mistakenly believed made Clark "the youngest offender ever executed in the United States, for *any* offence." The youth's actions were especially shocking because, far from being one of the "vagrant foreigners . . . the refuse and dregs of society" who commonly went to the gallows, Stephen was raised by "reputable parents" in a community "famed for steady habits, severe morality, and exemplary piety." He was, Cushing concluded, one of nature's "monsters" whose "precocious depravity" placed Essex County's and Massachusetts' feelings of "humanity" for the youth in conflict with their "sense of duty." And Bostonians worried whether executing the youth would "affect our reputation for *Humanity* with our sister States."[112] His execution was just, but only barely.

Race was never an issue in Clark's arson, but because he was a local Yankee the severity of his punishment seemed especially significant. Though Cushing did not know it, since 1674, when Massachusetts executed a seventeen-year-old white youth, the only juveniles executed in New York or

New England were persons of color convicted of murder: the twelve-year-old Connecticut Indian Hannah Ocuish in 1787 and the seventeen-year-old New York Indian John Tuhi in 1817, just four years before Clark. Later, in 1828, 1837, and 1844, New Jersey would execute three more children, aged twelve, fifteen, and sixteen years—all black and all for murder. The only white youth was a seventeen-year-old Irish immigrant, Michael Jennings, executed in Connecticut in 1854 after robbing his employer's home and murdering his wife, stabbing her repeatedly. In all these cases, though race and ethnic prejudice mattered, many officials and the public anguished over executing such youthful offenders.[113] Reversion to the old severity seemed justified only because the convicts appeared incorrigible—youths whose vices could not be reformed. Finding safety in tradition, society applied the old rules.

But though authorities followed the law, they accepted, indeed shared, public revulsion at the policy. It offended their underlying belief that because children and youth, like women, were *naturally* irresponsible they deserved leniency and protection. In 1830 when Theron Cheney, a white fourteen-year-old Massachusetts boy—"youthful in appearance even within that age"—committed armed robbery on another boy and was convicted and sentenced to hang, observers shuddered at such punishment. There were "so many extenuating circumstances, that the mercy of the Executive," many hoped would "save him from a violent death." Cheney was "a mere boy" who "had but indistinct conceptions of his deed, or the nature of the wrong." And his crime, after all, was "not so heinous as the crimes which the public is generally satisfied to expiated by death." Even the jury that convicted Cheney "signed a petition in his favor," and the boy did not hang.[114] Indeed in 1837, after Massachusetts Supreme Judicial Court chief justice Lemuel Shaw, according to law, sentenced fourteen-year-old Michael Monahon to hang for setting fire to the Cambridge almshouse, killing one resident, mercy prevailed. Monahon, like Stephen Clark and Theron Cheney, had "voluntarily" confessed, but Governor Edward Everett—a future U.S. secretary of state, Harvard president, U.S. senator, and Gettysburg orator—commuted the boy's sentence to life at hard labor "in consequence of his extreme youth."[115] Statute law lagged behind sentiment everywhere, so authorities retreated from enforcing statutes fully.

VI

Conflating women with children, classifying both as naturally less responsible than men and therefore properly the wards of their husbands and fathers—their natural and legal guardians—was paradoxical. Official ambivalence grew out of deep contradictions regarding women's actual roles in society. All Americans did not hold ambivalent views—but many subscribed to conflicting and inconsistent ideas—and collectively Americans displayed contradictory ideas and practices. Just as some rejected the natural inferiority of nonwhites, some challenged the conventional notion of female submission, affirming women's natural equality. With each passing decade, from the 1820s through the 1860s and beyond, women and male allies devised challenges to women's subordinate status. Women did not win equal citizenship in the nineteenth century, or perhaps even the twentieth century, but their emergence as powerful actors in the public sphere belied coverture and patriarchy.[116]

The pillars sustaining the movement for women's equal rights were not new. During the eighteenth century women closed the literacy gap with men and came to achieve preeminence in piety. Though arguably women's religiosity reflected subservience to male clergy, in fact whatever formal roles denominations prescribed, religion provided women with the moral self-assurance necessary to challenge political patriarchy by pursuing moral reform, temperance, antislavery, and women's rights. Though men barred women from learned professions, they could not block women from having opinions. In elections the laws that excluded women from voting kept them spectators, useful only to swell the ranks at political rallies. But as writers and face-to-face organizers they shaped public opinion, playing a central role in popular lobbying. By the 1840s women's politics tackled the central obstacles to equal citizenship: property rights and the franchise.[117]

During the independence movement women opened the path by signing political covenants aimed at Britain in the 1760s and 1770s. Some saw women signatories as curiosities to ridicule, but in Massachusetts and North Carolina hundreds of women acted with intentions as serious as the Whigs who solicited their support.[118] In the first decades after independence women routinely petitioned government, a right no one questioned. If, for example, they sought divorce or claimed property, laws directed women to petition a court or a legislature. Widows routinely petitioned for their husbands' military pensions. In the first decades of the nineteenth century women even petitioned to incorporate their charitable associations. No one challenged these entries into civil society.

But when women sought to exercise the franchise they met opposition rooted in coverture and patriarchy. One early case came from the Middleboro, Massachusetts, Congregational church, separated from Abigail Adams's letter to John by three years and thirty miles. In 1779 the Reverend Abram Camp, a recent Yale graduate, asked that the women church members vote on his invitation to settle as pastor. When five male members voted against this "decided innovation," he responded by turning down the invitation. Consequently the congregation selected another Yale graduate.[119]

Abigail Adams's belief that women should exercise power by voting was too radical even in a church where they were members. Because women constituted the majority of members in denominations where "conversion" was a condition of membership, allowing their vote would have given women control of many churches. In Massachusetts, Connecticut, and New Hampshire, where churches were tax-supported agencies of morality and social order, officials quashed the idea. And women did not, evidently, challenge this exclusion from the church franchise.

When it came to state power, however, as Abigail Adams predicted, women complained. During the war she had pointed out that though women were "deprived of a voice in Legislation, [and] obliged to submit to those Laws which are imposed upon us," they nevertheless remained engaged in "the publick Welfare." Indeed "all History and every age," she declared, "exhibit our fortitude." In response to this stream of Revolutionary ideology one state enfranchised propertied women equally with men in the 1790s. But though a reaction reversed the practice a dozen years later, advocates for women's equal rights did not vanish. During the state constitutional conventions of the 1820s when delegates adjusted Revolutionary era suffrage restrictions, women's vote became an issue. By 1820 a generation of popular politics, a growing population, and the market economy had stripped the property-based yeoman republic of legitimacy, making property qualifications contentious and ineffective.[120] State after state came to eliminate property requirements for voting, erasing a key justification for denying women's suffrage. In the past opponents had argued that single women and widows were exceptions—anomalies—because most females moved from daughters to wives seamlessly under coverture. But if property ownership was no longer required for voting, barring women and people of color needed a different justification. "Natural" differences and "natural" inequality became that justification.

For Jeffersonian Republicans who claimed that the franchise was a natural right, arguments to restrict voting to white men were awkward. As the historian Rosemarie Zagarri reports, women made the logical claim that they were as qualified to vote as propertyless men. And Federalists who wanted to block Jeffersonian reform argued that making suffrage a matter of natural rights philosophy would open elections indiscriminately. A Rhode Island legislative report complained that removing limits on suffrage would make voting "common to all, without distinction of age, sex, or color." A New York constitutional convention delegate acidly noted in 1821 that the natural rights principle that once permitted New Jersey women to vote would require New York to "admit negresses as well as negroes to participate in the right of suffrage," as well as "Minors" and "aliens."[121] Jeffersonians responded by redefining natural rights pragmatically. They did not resurrect the reasoning Virginia's legislators used to exclude slaves from their 1776 Bill of Rights by claiming women and blacks were not members of society. Instead they stigmatized them for their intrinsic and organic, natural political incompetence. White boys matured out of their "natural" disqualification, but women and people of color could never escape their inborn disability.

When this discussion moved to Virginia's constitutional convention in 1829, one woman protested. "A Virginia Freewoman" declared "astonishment and indignation" because the gentlemen delegates refused to defend "the Rights of women." Implicitly accepting coverture, this "Freewoman" argued that single women should vote. At a time when "so many others are recovering their long-lost Rights," she asked, "why should we alone be excluded?" The state, she complained, was turning a "natural right" into "a privilege." To advocates for women and people of color, Democratic-Republican reasoning defending universal white manhood suffrage appeared inconsistent and contradictory. Yet by 1828 Noah Webster, the old Federalist and dictionary writer, specified a gendered definition of a United States citizen: "a person, native or naturalized, who has the privilege of exercising the elective franchise, or the qualifications which enable *him* to vote for rulers, and to purchase and hold real estate."[122] Whether women and persons of color were citizens of towns, cities, counties, or states varied, but full citizenship privileges belonged almost exclusively to white men.

Ironically, just as the formal exclusion of women from political power was being reinforced, women seized a central role in American politics by organizing mass petitions. Excluded from voting, they deployed their long-held and hitherto unquestioned petitioning right to assert political power. Women began by collaborating with men in the temperance movement. Even before 1820 women began to sign antialcohol petitions initiated and signed by men. As the movement developed in the 1820s men welcomed women into the American Temperance Union. In time, women organized their own chapters, deferring to concerns about mixing the sexes. By the 1830s in scattered localities reaching from Delaware to Maine hundreds of women signed petitions to local and state officials to restrict alcohol sales.[123]

During the same period men enlisted women to help stop Cherokee removal from Cherokee lands in Tennessee, Georgia, and Alabama. In response, Catharine Beecher, leading a circle of activist Hartford women, secretly drafted a letter to women's charitable societies nationwide, urging women to organize public meetings and petition Congress for the Cherokees. Beecher's circle believed that their intervention as women was so radical that they concealed their arrangements. They distributed multiple copies of Beecher's printed circular letter via chain letters to female acquaintances all over the northern and western states. To hide the letter's origin they arranged to post their letters not in their hometown, Hartford, but in four other cities, including New York and Philadelphia.[124]

Beecher's circle recognized that they were violating gender boundaries and magnifying their offense by mobilizing other women, so Beecher's text used the language of female deference to shield their "Circular: Addressed to the Benevolent Ladies of the U. States." Turning women's exclusion from voting to advantage, Beecher's letter claimed that men protected women "from the blinding influence of party spirit, and the asperities of political violence." Indeed, though entering a political controversy, Beecher and her collaborators struck a submissive pose. Women had "nothing to do with any struggle for power, nor any right to dictate the decisions of those that rule over them." Admitting that their plea might be *"forbidden,"* they hoped that "female petitioners can lawfully be heard, even by the highest rulers of our land." As custodians of "the sweet charities of life" and *"the empire of affection,"* they boldly aimed to influence Congress. Appearing to accept conventional gender boundaries, the circular urged women to "exert that influence in society which falls within her lawful province.[125] Shrewdly, Beecher adapted the Quakers' antislavery petitioning technique to the cause of the Cherokees—while also opening a direct path for women in political contests. In following decades the thousands of signatures garnered by Beecher's Cherokee circular would be multiplied to hundreds of thousands as the antislavery movement mobilized the unfranchised to shape national politics.[126]

Some congressional supporters of Cherokee removal attacked women's intervention, ridiculing "the benevolent females." But others, including removal advocates who scorned the Cherokees' defenders, accepted the legitimacy of the ladies' effort. William Drayton, a South Carolina representative, denounced the Beecher petition because it "grossly violates common propriety and common decency" by charging Georgia with bad faith. But Drayton recognized that the petitioners, "in common with other citizens, have the constitutional right to petition Congress for the redress of grievances" and "to decide what are the proper occasions for its exercise." Though their petition and the Cherokee cause failed, women had established a beachhead in national politics that they would not relinquish.[127] Petitions were an ideal tactic for engaging the unfranchised in politics.

So when abolitionists built a mass movement to pressure Congress, in addition to mass mailings and scores of public meetings, they turned to petitions. A few hundred "apolitical" Quakers had petitioned Parliament as early as 1783 to abolish the slave trade. Now, fifty years later, hundreds of thousands of women and children joined with men to bombard Congress with abolition petitions. Some fifteen thousand women signed petitions to their congressmen in 1836 calling for an end to slavery, and when the House of Representatives answered the abolitionists' petitioning campaign with a Gag Rule, forbidding representatives to read petitions on the floor of Congress, abolitionists redoubled their efforts. The next year, when a women's national convention organized petitioning throughout the North, more than two hundred thousand women signed.[128] Northern as well as southern voices excoriated the abolitionists, singling out women's public efforts as ipso facto indecent.

The South Carolina slaveholder's daughter, Angelina Grimké, a leading abolitionist, rejected such arguments. Invited to testify before a Massachusetts legislative committee in 1838, Grimké declared that as "a citizen" of the Republic she must speak because the "honor, happiness, and well-being" of women, not less than men, were "bound up in its politics, government and laws." Grimké did not assert equal rights for women citizens, but she proclaimed their public role. "Are we aliens, because we are *women?*" she asked. "Have women no country—no interests staked in the public weal—no liabilities or common peril—no partnership in a nation's shame?"[129] Because the issues were "political" women were duty-bound to speak publicly, in the press, and with their signatures.

In Massachusetts, Grimké spoke before approving audiences, so her declaration of the citizen-woman's political role might be controversial but worthy of attention. Not so in Congress, where a North Carolina Jacksonian, the lawyer Jesse Atherton Bynum, dismissively classed women's political voice with "children, boys, or lunatics." America's founders, he claimed, could not have imagined women petitioning, though actually the founders handled women's pension and divorce petitions routinely, women's petitions being part of the colonial and English legacy. But for Bynum women, like "children, boys, or lunatics," should have no voice since they did not face military service or the tax consequences of politics.[130]

This Princeton graduate spoke supported by Jefferson's words. Defending political coverture, Jefferson rejected women's political voice. Because, like infants and slaves, women "had no will [they] could be permitted to exercise none in the popular assembly; and of course, could delegate none to an agent in a representative assembly." This view of female political disqualification dominated the United States in the 1830s. Even Catharine Beecher, disturbed by the acrimony of slavery politics, surrendered. Denouncing Grimké's abolition politics, she defended Drayton's and Bynum's principle of "decorum" as a constitutional standard. Retreating, she declared that men, not women, should rule. In the divine hierarchy "one sex [is] the superior . . . the other the subordinate," and as a consequence, "all the power and all the conquests that are lawful to woman, are those only which appeal to the kindly, generous, peaceful and benevolent principles." "Woman," Beecher proclaimed, "is to win everything by peace and love . . . in the domestic and social circle." What was best for society—"the sacred protection of religion," "the generous promptings of chivalry," "the poetry of romantic gallantry"—all depended on "woman's retaining her place as dependent and defenseless." The petition movement she helped launch was misguided: "In this country, petitions to congress, in reference to the official duties of legislators, seem IN ALL CASES, to fall entirely without the sphere of female duty."[131]

But if Beecher and the majority stood with Jefferson and the Jacksonians, Grimké also found support and not only from radical abolitionists. Abigail Adams's son, John Quincy Adams, the president turned congressman, vigorously defended women's right and everyone's right—even slaves—to petition. When a House colleague argued that women possessed no such right because they had no right to vote, Adams reversed the argument. Some states had considered women's suffrage before they withheld it, and women might indeed possess that right. Adams suggested that their exclusion from voting might be merely customary—not due to natural disqualification. Abigail Adams's son shared the common view that women were naturally kind, benevolent, and compassionate, and he rejected the idea of women routinely engaging in politics, but he refused to believe that women's nature required political submission.[132]

In light of women's past political marginalization, debating women's rights in Congress was historic. Banking, internal improvements, and sectional issues like the tariff, slavery, and slavery expansion were central con-tests for Whigs and Democrats, but the movement to recognize women's rights now became a prominent and permanent part of antebellum politics. Women and a few male allies made women's voting rights and full recogni-tion of their citizenship command attention. Attacking the wholesale denial of married women's property rights under coverture was their first priority.

In 1836, just as Congress was denying women the right to petition, New York legislators received two petitions calling for women's property rights: one from central New York carried thirty names, and another from New York City was signed by a recent Polish Jewish immigrant, Ernestine Po-lowsky Rose, and four other women.[133] Albany legislators accepted the peti-tions, but that was all. Only after the Panic of 1837 and the resulting wave of bankruptcies did state legislatures reconsider property in marriage. And in acting to separate a wife's property from her husband's, they aimed to pro-tect families from a husband's creditors. Nevertheless, compared with the long-standing coverture regime, the statutes of the 1840s and after led to sig-nificant changes in women's control of property. Although a woman's earn-ings and any property she owned remained subject to a husband's control as "family property," men could no longer "dispose of assets wives brought to a marriage or will them away." Instead a wife could use her own property and transfer its ownership. And if, like Anne Parker Cowper or Emeline Hunt Shaw, her marriage failed, now she could control her property and its earnings.[134]

Women remained legally subordinate in marriage, but once they con-trolled property, coverture and the related system of political disqualification began to falter. When the consequences of the new property laws played out in succeeding decades, women came to control increasing wealth. Empow-ering women by creating loopholes in coverture was rarely legislators' inten-tion, but that would be the result.[135] Indeed from the standpoint of accepted theories of representative government these legal changes made women's incomplete citizenship increasingly paradoxical and inconsistent. The le-gal status of the growing numbers of single women resembled men's—they could enter contracts, buy and sell property, testify in court, and act as legal guardians—yet constitutions and statutes barred them from typical rights and duties of adult citizens as voters, jurors, and public officeholders.[136] In addition custom, often based on notions of decorum, could exclude women from occupations as well as public accommodations, transportation, and public events. Lydia Maria Child, for example, reported that authorities refused women tickets to a murderer's 1842 execution in New York City.[137] States like New York had moved executions inside prison walls partly to shield women and children from the spectacle of executions and the rough crowds who came to witness them. Women were welcome at some public events, as when Whigs in the 1840s and 1850s sought to enlarge popular support at rallies, but practices varied according to venue, occasion, time of day, and jurisdiction.[138] Gender stereotypes regarding what was and was not natural and suitable for women influenced even the most radical proponents of their equal rights.

Elisha P. Hurlbut, the forty-year-old New Yorker elected to the state's supreme court in 1847, balanced contradictory ideas in his influential 1848 *Essays on Human Rights and Their Political Guaranties*. He began declaring "the rights of man and the rights of woman are precisely one and the same." This was natural law, and American and British law "touching the Rights of Woman, are at variance with the laws of the Creator." He attacked coverture directly: men lost no rights when they married, whereas a woman, "his equal" before marriage, was "now his inferior." That was wrong. He declared the "right of suffrage to be "inherent" in nearly all literate people since they possessed the requisite "intelligence and moral impulse" for voting. The exclusion of vicious persons or those convicted of an "infamous crime" was proper, since elections must not be shaped by "all those persons whose moral and intellectual defects create the principal necessity for Government." It was also reasonable to delay suffrage until adulthood and to require residency so that voters would be reasonable and informed. But except for literacy, Hurlbut declared other barriers improper.[139]

Hurlbut noted that every state now agreed that limiting suffrage to property holders was wrong because people had many interests in government, not just property—and American elections proved that though capacity for political participation varied, the system worked. So there was no reason to bar women from voting. Women had no "mental defects" as a class; indeed,

Hurlbut claimed, "It is established by phrenological science that woman is endowed with precisely the same mental faculties as man." He admitted that the power of mental faculties differed: for women, he claimed superior morality, and for men, superior reason. And, he allowed, women "naturally" relied on men for protection and governance. But it did not follow that husbands, fathers, sons, and brothers could truly represent women. Married women's interests were distinct from their husbands' interests when it came to obedience, property, divorce, and child custody—issues that judges in Virginia and New York recognized in Ann Parker Cowper's and Emeline Hunt Shaw's divorces. As Hurlbut saw it, justifications for male suffrage applied equally to women. And as to single, taxpaying women, their rights should be recognized immediately. Unaware of New Jersey's history of women's suffrage, he urged that at first single women should be enfranchised to demonstrate the legitimacy of women's suffrage.[140]

Early in 1848 Hurlbut published his human rights essay, and that summer the Women's Rights Convention at Seneca Falls, New York, attacked the contradictions in American women's citizenship status while demonstrating the increased scope and intensity of the equal rights movement. At Seneca Falls the activists who gathered in July—a mixed-race assemblage of about three hundred women and men—mounted a direct challenge not only to coverture but to the whole structure of laws and customs blocking women's equal rights. Their eleven resolutions and shrewdly crafted "Declaration of Sentiments" asserted women's rights more comprehensively than ever before. Like proponents of women's subordination, advocates for women's equal rights grounded their assertions on the law of nature. The "Creator" had decreed "that woman is man's equal." The Seneca Falls resolutions declared that nature intended for a woman's "station" to be determined by her "conscience" and never to "place her in a position inferior to that of man."[141]

The bold resolutions were complicated by the fact that many American women, perhaps a majority, did not believe in their own equality. So the convention tried to reconcile each woman's "conscience" with equal status. Women who did not recognize their own equality "ought to be enlightened." Moreover, since men generally believed that women possessed "moral superiority," they must acknowledge women's right "to speak, and teach" in religious gatherings, notwithstanding Saint Paul's strictures to the contrary. In addition the double standard regarding virtuous and refined social behavior must end. Men must live by the same moral standard as women, and women must liberate themselves from the "corrupt customs" and "perverted application of Scriptures" that kept them vassals of men.[142]

These resolutions set the stage for the provocative "Declaration of Sentiments" manifesto adopted by the convention. This now-famous document followed the form and language of the Declaration of Independence, adapting it to men's subjugation of women. "We hold these truths to be self-evident," the Seneca Falls declaration proclaimed, "that all men and women are created equal." Now the "long train of abuses and usurpations" was not King George's; it was the work of "man toward woman," intended to achieve "an absolute tyranny over her." To "prove this," the 1848 declaration stated, "let facts be submitted to a candid world." This new declaration listed sixteen grievances, not the twenty-seven claimed in 1776.[143]

The grievances, chiefly by New Yorker Elizabeth Cady Stanton, were urgent. Man's denial of woman's "inalienable right to the elective franchise" headed the list. Consequently women must "submit to laws" in which they had no voice. This was outrageous because suffrage was "given to the most ignorant and degraded men—both natives and foreigners." Men had supplanted the natural equality of the sexes with their law of coverture, making married women "civilly dead," denying property rights, "even to the wages she earns." Man's law discounted women's vaunted moral superiority. It "made her, morally, an irresponsible being," because in her husband's presence a wife could "commit many crimes with impunity." Coverture erased wives' civil existence while diminishing their moral being. Like a child, a wife was "compelled to promise obedience" to a husband who could "deprive her of her liberty" and "administer chastisement." As Ann Parker Cowper knew, the only escapes from marital subjugation, separation and divorce, disregarded "the happiness of women," since children's guardianship went to husbands owing to "the supremacy of man." As for single women, man's government recognized her only when "profitable" by taxing her property.[144]

Men had systematically organized society to guarantee women's sub-servience. They "monopolized nearly all profitable employments" and "closed all the avenues to wealth and distinction," such as the learned professions. Further, men nourished "a false public sentiment" whereby "moral [sexual] delinquencies which exclude women from society, are not only tolerated but deemed of little account to man." Worst of all, man had brainwashed woman so as "to destroy her confidence in her own powers, to lessen her self-respect, and to make her willing to lead a dependent and abject life." By internalizing dependency and submissiveness, women held themselves down.[145]

The sixty-eight women and thirty-two men who signed on to these senti-ments knew that equal rights were an uphill struggle, but despite legal and constitutional obstacles they knew how to influence politics. In April 1848 reformers had won a partial victory when New York's legislature passed a married women's property act ending some of coverture's evils. Now, fol-lowing abolitionist methods, they resolved to "use every instrumentality" available. They would "employ agents, circulate tracts, petition the State and national Legislatures, and endeavor to enlist the pulpit and the press in our behalf." Like conventions of "people of color" organized in the 1830s, they hoped to inspire conventions throughout the United States.[146]

Their resolutions and declaration were not comprehensive. They omit-ted the law making a wife's nationality follow her husband's, which meant when an American woman married a foreigner and left the country, she lost U.S. citizenship. But the convention did address inequalities that touched all free women, and in newspapers the Seneca Falls manifesto reached a wide audience. Moreover, the convention-with-resolutions idea caught on. In 1850 and for a decade women's rights conventions were held almost annually in northern states: Massachusetts, New York, Pennsylvania, Ohio, and Indiana. Their proceedings varied, but the 1850 call to the Ohio Con-stitutional Convention to recognize "the right of suffrage [and] . . . all the political and legal rights which are guaranteed to men" was repeated. That year the National Woman's Rights Convention at Worcester, Massachusetts, resolved, "Women are clearly entitled to the right of suffrage, and to be considered eligible to office." The Worcester reformers included Samuel

J. May, the clergyman who championed Prudence Crandall's school, Jane Swisshelm, who cleverly used Paul's command that women keep silent to justify disobedience to her husband, and Elizabeth Cady Stanton, principal drafter of the Declaration of Sentiments. In the Northeast and where northeastern migrants settled the Old Northwest, the call for women's rights did not win majorities, but it echoed.[147]

When Paulina Kellogg Wright Davis published *The History of the National Woman's Rights Movement* in 1871, she claimed that the convention movement was especially important. Since the 1840s Whig and then Republican politicians had begun to listen to women's rights advocates; consequently the 1862 Homestead Act enabled single women to claim land equally with men. Davis proudly noted that Republican legislatures in Iowa and other western states approved referenda on women's suffrage, and in Kansas even Democrats supported the cause. In 1869 Wyoming and Utah Territories actually enfranchised women.

Moreover, since 1869, Republicans had appointed 1,400 women postmasters; Kansas, Indiana, Iowa, and Missouri had admitted women to the bar; and in Wyoming a woman became a judge. In Albany County, New York, women had served equally with men on both grand and petit juries. Numbers of women pastors and physicians were increasing, and universities in Illinois, Indiana, Iowa and Michigan were now enrolling women, as were Washington University in Saint Louis and Saint Lawrence University in northern New York.[148]

What Davis did not fully acknowledge was the opposition mobilized by the growing women's rights movement. So when Republicans supported a voting rights amendment to the Constitution in 1869 they omitted women, aiming only at discrimination based on race, color, or previous condition of servitude. Republicans had recently begun to embrace women's suffrage, but when a Republican-backed suffrage referendum lost in Kansas in 1867 and New York turned it down, they retreated. President Ulysses S. Grant's narrow victory in 1868 convinced Republicans that their future success could rest on black men's votes, but Kansas's referendum showed that supporting women was too risky.[149]

Republicans chose the path of expediency, not principle. In 1868 this Fourteenth Amendment to the Constitution declared, "All persons born or

Frank Howard's popular song "We'll Show You When We Come to Vote," published in 1869 at Toledo, Ohio, presented a favorable view of women voting. Courtesy, American Antiquarian Society.

naturalized in the United States . . . are citizens of the United States *and* of the State where they reside." And as citizens no state could "abridge" their "privileges or immunities," deprive them of "life, liberty, or property, without due process," or deny them "equal protection of the laws." But by protecting the rights of male citizens only in the second section women's

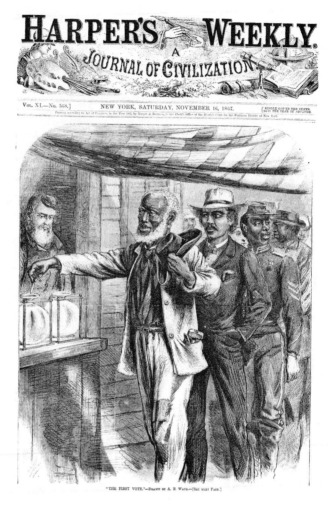

This dignified view of African Americans voting in the conquered
South aimed to give legitimacy to Republican efforts to sustain
equal voting rights. Courtesy, American Antiquarian Society.

rights were denied.[150] Two years later the Fifteenth Amendment, which became law early in 1870, a great landmark for men of color, became a bitter
defeat for women's rights. Elizabeth Cady Stanton and Susan B. Anthony
among many others felt betrayed. They had always believed that educated
white women like themselves deserved equal rights. Their 1848 declaration

had complained that the franchise belonged to "the most ignorant and degraded men—both natives and foreigners"; now they were mortified that
men raised as slaves, not educated as free people, joined that number—
while politically every woman was officially classed with children.[151]

This outcome demonstrated contradictions inherent in Americans' commitment to natural law for their political arrangements. Natural equality
led to conflicting political conclusions: a movement aimed at equal rights
based on natural law could be blocked by invoking natural law. In 1849
the chief justice of Massachusetts' highest court, Lemuel Shaw, ruled that
distinctions based on race, sex, and age were reasonable because they were
natural.[152] Indeed much as Chief Justice Taney had decreed in 1857 that
Revolutionary natural rights theory could not possibly have included people
of color, so Justice Joseph Bradley, a New Jersey lawyer named to the Supreme Court by President Grant in 1870, reasoned that even though Myra
Bradwell was the learned publisher of *Chicago Legal News* and passed
Illinois's bar exam "with high honors," women should be barred from becoming lawyers. His opinion for the Court majority in *Bradwell v. Illinois*
in 1873 upheld the Illinois Supreme Court judgment that "God designed
the sexes to occupy different spheres of action, and that it belonged to men
to make, apply and execute the laws." Only the old Ohio abolitionist Chief
Justice Salmon P. Chase dissented.[153]

Bradley and the majority went further. The Supreme Court presented
a "natural" defense of old coverture principles. Law, "as well as nature,"
Bradley declared, "always recognized a wide difference in the respective
spheres and destinies of man and woman." "Man," he said, was meant to
be "woman's protector and defender." Woman's "natural and proper timidity
and delicacy" made her unfit for many occupations. Bradley claimed that
"divine ordinance, as well as the nature of things," provided that "the domestic sphere . . . properly belongs to . . . womanhood." The very "idea of woman
adopting a distinct and independent career from that of her husband" was
truly "repugnant." The maxim that "a woman had no legal existence separate from her husband, who was regarded as her head," was the bedrock of
coverture, attested by the founders of the Republic. Bradley admitted that
single women were not subjected to coverture, but single women were "exceptional cases." According to "the law of the Creator," the Court opined,

"the paramount destiny and mission of woman are to fulfill the noble and benign offices of wife and mother."

Bradley and his colleagues recognized that some would view their judgment as retrograde, so they offered an apology of sorts. The Court professed to support "the humane movements of modern society . . . for woman's advancement," but only in "occupations adapted to her condition and sex." According to laws of nature, "not every citizen of ever age, sex and condition" was "qualified for every calling and position," so legislatures could properly regulate occupations by sex. Given the natural "destiny, and mission of woman" and man, Illinois properly concluded that the "decision and firmness which are presumed to predominate in the sterner sex"— men—should make law and public affairs a male monopoly. By prohibiting women from becoming lawyers, he argued, Illinois did not abridge "the privileges and immunities of citizens" as protected by the recent Fourteenth Amendment. For although that amendment had defined "all persons born or naturalized in the United States" as citizens, it did not empower women and maintained the standard twenty-one-year age requirement for male suffrage.[154]

VII

The Supreme Court judgment expressed the widespread belief in separate spheres for men and women. It was natural that men should be dominant outside the home and especially in public affairs. So majorities of men together with female collaborators resisted full recognition of women's rights. Ironically, however, four states—Indiana, Iowa, Kansas, and Missouri—had admitted women to the bar before Myra Bradwell's Illinois case came before the Court.[155] And despite the Supreme Court's pronouncement on women's unfitness for law, because the Bradwell decision upheld the right of legislatures to determine qualifications, women in those states would continue to practice law. In these and other western states women breached the wall of exclusion that so often likened their legal status to children. Indeed a few congressmen were ready to recognize women's rights, and when a House of Representatives committee considered Victoria Woodhull's 1871 petition to grant women suffrage based on the Fourteenth and Fifteenth Amendments, Massachusetts and Iowa congressmen supported a resolution "that women citizens, who are otherwise qualified by the laws of the State where they reside, are competent voters for Representatives in Congress." But the resolution failed.[156]

The majority in Congress and the Supreme Court spoke for the nation. The Revolution opened the prospect of equal rights for women theoretically; and as women took their place in the republic of letters, some of them, and a few men, began to press for equal rights in practice. But indifference or outright hostility blocked them, as in the backlash that ended women's voting in New Jersey.

MRS. WOODHULL ASSERTING HER RIGHT TO VOTE.—[FROM A SKETCH BY H. BALLING.]

Harper's Weekly depicted New York City Democrats
denying suffrage to Victoria Woodhull and her colleagues
while a black, an Irish, and a German man, among others,
voted. Courtesy, American Antiquarian Society.

In women's education, however, women's rights gained a major beach-head. Though many believed that a "separate spheres" curriculum would assure male supremacy and female subordination, in fact learning enabled women to challenge men from a more equal position. Like mathematics, geography, and natural philosophy, reason and logic had no gender. So even though law and custom shut women out of electoral politics, legal practice, and public office, women could not be silenced. As consumers and producers of print they rivaled men. And so women, abetted by male reformers, engaged in the temperance, abolition, and evangelical crusades. Then, using the tools of the unfranchised, they developed a full-scale movement. If women could not vote, they petitioned to express their views in state legislatures and Congress. They could not reward or punish legislators with their votes—but they could assert their beliefs in the public forum. And in 1848 the Seneca Falls convention demonstrated the movement's keen grasp of instruments for shaping public opinion: agents, tracts, petitions, the pulpit, and the press.[157]

The achievement was historic. While the national controversy over slavery had become the dominant national political debate, reformers brought women's equality into public discussion. Yet after the Union victory in 1865 resolved the question of slavery, majorities blocked the movement for equal recognition of women's rights. Reformers had begun to hammer at the edifice of patriarchy and coverture, and cracks had begun to appear as wives gained property and custodial rights in one or another state. But the structure stood. When the nation adopted the Fifteenth Amendment, enfranchising black men but leaving women—black and white—as the subjects of men, majorities meant to keep them in their place. Women were subordinate citizens. Three years later the Supreme Court gave its imprimatur. Ending political patriarchy would be a halting, generations-long story.

SEVEN

Equal Rights and Unequal People

All Men are by Nature Equal
But differ greatly in the sequel.
—*Nathaniel Ames*, An Astronomical Diary: or,
Almanack for the Year of Our Lord Christ, 1762 . . . , 1761

I am an aristocrat. I love liberty, I hate equality.
—*John Randolph of Roanoke, Virginia, to Nathan Loughborough, n.d.*

The picture that American society presents is . . .
covered with a democratic finish, beneath which . . .
one sees the old colors of aristocracy showing through.
—*Alexis de Tocqueville*, Democracy in America, 1835–40

Americans have a long-standing romance with the myth that the American Revolution bequeathed the promise of a classless society; yet the facts, they know, are otherwise. Birth mattered then and for succeeding generations. Even though Karl Marx's economic determinism and analysis of social classes have lost favor, most recognize that where one begins life contributes significantly to where one arrives. We doubt that birth and family determine social rank entirely, but hereditary advantages, like wealth and family status, or natural physical attributes, belie the notion that we enter the world equal. Tradition tells us we are equal in the eyes of God, but from a contemporary American perspective—perhaps a second Gilded Age—our equality may exist only in God's eyes.

Yet because social stratification in the United States has been dynamic, the power of the myth and the idea of equal rights have played major roles in shaping American society. Arguably, equal rights doctrine has tilted the United States toward social equality. By rejecting hereditary titles and some statutory privileges, all thirteen states and the U.S. Constitution created a more competitive stratification than Europeans knew. Nevertheless, from the beginning Americans enshrined one profoundly important hereditary privilege in constitutions and laws: private property. They called it a right, not a privilege; but however labeled, the heritability of property ensured a class structure resembling Britain. Except for master and slave—a momentous exception—Americans dispensed with hereditary titles, yet they maintained the structure of hereditary advantages exemplified by slavery and routinely practiced whenever property passed to heirs. As in Britain and Continental Europe, American society was divided between those with property and those without. Just as coverture survived the Revolution to shape gender rights, so did a property relations system that would shape social classes. But in contrast to coverture's erasure of married women's rights, American codes protected legal personhood and civic responsibility for free men. Moreover being propertyless was not a fixed condition; free men could acquire land and chattels. Consequently domestic and foreign observers were struck by American differences from the Old World class system. The vocabulary of republicanism combined with the language and practice of democracy to promote the mythology of a single class of free American people.

Given the realities of 1776 and 1787 this mythology was misleading. First, American law and custom severely curtailed the rights of people of color and women. In addition men had to own property to qualify as voters. Yet because reformers ended this class privilege by 1830, the mythology of classless America gained acceptance. Poor, uneducated, recently arrived immigrants could vote, so the United States was seen as the most democratic of nations. Yet scholars have seldom questioned an aspect of class privilege in American penal codes that challenged the mythology. Class ruled the dual system of punishment for convicts who could and could not discharge debts and pay fines. As with property-based suffrage, reformers abolished imprisonment for debt in the early decades of the nineteenth century. They also ended corporal punishments that had often been based on class: painful humiliation—often whipping—for the poor who could not pay fines or restitution. As with suffrage, post-Revolutionary reforms reinforced the classless idea. The Revolution and its "contagion of liberty" apparently propelled American society toward its democratic ideal.

Alexis de Tocqueville recognized a different reality in 1830, soon after Presidents Adams and Jefferson went to their graves. Tocqueville pointed to the Anglo-American practice of imprisonment or bail payment. "Such legislation," he recognized, "is directed against the poor and favors only the rich." Though ostensibly even-handed, Tocqueville objected that "the poor man does not always find bail, even in civil matters, and if he is constrained to go await justice in prison, his forced inaction soon reduces him to misery." The French aristocrat criticized this system because "the rich man . . . always succeeds in escaping imprisonment in civil matters," while in criminal cases he "easily escapes punishment," since "having furnished bail, he disappears." Tocqueville concluded: "All penalties that the law inflicts on him are reduced to fines." "What," he asked, "is more aristocratic than this?"[1] Because punishments differed based on money, American practice was plutocratic, not aristocratic, but certainly not egalitarian. Tocqueville, keenly aware of class distinctions in post-Revolutionary France, was quick to recognize ancien régime survivals in Jacksonian America.

To Americans, however, abolishing class privilege in voting rights overshadowed persistent class advantages in the justice system. The franchise made common men players in public affairs, courted by political parties. Voting also qualified men as jurors, so continuing class advantages in criminal justice and the bail system could be overlooked. Political parties courted voters, not poverty-stricken convicts, so public rhetoric neglected this disparity.

I

Egalitarian democracy was not the Revolution's legacy. Although American colonists possessed wider access to voting than Britons, every colony required land ownership. This requirement was deeply embedded in Revolutionaries' Whig ideology, a theory constructed around the inseparable bond between individual security and private property.[2] Colonists mobilized to resist Parliament and king because they believed that parliamentary taxation threatened private property, bulwark of their liberty. In theory, only men possessing independent means to provide for their households possessed liberty. If one's bread depended on the will of others, then subjects became dependents or "slaves." Only the procedure of consent could authorize government to take property, to tax. This reasoning sustained colonial voting requirements, usually the English standard: owning real estate earning at least forty shillings annually.

After 1776 the new state constitutions generally retained property requirements. John Adams explained the Revolutionary leadership's view on suffrage when he warned, "It is dangerous to open So fruitfull a Source of Controversy and Altercation, as would be opened by attempting to alter the Qualification of Voters." If voting rights became a matter of public debate, Adams feared, "every Man, who has not a Farthing, will demand an equal Voice with any other in all Acts of State." This, Adams and others schooled in Lockean principles believed would doom the United States to the vices of democracy—demagogy and disorder. Most delegates to the Massachusetts Constitutional Convention in 1779–80 shared this opinion, and when they addressed their "Friends and Countrymen" in the summer of 1780 they gave the reasons for restricting voting rights: "Persons who are Twenty one Years of age, and have no Property are either those who live upon a part of a Paternal estate, expecting the Fee [inheritance] thereof, who are but just entering into business, or *Those whose Idleness of Life and profligacy of manners will forever bar them from acquiring and possessing Property.*" The first group, they argued, would "think it safer for them to have their right of Voting . . . suspended for [a] small space of Time, than forever hereafter to have their Priviledges liable to the *control of Men, who will pay less regard to the Rights of Property because they have nothing to lose.*"[3] Men without property, the Massachusetts delegates explained, could not be trusted.

But not everyone hewed so closely to Whig theory, and some Massachusetts inhabitants complained bitterly. Reacting against the proposed Constitution, one town complained that young men, "neither profligate nor idle," would for years be barred from voting and that other "sensible, honest, and maturely industrious men" who "by numberless misfortunes never acquire and possess [sufficient] property" would also be kept "in some degree [of] slavery."[4] Another town, in a response drafted by the Revolutionary lawyer Joseph Hawley, one-time ally of Samuel and John Adams, argued that the suffrage restrictions were "absolutely repugnant to the genuine sense of the first article of the [Massachusetts] Declaration of Rights [where] . . . all men are declared 'to be born free and equal.'" The restriction meant that although adult men were counted for apportionment, "like brute beasts" they would be denied actual representation. Hawley, writing for Northampton, went further: "Shall these poor adult persons who are always to be taxed as high as our men of property . . . who have gone for us into the greatest perils and undergone infinite fatigues in the present war to preserve us from slavery, . . . some of them leaving at home their poor families, to endure the sufferings of hunger and nakedness, shall they now be treated like villains or African slaves? God forbid!"[5] The fact that Massachusetts's new constitution privileged propertied men for voting and officeholding was misguided according to citizens of Petersham, a later stronghold of Shays' Rebellion: "Riches and Dignity neither make the head wiser nor the heart better." The idle and profligate did not pose the gravest threat facing the new Republic; it was "the overgrown Rich we consider the most dangerous to the Liberties of a free State."[6] Such beliefs led some towns to reject the Massachusetts Constitution of 1780, but these towns were in a minority. As in almost every state, the constitution joined power and property.

The exception was Pennsylvania where, when the Revolutionary government tried to recruit soldiers, "every Man who has not a Farthing" demanded an equal voice in government. Later in many new states militiamen reasoned that if they were citizens to fight, they were citizens to vote. When it came to voting rights, representation, taxation and credit policies, and also public land policies, Americans divided according to interests. As James Madison explained in the *Federalist Papers*, "The most common and durable source of factions has been the various and unequal distribution of property."[7] And representation was the most fundamental right because it would determine who decided policy on every subject.

The role of common householders, "the people," was central. Nearly all leaders before 1820—men who favored the Constitution and those who opposed it, and later Federalists and Jeffersonian Republicans—believed "the people" ought to have the good sense to elect men as guides whose station provided the learning and knowledge of the world, as well as leisure, to conduct public business wisely. But other voices rejected prescribing deference for common men. In the year of independence a New Hampshire pamphlet, *The People the Best Governors; or, A Plan of Government Founded on the Just Principles of Natural Freedom,* laid out a more egalitarian view.

The premise was simple: "*God gave mankind freedom by nature, [and] made every man equal to his neighbor.*" Athenian democracy, not republican Rome, was the proper model: "*Tent makers, cobblers and common tradesmen composed the legislature at Athens,*" and so should "the *honest farmer and citizen*" govern the United States. It was "*the people,*" after all, who "*best know their own wants and necessities*" and so "*are best able to rule themselves.*" Admittedly, "the common people, and consequently their representatives, may not happen to be so learned and knowing as some others," but that did not disqualify from rule. Common men and their representatives might "chuse a council" of more learned men, but only to "advise, and prepare matters for the consideration of the people," not to exercise a veto. Even this learned council would be broadly representative because it would consist of "400 persons."[8]

According to *The People the Best Governors,* the franchise would be almost egalitarian according to 1776 standards. "The freemen of each incorporated town" would vote without regard to the property they owned or taxes they paid. Any requirement above freeman status would "make an inequality among the people, and set up a number of lords over the rest." The same principles applied to representatives. "Social virtue and knowledge," not wealth or lineage, were "the best, and only necessary qualifications." A property requirement for representatives would "root out virtue."[9] *The People the Best Governors* envisioned a yeoman republic according to democratic principles.

Americans understood social class as the division between the few, whose wealth or professions supported them, and the many, whose physical labor supplied their needs. Though this class division sometimes chafed, Americans accepted inequalities of wealth because they were committed to the pursuit of opportunity and the accumulation of property. Few questioned the heritability of wealth or sought its redistribution. Instead they pursued equal opportunity to prosper; they pursued social *in*equality, not leveling.[10] Sometimes there were calls to limit disparities between the few and the many, as when an early version of the Pennsylvania Declaration of Rights warned in 1776 "that an enormous Proportion of Property vested in a few Individuals is dangerous to the Rights, and destructive of the Common Happiness, of Mankind." But Pennsylvania's legislature dropped this language and did nothing to equalize property.[11] Later, in the 1780s, when conflicts between debtors and creditors erupted, friction between the few and the many flared from North Carolina to Maine, resulting in Shays' Rebellion in Massachusetts. Farmers and tradesmen complained when states raised taxes from the many to enrich the few who invested—or speculated—in public debt. Even after the ratification of the U.S. Constitution in 1788 extreme disparities of wealth could be seen as challenging the Republic's health.

Nor was this concern limited to radicals like Thomas Paine. Congressman James Madison, the Virginia planter who shaped the Constitution and steered the Bill of Rights through Congress in 1789, believed that great concentrations of wealth endangered the United States. Madison ranked high among the learned few, but he argued that "a political equality" must be established among all "interests" in "political society." The nation must have no privileged classes. Practically speaking, this meant that government must never award "*unnecessary* opportunities . . . to increase the inequality of property" or support "an immoderate, and especially an unmerited, accumulation of riches." Instead laws should "reduce extreme wealth towards a state of mediocrity, and raise extreme indigence towards a state of comfort." Madison was no leveler: this aim must be pursued "without violating the rights of property." But Madison, like Jefferson and others, believed that Treasury secretary Alexander Hamilton's proposal to consolidate state and Continental Revolutionary War debts in a national debt would "favor one interest"—debt speculators—"at the expense of another"—every taxpaying landowner.[12]

In the states conflicts pitting the few against the many could be sharp. In Connecticut, where a majority were farmers, mechanics complained that the "faculty tax," a head tax laid on them for their skills because they seldom paid taxes on land, violated "the natural and equal rights of man."

Walter Brewster, a shoemaker in Canterbury, tried to rally "Brother Mechanics" in 1791 by denouncing the privileges of men of learning, attorneys especially, written into law. These men, the shoemaker argued, "should be assessed for their faculty to make money faster than mechanics; while they live like gentlemen of leisure." Brewster declared that such propertied men and their sons with "classic education" seldom became mechanics. He did not call learned men parasites, but he railed at their "redundancy." "Priests, Lawyers and Doctors," he complained, "are thick enough to ride two upon a horse." Because of the faculty tax, Brewster protested that men joined the "idle herd of speculating drones, who practice every art on the unsuspecting Peasant." Governor Samuel Huntington and Connecticut legislators deserved blame for taxing mechanics. They showed that "*Might* generally overcomes *Right*." Connecticut was following the "universal tendency of all laws, in all countries, to assist those who have property and power, against those who have none."[13]

Brewster's analysis of Connecticut politics reflected Madison's observation, "Knowledge will forever govern ignorance," leading to the shoemaker's discouraging conclusion:

> This law was made because . . . mechanics in general are poor and illiterate; therefore cannot get the suffrages of the people to sit in the general court [legislature], and this law is calculated forever to keep him out of that office which would enable him to represent himself, and his poor brother mechanics: but should he obtain a seat, it is ten to one if he dare speak, for he is illiterate. But the attorney has language to cloath his ideas in communicative terms, to prepossess the heart through the medium of the ear, and is sure to represent himself and get every thing done which may be to his advantage; and thus we see almost every post of honor and profit filled by attornies.[14]

Brewster called on his "Brother Mechanics" to serve as legislators. In every town they should elect "one mechanic . . . who is a man of reason, and durst advocate his right before the general court." He recognized this remedy was

impossible because although "you are all strong enough, and have property enough to bear assessing" for the faculty tax, you cannot vote because
"you are not all freemen, you have not the requisite property"—the forty-
shilling freehold. Brewster, the disillusioned shoemaker, signed his open
letter to cooper-turned-lawyer Governor Huntington, "A Mechanic, not yet
a Free-Man."[15]

Barred from voting by the property requirement, Walter Brewster and
fellow mechanics could not repeal the poll tax, but they found allies who
labored with their hands and shared their views. Soon after Brewster's complaint a farmer, "A Freeman of the State," made common cause with the
1,400 mechanics from twenty towns protesting a tax that did not give "equal
justice to every Class of People." The legislators had "taken care to clear
themselves from the poll-tax" and all state officials, clergymen, and Yale
faculty and students—"so that this burthen falls principally on the farmer
and the mechanic." According to the colonial era law, the man who sent his
son to Yale paid no tax for that son since the boy was not earning, whereas
artisans and farmers paid tax for sons sixteen years and older, as did laborers
and apprentices.[16] These exemptions smacked of privilege. Nevertheless,
despite the mechanics and farmers' challenge, the law stood. Aggrieved
mechanics and other unfranchised white men won relief only when Connecticut adopted a new constitution in 1818. Now voters were required to be
men and citizens of the United States eligible for militia service or taxpaying men of color.[17]

But even though the privileges of property survived, egalitarian ideas and
mythology flourished. In 1793, before the Jacobin guillotine came to terrify
elite Americans, the New Jersey lawyer and congressman Elias Boudinot
extolled American equality with utopian enthusiasm. Celebrating American independence before his state's hereditary Society of the Cincinnati,
he proclaimed, "The road to honors, riches, usefulness and fame, in this
happy country, is open equally to all." Unlike monarchies with their privileged aristocrats, "the meanest citizen of America, educates his beloved
child with a well founded hope, that . . . he may rationally aspire to the
command of our armies, a place in the cabinet, or even to the filling of
the presidential chair." According to the Philadelphia-born grandson of a

Huguenot immigrant, "he stands on equal ground . . . with the richest of his fellow citizens." In Boudinot's mythical United States "the child of the poorest laborer, by enjoying the means of education (afforded in almost every corner of this happy land) is trained up for, and is encouraged to look forward to a share in legislation." Ironically, in New Jersey the meanest white citizens and laborers could not vote until 1807, and in Connecticut and Massachusetts, the states where poor men could most often provide children with tax-supported education, such citizens would not vote for a generation. Boudinot, who also declared "the Rights of Women . . . are now heard as familiar terms in every part of the United States," pictured an egalitarian ideal, not reality.[18]

One wonders how widely that ideal was shared. That common men shared some egalitarian beliefs is suggested by the 1,400 Connecticut mechanics who petitioned against the poll tax in 1792. But nothing in their petitions suggests that they wanted to extend voting rights to the very poorest people, women, or men of color. Expressions of political ideas from the lower social tiers are rare, but the Shays and Pennsylvania Whiskey Rebellion insurgents, as well as the landlord-tenant battles of the Hudson Valley and Maine frontier, supply convincing evidence that some common men, often possessing little or no property, were convinced that government did not fairly represent them.

But critics' beliefs regarding equal rights were mixed. In the late 1790s William Manning, a middling farmer and owner of 137 Massachusetts acres, saw society as divided between "the few," championed by Federalists, who pursued "monarchy or aristocracy," and "the many," defended by Republicans. Manning shared the widespread hostility to lawyers as "most dangerous to liberty and the least to be trusted of any profession." But in spite of his strong identification with the "many" whose "bodily labors" produced "food, clothing, shelter," he acknowledged that even without physical labor "the merchant, the physician, lawyer and divine, the philosopher and schoolmaster, the judicial and executive officers, and many others" earned their livelihoods "honestly and for the benefit of the community." He was convinced that "one-third part of those [few] that live without labor are true republicans and friends to the rights and liberties of the Many."[19] Though the United States was divided between the few and the many, the separation was far from complete.

Like the author of *The People the Best Rulers*, Manning complained that superior learning enabled the few to exploit "the ignorance and superstition of . . . the Many." They magnified their power by organizing themselves in "Chambers of Commerce," "medical societies," and ministerial and bar associations, while the "turbulent and changing" many were unorganized. Their ignorance made the many vulnerable to manipulation by the learned few. Yet Manning also boasted, "We are the most knowing and the best acquainted with the true principles of liberty and a free government of any people on earth." And although he railed against the disproportionate wealth and power of the few, he admitted that compared with Europe, "we are on an equality as to property."[20] Manning and critics like him did not share Boudinot's inflated mythology of American equal rights and opportunities, but their criticisms expressed their aspiration for its fulfillment.

In time, as states revised their constitutions, equal voting rights became widespread for white men. Although as of 1790 only Pennsylvania and the new state of Vermont (admitted in 1791) had no property requirements, thereafter every new state, from Kentucky (1792), Tennessee (1796), and Ohio (1803) onward did the same. But race restrictions multiplied as, from Ohio onward, every new state barred nonwhites from voting. Congress enacted this new consensus in 1808, ending its 1787 Northwest Territory voting requirement of fifty acres and instead enfranchising all taxpaying free white men—*citizens and aliens alike.* Among the original states, however, property requirements lasted to 1821 in New York and Massachusetts and until 1850 in Virginia. Meanwhile Connecticut (1818), New York (1821), North Carolina (1835), and Pennsylvania (1838) erected racial barriers. So far as white men were concerned, vestiges of privilege touching residency and citizenship remained in few jurisdictions. By the 1840s and 1850s midwestern states, following the territories, enfranchised white aliens even if they were resident for just a single year. Among white men, only "paupers" and felons were widely excluded.[21] By this time, because exclusion of women and people of color now needed defense, voting was often defined as a "social" rather than a "natural" right and sometimes connected to bearing arms to defend the state. By enfranchising white men, slave states reinforced race solidarity in the event of slave uprisings like those of South Carolina's Denmark Vesey in 1822 and Virginia's Nat Turner in 1831. Westerners believed that a generous franchise attracted settlers and raised land values. Democrats saw these opportunities first, but Whigs followed.[22]

Since the 1770s voting rights had been controversial; but for white men movement had been in the direction of equal rights for three generations. But by the middle of the nineteenth century advocacy for blacks, women, immigrants, laborers, and factory workers was generating a backlash. In the Northeast voting "expansionists" faced opposition from "restrictionists who claimed that black, poor, urban, and immigrant voters corrupted democracy. In 1855 and 1857 Connecticut and Massachusetts introduced new requirements aimed at recent, chiefly Irish Catholic, immigrants. Now voters had to be able to read the Constitution and sign their names, though men who had previously voted or were over age 60 were exempted. In addition, though nativists failed to add a fourteen-year waiting period before naturalized citizens could vote, these states introduced a two-year delay following the five-year naturalization process. This new waiting period, fueled by the anti-Catholic nativism of the 1850s, was rescinded in the 1860s as both Republicans and Democrats appealed to new citizens, but the literacy test remained—a device many states would later use to exclude black voters.[23]

The most significant moments in the movement toward equal rights came when the great post–Civil War amendments—the Thirteenth, abolishing slavery; the Fourteenth, requiring equal protection of the laws; and the Fifteenth, stating that "the right of citizens . . . to vote shall not be denied or abridged by the United States or any State on account of race, color, or previous condition of servitude"—won approval in 1865, 1868, and 1870. It is hard to exaggerate their importance. By abolishing slavery without compensation the Thirteenth Amendment terminated a two-centuries-old hereditary class system and erased property rights defended by the Constitution for three generations. And the Fourteenth Amendment, by recognizing the citizenship, national *and* state, of everyone born or naturalized in the United States, explicitly reversed the Dred Scott decision denying negro citizenship. Even more remarkable, and unexpected because black enfranchisement in states had so generally failed, the Fifteenth Amendment prohibited race-based suffrage. The historian Alexander Keyssar reported that a majority of Democrats joined with a minority of Republicans between 1863 and 1870 to defeat black suffrage "in more than fifteen northern states and territories," and during this decade just one state reversed its old policy by enfranchising black men. That was Iowa, which acted by referendum in 1868.[24]

Two years later the Republicans, seeking to assure victories in the South, adopted Iowa's barrier to racial voting tests. By enacting the Fifteenth Amendment the Republican Congress and president created a new Constitutional standard. In exchange for controlling Congress, Republicans accepted white backlash. In 1872 their military hero Ulysses Grant won reelection and Congress remained Republican, but in 1874 Democrats—friendly to immigrants and hostile to people of color—gained control of the House of Representatives, winning majorities of both houses in 1878. Equal rights for *white* men commanded far more support than equal rights for *all* men— or for women. Yet considering the inequalities prevailing in 1776, this movement toward equal voting rights was momentous and provided a foundation for future equal rights measures.

II

The significance of equalization of men's voting rights is striking compared to the uneven history of debtor-creditor relations and, as Tocqueville noted, policies concerning imprisonment for debt. Historically, English and colonial law placed the onus of debt squarely on the debtor. Because debt payment was understood to be a matter of personal honor, the law presumed that delinquent debtors were vicious or fraudulent. By the mid-eighteenth century, however, in Britain and its colonies merchants and lawyers recognized that commercial culture was supplanting honor culture in the marketplace. Investments and trade operated according to calculations of profit and loss more than personal honor. The Milanese reformer Beccaria, whose treatise *On Crimes and Punishments* swept the Atlantic world in the 1760s and 1770s, called imprisonment of honest debtors "barbarous," and some argued that withholding forgiveness from debtors was "unchristian." But the law, sustained by creditor support, possessed a powerful inertia. In England and in several colonies judicial rulings and reformist legislation produced only fleeting alterations of policies that presumed debtor guilt.[25]

Revolutionary economic and political upheavals generated substantial attempts to enable creditors to coerce debtors by threatening imprisonment. At the national level the Treaty of 1783 enabled American debtors to escape paying debts to British merchants because, though the treaty stipulated that "creditors on either side shall meet with no lawful impediment to the recovery of the full value in sterling money of all bona fide debts," British creditors could pursue claims against American debtors only in state courts where debtors held sway. In effect, the treaty erased prewar debts, especially for Chesapeake planters.[26]

In states where merchants were influential, New York and Pennsylvania, reformers actively sought to relieve debtors. A 1784 New York law briefly offered full bankruptcy relief for currently imprisoned debtors, regardless of occupation or size of debt. This law was replaced in 1786 by an act favoring small debtors (those who owed less than £15). They were released from jail, whereas those owing greater sums remained incarcerated. Three years later this prodebtor law was partially reversed: debtors under £10 could be freed only after thirty days in jail, and anyone owing £10 to £200 could not be released unless they assigned their property to creditors, who had to agree to their release. Wealthy debtors disliked assigning their property, because then it could no longer earn needed cash. If the debt was more than £200, the debtor remained in jail. After the number of imprisoned debtors grew, in 1791 the legislature tightened its release policy, raising the barrier to release from £200 to £1,000. By this time, as speculations multiplied the numbers of honest debtor inmates, debtors' benevolent societies formed in New York and Philadelphia to donate food, clothing, and fuel to relieve jailhouse suffering.[27] Reformers also worked to create debtor jails, separate from those for common criminals. Friends of debtors tried to soften the law's impact.

By the time Shays' Rebellion erupted in Massachusetts in 1786 there was no escaping the debtor-creditor conflict. The Massachusetts struggle was in some ways the same clash between the few and the many that played out more peacefully elsewhere; yet Massachusetts insurgents did not repudiate their debts or challenge unequal distribution of property by leveling. Instead they aimed to delay legal proceedings to gain time to pay creditors. The many accepted the legitimacy of debts they owed. Common farmers and artisans were used to living in a web of credit and debt where they were simultaneously lenders and borrowers with neighbors, relying on book credit from merchants. To deny their debts was as alien to their moral economy as being thrown off their land because they could not make timely payment. What was new and disturbing was the extent to which commercial and real estate speculations now put long chains of borrowers and creditors at risk. When someone at the top could not pay his debts, a cascade of defaults spread among merchants and speculators who then wreaked havoc involuntarily by calling in the debts of farmers and tradesmen.

In this marketplace economy unfamiliar principles and priorities ruled. And the contest between debtor and creditor was as likely to be among the wealthy few as between those few and the many. The great speculations of the 1790s, which landed a score of prominent leaders in debtor's prison, led to fresh efforts to change American policy on debt. Recognizing the importance of credit relations for the national economy, the drafters of the Constitution had empowered Congress to establish "uniform Laws on the subject of Bankruptcies throughout the United States."[28] So when, as historian Bruce Mann explains, an "epidemic" of business failures overtook speculators in commercial paper and land, with Philadelphia, the nation's capital, seeing "150 failures in six weeks," and sixty-seven new debtors imprisoned in a two-week period, action seemed imperative.[29] Once the speculative bubble burst, virtually every major speculator went to jail. As of January 1798, Thomas Jefferson, no friend to commercial adventurers but personally familiar with debt, remarked, "The prison is full of the most reputable merchants."[30] Speculation by gentlemen had become so legitimate that insolvency was seen as a business miscalculation, not a moral failure akin to criminal fraud.

As real as the crisis was for some gentlemen, it was less urgent for wealthy debtors because, unlike poor debtors, they were rarely crowded in dirty prisons with criminals. They had alternatives. One was to "keep close" at home where they could not be served with a "bill of attachment" for property. Because writs could not be served on the Sabbath, this mild house arrest allowed debtors to go for religious services or recreation on Sundays. If the debtor was not fearful that his creditors would seize and hold him overnight to serve papers on Monday, he might visit and exercise outdoors. This was the experience of the nation's most prominent debtor, Robert Morris—signer of the Declaration of Independence, Articles of Confederation, and Constitution—who had been superintendent of finance for the Continental Congress and U.S. senator from Pennsylvania. But after avoiding arrest for months on his suburban estate, Morris was finally seized and locked up in Philadelphia's Prune Street jail.

Initially Morris suffered: "I sleep in another persons bed. I occupy other peoples rooms." Having no space assigned to him, he complained that he could not think or write without interruption. But after a week's discomfort he rented the jail's best room and furnished it with a bed, a trunk of clothes, mirrors, writing desks, eight chairs, a settee, and a mahogany table, as well as office equipment, account books, and correspondence, including twenty years' accumulation of papers. In jail Morris could work to straighten out his affairs, and to ease his suffering, his friends sent cases of wine. George Washington visited, and Morris even entertained the former president at dinner in the Prune Street jail room where he dwelled for over two years.[31]

Privileges purchased by wealthy debtors generated resentment visible in newspaper stories about how gentlemen lived in jail. A Philadelphia paper claimed that "a few capital bankrupts" in New York dwelled in apartments "furnished and decorated in a manner that vies with any drawing room." An astonished European discovered that men who "speculated wildly," losing not only their own money but "that of others," now lived "sumptuously" in jail, diverted by visitors and such "pleasures" as music and gaming. "Their whole punishment," he groaned, "consists in not being able to leave the prison."[32]

Conditions were ripe for reform, but divisions among the few and between the few and the many persisted. In Pennsylvania—where much distress centered—legislators allowed their state's bankruptcy law to lapse in 1793, anticipating passage of a uniform national law. But although congressmen drafted bills, they were repeatedly tabled. Predictably the radical Democratic-Republican journalist Benjamin Bache denounced speculators, taking pleasure in their troubles, and many who rejected Bache's politics also believed that speculators should suffer pain. The Massachusetts high Federalist and Speaker of the House Theodore Sedgwick, a friend of Washington and some jailed investors, declared that "he was not sorry that the bubble of speculation has burst." People like Sedgwick opposed legislative relief for all debtors, rich or poor. And those who, like Bache, wanted to relieve poor debtors, "men who produce by their industry," were unwilling to give a free pass to the few who got rich "by their *art* and *cunning*."[33]

The jailing of Morris and such notables as Supreme Court Justice James Wilson concentrated Federalist minds wonderfully, enabling them to stumble, haltingly, toward a law. During 1798 Congress debated a bankruptcy bill to relieve large commercial debtors. But though most Federalists supported it, the bill lost narrowly in the House because some southerners opposed. Consequently Federalists introduced a new bill at the beginning of 1800.[34]

The partisan and sectional cauldron in which Congress created the Bankruptcy Act of 1800 ignored poor debtors. Instead debates revolved around expansion of national power and the conflicting interests of southern landed gentlemen and northern businessmen. Federalists wanted the bankruptcy law to enhance the national government and judiciary, but they needed to accommodate landed southern Federalists, who defended state barriers to the seizure of debtors' land, as well as New Englanders who feared the act would weaken state laws for attaching debtors' property. No one represented poor debtors when Sedgwick worked out a compromise. Landed property would lose protection by closing a loophole that allowed debtors to protect assets by shifting them into land; however, bankruptcy judgments could be made by local juries, instead of a federal judge. Moreover the law would be temporary, expiring after five years.

Even after these accommodations, opponents who defeated the previous bankruptcy bill almost won. Speaker Sedgwick brought the Bankruptcy Act to vote when several opponents were absent but still lost his majority when eleven Federalists voted with the Republicans. Acting to break a tie, Sedgwick's vote carried the bill in the House. In the Senate, with difficulty, it also passed. Consequently traders, merchants, and brokers and who owed at least a thousand dollars could be forced into bankruptcy proceedings. Practically speaking, bankers and businessmen in Boston, New York, and Philadelphia could now collect from their counterparts in states like Kentucky and Tennessee.[35] The few enacted a bankruptcy bill for the few. The many would have to wait.

Indeed a durable national policy on bankruptcy would wait a full century. For even the temporary act of 1800 proved so unpopular that the Republican majority promptly repealed it. No bankruptcy law would again pass Congress until 1841, when Whigs controlled government.[36] That legislation proved even more ephemeral, being repealed in a year. In the states debtor-creditor politics were so interwoven with other issues that no national policy could succeed.

The plight of poor debtors remained bleak; improvement came slowly. Imprisoned New York City debtors celebrated the bankruptcy law of 1800, but it did nothing for them. Within the prison William Keteltas, a lawyer jailed for debt, briefly published a newspaper, the *Forlorn Hope*, giving voice to poor debtors. Keteltas argued that debtors were treated more harshly than criminals, who were fed and clothed, sometimes taught trades, and served fixed sentences; debtors, by contrast, were held for uncertain periods and required to pay for food and clothing. "Misfortune," it was said, "was no crime," yet a March 1800 jailhouse visitor found "eleven persons, confined in one room . . . who declared they had been four days without a morsel to eat." Lacking money for food, "nor friends to procure, even the means of food," they might have starved but for the intervention of the prison keeper and the Humane Society. For in New York, unlike some states, a creditor who jailed his debtor was not required "to pay a small pittance for his [the debtor's] support." Yet according to the *Forlorn Hope*, in New York "the unfeeling creditor may famish him [the debtor] to death."[37]

The New York prisoners had offered a July 4, 1799, toast wishing that "imprisonment for debt and personal slavery, solecisms [errors] in the chapter of American rights and privileges," would be no more. But no single law or court decision ended imprisonment for debt in the United States. Amelioration was a gradual process, propelled in part by creditors' and courts'

Forlorn Hope, a newspaper briefly published out of the New York City debtors' prison, sought reforms by appealing to the humane feelings of prosperous New Yorkers. Courtesy, American Antiquarian Society.

recognition that imprisonment for debt was expensive and ineffective. Nevertheless as Tocqueville observed, the system persisted. By the twentieth century American courts no longer imprisoned private debtors to satisfy private creditors, but they continued to imprison people who could not pay public fines or penalties—a practice that continues in spite of Supreme Court rulings in 1970, 1971, and 1983 declaring that imprisonment in lieu of paying a fine or court costs when a person cannot pay violates the equal protection clause of the Fourteenth Amendment.[38]

III

Given the British legal heritage and the primacy of property rights for Americans, one might expect wealth and social status to shape criminal law as well as debtor-creditor policies in the early Republic. Paradoxically, however, monarchy's defenders had long boasted that regardless of social rank every British subject was equal before the law, especially in criminal matters. The hanging of Lord Ferrers in 1760 for murdering his steward reinforced this mythology, as did the 1777 execution for forgery of William

Dodd, chaplain to King George III and tutor to the Earl of Chesterfield. In spite of Dodd's high clerical rank and aristocratic connections, and notwithstanding an unprecedented petitioning campaign in which twenty-three thousand Englishmen petitioned to save the fashionable clergyman, a crowd of thousands watched Dodd's ignominious hanging at Tyburn. Just as the occasional execution of an aristocrat in the seventeenth century fed the notion that no man was above the law in English justice, Dodd's punishment propelled the myth for later generations.[39] Ironically, forty years before Dodd's hanging, his friend Samuel Johnson penned ironic lines on the courtroom disparity between rich and poor: "All crimes are safe, but hated Poverty. This, only this, the rigid Law pursues."[40] Less genteel folk

David Claypool Johnston's sketch of a poor mother being turned away heartlessly suggests the boundary between the poor and the prosperous in Boston in the 1830s. Courtesy, American Antiquarian Society.

used ballads and newspaper satire to rail against the advantages wealth and rank enjoyed at the bar of justice.

In the United States poverty was more often understood as a temporary condition than in Britain, and the poor constituted a smaller proportion of free people. Moreover the distance between the wealthy and middle-class farmers and artisans was narrower. The boundary between the few and the many was substantial in the new Republic, but it was blurred and porous. Consequently Americans widely accepted the myth that theirs was a land of equal justice. American courts regularly supplied poor defendants with prominent attorneys in capital cases, and occasionally governors and legislatures reversed convictions of the poor or pardoned them. Yet no one claimed that American criminal courts *always* meted out equal justice, so the question of impartial justice was always present.

One cannot determine how often American criminal courts dispensed justice fairly, providing equal rights to defendants. Comparisons among criminal cases cannot be exact because circumstances were too various—the facts and their contexts, the defendant(s), the witnesses, evidence, the law, and court officials, including judges, prosecutors, defense attorneys, and jurors. Nevertheless criminal trials are instructive for assessing whether different classes of people possessed equal rights. Capital cases can be especially revealing because their gravity demanded the most from court officials and commanded public scrutiny. Though precise assessments are beyond reach, considering when courts operated impartially and when they did not is instructive.

When respectable white men faced accusations of murdering members of their own class they could not expect preferred treatment. Public opinion no less than duty demanded rigorous prosecutions. Like poor men, respectable defendants could expect prominent attorneys to defend them. Consequently, just as the prosecutor tried the defendant's character, defense attorneys challenged the victim's character. In the 1801 case of twenty-one-year-old Jason Fairbanks, convicted for murdering his eighteen-year-old girlfriend, Elizabeth Fales, both belonged to respected families. The prosecutor, Massachusetts attorney general James Sullivan, could not disparage Fairbanks's social rank because he came from the property-owning class of the jurors—but he could assign to Fairbanks the stereotypical faults of privileged youth, idleness and dissipation. Fairbanks's chief defender, the prominent Boston attorney Harrison Gray Otis, had just returned from Congress. Like Sullivan, he could not criticize the victim's origins because she enjoyed a reputation for virtue in the same social class. So Otis used romantic novels to diminish her character. Elizabeth was, he claimed, so disappointed by her romance with Fairbanks that she took her own life. Casting doubt on this suicide narrative were the nine or more fatal wounds to her chest, arms, back, throat, and thumb—all inflicted with the dull two-and-a-half-inch blade of Fairbanks's penknife. Fairbanks himself suffered multiple wounds from that knife due to what he said was his own suicide attempt.[41]

The jury spent all night weighing the attorneys' eloquence and the evidence. Fairbanks's defender, Otis, constructed his defense based on class, portraying the young man as a tragic victim. "The piety and exemplary virtues of his parents . . . his early education under virtuous preceptors—the habits and character of the village—his own character without a stain—even the character of *the nation*" argued against the guilt of "this stripling." Convicting Jason would condemn not only the "*unhappy* youth" but his family and community. Responding, prosecutor Sullivan stripped away class and community, describing Jason as "a person of great depravity of morals. . . . He had a heart void of social duty, and [he was] fatally bent on mischief." The justices were silent regarding the defendant's class and character when they charged the jury, but they declared it impossible for the victim to wound herself in the back "in place and form as described by the witnesses." Perhaps this last fact—not class or character—was decisive. After nightlong deliberations, the jury delivered a unanimous guilty verdict.[42] Though the prisoner's defenders invoked class solidarity for their client, they failed. The victim was equally respectable and truly virtuous. Thirty years later in a similar New Jersey case, a master stonemason, twenty-nine-year-old Joel Clough, was convicted for the fatal stabbing of a virtuous twenty-eight-year-old widow, Mary Hamilton, after she spurned his marriage proposal. Like Fairbanks and Fales, Clough and Hamilton were both respectable, so the fact that Clough possessed genteel manners did not make his insanity defense persuasive, though after the verdict the judge told Clough that jurors, his social equals, "most ardently and fervently desired to find you innocent."[43]

Even-handed justice seemed especially prized when perpetrator and victim shared elevated status. Such cases commanded the closest public scrutiny, putting the criminal justice system itself on trial. One notorious example was the 1830 murder trial of men from leading families in Salem, Massachusetts, a seaport of fourteen thousand residents. Two defendants were twenty-six-year-old Richard Jr. ("Dick") and twenty-four-year-old George, sons of Richard Crowninshield and born at the apex of Salem's merchant aristocracy. As nephews of deceased Congressman Jacob Crowninshield and his brothers Benjamin and George, one a member of Congress and former secretary of the navy, the other a shipping magnate, Dick and George Crowninshield were Salem aristocrats. Their father, Richard, youngest of these Crowninshield brothers, was a woolen manufacturer who married an Irish hotel maid. According to his clergyman, William Bentley, who boarded in another Crowninshield household, Richard Crowninshield was a one-time bankrupt involved in a "fraudulent conveyance." When one of Richard's daughters eloped "with two Irishmen," the clergyman was appalled. The Crowninshields were distinguished and wealthy, but Bentley believed that "this family exhibit something yet unknown in this part of the country for want of domestic economy, education of children, management of affairs & conduct among their servants and neighbors."[44] Less than a dozen years after Bentley's observation the next generation was at the center of a shocking murder mystery.

The other two respectable gentlemen, twenty-seven-year-old Joseph Jenkins Knapp Jr. and his twenty-year-old brother John Francis ("Frank") Knapp, came from lower in the same social circle. Their father, a ship captain and merchant of modest pedigree, sent Joseph Jr. to sea as a teenager before making him, at age twenty, master of a ship. He became such an accomplished mariner that at age twenty-two Joseph Jr. was admitted into Salem's East-India Marine Society, which normally required mastering a ship from Salem to the Indies. Now he sailed for one of Salem's wealthiest merchants, old Captain Joseph White. White had employed his father, Joseph Sr., loaned him money, and sold the father his old house. But in 1827 when Joseph Knapp Jr. married White's grandniece, Mary Beckford, the old captain pronounced him a fortune hunter, vowing to cut the Beckfords out of his will.[45] It would be Captain White's fortune—made partly in the slave trade after Massachusetts outlawed slaving in 1788—that led to murder.[46]

Joseph's younger brother, Frank, was friendly with the Crowninshield brothers, Dick and George. In 1827 they encouraged Frank, then seventeen, to steal three hundred dollars from his father to finance a vacation to New York City. After spending that money, the three young gentlemen tried theft, but they were arrested and jailed.[47] Evidently their fathers, Crowninshield and Knapp, secured their release—demonstrating privilege at work. The three then separated, but by 1830 Frank, Dick, and George had returned to Salem and neighboring Danvers, and none had found a career. Now Captain Joseph Knapp's business was sliding into bankruptcy, and Captain White owned his mortgage.[48] So when Joseph Jr. learned that White's new will cut off his Beckford in-laws, he determined to steal and destroy that will. Captain White's death would then erase his father's debt and make his mother-in-law and wife rich. So after pilfering and destroying a copy of the will, Joseph Jr. enlisted Frank in a plot to murder the captain. But the Knapp brothers hesitated to do the killing; White was their neighbor and kinsman, and their family lived in his former house. Yet they felt no fondness for White—decades earlier the Reverend Bentley had called him a "horrid" man—and so they offered the Crowninshield brothers a thousand dollars to do the deed.[49] The Crowninshields had no association with Captain White and no motive to attack him. They would not be suspected.

On April 6, 1830, eighty-two-year-old Captain Joseph White was bludgeoned and stabbed to death in his bed. No arrests were made. But a week later a letter arrived accusing the Crowninshields, who were promptly jailed. Later still Joseph Knapp Sr. received a blackmail letter touching his sons, and because his son Joseph Jr. dismissed it, the trusting father handed it over to the authorities. When the blackmailer was later identified and questioned, he testified that he had overheard the Crowninshields discussing the Knapps' plan to murder White. Now the Knapp brothers joined the Crowninshields in the Salem jail.[50]

The trials that followed—two for Frank Knapp and one each for Joseph Knapp Jr. and George Crowninshield, represented the state's effort to convict Captain White's murderers notwithstanding a variety of legal tangles created by the four-part conspiracy wherein one principal, Dick Crownin-shield, committed suicide in jail, and another, Joseph Knapp Jr., confessed to a clergyman in exchange for a doubtful offer of immunity from prose-cution—a confession he retracted. So eager was the seventy-nine-year-old Massachusetts attorney general Perez Morton to win convictions that he accepted the offer of Captain White's nephew and heir, Stephen White, to pay Senator Daniel Webster a thousand dollars to lead the prosecution. Ear-lier that year Webster had famously proclaimed in Congress: "Liberty and Union, now and forever, one and inseparable!" Webster was at the height of his oratorical powers, and his summary speech at the trial gained lasting fame among lawyers.[51]

The trials occupied summer and fall in 1830, commanding extensive newspaper coverage in New England and the nation. The Salem court-room was packed, and crowds surrounded the courthouse. Reportedly, Webster "literally sent a thrill through the veins of those who heard him."[52] But as murder details emerged, the clamor for guilty verdicts clashed with legal procedures. So when Frank Knapp's trial ended in a hung jury on Friday, August 13, some demanded the names of jurors who voted to acquit. Lawyers, too, were targeted because they argued technicalities so "that a rogue should entirely escape." Consequently, when the defense asked to postpone the retrial, the judges denied the request, ordering Frank Knapp to stand trial again the next day.[53]

Few were surprised when Frank Knapp's weeklong second trial led to conviction and a death sentence. That his brother testified, "Frank told me two or three times that I had better let the business alone," counted for naught. Knapp's defense attorney argued that "the community was against" his client, and a Massachusetts newspaper reported that "judicious profes-sional men, . . . witnesses of the state of feeling in Salem," believed that "*street discussion* of the evidence" shaped the verdict. So if strict legal stan-dards were the measure of a fair trial, Knapp's rights were sacrificed. Pub-lic opinion decided that fastidious adherence to legal rules would allow a gentleman to get away with murder.[54]

After Frank Knapp's conviction, his older brother's condemnation was almost certain, since the evidence against him was even stronger. When the judges ruled that Joseph Jr.'s jailhouse confessions could be entered as evidence, his defense collapsed. A Boston newspaper commented: "There is, of course, no chance for the prisoner—and there certainly appears to be no sympathy for him." As with Frank, the jury found him guilty, and the public was satisfied.[55] The state had now sent two sons of a ship master and merchant—brothers of a Harvard-educated lawyer—to the gallows. And one from the distinguished Crowninshield family had, as Daniel Webster put it, confessed his guilt by committing suicide.[56]

Immediately after Joseph Knapp Jr.'s conviction, the fourth member of the gentlemen's quartet, George Crowninshield, came to trial. Like Frank Knapp, George was tried twice, but he escaped death. He came to trial right after Joseph's sentencing, seven months after Captain White's murder, five months since Dick's suicide, and seven weeks after Frank Knapp's execution. Public excitement had moderated, and the case against George depended on a single disreputable witness, the Knapps' blackmailer, a convict who had served two years in Maine for breaking and entering. Since even he could not place the George near the murder scene and several witnesses swore that the prisoner had been elsewhere the night of the crime, the jury doubted that George Crowninshield was an accessory to murder. His acquittal was greeted "by the cheering of a portion of the spectators."[57]

Still Attorney General Morton pursued George, immediately charging the congressman's nephew with "misprision of Felony, or concealment of the knowledge, before and after the fact with a wicked and malicious purpose." At this point Crowninshield's elite status won the preferred treatment Tocqueville criticized: he was released on his own recognizance on a five-hundred-dollar bond his father guaranteed. George's bail "excited great astonishment among many people" because it was "too low, [and made] for the very purpose of enabling him to clear the coast."[58] And if the Crowninshields were not confident of a second acquittal, perhaps George would have fled rather than face prison. But George did not flee. Two weeks later he stood trial for the lesser offense of misprision, and the jury took just thirty minutes to find him "NOT GUILTY."[59] Passions had cooled, and George Crowninshield's class status arguably helped keep him out of prison.

But perhaps, as the jury determined, it was impossible to *prove* him guilty since his brother was dead. In his final jail-cell letter to George, the guilty

Richard not only asked forgiveness for "what I have caused you" but prayed that his younger brother's "innocence" would keep him "safe through this trial!" One observer remarked, "All knew he [George] had been led astray by Richard who had acquired absolute control over him from his youth." Some concluded that George was merely a follower and that since three perpetrators had already died he did not require further punishment. Less than a year later his neighbor Nathaniel Hawthorne reported, "George Crowninshield still lives at his father's and seems not at all cast down by what has taken place. I saw him walk by our house, arm-in-arm with a girl."[60]

Twenty years later an even more sensational elite murder fascinated a national audience. The jurisdiction was again Massachusetts, and the site was Boston, the nation's third largest city with 137,000 inhabitants. The victim was the hugely wealthy fifty-four-year-old bachelor Dr. George Parkman, an austere, thrifty workaholic. Parkman, a Harvard graduate, did medical training in Europe, where he studied mental illness. After serving as a surgeon during the War of 1812, Parkman persuaded Bostonians to create a mental hospital under his supervision. But when the Massachusetts General Hospital took over his asylum, it let Parkman go.[61] Then after his father died, making him executor of a vast estate, Parkman managed real estate investments and moneylending, chiefly mortgages. An active philanthropist, Parkman assisted the poor and the sick and donated land for Harvard's medical school. A fellow physician, Dr. Oliver Wendell Holmes, dean of Harvard Medical College, said of Parkman, "He abstained while others indulged, he walked while others rode, he worked while others slept." Master of a "princely fortune," Parkman lived modestly in his grand, four-story family mansion.[62]

One of Parkman's borrowers was his old friend fifty-nine-year-old Dr. John White Webster, like Parkman a physician and Harvard College graduate. In 1837 Parkman had recommended Webster's appointment as professor of chemistry and mineralogy at Harvard Medical College. Webster, too, came from a wealthy Boston family, although the fortune was more recent and smaller than Parkman's. And unlike Parkman, Webster lived extravagantly, building a Cambridge mansion after inheriting fifty thousand dollars in 1834. Although successfully employed as a professor and physician, Webster lost his mansion to creditors and by the 1840s was renting a house and borrowing to pay the bills. With a wife who gave expensive parties and three unmarried daughters to present in Boston society, Webster lived way beyond his means.[63]

Webster might have continued on had Parkman not learned early in November 1849 that the mineral collection Webster pledged to him as collateral for a loan was already pledged to support another loan. This fraudulent double-pledging outraged Parkman, and, old friend or not, he demanded immediate payment of his overdue loan. So when Webster asked Parkman to meet him at his medical college laboratory on Friday, November 23, 1849, the professor faced a strong-willed, righteous benefactor and creditor. According to Webster, Parkman demanded full payment and promised that otherwise he would use his influence to sack the professor. Parkman threatened to ruin Webster professionally, crushing him and his family socially and financially.[64]

Webster answered Parkman's demands with a two-foot piece of wood, clubbing his head so hard that Parkman fell bleeding and lifeless. When Webster realized that he had killed Parkman, he locked his laboratory door and, cutting the corpse apart, disposed of the remains in his laboratory. Then he returned to Cambridge and a party at another professor's house.[65] The next day, Saturday, Parkman's family called for a search. That evening, Webster read of Parkman's disappearance, so, conscious that several people knew he had met with Parkman, he covered his tracks by telling police the next day that after their meeting Parkman had said he was going to Cambridge. The following day a Parkman kinsman offered a three-thousand-dollar reward for anyone who could find Parkman alive. Because he was last seen at the medical college, Boston police concentrated on the college building and its neighborhood, where the missing man had many poor Irish tenants who might have killed their rent-collecting landlord.[66]

That week police visited Webster's laboratory twice, coming away suspicious, though lacking evidence. But the janitor, Ephraim Littlefield, was even more suspicious. He had seen Parkman enter the building and had earlier heard the two men arguing. So when, five days after Parkman's disappearance, Littlefield saw one of the twenty-eight thousand reward notices promising a thousand dollars "for information that leads to the recovery of his body," the janitor turned sleuth. Two days later, having chiseled through five layers of brick, he found major body parts in Webster's privy. Consequently the police arrested Webster who, after asking if they had found "the *whole* of the body," went on to exclaim, "I am a ruined man!" before swallowing a strychnine pill.[67] After collecting additional evidence, the attorney general brought a murder indictment to a grand jury that unanimously voted Webster must stand trial.

According to twenty-first-century standards Dr. Webster could not have received a fair trial anywhere near Boston. Parkman's murder, like Captain Joseph White's, demanded redress for an assault on respectable Massachusetts. And with extensive newspaper coverage and local gossip broadcasting grisly facts and rumors to eager audiences, the public rushed to judgment. As scraps of information accumulated, enterprising printers kept the public abreast of the case.

Early in 1850 one pamphleteer issued a pretrial verdict on Webster, *The Boston Tragedy! An Expose of the Evidence in the Case of the Parkman Murder!* Based chiefly on leaks from the coroner's and grand juries, it presented significant evidence against Webster and attacked his character. Webster failed to honor provisions in his father's will directing an annual payment of $50 to an orphaned "near relative" who was receiving public support in the almshouse—an $800 cumulative default—though Webster's $1,900 Harvard salary was supplemented by payments from his father's estate. Moreover his religious beliefs were offensive: "Webster is a professed materialist—believing only in human existence, and, at death, annihilation of the soul." The great lawyer Rufus Choate, it was said, refused the professor's defense because he "thought Webster's a desperate case." And Senator Daniel Webster had reportedly declined a $2,000 defense fee. Moreover, though the pamphleteer did not know it, Charles Francis Adams and Charles Sumner also refused to defend Webster, as did Congressman Benjamin Curtis, soon to be appointed to the U.S. Supreme Court where he would dissent from Taney in *Dred Scott.* According to the pamphlet, Massachusetts governor George Briggs, a lawyer and twelve-year congressman, had asserted that "he could come to no other conclusion than that Webster was a guilty man." Webster had friends, and the New York *Herald* called Massachusetts's proceedings "star-chamber-like" and Boston's police "stupid, foolish and imbecile." But the *Expose* concluded that "the facts . . . will startle everybody, and the confessions of Mr. Webster at the time he was arrested, will convince the jury and the world that he is guilty."[68] Given this local judgment, convincing jurors of Webster's innocence would prove an enormous challenge.

To defend Webster the Massachusetts Supreme Judicial Court, which tried all capital cases, appointed Pliny Merrick, a fifty-five-year-old former judge who would soon join their bench, and Edward D. Sohier, like Merrick an experienced Harvard graduate. Given the assertions that their client was the last person to see Parkman alive and that body parts were discovered in Webster's laboratory, Merrick and Sohier did not deny all possibility that Webster killed Parkman; instead, they cast doubt on that conclusion. The human remains in the laboratory might not be Parkman's, and they brought witnesses who testified that they saw Parkman *after* he left Webster's laboratory. The prosecution's evidence, they argued, was merely circumstantial and inconclusive. Their blue-ribbon witnesses swore that Webster's character and temperament could not be murderous.[69]

But recognizing the facts that Attorney General John H. Clifford would present, including evidence emphasizing Webster's motives, and the implausible, inconsistent, and self-serving portions of the professor's account, Merrick and Sohier presented a "fallback" argument of possible manslaughter to save Webster's life. If the jury concluded that Webster killed Parkman in an angry outburst, without malicious intent, his crime was manslaughter, not murder, and jurors could imprison instead of hanging him. Webster seemed confident of acquittal; but his lawyers were duty-bound to present arguments enabling jurors, mostly tradesmen, to convict Webster merely of homicide, not murder. With anti-death-penalty sentiment powerful in Massachusetts, this was prudent. One prosecutor was ambivalent about executions, and one juror explicitly opposed capital punishment though, when questioned, "did not think his opinions would interfere with his doing his duty as a juror."[70]

The trial lasted eleven days, and so many people wanted to watch it that the sheriff issued tickets allowing tens of thousands of men and women a ten-minute glimpse of the proceedings.[71] Prosecution lasted seven days and presented dozens of witnesses. Though the defense challenged some circumstantial evidence effectively—the body parts might not be Parkman's—the quantity and specificity of prosecution testimony put Webster's lawyers at a grave disadvantage. Their witness list was much shorter, and though they brought eminent men to testify for Webster's character and temperament, they depended more on rhetoric than on evidence during their two-day defense.

When the jury found Webster guilty after only a couple of hours, criticism of the trial came quickly—especially from New York and Philadelphia. A New York City lawyer argued that the defense attorneys tried to curry favor with the court and Boston's bar instead of freeing their client. They blundered by introducing manslaughter instead of denying Webster's role in the homicide. They should have played up social class by pointing suspicion at the janitor who had access to Webster's laboratory. In Massachusetts the anti-capital-punishment crusader Lysander Spooner attacked the court's exclusion of three death penalty opponents from the jury. The court thus "packed" the jury against Webster, denying his right to a jury selected from the community that included capital punishment opponents. For like-minded people this argument, though contrary to standard policy and majority opinion, was decisive.

More telling was lawyers' criticism of Chief Justice Shaw's treatment of "reasonable doubt" and the distinction between manslaughter and murder in his charge to the jury. Prosecutors and judges routinely explained that "reasonable doubt" did not mean all possible doubt. But Shaw emphasized circumstantial evidence—telling the jurors that if a consistent chain of evidence led to "a reasonable and moral certainty," they could convict. Critics charged that there was no consistent chain of evidence.[72]

Chief Justice Shaw's explanation of murder was not new. Lacking contrary evidence, he explained, English precedent and his own ruling five years earlier, said that malicious intent could be implied from a defendant's motives and actions before, during, and after the assault. But according to Harvard Law School professor Joel Parker, this reasoning reversed the sacred standard of presumed innocence, because instead of requiring the prosecution to prove malice, the defendant would need to prove its absence.

In addition the example Shaw gave—the use of chloroform—was heavily criticized. Shaw appeared to suggest that Webster used chloroform; though Shaw may have preferred to avoid illustrating his point by repeating the prosecution's argument of murder with a wooden club. Chief Justice Shaw had come to prominence in the rough, argumentative world of politics and law, but rarely had his pronouncements met with such sharp criticism.[73]

Following Webster's conviction, sympathy for the condemned man surged, and 2,200 men and women petitioned to commute his sentence, including 1,476 New York State opponents of the death penalty and others as distant as Michigan. Critics in New York and Philadelphia denounced the proceedings as reminders of Puritan persecution of witches and Quakers. The rising Harvard Law graduate Stephen H. Phillips wrote in the *Massachusetts Monthly Law Reporter* that because Webster was so prominent, "it was very easy to raise a cry against the Court if any unusual leniency should be shown to him." Public opinion, Phillips claimed, "forced the Court into THE OPPOSITE EXTREME." Public order required authorities to solve the crime quickly with "a verdict as would correspond with public opinion." Consequently "the intensity of public excitement prevented a fair trial." One commentator claimed that justice "had been seriously prejudiced by his [Webster's] social position": the desire "not so show him any undue favor on account of it, has unconsciously operated to deprive" Webster of the sympathy given to "criminals of a different rank."[74]

Contemporary critics properly argued that the trial was flawed. But Webster's confession after his conviction, when he hoped for a pardon, left no doubt that he committed homicide if not murder and tried to hide it. Social class raised the public profile of the case. The victim's high status led to aggressive prosecution, while the defendant's comparable stature cut two ways. Because Webster was well born, wealthy, and an accomplished insider in Boston, he enjoyed support from prominent friends at the trial, including Harvard's president. Afterwards a dozen or more Boston notables petitioned to save his life. Simultaneously the popular demand for "equal justice" prohibited the appearance of favoritism for the Harvard professor. Yet had circumstances been otherwise and Parkman's killer been one of his poor Irish-born tenants, as was briefly rumored, "Paddy's" conviction and execution would never have generated comparable public attention, sympathy, or clemency petitions. Criminal trials could be sites for the expression of equal rights, but whether they were that—or occasions for class privilege and political advocacy—depended on the case, the crime and its locality, the participants, and the trial jurisdiction.

An 1827 homicide in Pierstown, New York, a hamlet near Cooperstown, illustrates how justice could operate when a farm and sawmill owner, Levi Kelley, killed his tenant. Kelley, a nephew of town founder William Cooper and first cousin of novelist James Fenimore Cooper, was a "reputable" forty-seven-year-old "in easy circumstances" who owned a sawmill, a house and barn, woodland, and meadow as well as horses, cows, hogs and sheep. Kelley's father, an Irish immigrant to Philadelphia, had married William Cooper's sister Ann, but his death left her with three sons in 1787, the oldest being seven-year-old Levi. Assisted by Squire Cooper, the family moved to Cooperstown, where in 1802 Levi purchased a village lot from his uncle for fifty dollars. Trained as a cabinetmaker and joiner, the ambitious Kelley bought a half-interest in a saw mill for five hundred dollars in 1810. By 1816 he prospered sufficiently to buy a half-interest in another saw mill on seventy acres in neighboring Middlefield for two thousand dollars. By the 1820s Levi, married but without children, achieved modest success. His household included emblems of gentility—a high-post bed, a secretary desk, a tall clock, and a "Library of Books." Kelley also owned a gun.[75]

His victim, Abraham Spafard, was a forty-eight-year-old Connecticut native. With his wife, Sally, Spafard had lived with fifteen different families before moving into a room in Kelley's house with their children in April 1827.[76] After a few months the short-tempered Kelley was finding fault with his tenant—a tree cut down to repair a wagon, damage to a wooden gate, a two-dollar debt, and, most explosively, Spafard's unloading oats in the "wrong" part of Kelley's barn. Spafard explained he had not known where Kelley wanted the oats, but Kelley responded, "It is your business to come and ask me—I'm at the helm, remember, and you must do to please me." After Spafard apologized, Kelley made other complaints, shaking his fists. Spafard then cautioned Kelley not to "get in such a passion." Kelley's retort: "There is no harm in it as long as I don't touch you." But Spafard worried:

"I fear you will get so angry as to bring out your gun: you brought it out the other night to shoot my brother, I fear you will now bring it out to shoot me." Yet the conflict appeared finished.

Soon after Spafard went into his room for dinner, Kelley entered asking for John Clark, the twenty-year-old who that day worked for Spafard. Then Spafard's daughter "came running in" to report that Kelley was scuffling with Clark. "Father," she exclaimed, "Kelley will kill John: do go in and part them." So Spafard left dinner, entering Kelley's part of the house saying, "Stop, stop! let go of John." Kelley replied, "I won't. What! do you come into my house, d——n you?" Then, as Kelley held Clark "by the throat . . . up against the chimney," Spafard repeated, "Let go of him; you must not hurt him; he has been working for me, and I will not see him abused." When Kelley refused, Spafard grabbed Kelley "and took his hands from John's throat." Kelley then ordered Spafard "out of my house." As Spafard was leaving Kelley grabbed him by the collar and pushed him. A scrap ensued and Spafard, the stronger man, pinned Kelley, who had his hand on Spafard's throat. Now Mrs. Spafard persuaded her husband to release Kelley, and Spafard, freeing himself, returned to his room with his wife. Moments later Kelley burst in: "You think I an't a going to protect my own house, don't you, d——n you?" As Spafard faced the intruder, Kelley pointed the muzzle a foot from Spafard's chest and shot him—fatally.[77]

Ten weeks later Levi Kelley was tried for murder in Cooperstown before a special court of oyer and terminer. Kelley's attorneys, leaders of the county bar, agreed that Kelley had committed homicide but argued that his crime was only manslaughter because their client had responded to Spafard's "assault . . . with circumstances of indignity." Kelley had "resented [it] immediately and [acted] in the heat of blood." Trial testimony revealed that Kelley spoke to Spafard as a superior to an inferior; Spafard's confrontational responses enraged Kelley because the tenant refused him due deference. But thirty-five-year-old Judge Samuel Nelson, later appointed to the U.S. Supreme Court, told the jury that if after provocation "there was an interval of reflection, a reasonable time for the blood to cool," then "the crime would be murder." Two hours later they declared Kelley guilty. Spafard entered

Kelley's rooms only to stop the attack on John Clark, exonerating Spafard for his "assault" on Kelley. Because Spafard left Kelley after their "scuffle," and Kelley then fetched his gun, entered Spafard's room, and shot him, manslaughter did not fit the facts.[78] Spafard, the tenant, had stood up to the landlord Kelley, but in this trial Kelley's rank did not add to his rights.

Indeed when Judge Nelson—who thirty years later would side with Chief Justice Taney against Dred Scott—sentenced Kelley, he admonished that his transgression was increased because he enjoyed social advantages. Like Jason Fairbanks and the Knapp brothers, Kelley "had been born and educated in a well informed and christian community." He was part of "respectable society," and Nelson believed, erroneously, that Kelley could not claim "ignorance, nor want of early and paternal care in preparing you for life." Kelley possessed "reasonable abundance," a "beloved family," and "all the comforts and enjoyments of domestic happiness." Yet he abused his power and provoked conflicts. "You causelessly and violently attacked a boy" who was under Spafard's "care and protection." And Spafard had "as a citizen, and in humanity as a man," properly intervened. Nelson declared the tenant morally superior to the landlord. Whereas Spafard displayed "many amiable and estimable qualities . . . [and] christian virtues," Kelley's "irascible and impetuous passions, unreasonable and unfeeling conduct, assailed him [Spafard] in every mode your relative situation permitted." According to one newspaper, "The deceased sustained a fair character, was about fifty years of age, and has left a wife and a large family of children, destitute of property."[79] In this trial of character Levi Kelley, "respectable" nephew of Cooperstown's founder, ranked below the poor tenant.

IV

One must not conclude from trials like those of Fairbanks, the Knapps, Webster, and Kelley that when it came to social class "equal justice before the law" ruled American courts. Because when upper-class, well-connected men committed crimes against lower-class men they sometimes escaped punishment. And when men of any class assaulted or even murdered women of doubtful morals, trials might also end in acquittal. Verdicts rested on respectable white men deliberating on juries, men whose prejudices, with popular opinion, shaped their understanding of fairness and justice.

Class privilege emerged conspicuously in the highly publicized murder trial of Congressman Philemon T. Herbert. Public responses to this 1856 killing were shaped by the tinderbox election year—when warfare raged between proslavery and antislavery forces in Kansas and Free-Soil Republicans ran their first presidential candidate. The defendant, an anti-immigrant, anti-Catholic, Know-Nothing California Democrat, was an Alabama native and university graduate who would die fighting for the Confederacy. Two weeks before South Carolina congressman Preston Brooks beat antislavery Massachusetts senator Charles Sumner senseless at his Senate desk, Herbert fatally shot Thomas Keating.

The violence was brief. On May 8, 1856, at 11:30 a.m., Herbert entered the Willard Hotel dining room for breakfast, demanding, "Let us have it damned quick." His waiter, Jerry Riordan, brought part of the breakfast, explaining at that hour "it would be necessary . . . to get an order from the office to have an order sent up from the kitchen." Witnesses gave conflicting accounts of the fracas that followed. Apparently Herbert insulted Riordan and head waiter Thomas Keating, addressing each as "you damned Irish son-of-a-bitch," before brandishing his loaded revolver, walking up to Keating, and having words with him. Then Herbert struck Keating from behind with his fist. In the following melee Thomas Keating's brother, Patrick, and other waiters clashed with Herbert and his friends. Plates, chairs, and fists flew until Herbert shot Thomas Keating in the chest at close range, killing him. After Keating fell, waiters attacked Herbert before his friends extricated him. Then, with Keating dead on the floor, Herbert and his companions left to report the incident to a justice of the peace, who ordered Herbert's arrest.[80]

Herbert's trials—there were two—provided competing narratives. The prosecution witnesses, chiefly Keating's coworkers, testified that the arrogant and abusive Herbert struck first in word and deed. By punching Keating and threatening him with a loaded gun Herbert showed malicious intent before shooting. Herbert's defense argued that the congressman used his pistol in defense after he was attacked and feared for his life. One newspaper reported, "Mr. Herbert fired only when it became evident that it was the design of the waiters to kill him."[81] The jury's decision, however, rested on more than courtroom evidence and arguments. Herbert's trials tested equal justice under law, an ideal enshrined a century earlier in Lord Ferrers's London trial.

The challenge to equal justice began at Herbert's arraignment before Judge Thomas Hartley Crawford, a Pennsylvania ex-congressman and, like Herbert, a Democrat. Judge Crawford determined that *"a conviction for murder shall not take place."* He declared the appropriate charge to be manslaughter, though the grand jury actually charged Herbert with *"murder."* Still, the congressman could be optimistic: the prosecutor, Philip Barton Key, a personal friend and nephew of Chief Justice Taney, would be criticized for his gentle prosecution. During his trial Herbert was "surrounded by numerous personal and political friends," including congressmen and senators. When Crawford charged the jury he virtually directed acquittal by explaining that though the defendant might not face "imminent peril of life," if he reasonably believed that he "was in danger of death or of serious bodily harm from which he could not safely escape, he was justified in taking life." If jurors had "reasonable doubts . . . they must give the benefit to the defendant." Crawford remarked in "informal conversation . . . sufficiently loud to be heard all around . . . 'That for his part he looked upon the act [Herbert's homicide] as a clear case of self-defence." After lengthy deliberation the jury deadlocked. The grand jurors had voted a murder indictment, but no trial juror voted for murder: five decided that Herbert was guilty of manslaughter while seven preferred acquittal. It was a mistrial. So the prosecution called for a new trial.[82]

In Herbert's second trial the jurymen were new, but other participants were much as before. The chief difference was William P. Preston of Baltimore, the prominent anti-Know-Nothing Roman Catholic attorney who, experienced in criminal cases, joined the prosecution.[83] The new jury pool included seventy-nine men, but even after seventy-one were dismissed, two of those impaneled admitted that they had "formed or expressed opinions on the subject." One had even visited Herbert in jail. Nevertheless Judge

Crawford dismissed objections: they could render "an impartial verdict" because each man said he would "not be swayed by any bias." In the completed jury none bore a recognizably Irish surname.[84]

The evidence and arguments of the second trial mostly repeated the first. But the fresh prosecution attorney, Preston, introduced the theme of class. Likening Congressman Herbert's shooting of Keating to Lord Ferrers's shooting of his servant, Preston extolled England's "rigid observance of the rules of impartial justice." Though Ferrers was among "the most distinguished noblemen," English judges rejected his petition to be executed as befitted his rank, so "he died by the common hangman upon the gallows." Herbert was not Lord Ferrers, but, Preston argued, he was "a gentleman, a member of *Congress*' and his act "blots the American name, and imprints a stain upon the page of Congressional history." Herbert "struck down to death this poor, humble, toiling servant," making "the poor man's hearthstone desolate." The congressman "robbed a wife of her husband, and left her children fatherless." Though Herbert's defense claimed that Ferrers's case was irrelevant, Preston rejoined, "Even in aristocratic England, the descendant of the noble Earl of Essex, could not with impunity take the life of his servant."[85] In the democratic United States, he proclaimed, regardless of class, equal justice should be even more certain.

Preston wove class themes into his summary of the crime. Herbert, he said, called Keating "a damned Irish son of a b——" before approaching him, loaded pistol in hand. Keating might only be a "humble waiter," Preston admitted, "but he was still a man." So after Herbert addressed him with a "grossness and rudeness . . . so unsuited to the lips of a gentleman," Keating's reply, though less than genteel, was appropriate. Nothing in the dining room warranted display of a gun or justified its use. Preston expressed compassion for Herbert, "the unfortunate accused," but jurors must "do your duty to your country and God." Though sympathetic to the congressman, they must not, as Daniel Webster explained prosecuting Joseph Knapp, "'suffer the guilty to escape.'" If they freed Herbert "'they make themselves answerable for the augmented danger of the innocent.'"[86]

Many believed that Preston's performance was brilliant, and it was published for lawyers to study. The jury, however, was not convinced and promptly acquitted the congressman. Public responses divided according to political and ethnic allegiances. Herbert, the Know-Nothing Democrat, known to California opponents as "the Mariposa gambler," was reportedly supported by Democrats and President James Buchanan. During his trial "leading and distinguished Senators and Representatives were seen in the Court . . . extending their sympathy and countenance." In the House, Democratic colleagues defeated an attempted Republican inquiry into the shooting that could have ousted Herbert from Congress.[87] Though he was not a hero like South Carolina's Preston Brooks, southerners exonerated Herbert. As the *Charleston Standard* put it, so what if Herbert had irritated the waiters? His was "at the most a provocation of words, and such a provocation as a servant should not have the right to resent." As "menials" the waiters' duty was to accept their roles "quietly." According to an Alabama newspaper, because Herbert was "attacked by a mob of the waiters . . . there is no doubt he acted in self-defence." Herbert taught the waiters that "they are servants and not 'gentlemen' in disguise."[88]

But others condemned Herbert. Two thousand of his California constituents believed that he "deeply injured the fair fame of the State of California" and asked him to quit their state.[89] In Washington, D.C., one paper condemned his acquittal. This decision provided "much less than justice" because "social position" and "political connections" shielded Herbert.[90] The Republican press spoke bluntly. Judge Crawford's "partiality" had been "very glaring," according to Horace Greeley's *New York Tribune*; Herbert was "the culprit" in "a perfectly plain case of murder." The class bias of acquittal showed how the "Slave Power" regarded "free white laboring people of the country." Had the situations been reversed so that "the Irish waiter . . . killed Herbert, or any other person in Herbert's social position, the act would have been held to be murder, and the Irish waiter would have been hung for it." Likening Keating's death to the recent killing of a teacher by his wealthy Kentucky student—also tried and acquitted—the *Tribune* declared that it was now "a settled point in the slaveholding States that no 'gentleman,' that is to say no rich man, shall ever be held . . . to have committed a murder." Writing sarcastically under the headline "A Murderer Acquitted!" a western Pennsylvania newspaper declared, "It would be the most absurd thing imaginable to suppose that an *Honorable* member of Congress would be punished for murdering an humble individual like *Tom Keating*, a poor Irish servant." Comparing Herbert to Preston Brooks, the paper wondered whether Know-Nothings would present "the blood stained Herbert . . . with a *pistol*," just as "Brooks deserved the presentation of a *cane* for his assault on Sumner." Sarcastically the editor concluded, "Surely Herbert is entitled to a reward of merit equally appropriate."[91]

Congressman Herbert's exoneration involved more than class privilege—political partisanship, the sectional conflict over slavery, and Irish ethnicity all mattered—but it was Herbert's stature as a gentleman assailed by servants that rendered his respectable witnesses more credible than servant witnesses, giving his defense story credible veneer. Though the law prescribed equal rights, actual court proceedings could favor upper-class defendants over lower-class victims. This may have been especially characteristic of the South because of the elite's commitment to maintaining slave subordination, but elite privilege operated nationally. Certainly the common man's demand for equal justice was widespread and figured explicitly in the convictions of the Knapps and Webster, but these gentlemen's victims were the wealthiest of gentlemen. When victims were poor or disreputable, equal justice was never assured. And if the victim was a disreputable woman or person of color, white privilege and male privilege magnified class privilege. The murder trials and acquittals of the Reverend Ephraim Avery in 1833, Richard Robinson in 1836, and Albert Tirrell in 1845 were archetypal. Indeed, the miscarriage of justice in Robinson's trial for the murder of Helen Jewett remained notorious for a generation.[92]

With gender and sexual stereotypes influencing all-male court personnel, prosecutors faced difficult odds in trying to prove the guilt of "respectable men." Though the gentleman's story might be far-fetched, in an era when capital punishment was under attack jurors could embrace "reasonable doubt." Moreover when a woman's testimony conflicted with a respectable man's, hers might be dismissed. If the victim was a "fallen woman" and prosecutors relied on her associates for evidence, conviction was a longshot. Women were understood to be inherently flighty and fickle—unreliable compared to men.

When the Methodist clergyman Ephraim K. Avery, a married man with three children, was tried for murdering Sarah Cornell, a Fall River "factory girl," his motive was said to be ending their illicit relationship, which had left her pregnant. Cornell's corpse was found hanging from a post in Tiverton, Rhode Island, before Christmas, 1832. According to Attorney General Albert C. Greene, Avery strangled Cornell with a cord, tied her to the post to simulate suicide, and finally inflicted fatal wounds to her body. As with the Knapps and Professor Webster, murder evidence was circumstantial. In proceedings covered extensively by the press—two coroner's inquests, a grand jury indictment, and published trial testimony of nearly two hundred witnesses, as well as incriminating letters between Avery and Cornell— Avery appeared to be guilty.[93]

After a twenty-seven-day trial and seventeen hours' deliberation, however, the jury acquitted Avery.[94] They found reasonable doubt as to whether Sarah Cornell had committed suicide or died by an unknown assailant. Avery's attorneys, led by former U.S. senator Jeremiah Mason, whose five-hundred-dollar fee was paid by Methodists, succeeded for two reasons primarily.[95] First, the defense brought six expert medical witnesses to testify that although Cornell's corpse could have been disfigured by violence, post-mortem natural causes could also explain its appearance. The four matrons who described "bruising" and "prints of fingers" on Cornell were mistaken. Even midwives and women who regularly prepared corpses could not usefully appraise the victim's body. Such "ignorant persons" could not distinguish marks of violence from routine posthumous changes. As one expert physician put it, "Women are not good judges."[96] Testimony that Cornell had spoken of suicide supported the idea her death was, as the first coroner's inquest concluded, suicide.[97]

Even more telling was the defense attack on Cornell's character. Unlike Elizabeth Fales and Mary Hamilton, Cornell was no paragon of female virtue. Physicians from Lowell testified that they had treated her for gonorrhea and questioned her mental stability. Mill girls swore that Cornell had confessed to "a lewd life ever since she was 15 years old," having admitted behaving "improperly" with four men and "lying." They claimed she was angry at the reverend because, after she admitted sinning, he tried to separate her from the Methodists.[98] According to Avery's defenders Cornell was notorious, and mill girls, artisans, businessmen, professionals, and clerics all commended Avery's character.

To counter this disparaging portrait, Attorney General Greene, former Speaker of Rhode Island's legislature and future U.S. senator, defended Cornell and her class. He acknowledged that Cornell was once "a strange, wayward being, sinning and repenting, repenting and sinning," but she was never so depraved as to plot to blame Avery for her suicide. The story that Avery sought to dismiss her from Methodism was false; actually, he had signed a religious certificate for her. Moreover, for the past two years in Lowell "her character and conduct were irreproachable." Cornell was certainly "a Factory girl," part of "that class of women and children . . . usefully and honorably employed in the 130 Cotton Mills of this State." That class included seven thousand workers "indispensable to the industry" of Rhode Island. Her "rights" and their "rights" must be protected, "and their wrongs avenged.

The prosecution failed in the Rhode Island Supreme Judicial Court, but in the court of public opinion it succeeded. Wide newspaper coverage and twenty trial reports, narratives, and broadsides led most to conclude that Avery was guilty. Jurors were divided over suicide or murder. Though at first they leaned toward a guilty verdict, they finally decided that acquittal was better than deadlock and retrial. The Newport *Republican* paper claimed that the outcome "struck almost *every* one with astonishment." The law might have been served, but "*justice* [was] entirely withheld." Many believed that Avery's acquittal was technically legitimate; still, the *Republican* claimed that "nineteen twentieths of the public, find him guilty of the crime." With so many uncertainties, the distinction between "reasonable doubt" and "all possible doubt" was murky. The jurors' reluctance to hang Avery, a respectable clergyman, husband, and father, was understandable. Avery, the public recognized, was not the first guilty man acquitted in court.[99]

For New England Methodists the case did not end there. They had come to the embattled clergyman's aid, raising funds to defend him, testifying for him, and providing for his family. After the verdict the church promptly rehabilitated Avery with a twelve-page *Report of a Committee of the New*

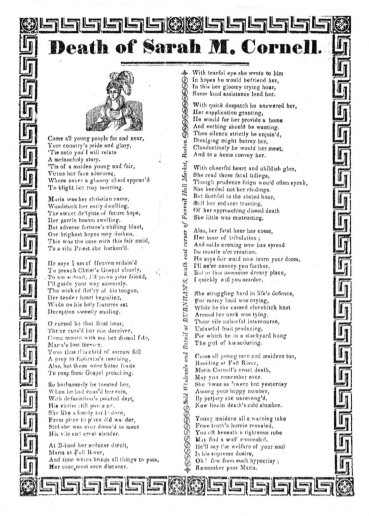

The sentimental verse on Sarah Cornell's demise, and the genteel image of her, elevated the mill girl to a plane of equality with the accused clergyman. Courtesy, American Antiquarian Society.

England Conference of the M. E. Church, on the Case of Rev. E. K. Avery, a Member of Said Conference. Avery's acquittal, they claimed, provided "clear evidence of innocence," regarding the murder as well as reports of "illicit intercourse." Believing that prejudice against their church propelled Avery's prosecution, they claimed his acquittal as victory.[100]

The public remained skeptical. In "the tribunal of the people," a Pawtucket editor wrote, the "verdict is against him." The Methodists had used "unprecedented efforts," including "false testimony." When Avery returned to Lowell to preach, "he was hung and burned in effigy," with "great numbers ready to mob him." The Lowell paper declared that Americans believed Avery to be guilty, so "guilty or not" he should not claim to be "an innocent and injured man" and try "to brow beat" public opinion. Though there was "reasonable doubt of his guilt," Avery escaped hanging only "by the skin of his teeth."[101] According to popular judgment this clerical gentleman had gotten away with murdering a mill girl: that might be the law, but it was not justice.

This perception that courts favored "gentlemen" in contests with "fallen" women was accurate. One infamous example—the murder of Helen Jewett—happened in New York City in 1836. Jewett, a polished twenty-three-year-old prostitute, had come from Maine and became entangled in a quasi-romantic relationship with a customer, Richard P. Robinson, a well-born nineteen-year-old clerk from Connecticut. When Jewett's corpse was found at Rosina Townshend's elegant brothel, there were three wounds to Jewett's head, apparently inflicted by a hatchet, and her room had been set ablaze. After police questioned Jewett's madam and coworkers, they connected Robinson to her death: he had visited Jewett that night, and police found a hatchet and cape associated with him in the backyard.

Robinson's trial reportedly "excited nearly as much attention, as did the trial of E. K. Avery."[102] The prosecutor, relying on physical and circumstantial evidence supplied largely by prostitutes, did not vigorously press the case, winning praise because he "went not a step further than . . . required by considerations of duty." In contrast, Robinson's defense, led by Ogden Hoffman—son of a New York Superior Court judge and himself a recent district attorney of New York County—called on respectable clerks, their employers, and professionals. His client was "scarcely beyond the age of boyhood"—a youth gone astray—still "in the eye of the law an infant," who lived "respectably" with his employer, a relative "who stood . . . in the relation of a father." The defense claimed that brothel-keeper Rosina Townshend was the likely murderer because she had recently increased her fire insurance. Her testimony and that of the other prostitutes must be dismissed because prostitutes were equivalent to "convicted felons" who ought not be regarded as "competent." Having "no conscience," they readily testified falsely.[103]

Circumstantial evidence pointed overwhelmingly to Robinson's guilt, but because a jury of fathers and businessmen determined the outcome, his exoneration was, according to the press, "anticipated." Robinson's talented and zealous defense overmatched the prosecutor. Judge Ogden Edwards—a grandson of Jonathan Edwards—charged the jury by declaring class prejudice the proper standard for evaluating testimony. Like Robinson's defenders, Judge Edwards told jurors that prostitutes' words were "not entitled to credit" without corroboration from "better sources," so whenever "the testimony of the dissolute females . . . came in collision with reputable witnesses" their statements "should be set aside and disregarded." When the trial ended past midnight on the fifth day, jurors asked the court to remain while they deliberated. After less than fifteen minutes' deliberation they acquitted Robinson—a verdict greeted by "a simultaneous burst of cheers from the spectators." The defendant, hitherto self-contained, "sank overpowered by his feelings, upon the neck of his venerable father, and wept like a child."[104]

In contrast to courtroom spectators, broader public responses were critical. Though the *New York Herald*, a merchants' paper, praised the verdict initially, most New York papers and those around the country condemned the outcome. Even the *Herald* switched when evidence of Robinson's bad character emerged. Ultimately the public concluded that class privilege and male privilege had defeated justice. That a horrific murder and a tainted trial in the 1830s should have been recognized as violating equal rights doctrine indicated the vitality of the Revolutionary legacy as well as the growing movement for women's rights.[105]

In Connecticut, near Robinson's family home, a "gentleman too elevated to be motivated by unworthy reasons," concluded that Judge Edwards "improperly" ruled out the prostitutes' testimony. Because Robinson consorted with prostitutes they were "good witnesses against *him*." Their testimony might be doubted in some circumstances, but because Robinson voluntarily associated with them, and "rogues" routinely testified for the prosecution, their testimony should be accepted. If all testimony from disreputable people was ruled out, then "shocking crimes must very often go unpunished." Men who patronized brothels lost any claim to gender and class privilege. The Connecticut gentleman partially recognized such privilege but argued that if Judge Edwards's principles ruled, "every crime committed in such a place is almost sure to escape the law," as with Helen Jewett's murder.[106]

Ten years later a Boston murder demonstrated that privileges of class and gender remained potent. Again the victim was a Maine prostitute, twenty-three-year-old Maria Bickford, and again a gentleman was charged. The weapon was a razor, not a hatchet, but again the bed was set afire to conceal the crime. The accused, Albert J. Tirrell, was a twenty-one-year-old married father of two children who left his family to live with Bickford, whom he had met in a brothel. She, having left her husband, joined Tirrell in Boston, where they lived as husband and wife. Nevertheless Bickford continued as a prostitute, and Tirrell, jealous and angry, killed her. He fled to Montreal, hoping to escape to England. But weather thwarted his plan, so he sailed to New York and New Orleans before being arrested and returned to Boston for trial.[107]

Tirrell's wealthy family hired Rufus Choate, the brilliant attorney who later chose not to defend Dr. Webster. The facts pointed to the young man as the murderer even more surely than they had for Robinson, Avery, and Webster, though again the evidence was circumstantial. Because the facts were so incriminating, Choate invented a novel defense: if Tirrell did kill Bickford, the homicide was not murder because Tirell suffered from somnambulism—sleepwalking—and thus might have killed her and set the fire unconsciously. As with temporary insanity, the somnambulist could not be accountable for actions during sleep. This line of argument was novel; however, the dean of Harvard Medical College and the head of the Massachusetts Lunatic Asylum testified to somnambulism as a mental disorder. Choate's inventive defense won praise, but Tirrell's case hinged on stereotypes of gender and class privilege that freed other killers of fallen women.[108]

As with Cornell and Jewett, Bickford's character was easily vilified, and Tirrell's attorneys mercilessly maligned the dead prostitute. In contrast, defense witnesses for Robinson and Tirrell testified to their virtues as young men who sadly fell victim to vicious women. The deaths of women need not be seen as murder when they might be suicide—an argument used in the cases of the upstanding Elizabeth Fales as well as Sarah Cornell and now Maria Bickford. Finally, the claim that prostitutes and brothel-keepers could not be trusted to tell the truth, Judge Edwards's argument in Robinson's case, possessed broad appeal. The Connecticut gentleman warned that without such testimony "shocking crimes must very often go unpunished," but as a juror who acquitted Tirrell explained: "We couldn't believe the testimony of them abandoned women. Now, could we?"[109]

In trials like those of Avery, Robinson, and Tirrell, gender and class privilege operated simultaneously, reinforcing each other. But as with Congressman Herbert's killing of the Irish waiter, class privilege alone could suffice to shield a defendant from equal justice. The same was true for gender privilege. When a man killed a woman of his own class he might be convicted, as Jason Fairbanks had been condemned for murdering Elizabeth Fales, but if the woman victim was impure, male juries commonly acquitted their own sex. The 1816 case of the sailor George Coombs, charged with murdering his companion Maria Henry (also called Maria Coombs) in Boston, shows how male privilege worked at the lowest social level.[110]

Coombs, was a War of 1812 veteran who served on the U.S.S. *Constitution*, and neither he nor his New Hampshire–bred victim was "respectable." The couple lived in Boston's North End in the meanest of dwellings, a "ten-foot building" divided in half to share with others, in this case prostitutes. There, on June 15, 1816, a household argument became an "affray." Afterward witnesses found George with Maria, who lay on their bed dying from internal bleeding. Witnesses overheard the conflict and viewed it through "a crack and a gimblet [sic] hole" in the partition, as well as from a window. Their reports led to Coombs's arrest and murder indictment.[111]

At trial, defense witnesses said that Maria Henry Coombs "was sometimes in liquor, and sometimes fractious and quarrelsome." Worse, she had a "furious temper," and one witness "heard her utter profane, and even filthy language." The defense attorney, John Gallison, claimed that Maria was intoxicated during the "affray." Admitting that George might have struck Maria, Gallison claimed without proof that "[blows] came as well from her, as from him." The fall that caused her fatal injury, he argued, probably resulted from her drunkenness, not action by George Coombs. The prosecution presented a very different account. Attorney General Perez Morton presented six witnesses who saw and heard how "Mrs. Coombs" received her injuries. They came from George, who knocked her down. One said, "Coombs kicked her on the left side," and another, "Coombs lifted his foot and kicked her, and she thereby fell out the back door." A third, who claimed that she "belonged to a different [higher] class of people," said that after Maria was down, he "stamped upon her twice." Three reported that during and after the fight Maria cried out to George, "You have killed me" and "George has killed me." When Gallison objected to this hearsay evidence, the court ruled it out as not "necessary" or "expedient," because witnesses said Coombs was the author of the assault.[112]

As the trial progressed it became apparent that the prosecution might fail because key witnesses could be discredited as belonging—in the arch phrase of one witness—"to the *Cyprian Family*" of dissolute women, as had, reputedly, the dead victim. Because the credibility of prostitutes as witnesses was unsettled in American courts during the period, even apart from jurors' prejudices, the case against George Coombs was doubtful, though the public believed in his guilt. In the Reverend Avery's trial the testimony of debauched women was challenged, and though a Connecticut gentleman gave a qualified defense of prostitutes' evidence, Judge Edwards in New York had dismissed their testimony in Robinson's case. Long before any of those proceedings, a Boston newspaper reported that Chief Justice Isaac Parker chose Coombs's trial for "establishing a new principle of evidence" in Massachusetts.[113]

When Parker charged the jury he claimed that "it has not been usual to inquire into the mode of life, or immoral habits of a witness, except only in point of veracity"—the witnesses' reputation for telling the truth. In this case Parker allowed defense attorney Gallison "to go into this enquiry." Though new, Parker said, "it may hereafter be a principle of our criminal law." Stopping short of Ogden Edwards's later requirement of reputable corroboration of prostitute testimony, Parker advised that "the Jury are not bound to disbelieve them" because of their immorality. He doubted that "they would be willing to perjure themselves" in a capital case, but added the caveat that "if they are contradicted by *honest people*," their testimony would carry "little credit." He directed the jury that only "if they stand uncontradicted, and if no motive can be assigned why they should tell a falsehood," could they be believed. Jurors should judge the prostitutes' credibility.[114]

Parker concluded with a summary favoring the prosecution's narrative. Coombs, he said, was guilty of "murder" if the jurors "believe these witnesses." Even if they did not believe all witnesses, it was "evident the deceased received great violence." Reminding them of the testimony, he asked: "Was she complaining? And complaining of the prisoner?" If Maria had fallen and if George caused the fall, he said, because it was not proved that "she made any attack on him, at least the offence would be manslaughter." The murder charge could be reasonably doubted, but the judge implied that the evidence warranted at least a manslaughter verdict.[115]

Yet after an hour's deliberation the jury returned an acquittal. The defense pathway Parker opened by allowing Gallison to call the victim an "abandoned woman," and then to impeach witnesses by stressing "their appearance and behaviour," had consequences. By challenging the witnesses' "regard for truth when every other moral attribute has failed," and by declaring that they lacked the "purity of mind which is necessary for a sacred regard to truth . . . [and] every principle of morality and honor," Gallison convinced the jurors that they must not convict Coombs.[116] Whether or not the jurors had personal experience with the truthfulness of prostitutes, they shared common prejudices. So they saved their fellow man, George Coombs, from hanging. Unlike the woman-killers Avery, Robinson, and Tirrell, Coombs was from the lowest class and "a stranger." Though onboard the *Constitution* he was "an orderly, peaceable man," as an officer testified, afterward Coombs took up with "an abandoned woman."[117] But because she and her witnesses possessed no moral standing, he enjoyed male privilege and so could abuse her—lethally—with impunity. In contrast, in

the same year in Middletown, Connecticut, a drunken husband was convicted and executed for fatally battering his wife.[118] Unlike Coombs's case,
however, the sexual morality of the victim and witnesses was not an issue in
the Connecticut case, so male privilege did not operate.

V

In American courts the motto was equality before the law, and the favored
emblem was the blindfolded goddess Justitia holding the scales of justice
in one hand and the sword of punishment in the other. But in 1776 when
American Revolutionaries proclaimed that "all men are created equal" and
declared that all mankind was "endowed with certain unalienable rights,"
they spoke abstractly, without closely considering the ultimate consequences
of their expansive rhetoric. So it is not surprising that when the exalted principle of equal rights collided with dominant assumptions about social class
and gender (not to mention color), principle often yielded to power and to
prejudice. Often, but not always. When it came to voting, the necessities
of political and military mobilization combined with Revolutionary ideas
to propel the realization of equal rights. The drive to eliminate property
barriers for suffrage began with American independence. Still, equal voting
rights for white men remained two generations in the future. And for free
men of color access to equal rights generally was severely limited, inconsistent, a matter for state-by-state determination according to shifting tides of
white sentiment. Almost a century after the Declaration of Independence
the Fifteenth Amendment created an equal national standard for all *men* in
1870, but states could exercise voting practices so as to deny suffrage where
most people of color lived—sometimes blocking poor white voters as well.
Regarding women, whatever promise the Declaration made for them was
readily challenged; so women's access to equal rights was barred by statute
and court judgments, regardless of a woman's social station. As with race,
access to equal rights for women was less a matter of class than one of prevailing beliefs about natural attributes.

The principle of equal rights to justice was tested repeatedly in American
courtrooms in thousands of jurisdictions during the decades between the

Declaration and the Civil War. And in a criminal justice system based on laws made by representative legislatures and intended to reflect public opinion through juries, prevailing beliefs and prejudices influenced decisions. Courtroom trials, after all, were popular theater—where prosecutors, advocates, and judges played starring roles and jurors could become centers of interest. In this system ideal, objective justice could never be realized, and social class—like race and gender—could never be erased from the minds of court officials. Yet under certain conditions judges and juries strove to meet the ideal of equal rights. Their reliance on time-tested procedures deriving from British jurisprudence created a significant barrier against judgments springing merely from popular sentiment. In an 1815 North Carolina case where a poor white man was tried for murdering a slave, the jury convicted the defendant and the judge sentenced him to hang. Procedure ruled. But an outpouring of more than a thousand white petitioners persuaded the governor to issue a pardon.[119] Here, as elsewhere, the tension between professional standards and procedural rules was reflected in the tension between courtroom justice and true justice out-of-doors. Popular criticism of lawyers, judges, and legal technicalities sometimes led the public to verdicts different from the courtroom. Yet when defendant and victim came from the same social class, and even when their social classes differed, courts often appeared to render equal justice.

Nevertheless the fact that courts sometimes played favorites, conspicuously in the cases of Richard Robinson, Albert Tirrell, and Philemon Herbert, was highly significant. In the first two cases, where the testimony of "fallen women" was effectively dismissed, enabling juries to acquit murderers, the operation of the sexual double-standard was blatant. When women fell from chastity their sworn testimony became, ipso facto, worthless, whereas the oaths of unchaste men remained valid. Congressman Zephaniah Swift had laid down the double standard rule in his 1795 treatise on Connecticut law: "when a female once breaks over the bounds of decency and virtue, and becomes abandoned, she is capable of going all lengths in iniquity," and the result was "total depravity." Men were different: "There are frequent instances of men," Swift declared, "who disregard the principles of chastity, but in other respects conduct [themselves] with propriety."[120] This tradition enabled lawyers for Robinson and Tirrell to annihilate the female victim's legitimacy, making her life worthless compared to the respectable, well-dressed man seated before the court. Even a disreputable defendant like Coombs who "married" a prostitute won juror sympathy. Juries were reluctant to send a man to death, or even to prison, for the sake of a worthless, vicious woman.

Similarly, class and connections could provide equivalent protection. Though in Philemon Herbert's trial for killing Michael Keating ethnicity surely entered the jurors' consciousness, Herbert's self-defense argument was based on the illegitimacy of a servant challenging a superior. For those committed to preserving slavery the need to punish insolence in a waiter was akin to the necessity of punishing every form of slave resistance—a matter of practical necessity and honor. To northerners who aimed to halt the spread of slavery or even abolish it, Herbert's expectation of "servile" behavior on the part of waiters was an attack on democratic principles and characteristic of southerners' movement to make their class system national. In the North, Americans recognized and accepted class divisions between gentlemen and their families and laboring men and their families—as well as a host of finer distinctions—but paradoxically this acceptance coexisted with a democratic belief in equality and equal rights. Just as Americans in the North and West rejected the hereditary aristocracy of Europe's social order, they also rejected the rigid, impermeable, and stark inequality of the slavery system.

Ironically, three years after Herbert killed Keating another Democratic congressman, Daniel E. Sickles of New York was charged with murder and acquitted after killing Philip Barton Key, the Washington district attorney who had prosecuted Herbert. Here, in a case involving men of the same class, honor—a variant of male privilege—secured the acquittal. Dueling had been fashionable among gentlemen at the beginning of the century, but after Vice President Aaron Burr killed Alexander Hamilton in an 1804 duel in New Jersey, in the Northeast the practice became scandalous. But in the South and Southwest dueling remained honorable. Before Andrew Jackson became president he killed a man in a duel; Senator Henry Clay of

Kentucky fought a duel; and after a Kentucky congressman killed another from Maine in an 1838 duel, Congress outlawed dueling in the District of Columbia. Yet as late as 1853 a California senator dueled with a former congressman; and in 1859 Sickles, a protégé of President Buchanan, shot Key because he was having an affair with Sickles's wife. This was no duel, but for a District of Columbia jury Sickles's defense of his honor overrode evidence of premeditated murder. Opinions were divided. Though Sickles's repeated, point-blank shots at the unarmed Key indicated murder, the jury accepted a temporary insanity defense. And Sickles' rough justice won applause for ridding the nation's capital of a notorious rake. Congressman Sickles's honor defense epitomized the sexual double standard because he was himself a notorious philanderer. In the 1840s the New York legislature censured him because he brought a known prostitute to its chambers. Later, when Sickles took a government post in London, leaving his pregnant wife at home, he brought this prostitute with him, even introducing her to Queen Victoria.[121] For Sickles "honor" was purely a matter of gender.

Indeed male honor practices appeared so pervasive that there is no reason to suppose that they were bounded by social class. But courtroom evidence suggests that honor was recognized formally only when respectable men defended it. Given the tens of thousands of assault prosecutions in the thousands of American jurisdictions in the decades between American independence and the Civil War there were probably many proceedings against disreputable men who attacked others of their own class to vindicate masculine honor. Such cases garnered little public attention. As Professor John Webster's biographer commented: "Men who occupy the lower walks of life, among whom we often find those who seem to be abandoned by society, are tried, condemned, and executed without exciting much public attention, or absorbing much of the public conversation." When members of the "respectable" classes engaged in violence, however, their behavior could not be ignored and the proceedings attracted publicity; for "when suspicion is directed to those whose position in society is elevated, . . . the case is entirely different."[122] As such the cases of Avery, Tirrell, Herbert, and Sickles accentuated public recognition of class and gender privilege. The fact that these forms of privilege were widely accepted, even though public sentiment in the North and Northwest called both into question, suggests that Tocqueville captured an important reality when he observed that although American society was "covered with a democratic finish . . . one sees the old colors of aristocracy showing through."

EIGHT

Equal Rights, Privilege, and
the Pursuit of Inequality

"The original right of men—the right to equality, which is adverse
to every species of subordination beside that which arises from
the difference of capacity, disposition, and virtue."
—*Democritus [Thomas Shippen], "Loose Thoughts on* GOVERNMENT*,"*
Virginia Gazette *(Williamsburg), June 7, 1776*

"The America of the past is gone forever. A new nation is to be
born from the agony through which the people are now passing.
This new nation is to be wholly free. Liberty, *equality before
the law* is to be the great corner-stone.
—*Isaac Newton Arnold,* Congressional Globe,
38th Congress, 1st Session, June 15, 1864, 2989

W hen the Continental Congress proclaimed, "All men are created
equal," the delegates meant equality before the law primarily. They
cast off the kinds of special privileges dispensed by monarchs and aristocrats
targeted by Thomas Paine's *Common Sense*. Instead of "favor," the corrupt
path to advancement in monarchies, "superior merit and capacity" would
propel men to eminence in the United States of America. Because Revolutionary leaders were instituting "the career open to talents," the inescapable
inequalities belonging to all societies would arise from merit only in the
new Republic, not "artificial" advantages of wealth and lineage. According
to a New Jersey congressman and former president of the Revolutionary

Continental Congress: "The road to honors, riches, usefulness and fame, in this happy country, is open equally to all." As the historian Gordon Wood long ago pointed out, for Americans equality did not mean leveling; it more nearly meant "equality of opportunity"—an idea that, Wood explained, "implied social differences and distinctions." Consequently, the ideal of "equal freeholders" collided with the stratification created by unequal merit and capacity in a land rich in opportunities.[1]

Nationalism demanded that Americans set themselves apart from Britain and distance themselves from all monarchies. American legislators believed that by abolishing hereditary titles and offices, as well as ancient privileges like primogeniture, entail, and monopolies, they promoted equal rights. Recognizing the fluidity of their own social and economic order, they professed confidence that no "artificial aristocrats or overgrown rich men" would survive across generations.[2] Though the Declaration of Independence never supposed that future Americans would or should be equal in their condition, many Revolutionaries believed that their enlightened reforms of monarchial corruption in government with its hereditary principle would reconcile the realities of social and economic inequality with equal rights before the law.

At the same time they accepted major, critical contradictions. The unequal privileges they eagerly abolished were, with the important exceptions of primogeniture and entail, privileges like titles and commercial monopolies that as colonials they had never possessed and could never have won from the crown. In contrast, they accepted the unequal advantages that accompanied hereditary private property and coverture, which they understood to be rights, not privileges. For Patriots, hereditary private property was the sine qua non of political liberty, so absolutely fundamental that they could view it only as a right, not a privilege—a sacred principle of their political independence. For them the idea that a man might spend his lifetime amassing property and then be barred from passing it to his heirs was utterly out of bounds. This was one reason the question of slave property was so intractable. Private property was sacrosanct—to be disposed of exclusively by its owner. It was a natural right.

This imaginary New York City street shows class and ethnic diversity in 1837. Elite Americans mingle with a German, a black chimneysweep and bootblack, an Irish laborer, and white and black women. Courtesy, American Antiquarian Society.

Coverture, closely linked to property rights, was similarly bred in the bone. No one who debated the Declaration of Independence in 1776— and not even Abigail Adams—challenged the legitimacy of coverture. So although the United States formally renounced hereditary privilege and aristocracy—proclaiming a title-free, classless republican society where virtue would determine rank—the nation and every state assured the perpetuation of social hierarchies through constitutions, statutes, and legal practice. Since, in addition to capital, propertied families also supplied their children with advantages of connections, manners, and education, the impact of republican reforms was more significant as ideology than policy. Although well-born women, like their brothers, enjoyed obvious advantages, coverture denied them equal rights to property and the political standing that property supplied.

Americans never proclaimed their perpetuation of class difference and advantages, and they erased the hereditary privilege of slave ownership in the northern states gradually by dividing the right to slave property between masters—who were allowed to command slave labor for a stated period of years—and the freed person, who possessed the remainder of his or her lifetime labor. Recognizing the contradiction between enslavement and republican liberty, the Confederation Congress sought to exclude it from the Northwest Territory. But even though the economy of the early Republic destabilized some inherited wealth, and economic expansion provided opportunities for economic and social mobility, key pillars of hereditary privilege continued. Now protected by the Constitution instead of Parliament, slavery, coverture, and the transmission of wealth across generations were sustained by national and state legislation and jurisprudence.

Judging from the contests over abolition and women's rights in the early Republic, the Revolution's "contagion of liberty" undermined the legitimacy of slavery and coverture, as it also undercut religious establishments and property requirements for voting. But John Locke and Patriot ideology justified hereditary private property. Some radicals, such as Thomas Paine, criticized great disparities of wealth and recommended progressive taxation on inheritances. Conservatives tarred such people as "levelers"; indeed no party made redistribution of property its mission. Abolitionists launched attacks on private property, but only on the single form of slave property. In the 1830s and 1840s, it is true, a handful of reformers complained that inherited concentrations of wealth threatened American democracy; and proponents of utopian communism, both Christian and secular, advocated voluntary renunciation of private property. But their criticisms never aroused popular support, and no party advocated laws restricting private property or its inheritance.[3]

Because the Revolutionary generation believed that it had opened the way for "careers open to talent," American rhetoric claimed that the new Republic had ended "artificial" sources of inequality. The new nation would encourage industry, talent, and character—the "natural," approved ways to earn distinction and prosperity. Even Alexis de Tocqueville, the visitor who recognized "the old colors of aristocracy" showing through the nation's "democratic finish" in criminal punishment and imprisonment for debt, believed that the abolition of entail and the workings of partible inheritance effectively ended hereditary privilege. "The families of the great landed property owners have almost all been swallowed up within the common mass," he declared, "Today the sons of these opulent citizens are men of commerce, attorneys, doctors. Most have fallen into the most profound obscurity." He concluded, wishfully perhaps, "The least trace of ranks and hereditary distinctions is destroyed; estate law has done its leveling everywhere."[4]

Tocqueville was not entirely mistaken. Because most families had numerous children, partible inheritance could undermine the preservation of hereditary wealth, especially when wealth was tied to land. The Revolution, moreover, bequeathed a belief in yeoman landholding that led to conflict over taxation and land titles acted out in frontier skirmishes and state legislatures. But the Revolutionary commitment to individual rights over collective family or community rights enabled wealth to survive and grow. Americans' commitment to individual possession of property furnished the foundation for the nation's ruling social and economic orthodoxy—competitive individualism. In contests between the collective rights of farmers to rivers and the individual rights of mill owners to build dams that restricted fish runs or prevent floods from fertilizing meadows, individual mill owners won court battles. Ironically, even collectives doing business as corporations sought and gained treatment as individual persons bearing the rights of individuals—beginning with the 1819 Supreme Court ruling in the Dartmouth College case and continuing thereafter, most notably in the Court's 1886 ruling that according to the Fourteenth Amendment the Southern Pacific Railway Corporation was a person possessing "equal protection of the laws." Such corporate "individuals" possessed all the rights of individual persons, though not all their responsibilities. In contrast to actual people, they enjoyed protections no man or woman could possess, such as immunity from punishment according to criminal penal codes. No corporation could be imprisoned for debt or jailed for a felony.

The Revolutionary commitment to the inviolability of private property, except through the mechanism of legislative consent, was absolute. This was why, even in states where slavery was abhorrent and slaves were set free, legislatures made allowances for the property rights of slaveholders by requiring slaves to pay off their childhood support through labor into adulthood. Like coverture, slavery was rooted in control of private property—a powerful and durable barrier that kept the contagion of liberty in quarantine.

In contrast, when it came to religious worship, ethnicity, and national origin, equal rights were easier to recognize. As we have seen, state declarations of rights and the First Amendment to the Constitution pointed to religious liberty, and though Protestant privilege did not vanish immediately, defenders of religious privilege were divided and forced to give way. It is significant that the most powerful resistance to full-blown religious liberty, whether in Virginia or New England, resulted from property questions—tax support and the ownership of meetinghouses and church silver. Defenders of the status quo yielded, finally, because opponents of tax-supported worship won majorities in state legislatures and constitutional conventions. Majorities of voters determined that religious worship would be a matter of individual not collective choice.

Extending equal rights to white foreigners and people of non-English ethnicity was almost a given. At its founding the United States was already a multilingual, multiethnic society. British ethnicities—English, Welsh, Scots, Irish—were the most common, but Germans, Dutch, French, Scandinavians, and others from around the Atlantic world had long been incorporated into colonial society, if not on an equal basis, then nearly so. Indeed it was American nationality that was the new creation, and for the period, it was inclusive. As early as January 1776 Thomas Paine had proclaimed, "Europe, and not England, is the parent country of America." A few years later the French immigrant J. Hector St. John de Crèvecoeur elaborated: "What then is the American, this new man? He is either an European, or the descendant of an European. . . . Here individuals of all nations are melted into a new race of men." Crèvecoeur went on to proclaim Paine's sanctuary of freedom ideal, describing the new nation as "this great American asylum."[5] This was not merely a romantic vision; to foster economic development many new states were eager to welcome European immigrants. So when Congress enacted the first Naturalization Act in 1790 it provided citizenship rapidly for white immigrants to the United States.

During the 1790s, when French radicalism became transatlantic and its revolution spread to Haiti, Federalists, especially in New England, challenged this welcoming policy. In addition, some in the South feared that West Indian planters, fleeing Haitian turmoil, might infect their region by bringing rebellious slaves into the country. But when Jeffersonians took power after 1800, the white asylum principle ruled once more. Stereotypical prejudices toward Irish, Italian, and a few other immigrant ethnicities sometimes operated in courtrooms, in the press, and out-of-doors, but legal procedures and legislation aimed to provide equal rights. And based on the evidence of capital trials, neither religion nor ethnicity provided major obstacles to equal rights.

But equal justice was more elusive when social class, gender, and race came into play. Here, too, the conditions for dispensing justice were various and dynamic. Even within a single state what happened in courtrooms was never uniform. Moreover justice depended in part on the circumstances of defendant and victim. Where they possessed equal social and moral stature courts appeared to provide equal justice. But where the victim or the defendant outranked the other significantly, then social and moral status shaped outcomes. Judges counseled jurors to shelve their prejudices, but neither judge nor jury could transcend the common assumptions of their time respecting race, class, and gender. Juries themselves, being composed of white male voters, embodied the very assumptions they might be asked to transcend. Moreover since courts relied so heavily on the reliability of witness testimony, rather than forensic evidence, "respectable" witnesses carried weight. In the extreme case, jurors could dismiss the testimony of prostitutes entirely, because such women were said to possess no self-respect and no commitment to truth. In many states people of color could not testify against whites if they could testify at all.

Although the impact of social class is difficult to assess, it cannot be doubted that it influenced outcomes. Legislation was supposed to operate uniformly within states and, where acts of Congress were concerned, across all states. But whatever legislatures and judicial rulings might prescribe, actual judgments depended not only on the locale in which a prosecutor issued an indictment and a defendant was tried but on the year and decade that trial took place. When Hannah Ocuish was tried for murder in New London in 1787, the fact that she was a local girl with a local record and reputation, one who was seen to threaten local safety, bore on the guilty verdict. So did the year, 1787, falling in a disordered, postwar period when executing women and children remained legitimate in the region. Just a few years later New Englanders would no longer execute a child, even a black child, for murder. And authorities in the region would also cease executing women for murdering newborn infants.

Circumstances of time and place were no less significant in 1821, when Stephen Merrill Clark was tried in Salem for committing arson. Salem was a port town just as vulnerable to fire as Newburyport, which the youth had set ablaze six months earlier when the town was recovering from the preceding decade's disastrous fire. As with Ocuish, the fact that the unrepentant Clark had a local record worked against him. And in the cases of Congressmen Philemon Herbert and Daniel Sickles, the time and place of their murder trials, late 1850s Washington, D.C., when rabid partisanship shaped perceptions, surely helped both men to win acquittals. Law was supposed to operate equally and objectively, but since it was embedded in society and politics, those ideals could never be fully realized. Because American institutions aimed to represent and respond to voters, popular politics magnified the influence of common belief and sentiment. Elected officials aligned with political parties played key roles, as did their appointees. Procedural rules enforced by legal professionals helped, but as with Judge Crawford in Herbert's trial, officials could be partisans.

The conditions under which equal rights ideals played out were inherently unstable. Decade by decade the multiplication of Protestant sects undermined majority support for any kind of religious establishment. American religious life, like American politics, came to operate according to the principles of free-market liberalism. Each religion was free to compete in the marketplace of faith, and often those best equipped to evangelize gained the most supporters. But whereas equal rights could emerge dominant in the context of religion, when it came to race and gender, change repeatedly meant conflict. At the moment of independence and for some time thereafter the free population of color had been so small that it posed no threat to white Americans' expectation of superiority and control. For whites the subordination of people of color as slaves had been a reality for several generations, so few gave much thought to the idea of equal rights for blacks and people of mixed race. But just as each passing decade brought new religious sects into society, so the number of free people of color grew, from hundreds to thousands to tens of thousands, and by the middle of the nineteenth century a constituency including hundreds of thousands. During the same decades the call for women's equal rights went from a handful of voices to the demands of hundreds of thousands of single women and wives across the North and Northwest.

The most widespread response to black and female self-assertion was resistance, led by white men. The justification for their backlash against Enlightenment principles of universal rights was a quasiscientific emphasis on "God-given," "natural," and hereditary characteristics of people of color and women. According to the emerging biological theory, nature itself decreed that nonwhites and women must be barred from full participation as citizens. Like children, they were "naturally dependent" on white men, whose generally superior wisdom and judgment made them the rightful and exclusive possessors of political authority. By the time of the Supreme Court's *Dred Scott* decision in 1857, almost a generation before the parallel

Bradwell judgment on women in 1873, leading jurists were coming to regard the Enlightenment doctrine of the Declaration of Independence, perhaps even the Constitution, as impossibly dated. During debate over Kansas and Nebraska, an Indiana senator, a native of northern New York, complained that the doctrine that "all men are created equal" was a "self-evident lie." As Rufus Choate, the Massachusetts lawyer and one-time U.S. senator declared in an 1856 open letter, the United States must not be ruled according to the "glittering and sounding generalities of natural right which make up the Declaration of Independence."[6] The Democrat Taney and the Whig Choate agreed: the men who created the United States were too wise to have subscribed literally to a simple doctrine of equal rights.

This new direction in natural rights thinking joined with the emerging romantic and humanitarian values that swept Europe and the transatlantic world in the early nineteenth century. Consequently, with harsh physical punishments generally falling out of favor (except for slaves), women and children, who had long been punished with equal severity to men, now warranted some protection, especially when they were white. By midcentury the only officials fighting to retain the lash were in the South, whose senators as late as the 1850s argued that whipping was necessary to discipline sailors in the U.S. Navy.[7] Significantly, they found whipping white sailors, though perhaps less frequent, to be no less legitimate than whipping sailors of color.

Indeed in spite of the popularity and power commanded by "natural" racial and gender stereotypes, their triumph over equal rights ideology was never complete. Challengers who advocated the causes of abolition, antislavery, and women's rights grounded their arguments on the "principles of 1776," whether it was Abigail Adams in that very year or Abraham Lincoln at Gettysburg four score and seven years later. The bedrock idea held that all citizens ought to possess the same rights and that there was a single, indivisible class of citizens. If persons of color or women were born in the United States, they were citizens who should enjoy the rights of citizens. Indeed from time to time in certain electoral situations states applied the equal rights agenda—even including suffrage—to immigrants and transients as well as to people of color.

In fact, of course, there was no single American citizenship. According to the terms of the Constitution citizenship was both state and national, and the two did not necessarily overlap or afford the same rights. According to Article 4, each state was bound to treat citizens of other states equally, but that standard never operated. In principle the United States should have recognized the citizens of every state as United States citizens equal to their own residents. But that was never true, and when it came to women and people of color, that standard failed. The United States issued citizenship papers to mariners of color so as to protect them from enslavement in southern ports and to identify them internationally, but passports to assist foreign travel were another matter. Until Congress acted in 1856, passports were issued by states and cities as well as the U.S. Department of State, and no fixed rules applied. Consequently when in 1857 the Supreme Court ruled in *Dred Scott* that "no negro" or descendant of a slave could be a United States citizen, the principle of equal citizenship based on race, practiced irregularly but practiced nonetheless, suffered a great setback. As for women, something like coverture governed citizenship as well as property. As the historian Linda Kerber has explained, women's rights as citizens were never clear-cut, and well into the twentieth century when a wife left the country, her citizenship followed that of her husband.[8]

A survey of the entire early national era from American independence through the Civil War makes clear that there were always struggles over equal rights but that policies and conditions were never truly stable. This was, in the first instance, owing to the decentralized and unstable character of American sovereignty, where state governments and the national government pursued varying and sometimes contradictory policies. The dynamic and uneven economic development of the United States both generated and reinforced instability. Consequently the status of equal rights in the early Republic resists comprehensive generalizations.

Nevertheless the movement toward equal rights for all Americans, however imperfect and incomplete, appeared strongest in the first generation after 1776. Virtually everywhere there was movement, both in rhetoric and in public policy, toward the recognition of all citizens—rich and poor, white and nonwhite, female and male, and regardless of religion and ethnicity. This movement was sometimes minimal, as when property restrictions for voting were reduced but retained or when religious establishments were enlarged to include additional Protestant sects. Advocates of equal rights could not celebrate when manumission laws were enacted, motivated as such laws were in part to further the individual liberty of masters in relation to their slaves. Nor did equal rights advocates cheer when propertied widows gained the right to vote in only a single state among a baker's dozen. But manumission laws, like gradual abolition statutes, recognized the legitimacy of black freedom and opened the way for the emergence of a class of free people of color who would press for the full panoply of equal rights. And recognition of the legitimacy of female voting, if only by a single state, embodied a critical principle that advocates for women's rights would press in coming decades.

In the two generations that followed, stretching from the start of the nineteenth century to its middle years, no broadly inclusive movement on behalf of equal rights could be sustained as the effort to spread "the contagion of liberty" became sharply divisive. White men fended off movements to extend equal rights to people of color and to women as they sought exclusive possession of the benefits of the Revolutionary contagion. Consequently the emergence of the inclusive revolutionary ideology of democratic equality— a legacy of the American and French Revolutions—required development of a theory to justify social stratification, not only in the United States but in the Western world. That theory, though rooted in older ideas, led to a doctrine of natural inequality according to race and sex. Contrary to the principle "that all men are created equal" and the French Declaration of the Rights of Man, this theory justified the denial of equal rights and laid the foundation for what some have called a *Herrenvolk* democracy in the American South and perhaps the entire United States.[9] The movement toward the elimination of property requirements for suffrage would triumph convincingly in all regions, as would the disestablishment of churches together with equal rights in religion. But a broad reaction against the growing population of free people of color led to new discriminatory laws and constitutional provisions that contradicted the principle of equal rights. From the perspective of written law as well as white majority opinion, the egalitarian ideas expressed in the Declaration of Independence could come to be seen as impractical and unrealistic—merely "glittering generalities."

Although circumstances regarding women's rights differed in important respects, they were in some ways analogous. The emergence of a vigorous movement advocating equal rights for women, like the movement against slavery and in favor of equal rights for people of color, deployed petitions, conventions, and energetic press advocacy. It also generated reactionary, self-righteous opposition. Though in some states the women's rights movement gained piecemeal victories regarding property rights, divorce, and even suffrage, at the national level the countermovement carried the day. The Fifteenth Amendment unequivocally excluded women from national voting rights, while three years later the *Bradwell* case—what might be called the "women's *Dred Scott*"—denied women's equality due to natural differences.

Likewise, the question of equal rights and social class remained unresolved. Although statute law, with few exceptions, was blind to wealth and class, justice and the workings of the social order were not.[10] The right to hereditary property, sacred to the Revolutionary generation, remained at the core of this continuing structure of unequal power and unequal rights. All the social and political advantages that flowed from hereditary wealth remained in place. Moreover just as Americans showed little interest in challenging the hallowed hereditary right to property, so they showed no inclination to expand on their understanding of rights laid out by the Radical Whigs of the independence movement. For Americans, equal rights remained fundamentally those rights that protected individuals against tyrannical government, not protection from one another.

And to a significant degree, for white men the generations that followed 1776 realized the universalism of the "all men are created equal" principle. Indeed by 1870 the United States had even enacted constitutional amendments that not only ended slavery but attacked discrimination against people of color. In light of the national practice of discriminating against people of color in law and custom, as well as the long, acrimonious conflict over slavery culminating in the Civil War, this realization of equal rights in the Constitution demonstrated the power of the universalism expressed in the Declaration of Independence. That it did not surmount the gender barrier was a consequence of the fact that nowhere in the United States was there a majority, let alone a national party, that regarded women's rights as essential for defending their own political, economic, or social interests. Sectionalism and partisan politics could and did undermine slavery and enfranchise people of color, but it did virtually nothing for women's rights.

In the United States and in France the democratic revolutions of the eighteenth century with their Bill of Rights and Declaration of the Rights of Man explicitly provided foundations for men's equality. Simultaneously an unintended consequence of their universal language was the path they created for women to demand equal rights and an end to coverture. Before those goals could be realized, men would have to be persuaded to yield voluntarily their political monopoly. From the 1830s onward, generations of women's rights reformers—looking backward to the language of the Declaration of Independence—took on that task, ultimately bringing the goal into sight.

But equality—equality of condition, including the realization of positive rights such as food, shelter, and healthcare—was a different story. When the Continental Congress proclaimed the rights to "life, liberty, and the pursuit of happiness," they meant the pursuit only, not the realization of well-being. The language, which Thomas Jefferson may have taken from his copy of John Locke's *Essay on Human Understanding*, concerned an individual's right to choose a path to satisfaction and contentment, not a "right to be happy." So it is fair to say that the early Republic's society of inequalities, of competition and stratification, was consistent with the Declaration. Some Revolutionaries worried that equal rights would be undermined by the great disparities of power that accompanied great disparities of wealth, and that the heritability of great wealth might lead to a hereditary aristocracy of wealth—a plutocracy. That was why Jefferson was so proud of Virginia's abolition of primogeniture and entail, and why he, like Thomas Paine among others, advocated partible inheritance and taxation levels based on wealth.[11] But Revolutionaries from George Washington down to minutemen farmers were also committed to the pursuit and accumulation of wealth, and its heritability. Privilege according to religion and national origin would be erased, and privileges supplied by color and gender perhaps in time. But according to the creators of the United States the advantages that flowed from property were rights, not privileges. And every free man had a right to pursue them.

NOTES

═══════

Chapter One. The Declaration of Independence and the Mystery of Equality

1. Quotations from Henry Steele Commager and Milton Cantor, eds., *Documents of American History*, vol. 1, *To 1898*, 10th ed. (Englewood Cliffs, N.J.: Prentice Hall, 1988), 100, 103; Danielle Allen, *Our Declaration: A Reading of the Declaration of Independence in Defense of Equality* (New York: Liveright, 2014), 119–22.

2. Pauline Maier, *American Scripture: Making the Declaration of Independence* (New York: Alfred A. Knopf, 1997), 123–36, 191–201; Gordon S. Wood, *The Radicalism of the American Revolution* (New York: Alfred A. Knopf, 1992), 232: "Equality was in fact the most radical and most powerful ideological force let loose in the Revolution"; Joseph J. Ellis, *Founding Brothers: The Revolutionary Generation* (New York: Alfred A. Knopf, 2000), 89; Michal J. Rozbicki, *Culture and Liberty in the Age of the American Revolution* (Charlottesville: University of Virginia Press, 2011).

3. "Draft of Instructions to the Virginia Delegates in the Continental Congress," manuscript text of *A Summary View of the Rights of British America* (Williamsburg, n.d. [1774]), in *Papers of Thomas Jefferson*, ed. Julian P. Boyd, vol. 1 (Princeton, N.J.: Princeton University Press, 1950), 121–37. Rozbicki, *Culture and Liberty*, argues that English "liberty" was rooted in "liberties," i.e., privileges.

4. Linda Colley, *Britons: Forging the Nation, 1797–1837* (New Haven: Yale University Press, 1992), 30–36, 43–54, 354, 368–69.

5. Maier, *American Scripture*, xvi–xviii, 87, 124, 136–37.

6. Richard D. Brown, *Revolutionary Politics in Massachusetts: The Boston Committee of Correspondence and the Towns, 1772–1774* (Cambridge, Mass.: Harvard University Press, 1970), 62.

7. Brown, *Revolutionary Politics*, 7; William G. McLoughlin, *New England Dissent: The Baptists and the Separation of Church and State* (Cambridge, Mass.: Harvard University Press, 1971).

8. Brown, *Revolutionary Politics*, 72–73; Lev. 19:15 (AV), renders the idea as: "Ye shall do no unrighteousness in judgment: thou shalt not respect the person of the poor, nor honour the person of the mighty: *but* in righteousness shalt thou judge thy neighbour."

9. Bernard Bailyn, *Ideological Origins of the American Revolution*, enlarged ed. (Cambridge, Mass.: Harvard University Press, 1992), 283; Rozbicki, *Culture and Liberty*.

10. Barry Alan Shain, ed., *The Declaration of Independence in Historical Context* (New Haven: Yale University Press, 2014), 212. Shain reports that Congress recognized that the appeal to "laws of nature," asserted in the Suffolk County Resolves, was radical (209, 221–22). See also his "Rights Natural and Rights Civil in the Declaration of Independence," in *The Nature of Rights at the American Founding and Beyond* (Charlottesville: University of Virginia Press, 2007), 137–38.

11. Commager and Cantor, *Documents*, 79, 84, italics added. Bailyn develops this idea in *Ideological Origins*, 307.

12. Commager and Cantor, *Documents*, 92.

13. Thomas Paine, *Common Sense*, ed. Isaac Kramnick (New York: Penguin Books, 1986). For Adams on Paine, see *Diary and Autobiography of John Adams*, ed. L. H. Butterfield, Leonard C. Faber, and Wendell D. Garrett, vol. 4 (Cambridge, Mass.: Harvard University Press, 1961), 330–34; and for George Washington's and John Adams's reactions to *Common Sense*, see Bailyn, *Ideological Origins*, 288–89.

14. Commager and Cantor, *Documents*, 103, italics added.

15. Paul Finkelman, *Slavery and the Founders: Race and Liberty in the Age of Jefferson* (Armonk, N.Y.: M. E. Sharpe, 1996); Edmund S. Morgan, *American Slavery, American Freedom: The Ordeal of Colonial Virginia* (New York: W. W. Norton, 1975), 379–80; Shain, *Declaration of Independence*, 209, 221–22; Rogers Smith, *Civic Ideals: Conflicting Visions of Citizenship in U.S. History* (New Haven: Yale University Press, 1997), 1, 3, 8, 9.

16. Arthur Lee and Francis Fauquier (1760) in Andrew Levy, *The First Emancipator: The Forgotten Story of Robert Carter, the Founding Father Who Freed His Slaves* (New York: Random House, 2005), 19, 23; Boyd, *Papers of Thomas Jefferson*, 130; Continental "Association," Oct. 20, 1774, in Commager and Cantor, *Documents*, 85; *Strictures upon the Declaration of the Congress at Philadelphia*, quoted in Bailyn, *Ideological Origins*, 246; "How is it that we hear the loudest *yelps* for liberty among the drivers of negroes?," Samuel Johnson, "Taxation Not Tyranny," in *Yale Edition of the Works of Samuel Johnson*, vol. 10 (New Haven: Yale University Press, 1977), 454.

17. John Adams to Timothy Pickering, Aug. 6, 1822, in *Works of John Adams*, ed. Charles Francis Adams, vol. 2 (1850–56; reprint, Freeport, N.Y.: Books for Libraries Press, 1969), 514n; Boyd, *Papers of Thomas Jefferson*, 317–18.

18. Boyd, *Papers of Thomas Jefferson*, 314–15; William Gordon, "Letter V," *Independent Chronicle* (Boston), Oct. 3, 1776, 1.

19. Alexander Saxton, *The Rise and Fall of the White Republic: Class Politics and Mass Culture in Nineteenth-Century America* (London: Verso, 1990), 30; James Otis, *Rights of the British Colonies Asserted and Proved* (Boston, 1764), 43. Three London reprints followed.

20. George H. Moore, *Notes on the History of Slavery in Massachusetts* (New York, 1866; reprint, New York: Negro Universities Press, 1968), 124–25.

21. Moore, *Notes on the History of Slavery*, 131–32 (italics added), 133–36; Conrad Edick Wright, *Revolutionary Generation: Harvard Men and the Consequences of Independence* (Amherst: University of Massachusetts Press, 2005), 57.

22. Moore, *Notes on the History of Slavery*, 145–46.

23. Moore, *Notes on the History of Slavery*, 149–50, 153.

24. Moore, *Notes on the History of Slavery*, 180–81; Oscar and Mary Handlin, eds., *The Popular Sources of Political Authority: Documents on the Massachusetts Constitution of 1780* (Cambridge, Mass.: Harvard University Press, 1966), 442; Paul Finkelman, *An Imperfect Union: Slavery, Federalism, and Comity* (Chapel Hill: University of North Carolina Press, 1981), 41; Gloria McCahon Whiting, "'The Negroes Have Left': African Americans and the Politics of Emancipation in Massachusetts," paper presented at Massachusetts Historical Society conference on American Revolution, Apr. 10, 2015.

25. Louis B. Wright, ed., *The Prose Works of William Byrd of Westover: Narratives of a Colonial Virginian* (Cambridge, Mass.: Harvard University Press, 1966), 221. Cited in Wood, *Radicalism of the American Revolution*, 235.

26. Levy, *First Emancipator*, 19; *Journals of the House of Burgesses*, Apr. 1, 1772, 131.

27. Boyd, *Papers of Thomas Jefferson*, 130; Melvin Patrick Ely, *Israel on the Appomattox: A Southern Experiment in Black Freedom from the 1790s through the Civil War* (New York: Alfred A. Knopf, 2004), 33.

28. On Carter, see Levy, *First Emancipator*, 117–18, 138, 180; on Randolph, see Ely, *Israel on the Appomattox*, 27–29; on Washington, see Joseph J. Ellis, *His Excellency: George Washington* (New York: Alfred A. Knopf, 2004), 162–64; and François Furstenberg, *In the Name of the Father: Washington's Legacy, Slavery, and the Making of the Nation* (New York: Penguin, 2006). Manumission of Washington's slaves followed the death of his wife, Martha, whose slaves remained enslaved owing to entail restrictions.

29. Ferdinando Fairfax, "Plan for Liberating the Negroes within the United States," *The American Museum, or Universal Magazine* (Philadelphia), December 1790, 285–87. Fairfax dated his plan Richmond, March 6, 1790. Italics added.

30. St. George Tucker, *A Dissertation on Slavery: With a Proposal for the Gradual Abolition of It, in the State of Virginia* (Philadelphia: Mathew Carey, 1796). Tucker

systematically explored the demography of slavery and other approaches, including Massachusetts' abolition. See "Queries Respecting the Slavery and Emancipation of Negroes in Massachusetts, Proposed by the Hon. Judge Tucker of Virginia, and Answered by the Rev. Dr. Belknap," *Collections of the Massachusetts Historical Society for the Year 1795*, 1st ser., vol. 4 (Boston, 1795; reprinted 1835), 191–211.

31. William W. Hening and William Munford, *Reports of Cases Argued and Determined in the Supreme Court of Appeals of Virginia: With Select Cases Relating Chiefly to Points of Practice, Decided at the Superior Court of Chancery for the Richmond District, part 1, vol. 1* (Richmond, 1807), 134.

32. Hening and Munford, *Reports of Cases*, 139,141.

33. Hening and Munford, *Reports of Cases*, 141; Tucker, *Dissertation on Slavery*, t.p.

34. *Virginia Herald* (Fredericksburg), Sept. 23, 1800; James Sidbury, *Ploughshares into Swords: Race, Rebellion, and Identity in Gabriel's Virginia, 1730–1810* (Cambridge: Cambridge University Press, 1997), 129; Ira Berlin, *Many Thousands Gone: The First Two Centuries of Slavery in North America* (Cambridge, Mass.: Harvard University Press, 1998), 284.

35. Thomas Jefferson, *Notes on the State of Virginia* (1785), intro. Thomas Perkins Abernathy (New York: Harper Torchbooks, 1964), 133; Bruce Dain, *A Hideous Monster of the Mind: American Race Theory in the Early Republic* (Cambridge, Mass.: Harvard University Press, 2002), chap. 1 ("The Face of Nature").

36. Jefferson, *Notes on the State of Virginia*, 133–35.

37. Jefferson to Benjamin Banneker, Philadelphia, Aug. 30, 1791, in *Thomas Jefferson: Writings*, ed. Merrill D. Peterson (New York: Library of America, 1984), 982. For Jefferson's growing belief in natural inferiority of blacks to whites and Indians, see Johann N. Neem, "'To Diffuse Knowledge More Generally through the Mass of the People': Thomas Jefferson on Individual Freedom and the Distribution of Knowledge," in *Light and Liberty: Thomas Jefferson and the Power of Knowledge*, ed. Robert M. S. McDonald (Charlottesville: University of Virginia Press, 2012), 65–67.

38. Jefferson to Henri Gregoire, Washington, Feb. 25, 1809, in Peterson, *Jefferson Writings*, 1202; Hening and Munford, *Reports of Cases*, 139; Jefferson to Joel Barlow, Oct. 8, 1809, in *Writings of Thomas Jefferson*, ed. Andrew A. Lipscomb and Albert Ellery Bergh, vol. 12 (Washington, D.C.: Thomas Jefferson Memorial Association, 1903), 322.

39. Richard D. Brown, *Major Problems in the Era of the American Revolution, 1760–1791* (New York: Houghton Mifflin, 2000), 171, 261–62; Benjamin Rush, "An Account of the Vices Peculiar to the Indians of North America," in *Essays, Literary, Moral and Philosophical* (1798), ed. Michael Meranze (1806 ed.; reprint, Schenectady, N.Y.: Union College Press, 1988).

40. Frank Lambert, *The Founding Fathers and the Place of Religion in America* (Princeton, N.J.: Princeton University Press, 2003), 129.

41. First Continental Congress, "Address to the People of Great Britain, October 21, 1774," and Second Continental Congress, "To the Oppressed Inhabitants of Canada, May 29, 1775," in Shain, *Declaration of Independence in Historical Context*, 198, 265–66.

42. Bailyn, *Ideological Origins*, 258–60.

43. Commager and Cantor, *Documents*, 104.

44. Lambert, *Founding Fathers*, 226–27, 229–35; Commager and Cantor, *Documents*, 125–26.

45. Bailyn, *Ideological Origins*, 263–64.

46. Brown, *Major Problems*, 353–54, italics added.

47. John Leland, *The Connecticut Dissenters' Strong Box: No.* 1 (New London, 1791), in *Political Sermons of the American Founding Era, 1730–1805*, ed. Ellis Sandoz (Indianapolis: Liberty Press, 1991), 1092–93; Brown, *Major Problems*, 356, 365.

48. Brown, *Major Problems*, 365; John Milton, *Areopagitica* (London, 1644): "And though all the winds of doctrine were let loose to play upon the earth, so Truth be in the field, we do injuriously by licensing and prohibiting to misdoubt her strength. Let her and Falsehood grapple; who ever knew Truth put to the worse in a free and open encounter? Her confuting is the best and surest suppressing."

49. Thomas Anbury in Morgan, *American Slavery, American Freedom*, 378–79; Wood, *Radicalism of the American Revolution*, 233, 243.

50. Holly Brewer, "Entailing Aristocracy in Colonial Virginia: 'Ancient Feudal Restraints' and Revolutionary Reform," *William and Mary Quarterly*, 3rd ser., 54 (1997): 307–46; Steven Rosswurm, *Arms, Country, and Class: The Philadelphia Militia and "Lower Sort" during the American Revolution, 1775–1783* (New Brunswick, N.J.: Rutgers University Press, 1987), 104; Gary B. Nash, *The Unknown American Revolution: The Unruly Birth of Democracy and the Struggle to Create America* (New York: Viking, 2005), 275–76.

51. Jefferson, *Notes on the State of Virginia*, 140; Wood, *Radicalism of the American Revolution*, 237, 101. See also Michal Jan Rozbicki, "Rethinking the American Revolution: Politics and the Symbolic Foundations of Reality," *Historically Speaking* 13 (April 2012): 8–10.

52. Wood, *Radicalism of the American Revolution*, 233–34.

53. Allen, *Our Declaration*, 268–69.

54. Jonathan Boucher in Bailyn, *Ideological Origins*, 316.

55. Alexander Hamilton, John Jay, and James Madison, *The Federalist*, ed. Benjamin F. Wright (Cambridge, Mass.: Harvard University Press, 1961), 94.

56. "If a nation expects to be ignorant & free, in a state of civilisation, it expects what never was & never will be." Jefferson to Charles Yancey, Monticello, Jan. 6, 1816, in *Papers of Thomas Jefferson, Retirement Series*, ed. J. Jefferson Looney, vol. 9 (Princeton, N.J.: Princeton University Press, 2012), 331.

Chapter Two. Contending for Religious Equality

1. Frank Lambert, *The Founding Fathers and the Place of Religion in America* (Princeton, N.J.: Princeton University Press, 2003), 178–79.
2. *Wikipedia*, s.v. "Jew Bill of 1753"; Lambert, *Founding Fathers*, 133. Elaine F. Crane reports intolerance toward Jews in Rhode Island: "Uneasy Coexistence: Religious Tensions in Eighteenth Century Newport," *Newport History* 53 (Summer 1980): 101–11. According to Jacob Rader Marcus, ed., *The Colonial American Jew*, *1492–1776*, vol. 1 (Detroit: Wayne State University Press, 1970), 265, in 1783 only one state had Jewish citizens.
3. Lambert, *Founding Fathers*, 220.
4. Attribution to Mason and Madison includes Garrett Ward Sheldon and Daniel L. Dreisbach, eds., *Religion and Political Culture in Jefferson's Virginia* (Lanham, Md.: Rowman and Littlefield, 2000), 137–40. Text from Henry Steele Commager and Milton Cantor, eds., *Documents of American History*, vol. 1, *To 1898*, 10th ed. (Englewood Cliffs: Prentice Hall, 1988), 104.
5. New Jersey Constitution of 1776, *New-York Gazette and the Weekly Mercury*, July 22, 1776, 2:2; Pennsylvania Declaration of Rights, Sept. 18, 1776, available at http://avalon.law.yale.edu/18th_century/pa08.asp; North Carolina Declaration of Rights, Dec. 18, 1776, available at http://avalon.law.yale.edu/18th_century/nc07.asp.
6. Lambert, *Founding Fathers*, 208, 220. Lambert sees two alternatives: the tolerationist status quo or full religious liberty and equality.
7. Jason K. Duncan, *Citizens as Papists: The Politics of Anti-Catholicism in New York, 1685–1821* (New York: Fordham University Press, 2005), 28. See also Mark Douglas McGarvie, *One Nation under Law: America's Early National Struggles to Separate Church and State* (DeKalb, Ill.: Northern Illinois University Press, 2004), chap. 5 ("Revolutionary Era Disestablishment: The Case of New York State"), 97–130.
8. Commager and Cantor, *Documents of American History*, 91; Duncan, *Citizens as Papists*, 38.
9. Owen Stanwood, "Catholics, Protestants, and the Clash of Civilizations in Early America," in *The First Prejudice: Religious Tolerance and Intolerance in Early America*, ed. Chris Beneke and Christopher S. Grenda (Philadelphia: University of Pennsylvania Press, 2011), 218–40; Thomas Paine, *Common Sense*, ed. Edward Larkin (Peterborough, Ont.: Broadview Press, 2004), 53, 56; William Pencak, *Jews and Gentiles in Early America, 1654–1800* (Ann Arbor: University of Michigan Press, 2005), 9.
10. New York State Constitution, Apr. 20, 1777, available at http://avalon.law.yale.edu/18th_century/ny01. arts. 35, 39.
11. New York State Constitution, art. 38.
12. Duncan, *Citizens as Papists*, 41, 51–53.
13. Duncan, *Citizens as Papists*, 41, 54, 119, 121–25, 130, 181.

14. Jonathan D. Sarna, *American Judaism: A History* (New Haven: Yale University Press, 2004), 65.

15. Morton Borden, *Jews, Turks, and Infidels* (Chapel Hill: University of North Carolina Press, 1984), 51.

16. Thomas Jefferson, *Writings*, ed. Merrill Peterson (New York: Library of America, 1984), 344; Lambert, *Founding Fathers*, 227, 228, 232.

17. Dumas Malone, *Jefferson the Virginian*, vol. 1 of *Jefferson and His Time* (Boston: Little, Brown, 1948), 275, 277. For Patrick Henry's religious identification, see George F. Willison, *Patrick Henry and His World* (Garden City, N.Y.: Doubleday, 1969), 314.

18. Malone, *Jefferson the Virginian*, 275–76; Lambert, *Founding Fathers*, 227, 229, 233.

19. Lambert, *Founding Fathers*, 229–30. Daniel L. Dreisbach, "Church-State Debate in the Virginia Legislature: From the Declaration of Rights to the Statute for Establishing Religious Freedom," in Sheldon and Dreisbach, *Religion and Political Culture*, 149–50.

20. Washington to George Mason, Mount Vernon, Oct. 3, 1785, in *The Papers of George Mason*, ed. Robert A. Rutland et al., vol. 2 (Chapel Hill: University of North Carolina Press, 1970), 832. On Washington's religious beliefs, see Peter R. Henriques, *Realistic Visionary: A Portrait of George Washington* (Charlottesville: University of Virginia Press, 2006), 167–85.

21. Robert A. Rutland et al., eds., *The Papers of James Madison*, vol. 8 (Chicago: University of Chicago Press, 1973), 295–97. Text of religious liberty broadside was ten pages in Isaiah Thomas's 1786 reprinting.

22. Rutland et al., *Papers of James Madison*, 299–301.

23. Rutland et al., *Papers of James Madison*, 302–4.

24. Rutland et al., *Papers of James Madison*, 297; *Pennsylvania Packet and Daily Advertiser* (Philadelphia), Sept. 21, 1785, 3:2, dated Richmond, August 27.

25. Charles Ramsdell Lingley, *The Transition in Virginia from Colony to Commonwealth* (New York: Columbia University and Longmans, Green, 1910), 205; Rhys Isaac, "'The Rage of Malice of the Old Serpent Devil': The Dissenters and the Making and Remaking of the Virginia Statute for Religious Freedom," in *The Virginia Statute for Religious Freedom: Its Evolution and Consequences*, ed. Merrill D. Petersen and Robert C. Vaughn (Cambridge: Cambridge University Press, 1988), 150.

26. Text from Peterson and Vaughn, *Virginia Statute for Religious Freedom*, xvii–xviii.

27. Sheldon and Dreisbach, *Religion and Political Culture*, 163–64n140. The bill first passed December 17, 1785. Jefferson's retrospective views on the law in his "Autobiography" between January 6, 1821, and July 1821, are in *Thomas Jefferson: Writings*, ed. Merrill D. Peterson (New York: Library of America, 1984), 40. Madison's similar retrospective views from his detached memoranda, 1819, are in *James Madison: Writings*, ed. Jack Rakove (New York: Library of America, 1999), 761.

28. Constitution of Pennsylvania, Sept. 28, 1776, available at http://avalon.law.yale. edu/18th_century/pa08.asp. "Petition of the Philadelphia Synagogue to Council of Censors of Pennsylvania," Dec. 23, 1783, in *Church and State in the United States*, ed. Anson Phelps Stokes, vol. 1 (New York: Harper and Brothers, 1950), 287–89. William Pencak argues that Pennsylvania exclusion of Jews was a deliberate anti-Semitic policy in "Anti-Semitism, Toleration, and Appreciation: The Changing Relations of Jews and Gentiles in Early America," in Beneke and Grenda, *First Prejudice*, 241–62, esp. 250.

29. *Pennsylvania Packet, and General Advertiser* (Philadelphia), Jan. 17, 1784, 3:2; Pennsylvania Constitution of 1790, art. 9, secs. 3, 4.

30. "The Last Will and Testament of Charles Lee, Esquire, Late Major General in the American Army," *New-York Packet, and the American Advertiser*, Feb. 9, 1784, 2:3–4. Lee wrote the will in 1782 and died in October 1783.

31. North Carolina Declaration of Rights and Constitution, Dec. 18, 1776, art. 19, copied art. 2 of the Pennsylvania declaration. The antiestablishment provision is art. 34 of the North Carolina Constitution. The exclusion of clergymen is addressed in arts. 31, 33.

32. *Proceedings and Debates of the Convention of North-Carolina, Called to Amend the Constitution of the State, . . . 1835* (Raleigh, 1836), 318–19; Samuel A. Ashe, Stephen B. Weeks, and Charles L. Van Noppen, eds., *Biographical History of North Carolina from Colonial Times to the Present*, vol. 2 (Greensboro, N.C.: Charles L. Van Noppen, 1905), 31; Leon Huhner, "The Struggle for Religious Liberty in North Carolina, with Special Reference to the Jews," *American Jewish Historical Society Publications* 16 (1907): 46, 46n; John S. Watterson, "Revolutionary Non-Conformist: Thomas Burke of North Carolina," *South Dakota State History* 6 (1976): 334–52, said that Burke was probably not Catholic, but 1835 testimony asserts that his Catholicism was well known.

33. Martin H. Brinkley, "A Brief History of the North Carolina Supreme Court," *NCpedia*, http://ncpedia.org/supreme-court-north-carolina; William S. Powell, ed., *Dictionary of North Carolina Biography*, 6 vols. (Chapel Hill: University of North Carolina Press, 1986–96), 2:283–85, 4:211.

34. Biographical Directory of the United States Congress, bioguide.congress.gov, s.v. "Gaston, William," and "Manly, Matthias Evans"; Huhner, "Struggle for Religious Liberty," 48.

35. "Address in the Committee of the Whole of the House of Commons of North Carolina, December 6, 1809," in A *Documentary History of the Jews in the United States, 1654–1875*, ed. Morris U. Schappes (New York: Citadel Press, 1950), 122–25, esp. 122–23. Henry, son of Joel and Amelia Henry of Beaufort, Carteret County, applied to marry Esther Whithurst, Feb. 9, 1801; listed as freemason, Beaufort, 1807; Schappes, *Documentary History*, 597n2. Huhner, "Struggle for Religious Liberty," 51, on reporting Henry's speech.

36. Huhner, "Struggle for Religious Liberty," 123–25. Variant versions of the Golden Rule appear in the Old Testament, Lev. 19:18 ("Thou shalt love thy neighbor as thyself"), and in the New Testament, Matt. 7:12 and Lk. 6:46.

37. Borden, *Jews, Turks, and Infidels*, 44–45, 44–50.

38. William G. McLoughlin, *New England Dissent, 1630–1833: The Baptists and the Separation of Church and State* (Cambridge, Mass.: Harvard University Press, 1971), 556–67, 565.

39. McLoughlin, *New England Dissent*, 594–95, 596–97; Phillips Payson, *A Sermon Preached before the Honorable Council, and the Honorable House of Representatives, of the State of Massachusetts-Bay . . . May 27, 1778* (Boston, 1778), 20.

40. McLoughlin, *New England Dissent*, 597–99.

41. McLoughlin, *New England Dissent*, 602–3, 607, 610. The restriction against Catholic office-holding was lifted by the legislature in 1820. Catherine B. Shannon, "'With Good Will Doing Service': The Charitable Irish Society of Boston (1737–1857)," *Historical Journal of Massachusetts* 43 (2015): 106.

42. Oscar Handlin and Mary Handlin, eds., *The Popular Sources of Political Authority: Documents on the Massachusetts Constitution of 1780* (Cambridge, Mass.: Harvard University Press, 1966), 442–43.

43. Handlin and Handlin, *Popular Sources*, 443.

44. Handlin and Handlin, *Popular Sources*, 657–58.

45. Handlin and Handlin, *Popular Sources*, 632–33.

46. Handlin and Handlin, *Popular Sources*, 691. According to the *Return of the Whole Number of Persons within the Several Districts of the United States . . . Second Census [1800] . . .* (n.p., n.d.), 9, Fitchburg had 1,392 persons: 346 free white males aged sixteen years and over.

47. Handlin, *Popular Sources*, 651, 652–53, 659, 1084, 1088, 1098–99, 1101–2, 1104, 1124–25. The Supreme Judicial Court favored Congregational establishment; it upheld contracts for clerical salaries of incorporated parishes. Previously all parish ratepayers were taxable for salaries; so if some ratepayers could opt out, the contract was undermined.

48. Handlin and Handlin, *Popular Sources*, 1156, 1164.

49. Handlin and Handlin, *Popular Sources*, 1189–93.

50. Handlin and Handlin, *Popular Sources*, 1200–1201. McLoughlin, *New England Dissent*, 1203, compares the act to general incorporation laws; Sarah Barringer Gordon, "The First Disestablishment: Limits on Church Power and Property before the Civil War," *University of Pennsylvania Law Review* 162 (2014): 307–72.

51. Ronald F. Banks, *Maine Becomes a State: The Movement to Separate Maine from Massachusetts, 1785–1820* (Middletown, Conn.: Wesleyan University Press for the Maine Historical Society, 1970), 155–56, 180.

52. McLoughlin, *New England Dissent*, 1248, 1259.

53. Nancy Lusignan Schultz, *Fire and Roses: The Burning of the Charlestown Convent, 1834* (New York: Free Press, 2000); Daniel A. Cohen, "Alvah Kelley's Cow: House-hold Feuds, Proprietary Rights, and the Charlestown Convent Riot," *New England Quarterly* 74 (2001): 531–79; Leonard W. Levy, *Blasphemy: Verbal Offense against the Sacred from Moses to Salman Rushdie* (New York: Alfred A. Knopf, 1993), 400–401, 413–23; Henry Steele Commager, "The Blasphemy of Abner Kneeland," *New England Quarterly* 8 (1935): 32; Borden, *Jews, Turks, and Infidels*, 101. See also Christopher Grasso, "The Boundaries of Toleration and Tolerance: Religious Infidelity in the Early American Republic," in Beneke and Grenda, *First Prejudice*, 286–302.

54. Levy, *Blasphemy*, 419–22, 422–23.

55. Levy, *Blasphemy*, 423.

56. McLoughlin, *New England Dissent*, 917, 919, 921, 922, 931.

57. McLoughlin, *New England Dissent*, 894; Borden, *Jews, Turks, and Infidels*, 33–34. Borden notes New Hampshire's 1850 constitutional convention, when anti-Catholic nativism flourished. Voters retained the Protestant test: 12,082 to 9,566. In 1876 voters ended the test: 28,477 to 14, 231. Voters removed "Protestant" from the Constitution in 1968: 142,112 to 67,697. Article 3 of the 1777 Vermont Constitution's "Declaration of Rights" guaranteed civil rights to "protestant" men. The 1786 Constitution dropped "protestant" but retained encouragement for Christian worship, renewed in the 1793 Vermont Constitution. The current constitution reads: "Every sect or denomination of Christians ought to observe the Sabbath or Lord's day, and keep up some sort of religious worship, which to them shall seem most agreeable to the revealed will of God." Vermont Constitution, chap. 1, art. 3.

58. Borden, *Jews, Turks, and Infidels*, 37–40, 13, 29; Jonathan D. Sarna and David G. Dalin, *Religion and State in the American Jewish Experience* (South Bend, Ind.: University of Notre Dame Press, 1997), 94–97.

59. Borden, *Jews, Turks, and Infidels*, 17–18. Article 6, sec. 3, of the Constitution in Commager and Cantor, *Documents of American History*, 145.

60. Michael I. Meyerson, *Endowed by Our Creator: The Birth of Religious Freedom in America* (New Haven: Yale University Press, 2012), 181–85, chap. 6 ("Freedom of Religion in the New Nation"), 180–235; Commager and Cantor, *Documents of American History*, 173. Phrase order reversed: Henriques, *Realistic Visionary*, 174, 176–79; Washington to Mason, Mount Vernon, Oct. 3, 1785. See also Chris Beneke, "The 'Catholic Spirit Prevailing in Our Country': America's Moderate Religious Revolution," in Beneke and Grenda, *First Prejudice*, 265–85.

61. Article 11 of the treaty, *Gazette of the United States*, June 16, 1797, 3:3.

62. Jefferson to Messrs. Nehemiah Dodge and Others, A Committee of the Danbury Baptist Association, in the State of Connecticut, Jan. 1, 1802, in Peterson, *Jefferson: Writings*, 510; "Speech in Congress Proposing Constitutional Amendments," June 8, 1789, in Rakove, *Madison: Writings*, 450–51; Detached memorandum on

"Monopolies. Perpetuities. Corporations. Ecclesiastical Endowments," in Rakove, *Madison: Writings*, 763.

63. Nathan O. Hatch, *The Democratization of American Christianity* (New Haven: Yale University Press, 1989); Christine Leigh Heyrman, *Southern Cross: The Beginnings of the Bible Belt* (New York: Alfred A. Knopf, 1997).

64. Peterson and Vaughn, eds., *Virginia Statute for Religious Freedom*, xviii; Sean Wilentz, *The Rise of American Democracy: Jefferson to Lincoln* (New York: W. W. Norton, 2005), 450. One anomaly was the survival in some states of Britain's ancient "Benefit of Clergy," whereby convicts could occasionally be saved from the gallows by swearing a Christian oath. It survived in North and South Carolina until Reconstruction. Maryland and Virginia abolished it after the Revolution, but Virginia retained it for slaves to 1848. Jeffrey K. Sawyer, "Benefit of Clergy in Maryland and Virginia," *American Journal of Legal History* 34 (1990): 49–68; Richard B. Morris, "Benefit of Clergy in America and Related Matters," *University of Pennsylvania Law Review* 105 (1957): 436–38.

Chapter Three. Equal Justice for Irishmen and Other Foreigners

1. Linda Colley, *Britons: Forging the Nation, 1707–1837* (New Haven: Yale University Press, 1992).

2. *The True-Born Englishman: A Satyr* (n.p. [London], 1701). Maximillian [sic] E. Novak, *Daniel Defoe, Master of Fictions: His Life and Ideas* (Oxford: Oxford University Press, 2001), 148–49; Paula R. Backscheider, *Daniel Defoe: His Life* (Baltimore: Johns Hopkins University Press, 1989), 75, calls this satire "the great literary triumph of Defoe's lifetime," reporting fifty editions by 1750; John Tutchin in Novak, *Daniel Defoe*, 149; *True-Born Englishman*, 4, 6, 7.

3. Frank Lambert, *The Founding Fathers and the Place of Religion in America* (Princeton, N.J.: Princeton University Press, 2003), 133.

4. Leonard W. Labaree and Whitfield Bell, eds., *Papers of Benjamin Franklin*, vol. 4, *July 1, 1750, through June 30, 1753* (New Haven: Yale University Press, 1961), 234. Franklin wrote *Observations* in 1751; first publication, Boston, 1755; additional printings through 1769. Thomas Malthus quoted Franklin's *Observations*; Adam Smith owned two copies. Franklin set up a German press for the growing Pennsylvania German market.

5. Labaree and Bell, *Papers of Benjamin Franklin*, 234.

6. Thomas Paine, *Common Sense*, ed. Edward Larkin (Peterborough, Ont.: Broadview, 2004), 64, 76.

7. J. Hector St. John de Crèvecoeur, *Letters from an American Farmer; Describing Certain Provincial Situations, Manners, and Customs . . . of the British Colonies in North America* (London, 1782), 48, 49, 50. Within two years the work, patronized by Benjamin Franklin, had eight editions in five countries.

8. Crèvecoeur, *Letters from an American Farmer*, 52, 51.

9. *Statutes at Large, First Congress of the United States*, 2nd Sess., chap. 3, 103–4. Citizenship requires a year's residency in the state where citizenship was claimed; a child must also be a U.S. resident.

10. U.S. Congress, *Debates and Proceedings in the Congress of the United States . . . Third Congress . . . December 2, 1793, to March 3, 1795 . . .* (Washington, D.C.: Gales and Seaton, 1849), 1034–35.

11. U.S. Congress, *Debates and Proceedings*, 1034–35.

12. U.S. Constitution, art. 1, sec. 9. In Henry Steele Commager and Milton Cantor, eds., *Documents of American History*, vol. 1, *To 1898*, 10th ed. (Englewood Cliffs, N.J.: Prentice Hall, 1988), 142; U.S. Congress, *Debates and Proceedings*, 1039, 1040, 1041, 1054, 1057. Vote: 63 opposed, 28 in favor (from New York and New England).

13. U.S. Congress, *Debates and Proceedings*, 1057. Vote: 59 in favor, 32 opposed (mostly from the North); U.S. Congress, *Debates and Proceedings*, statute 2 (Jan. 29, 1795), chap. 20, 414.

14. U.S. Congress, *Debates and Proceedings*, 1066; U.S. Congress, *Debates and Proceedings*, statute 2 (Jan. 29, 1795), chap. 20, 414.

15. U.S. Congress, *Debates and Proceedings in the Congress of the United States . . . Fifth Congress . . . May 15, 1797, to March 3, 1799 . . .* (Washington, D.C.: Gales and Seaton, 1851), 422 (July 1, 1797).

16. U.S. Congress, *Debates and Proceedings*, 424 (July 1, 1797). Harper, a 1765 native of Virginia, moved with his parents to North Carolina as a child, graduated from Princeton, and later moved to Baltimore. He served as U.S. senator from Maryland in 1815–16.

17. U.S. Congress, *Debates and Proceedings*, 1568 (May 1798).

18. U.S. Congress, *Debates and Proceedings*, 429–30 (July 1, 1797). Otis, born in 1765, served as U.S. senator from Massachusetts, 1817–22.

19. U.S. Congress, *Debates and Proceedings*, 1570. Otis excepted present naturalized citizens.

20. U.S. Congress, *Debates and Proceedings*, 1570 and 426–27 (July 1, 1797). Thatcher, a 1754 Massachusetts native, served in Congress from 1787 to 1801 and resided in Maine.

21. U.S. Congress, *Debates and Proceedings*, 427 (July 1, 1797). McDowell (1756–1801) was a Virginia native brought to North Carolina in 1758; U.S. Congress, *Debates and Proceedings*, 1573 (May 3, 1798), 425 (July 1, 1797). Macon (1757–1837), a North Carolina native, served in the U.S. House and Senate, 1791–1828. U.S. Congress, *Debates and Proceedings*, 462–63 (July 8, 1797). Holmes (1769–1832), a Pennsylvania native, moved to Virginia as a child; he served as U.S. representative from Virginia, 1797–1809, and as U.S. senator from Mississippi, 1820–25. His proposal failed. U.S. Congress, *Debates and Proceedings*, 426 (July 1, 1797). Lyon (1749–1822)

immigrated to Connecticut in 1765 as an indentured farm laborer. He moved to Vermont in 1774 and served as U.S. representative, first from Vermont, 1797–1801, and later from Kentucky, 1803–11.

22. U.S. Congress, *Debates and Proceedings*, 426 (July 1, 1797).

23. U.S. Congress, *Debates and Proceedings*, 423–24 (July 1, 1797). On John Swanwick, see Harry Marlin Tinkcom, *The Republicans and Federalists in Pennsylvania, 1790–1801* (Harrisburg: Pennsylvania Historical and Museum Commission, 1950), 85, 142, 160–61, 173.

24. U.S. Congress, *Debates and Proceedings*, 428, 431. Vote July 1, 1797: 46 for tax, 42 opposed.

25. "Memorial and Address of the People Called Quakers from Their Yearly Meeting Held in Philadelphia . . . from the 25th of the 9th Month, to the 29th of the Same Inclusive, 1797," in U.S. Congress, *Debates and Proceedings*, 657; whole debate on 656–70, 661 (Nov. 30, 1797), 945–1033.

26. U.S. Congress, *Debates and Proceedings*, 1579 (May 3, 1798), 1631 (May 8, 1798), 1776 (May 21, 1798).

27. U.S. Congress, *Debates and Proceedings*, 570–572 (June 25, 1798). James Madison to Thomas Jefferson, May 20, 1798, in *The Papers of James Madison*, ed. David B. Mattern, J. C. A. Stagg, Jeanne K. Cross, and Susan Holbrook Perdue, vol. 17 (Charlottesville: University Press of Virginia, 1991), 133–34.

28. U.S. Congress, *Debates and Proceedings*, 2019 (June 21, 1798). Otis's word order was altered so that his use of "trial by jury" replaces his later use of "this," followed by "as well as other advantages"; Otis, U.S. Congress, *Debates and Proceedings*, 429–30 (July 1, 1797).

29. Stanley Elkins and Eric McKitrick, *The Age of Federalism* (New York: Oxford University Press, 1983), 703–11; Lawrence W. Levy, *Emergence of a Free Press* (New York: Oxford University Press, 1985), chap. 8.

30. U.S. Congress, *Debates and Proceedings*, 566–69 (June 18, 1798).

31. U.S. Congress, *Debates and Proceedings*, 566–69 (June 18, 1798); U.S. Congress, *Debates and Proceedings*, 422, 424 (July 1, 1797).

32. Frank George Franklin, *The Legislative History of Naturalization in the United States* (1906; reprint, New York: Arno, 1969), 97.

33. U.S. Congress, *Public Statutes at Large of the United States of America . . .* , vol. 2 (Boston: Little and Brown, 1845), 153–55 (Apr. 14, 1802). The gender-neutral use of "he or she" is notable, a first for U.S. naturalization law.

34. U.S. Congress, *Public Statutes*, 153 (Apr. 14, 1802. James H. Kettner, *The Development of American Citizenship, 1608–1870* (Chapel Hill: University of North Carolina Press for the Institute of Early American History and Culture, 1978), 246; Franklin, *Legislative History of Naturalization*, 109. One further naturalization law was enacted on June 18, 1813, to allow British subjects who, before the War of 1812,

had begun naturalization proceedings or were eligible to become citizens though otherwise regarded as "enemy aliens" excluded from citizenship. Franklin, *Legislative History of Naturalization*, 128.

35. Alexander Hamilton, John Jay, and James Madison, *The Federalist*, ed. Benjamin F. Wright (Cambridge, Mass.: Harvard University Press, 1961), 94.

36. Ruth Wallis Herndon, *Unwelcome Americans: Living on the Margin in Early New England* (Philadelphia: University of Pennsylvania Press, 2001), 13, 175. Herndon found four immigrants in her 1750–1800 sample: one Englishman, one German, one Irishman, and one West African.

37. *Boston Gazette*, Nov. 10, 1783, 3; *Boston Independent Ledger and Advertiser*, Jan. 19, 1784, 3; *Salem Gazette*, Jan. 22, 1784, 3; *The Life, Last Words, and Dying Speech of Cassumo Garcelli . . . January 15, 1784* (Boston, n.d.).

38. *American Bloody Register: Containing a True and Complete History of the Lives, Last Words, and Dying Confessions of Three of the Most Noted Criminals . . . Richard Barrick and John Sullivan, High way Robbers. Together with the Dying Confession of Alexander White, a Murderer and Pirate . . .* (Boston: E. Russell, 1784), 7. Also Daniel A. Cohen, *Pillars of Salt, Monuments of Grace: New England Crime Literature and the Origins of American Popular Culture, 1674–1860* (New York: Oxford University Press, 1993), 123–24.

39. Timothy Hilliard, *Paradise Promised, by a Dying Saviour, to the Penitent Thief on the Cross* (Boston, 1785; reprint, Newburyport, Mass., 1785), 7.

40. On Grout and Coven, see *The Life, Last Words and Dying Speech of Dirick Grout, a Dutchman, of New-York State, Aged 36; and Francis Coven, a Frenchman, Belonging to Marseilles, Aged 22; Who Were Executed This Day, Pursuant to Their Sentence, for the Crime of Burglary, Thursday, October 28, 1784* (n.p., n.d.). Also *Massachusetts Centinel and Republican Journal* (Boston), Sept. 15, 1784, 3; *Massachusetts Spy or Worcester Gazette*, Sept. 23, 1784, 3; *Independent Chronicle* (Boston), Oct. 14, 1784, 3. *Independent Chronicle* reprinted: *Independent Ledger* (Boston), *Salem Gazette*, *Essex Journal* (Newburyport), *South Carolina Gazette and General Advertiser* (Charleston), *New Hampshire Gazette* (Portsmouth), *Providence Gazette*, *Pennsylvania Packet* (Philadelphia), *Vermont Journal* (Windsor), *Massachusetts Spy* (Worcester), and others.

41. *American Herald* (Boston), Nov. 15, 1784, 3. The same article was reprinted in Philadelphia's *Independent Gazetteer*, Dec. 4, 1784, 2.

42. *Life, Last Words and Dying Speech of John Sheehan, Who Was Executed at Boston, on Thursday, November Twenty-Second, 1787, for Burglary* (Boston: E. Russell, n.d. [1784]); *Independent Chronicle and the Universal Advertiser* (Boston), Nov. 30, 1787, 3.

43. *Independent Chronicle and the Universal Advertiser* (Boston), Nov. 30, 1787, 3; *American Mercury* (Hartford), Dec. 3, 1787, 3. Identical reports in Philadelphia's

Independent Gazetteer, Dec. 6, 1787, 2; *Pennsylvania Packet* (Philadelphia), Dec. 7, 1787, 2; and *Vermont Journal* (Windsor), Dec. 31, 1787, 3.

44. Significant anti-Catholicism was reported after 1815 when Protestant Orangemen from Northern Ireland clashed with Catholics from Southern Ireland in New York, Philadelphia, and elsewhere. David Noel Doyle, *Ireland, Irishmen and Revolutionary America, 1760–1820* (Dublin: Mercier, 1981), 212.

45. Colley, *Britons*, 326–28.

46. Doyle, *Ireland, Irishmen*, 62.

47. Doyle, *Ireland, Irishmen*, 101; Thomas Archdeacon, *Becoming American: An Ethnic History* (New York: Free Press, 1983), 25, 26. The Charitable Irish Society, formed in Boston in 1737, originally assisted Presbyterians from Northern Ireland; but later included Catholics from the south in its mission. Catherine B. Shannon, "The Charitable Irish Society of Boston, (1737–1857)," *Historical Journal of Massachusetts* 43 (2015): 94–123.

48. Charles Woodmason in Doyle, *Ireland, Irishmen*, 87.

49. Doyle, *Ireland, Irishmen*, ix, 80.

50. Kerby A. Miller, Arnold Schrier, Bruce D. Boling, and David N. Doyle, eds., *Irish Immigrants in the Land of Canaan* (New York: Oxford University Press, 2003), 625. Douglas Bradburn, *The Citizenship Revolution: Politics and the Creation of the American Union* (Charlottesville: University Press of Virginia, 2009), 234, says that the term "Scotch-Irish" dates chiefly after 1850.

51. Robert Secor, "Ethnic Humor in Early American Almanacs," in *A Mixed Race: Ethnicity in Early America*, ed. Frank Shuffleton (New York: Oxford, 1993), 163–93, esp. 177–81.

52. Doyle, *Ireland, Irishmen*, 182. Andrew Jackson, elected president in 1828, was the son of Scots-Irish immigrants to South Carolina in 1765, two years before his birth.

53. Michael J. O'Brien, *A Hidden Phase of American History: Ireland's Part in America's Struggle for Liberty* (New York: Dodd, Mead, 1919), 168.

54. Newspaper accounts in the *Courier* (Boston), Aug. 19, 1795, and *Salem Gazette*, Nov. 11, 1795; Nathaniel Fisher, *A Sermon Delivered at Salem, January 14, 1796, Occasioned by the Execution of Henry Blackburn on That Day for the Murder of George Wilkinson* (Salem, 1796), 18. The Reverend William Bentley referred to Wilkinson as "a young English seaman." *Diary of William Bentley, D.D., Pastor of the East Church, Salem, Massachusetts*, vol. 2, January 1793–December 1802 (Gloucester: Peter Smith, 1962), 157.

55. *A Sermon Preached at the Execution of Matthias Gotleib [sic], for Murder; at Newton, October 28, 1796* (Newton, N.J.: 1796), 2, 3, 4–8; Daniel Allen Hearn, *Legal Executions in New Jersey, 1691–1963* (Jefferson, N.C.: McFarland, 2005), 63, 428.

56. Search of "Cutlip" and "1796" in America's Historical Newspapers, series 1–6.

57. *Hampshire Gazette* (Northampton, Mass.), Oct. 5, 1796, 3:2; *American Intelligencer* (West Springfield, Mass.), Oct. 4, 1796, 3:3; *Massachusetts Spy: Or, the Worcester*

Gazette, Oct. 12, 1796, 3:1; Doron Ben-Atar and Richard D. Brown, *Taming Lust: Crimes against Nature in the Early Republic* (Philadelphia: University of Pennsylvania Press, 2014), 41–50, 129–37.

58. Petitions in Governor's Council Pardon File, John Farrell, 1796, Massachusetts Archives.

59. Francisco Dos Santos, *A Full and Particular Account of the Trial of Francisco Dos Santos, Alias Francisco Son for the Murder of Archibald Graham . . . Held in the City of New-York, Jan. 9, 1806 . . . to Which is Added a Short Account of His Life, Together with His Confession . . .* (New York: n.p., 1806), 3, 17. Also Daniel Allen Hearn, *Legal Executions in New York State: A Comprehensive Reference, 1639–1963* (Jefferson, N.C.: McFarland, 1997), 30, 296.

60. Dos Santos, *Trial of Francisco dos Santos,* 10, 17, 21–23.

61. On Morton, see J. Jefferson Looney and Ruth L. Woodward, *Princetonians, 1791–1794: A Biographical Dictionary* (Princeton, N.J.: Princeton University Press, 1991), 198–203. Morton (1775–1810) was among the first Americans named after George Washington. By 1806 he was prominent, connected to the Schuylers and Alexander Hamilton's family through marriage. In 1797 he eloped with Cornelia Schuyler from Albany to Stockbridge, Massachusetts, where the prominent Federalist congressman Theodore Sedgwick arranged their marriage and assisted in reconciling her father to the match.

62. Looney and Woodward, *Princetonians, 1791–1794,* 19.

63. *Hampshire Federalist* (Springfield, Mass.), Mar. 11, 1806, 3:2.

64. *Hampshire Federalist* (Springfield, Mass.), Mar. 11, 1806, 3:2; *Republican Spy* (Northampton, Mass.), Mar. 29, 1806, 3; and the *Reporter* (Brattleboro, Vt.), May 3, 1806, 2. The case produced neither trial report nor execution sermon to elaborate. The inflammatory possibilities of such a trial are evident in the case of Bathsheba Spooner and her foreign, in this instance British, confederates for the 1778 murder of her husband. See Deborah Navas, *Murdered by His Wife: A History with Documentation of the Joshua Spooner Murder and Execution of His Wife, Bathsheba, Who Was Hanged in Worcester, Massachusetts, July 2, 1778* (Amherst: University of Massachusetts Press, 1999).

65. [Dominic Daley and James Halligan], *Report of the Trial of Dominic Daley and James Halligan for the Murder of Marcus Lyon, . . . April 1806* (Northampton, Mass., 1806), 9. Modern distance measurement: 116 miles; Richard D. Brown, "'Tried, Convicted, and Condemned, in Almost Every Bar-Room and Barber's Shop': Anti-Irish Prejudice in the Trial of Dominic Daley and James Halligan, Northampton, Massachusetts, 1806," *New England Quarterly* 84 (2011): 205–33.

66. Irene Quenzler Brown and Richard D. Brown, *The Hanging of Ephraim Wheeler: A Story of Rape, Incest, and Justice in Early America* (Cambridge, Mass.: Harvard University Press, 2003), 361n45.

67. "Ezra Witter," in Franklin B. Dexter, *Biographical Sketches of the Graduates of Yale College with the Annals of the College History*, vol. 5, June 1792–September 1805 (New York: Henry Holt, 1911), 94–95.

68. Ezra Witter, *A Discourse Delivered in Wilbraham, November 17, 1805, Occasioned by the Murder of Marcus Lyon* (Springfield, Mass., n.d. [1805?]), 8. Possibly Witter was the anonymous letter writer in *Hampshire Federalist*, Mar. 11, 1806.

69. Witter, *Discourse*, 13. Word order of "state-prisons" and "crowded" here reversed.

70. Witter, *Discourse*, 13, 14.

71. [Daley and Halligan], *Report of the Trial*, 32. In 1800 gentlemen of the Connecticut Academy of Arts and Sciences asked local leaders to enumerate their capital criminals, suicides, and poor and to report whether they were "natives or foreigners." Christopher P. Bickford, *Voices of the New Republic: Connecticut Towns, 1800–1832* (New Haven: Connecticut Academy of Arts and Sciences, 2003), first solicitation to Connecticut towns, 6, 9.

72. William Lincoln, *History of Worcester, Massachusetts, from Its Earliest Settlements to September 1836* (1836; reprint, Worcester, Mass.: Charles Hersey, 1862), 199–200. Blake's political identification from his *Oration, Pronounced at Worcester, on the Anniversary of American independence: July 4, 1796* (Worcester, Mass., 1796).

73. Halligan's other attorney was Jabez Upham. Daley's attorneys were Thomas Gold and Edward Upham. *Report of the Trial*, 6.

74. [Daley and Halligan], *Report of the Trial*, 24. Ages in *Hampshire Federalist* (Springfield, Mass.), June 10, 1806, 3.

75. [Daley and Halligan], *Report of the Trial*, 21, 22; "this lad," 48, 49.

76. [Daley and Halligan], *Report of the Trial*, 34.

77. [Daley and Halligan], *Report of the Trial*, 32, 33.

78. [Daley and Halligan], *Report of the Trial*, 34–35.

79. [Daley and Halligan], *Report of the Trial*, 52–53. When Irish immigrants became more numerous in the decades after 1830, prejudice increased; see Charles and Tess Hoffman, *Brotherly Love: Murder and the Politics of Prejudice in Nineteenth-Century Rhode Island* (Amherst: University of Massachusetts Press, 1993).

80. [Daley and Halligan], *Report of the Trial*, 63, 65. Blake's defense covers pp. 28–65. The text says that Blake supplied it in writing (from memory) to the lawyer, who compiled the report. In November and December 1805, New York newspapers advertised an Irish edition of Curran's speeches, including the one Blake quoted. Curran's popularity is evident in that his speech opposing standing armies was reprinted in a Jeffersonian paper in Richmond, Va., in 1802, and in Isaac Riley's publication in 1809 and 1811 of a two-volume New York City edition of Curran's speeches.

81. Blake and other defense attorneys were praised in [Dominic Daley and James Halligan], *Brief Account of the Murder of Marcus Lyon* (Palmer, Mass., n.d. [1806]), 11.

Two editions of this pamphlet appeared. The first sixteen-page edition is held at the Forbes Library, Northampton. The second fourteen-page edition held by American Antiquarian Society lacks the elegy for the convicts.

82. [Daley and Halligan], *Report of the Trial*, 67, 75, 79, 80, 81, 86.

83. Ann Daley, "Petition for the Pardon of Her Son Dominick Daley under Sentence of Death in Hampshire County," Pardons Not Granted file, 1780–1820, Massachusetts Archives. Caleb Strong endorsed the petition, stating that the Council advised him not to grant the petition.

84. *Hampshire Federalist* (Springfield, Mass.), June 10, 1806, 3. The text is 1 John 3:15, a broad statement on divine love, sinfulness, and human responsibility. This contemporary evidence of Cheverus's text presents the thrust of his sermon. Scott D. Seay, *Hanging between Heaven and Earth: Capital Crime, Execution Preaching, and Theology in Early New England* (DeKalb: Northern Illinois University Press, 2009), compiled a database of all printed execution sermons in the colonies and the United States and found that Cheverus was the only person who chose this or any text from John.

85. James Russell Trumbull, *History of Northampton, Massachusetts, from Its Settlement in 1654*, vol. 2 (Northampton, Mass.: n.p., 1902), 589–92. The full text of Cheverus's sermon is lost. It is not in any U.S. Catholic archive. Cheverus returned to France, but his ship and papers were lost at sea. He rose to the rank of cardinal, so his papers could be in the Vatican. The passage quoted by Trumbull is from the paragraph reportedly from Cheverus's sermon in M. Hamon [André Jean Marie], *The Life of Cardinal Cheverus, Archbishop of Bordeaux, and Formerly Bishop of Boston*, from the French of J. Huen-Dubourg [pseudo.], trans. E. Stewart (Boston: n.p., 1839), 87. This was Trumbull's chief source for Cheverus in Northampton. The authenticity of the text cannot be verified and, having passed through translation by both French and English writers, may be doubted. Publication in Boston within possible memory of the event, and reproduction by a Northampton historian familiar with oral traditions, provide credibility.

86. Trumbull, *History of Northampton*, 591. Trumbull's account follows Hamon's *Life of Cardinal Cheverus* almost verbatim.

87. *Hampshire Federalist* (Springfield, Mass., June 10, 1806), 3; *Boston Gazette*, June 12, 1806, 2; *Portsmouth (N.H.) Oracle*, June 14, 1806, 3; *Reporter* (Brattleboro, Vt.), June 14, 1806, 3; *Salem Register*, June 16, 1806, 3; *Salem Gazette*, June 17, 1806, 3; *Courier* (Norwich, Conn.), June 18, 1806, 3; *Freeman's Friend* (Salem, Me.), June 18, 1806, 3; *Eastern Argus* (Portland, Me.), June 19, 1806, 2; *Haverhill (Mass.) Museum*, June 24, 1806, 4; *Post-Boy* (Windsor, Vt.), June 24, 1806, 199. At least four papers reported the execution without mentioning a nationality, and several carried advertisements for the printed trial report but did not report the execution.

88. *Brief Account of the Murder of Marcus Lyon*, 9.

89. *Trial of Frederick Eberle and Others, at a Nisi Prius Court, Held at Philadelphia, July 1816* (Philadelphia, 1817), 17, 134; Friederike Baer, *The Trial of Frederick Eberle: Language, Patriotism, and Citizenship in Philadelphia's German Community* (New York: New York University Press, 2008), esp. chap. 3, "Germans and Anglicized Eyrisch-Germans: The Parties," 69–94.

90. Baer, *Trial of Frederick Eberle*, 177; Sarah Barringer Gordon, "The First Disestablishment: Limits on Church Power and Property before the Civil War," *University of Pennsylvania Law Review* 162 (2014): 307–72.

91. *Report of the Trial of Henry Phillips, for the Murder of Gaspard Denegri, . . . 9th and 10th Jan. 1817. With the Address of the Chief Justice to the Prisoner, in Pronouncing Sentence of Death, and an Appendix Containing a Concise History of the Prisoner's Life* (Boston: Russell, Cutler, 1817), 4, 5; report of M'Cann acquittal in *Hampden Federalist* (Springfield, Mass.), Mar. 22, 1817, 2.

92. *Report of the Trial of Henry Phillips*, 6.

93. *Report of the Trial of Henry Phillips*, 50, 51.

94. Henry Phillips, *Trial of Henry Phillips for the Murder of Gaspard Dennegri* [Boston: Bangs, 1817], 5. This twenty-four-page account was advertised January 15, five days after the trial ended; the forty-eight-page account by Russell, Cutler, advertised as "just published," was issued January 30.

95. *Trial of Henry Phillips*, 7, 27.

96. *Trial of Henry Phillips*, 41–42.

97. *Boston Daily Advertiser and Repertory*, Jan. 23, 1817, 2; *Trial of Henry Phillips*, 17; Lemuel Shaw and George Sullivan to Governor John Brooks, Boston, Jan. 18, 1817, Inactive Pardons and Pardons Not Granted collection, re: Henry Phillips, Massachusetts Archives.

98. Shubael Bell and 136 others, Petition to Gov. John Brooks, et al., Jan. 29, 1817, and Henry Phillips, Petition to Gov. John Brooks, et al., Jan. 29, 1817 (in hand of Lemuel Shaw, attested by him and S. Bell, Gaoler), Inactive Pardons and Pardons Not Granted collection, re: Henry Phillips, Massachusetts Archives.

99. *Report of the Trial of George Ryan, before the Superior Court, at Charlestown, N.H., in the County of Cheshire, May Term . . . 1811 . . . for Highway Robbery* (Keene, N.H., n.d.). Many New England newspapers reported this episode without mentioning Ireland or the Irish, e.g., *New England Palladium* (Boston), Mar. 15, 1811, 1; William M'Donnough, *Trial of William M'Donnough, on an Indictment for the Murder of His Wife, Elizabeth M'Donnough, before the Hon. Supreme Judicial Court, . . . at November Term, Holden at Boston . . . on the Fourth Tuesday of November, 1817 . . . from Minutes Taken at the Trial, by a Gentleman of the Bar* (Boston, 1817), 5, 8, 15, 53; *Boston Repertory*, Jan. 20, 1818, 2.

100. Stephen Murphy and John Doyle, *Report of the Trials of Stephen Murphy and John Doyle, before the Supreme Judicial Court, at Dedham, Oct. 23, 1817, for the Rape*

of Rebecca Day, Jun., on the 10th Aug. 1817. By a Gentleman of the Norfolk Bar (Boston, 1817), 7, 16, 21.

101. Michael Powers, *Life of Michael Powers, Now under Sentence of Death, for the Murder of Timothy Kennedy* (Boston, 1820), 5–7. The crime and Powers's flight, capture, and trial were covered in press accounts from Portland, Maine, to Richmond, Virginia. Accounts began with the *Boston Daily Advertiser* or the *Boston Patriot and Daily Mercantile Advertiser* but were often abbreviated. Shortened accounts often omitted an Irish reference.

102. *Repertory* (Boston), Mar. 9, 1820, 4. Between 1811 and 1831 the paper was also known as the *Repertory and General Advertiser, Boston Advertiser*, and *Boston Daily Advertiser.*

103. John Wood Sweet, *Bodies Politic: Negotiating Race in the American North, 1730–1830* (Baltimore: Johns Hopkins University Press, 2003), 309–10. Hugh Henry Brackenridge, *American Chivalry*, was published in several parts: 1792, 1795, 1805, 1815.

104. "Irish Emigrants," *Essex Patriot* (Elizabeth-town, New Jersey), May 31, 1817, 1.

105. "Irish Emigrants," 1; Alexander Keyssar, *The Right to Vote: The Contested History of Democracy in the United States* (New York: Basic Books, 2000), 32.

106. *Trial of Henry Phillips*, 6.

107. Michael Martin, *Trial of Michael Martin, for Highway Robbery, before the Supreme Judicial Court of Massachusetts, for the County of Middlesex, October Term, 1821. Reported by F. W. Waldo, Esq.* (Boston, 1821), 5, 6.

108. [Redford Webster], *Miscellaneous Remarks on the Police of Boston; as Respects Paupers; Alms and Work House; Classes of Poor and Beggars; Laws Respecting Them; Charitable Societies; Evils of the Justiciary; Imprisonment for Debt; Remedies* (Boston, 1814), 5, 8, 14, 15, 24. The whole report is forty-two pages. Connecticut leaders showed the same concern and tracked capital crimes and suicides "and whether committed by natives or foreigners." They counted the poor, "whether natives or foreigners," as well as "free blacks; their number, vices and modes of life, their industry and success in acquiring property; whether those born free are more ingenious, industrious and virtuous, than those who were emancipated after arriving to adult years." Bickford, *Voices of the New Republic*, 6, 9.

109. [Webster], *Miscellaneous Remarks*, 8, 32. "Flagitious" means "atrocious" or "infamous."

Chapter Four. People of Color and the Promise Betrayed

1. Benjamin Howard, *Report of the Decision of the Supreme Court of the United States . . . in the Case of Dred Scott . . . December Term, 1856* (Washington, D.C.: C. Wendell, 1857), 16, 18. Joseph J. Ellis, *Founding Brothers: The Revolutionary Generation* (New York: Alfred A. Knopf, 2000), 89, observes: "However utopian and

excessive the natural rights section of the Declaration . . . might appear later on," the Declaration "was an unambiguous tract for abolition."

2. [Redford Webster], *Miscellaneous Remarks on the Police of the Poor of Boston; as Respects Paupers; Alms and Work House; Classes of Poor and Beggars; . . .* (Boston, 1814), 14.

3. Abraham Lincoln, Charleston, Ill., Sept. 15, 1858, in *The Lincoln-Douglas Debates*, ed. Harold Holzer (New York: HarperCollins, 1993), 189.

4. Wendell Phillips, *The Constitution a Pro-Slavery Compact; or, Selections from the Madison Papers, &c.* (New York: American Anti-Slavery Society, 1844).

5. Christopher Leslie Brown, *Moral Capital: Foundations of British Abolitionism* (Chapel Hill: University of North Carolina Press for the Omohundro Institute of Early American History and Culture, 2006), 96–98. William M. Wiecek, *The Sources of Antislavery Constitutionalism in America, 1760–1848* (Ithaca, N.Y.: Cornell University Press, 1977), 32–35. Wiecek, *Sources*, 34, quotes Cowper's verse, which is in *Task*, (London, 1785), bk. 2, ll. 40ff.

6. *Virginia Gazette* (Williamsburg), Aug. 20, 1772, 1:2. Wiecek quotes part of this in *Sources of Antislavery*, 34.

7. William Wetmore, Minutes of the Trial, Essex Inferior Court, Newburyport, October 1773, *Caesar v. Greenleaf*, argument of [John] Lowell, Massachusetts Historical Society Digital Editions, DocLJA02d027, 1773-10.

8. James Thomson's poem was set to music by Thomas Arne in 1740 and performed in London in 1745. The poem reads: "Britons never shall be slaves"; the lyric for "Rule Britannia!" repeats "never." See Linda Colley, *Britons: Forging the Nation, 1707–1837* (New Haven: Yale University Press, 1992), 3, 386n1. On *Somersett* in Anglo-American politics, see Van Gosse, "'As a Nation, the English Are Our Friends': The Emergence of African American Politics in the British Atlantic World, 1772–1861," *American Historical Review* 113 (2008): 1003–28.

9. James Otis, *The Rights of the British Colonies Asserted and Proved* (Boston, 1764), 29. Otis cited Montesquieu's criticism of race-based slavery in his 1748 *Spirit of the Laws*, published in Edinburgh and London in 1750.

10. "A History of the Dividing Line betwixt Virginia and North Carolina Run in the Year of Our Lord 1728," in *The Prose Works of William Byrd of Westover: Narratives of Colonial Virginia*, ed. Louis B. Wright (Cambridge, Mass.: Harvard University Press, 1966), 221.

11. Jeff Broadwater, *George Mason: Forgotten Founder* (Chapel Hill: University of North Carolina Press, 2006), 34; extract from address in the *Virginia Gazette*, Mar. 19, 1767; "By a Respectable Member of the Community" [Philadelphia? Printed for Joseph Crukshank? 1770?], 1, italics Lee's.

12. Patrick Henry to Robert Pleasants, Hanover, Jan. 18, 1773, in *Patrick Henry: Life, Correspondence and Speeches*, ed. William Wirt Henry, vol. 1 (New York, 1891), 152. Pleasants (1723–1801) was a Virginia planter and Quaker abolitionist who furnished

Henry with Anthony Benezet's *Caution and Warning to Great Britain and Her Colonies, in a Short Representation of the Calamitous State of the Enslaved Negroes in the British Dominions. Collected from Various Authors, and Submitted to the Serious Consideration of All, More Especially of Those in Power* [Philadelphia? 1770?].

13. Henry to Pleasants, italics added.

14. Eva Sheppard Wolf, *Race and Liberty in the New Nation: Emancipation in Virginia from the Revolution to Nat Turner's Rebellion* (Baton Rouge: Louisiana University Press, 2006), 21.

15. Pauline Maier, *American Scripture: Making the Declaration of Independence* (New York: Alfred A. Knopf, 1997), 146–47. Samuel Johnson asked: "How is it that we hear the loudest yelps for liberty among the drivers of negroes?" *Taxation no Tyranny: An Answer to the Resolutions and Address of the American Colonies*, 4th ed. (London, 1775), 89.

16. Wolf, *Race and Liberty*, 23.

17. "The Association, October 20, 1774," in *Documents of American History*, ed. Henry Steele Commager and Milton Cantor, vol. 1: *To 1898*, 10th ed. (Englewood Cliffs, N.J.: Prentice Hall, 1988), 85.

18. Wolf, *Race and Liberty*, 25–26.

19. Richard A. Wilson and Richard D. Brown, eds., *Humanitarianism and Suffering: The Mobilization of Empathy* (New York: Cambridge University Press, 2009), intro.; John W. Sweet, *Bodies Politic: Negotiating Race in the American North, 1730–1830* (Baltimore: Johns Hopkins University Press, 2003), 240, argues "in the era of the American Revolution, public support for slavery was challenged less by concepts of liberty or equality than by humanitarian sensibility." This seems persuasive through 1776, but the balance shifted toward liberty and equality, although the humanitarian impulse continued to influence antislavery and abolition, 1776–1865.

20. Broadwater, *George Mason*, 84.

21. Broadwater, *George Mason*, 84. The exclusion applied to *slaves*, not blacks or free people of color. Conflating these categories was not unusual in the late eighteenth century, an inaccuracy that such distinguished scholars as William Wiecek have accepted. Wiecek, *Sources of Antislavery*, 52. Gordon S. Wood, *The Radicalism of the American Revolution* (New York: Alfred A. Knopf, 1992), 234, says that "equal" in George Mason's Bill of Rights and in the Declaration of Independence meant that no one should be dependent on the will of another.

22. "Edmund Randolph's Essay on the Revolutionary History of Virginia, 1774–1782," *Virginia Magazine of History and Biography* 11 (1936): 45. Randolph was Jefferson's second cousin.

23. Maier, *American Scripture*, 165, 168. "Before 1840, Americans viewed the Declaration as being rhetorical or hortatory, rather than as a substantive and operative component of the constitution." Wiecek, *Sources of Antislavery*, 264.

24. Italics added. Drayton in Hezekiah Niles, *Principles and Acts of the Revolution in America* (Baltimore: W. O. Niles, 1822), 100. The vote of June 25, 1778, is in Peter M. Bergman and Jean McCarroll, eds., *The Negro in the Continental Congress* (New York: Bergman, 1969), 31–32 (*Journals of the Continental Congress*, 9:652, 653). For the absent Delaware and North Carolina delegates, see Merrill Jensen, *The Articles of Confederation: An Interpretation of the Constitutional History of the American Revolution, 1774–1781* (Madison: University of Wisconsin Press, 1940), 195. See Jack Rakove, *The Beginnings of National Politics: An Interpretive History of the Continental Congress* (New York: Alfred A. Knopf, 1979), 187. Jensen and Rakove are silent on inclusive or exclusive language.

25. Paul Finkelman, *Slavery and the Founders: Race and Liberty in the Age of Jefferson* (Armonk, N.Y.: M. E. Sharpe, 1996), 118–19; Gregory D. Massey, "The Limits of Antislavery Thought in the Revolutionary Lower South: John Laurens and Henry Laurens," *Journal of Southern History* 63 (1997): 495–530.

26. Virginia Constitution, June 29, 1776.

27. Gaston's ruling in *State v. Manuel* case of 1838 cited by Associate U.S. Supreme Court Justice Benjamin Curtis dissenting in *Scott v. Sandford* (1857). Gaston (1778–1844) was born Catholic and was an active Catholic layman who graduated from Princeton in 1796. A Federalist, he served in the North Carolina legislature and in Congress (1813–17). At the 1835 Constitutional Convention, Gaston opposed disfranchisement of people of color and advocated ending the state's requirement that public officials be Protestants, a requirement his own career contradicted. Ratification of North Carolina's constitutional amendments divided voters: 55 percent supported revisions; 45 percent opposed them.

28. Douglas Bradburn, *The Citizenship Revolution: Politics and the Creation of the American Union* (Charlottesville: University of Virginia Press, 2009), 245; Associate U.S. Supreme Court Justice Benjamin Curtis's dissent in *Scott v. Sandford* listed these states with Massachusetts.

29. Pennsylvania Constitution, Sept. 28, 1776, Declaration of Rights, art. 7. The Frame of Government, sec. 6, provides, "Every freeman of the full age of twenty-one Years, having resided in this state for the space of one whole Year next before the day of election for representatives, and paid public taxes during that time, shall enjoy the right of an elector: Provided always that the sons of freeholders of the age of twenty-one years shall be intitled to vote although they have not paid taxes." The 1790 constitution lengthened the residence requirement to two years. Julie Winch, "'Free Men and 'Freemen': Black Voting Rights in Pennsylvania, 1790–1870," Historical Society of Pennsylvania, *Legacies* 8, no. 2 (2008): 14–19. According to Paul Finkelman, *An Imperfect Union: Slavery, Federalism, and Comity* (Chapel Hill: University of North Carolina Press, 1981), 195n, after 1783, Connecticut and Rhode Island alone among northern states denied free black suffrage. These states did not

create constitutions during the Revolutionary era, relying instead on their colonial charters of the 1660s.

30. John Hancock, *The Great Question for the People! Essays on the Elective Franchise; or, Who Has the Right to Vote?* (Philadelphia: Merrihew and Son, 1865), 23, italics Hancock's.

31. David Skillin Bogen, "The Maryland Context of *Dred Scott*: The Decline in the Legal Status of Maryland Free Blacks, 1776–1810," *American Journal of Legal History* 34 (1990): 387, 387–90, 396–400; Sweet, *Bodies Politic*, 223.

32. David Brion Davis, *The Problem of Slavery in the Age of Emancipation* (New York: Alfred A. Knopf, 2014), chaps. 3–6.

33. Wolf, *Race and Liberty*, 3. The 1723 law replaced a 1691 statute that permitted manumission if masters paid for ex-slave to leave Virginia. See also Linda Rowe, "After 1723, Manumission Takes Careful Planning and Plenty of Savvy," *Colonial Williamsburg Interpreter* 25, no. 2 (2004). During the eighteenth century "meritorious services" meant outstanding character and service. Manumission was also by will, although that required a petition to the Governor and Council. From 1723 to 1773 there were just twenty petitions, some of which were rejected. See also Sweet, *Bodies Politic*, 223.

34. Sweet, *Bodies Politic*, 202, 215.

35. Wolf, *Race and Liberty*, 35, 36, 39, 45.

36. Wolf, *Race and Liberty*, 39, 44, 63, 64.

37. Wolf, *Race and Liberty*, chap. 2. In 1798 the Revolutionary war officer Thaddeus Kościuszko directed Jefferson, as executor of his American will, to use his assets to purchase freedom for slaves, providing them with land and implements as independent farmers. Gary B. Nash and Graham Russell Gao Hodges, *Friends of Liberty: Thomas Jefferson, Tadeusz Kościuszko, and Agrippa Hull* (New York: Basic Books, 2008), 163.

38. Wolf, *Race and Liberty*, 130; William Waller Hening and William Munford, *Reports of Cases Argued and Determined by the Supreme Court of Appeals of Virginia: With Select Cases Relating Chiefly to Points of Practice, Decided by the Superior Court of Chancery for the Richmond District*, vol. 1 (Philadelphia: [Smith and Maxwell], 1808), 134–44. Reversal on 144. Also Imogene E. Brown, *American Aristides: A Biography of George Wythe* (Rutherford, N.J.: Fairleigh Dickinson University Press, 1981), 266–67.

39. James Monroe to Thomas Jefferson, Richmond, June 11, 1802, in *The Papers of Thomas Jefferson*, vol. 37, *4 March to 30 June, 1802*, ed. Barbara Oberg (Princeton, N.J.: Princeton University Press, 2010), 589, italics added. Matthew Mason, *Slavery and Politics in the Early American Republic* (Chapel Hill: University of North Carolina Press, 2006), 19, quotes the letter.

40. Leon F. Litwack, *North of Slavery* (Chicago: University of Chicago Press, 1961), 72; Peter Onuf, *Statehood and Union: A History of the Northwest Ordinance* (Bloom-

ington: Indiana University Press, 1987), chap. 6, "Slavery and Freedom;" Stephen Middleton, *The Black Laws: Race and Legal Process in Early Ohio* (Athens: Ohio University Press, 2005), 42–73.

41. Paul Finkelman, ed., *Encyclopedia of African American History, 1619–1895* (New York: Oxford University Press, 2006), 153; Onuf, *Statehood and Union*, 116–18.

42. Donald S. Spencer, "Edward Coles: Virginia Gentleman in Frontier Politics," *Journal of the Illinois State Historical Society* 61, no. 2 (1968): 152–58; 57 percent (6,640) of voters rejected the convention; 43 percent (4,972) approved.

43. David Ress, *Governor Edward Coles and the Vote to Forbid Slavery in Illinois, 1823–1824* (Jefferson, N.C.: McFarland, 2006), 105, 163; Onuf, *Statehood and Union*, 123–26.

44. Sean Wilentz, *The Rise of American Democracy: Jefferson to Lincoln* (New York: W. W. Norton, 2005), 192–94, treats New York and Connecticut. In the Connecticut Constitutional Convention of 1818, Stephen Mix Mitchell (1743–1835), delegate to the Continental Congress (1785–88) and Connecticut's 1788 ratifying convention, sought unsuccessfully to delete "white" from the suffrage qualification. Mitchell served on the Connecticut Supreme Court, 1795–1807, and as chief justice, 1807–14.

45. Sweet, *Bodies Politic*, 267.

46. Lacey K. Ford Jr., "Making the 'White Man's Country' White: Race, Slavery, and State Building in the Jacksonian South," *Journal of the Early Republic* 19 (1999): 731–34; John Hope Franklin, *The Free Negro in North Carolina, 1790–1860* (1943; reprint, New York: W. W. Norton, 1971), 112–14, shows that western North Carolina generally favored continued black voting, whereas eastern residents generally disapproved.

47. Wilentz, *Rise of American Democracy*, 542, 551; Paul Goodman, *Of One Blood: Abolitionism and the Origins of Social Equality* (Berkeley: University of California Press, 1998), 7.

48. Chilton Williamson, *American Suffrage: From Property to Democracy* (Princeton, N.J.: Princeton University Press, 1960); Richard Sisson, Christian Zacher, Andrew and Robert Lee Cayton, eds., *The American Midwest: An Interpretive Encyclopedia* (Bloomington: Indiana University Press, 2006), 1556; Paul Finkelman, "The Promise of Equality and the Limits of Law," in *The History of Michigan Law*, ed. Paul Finkelman and Martin J. Hershock (Athens: Ohio University Press, 2007), 190; Ray A. Brown, "The Making of the Wisconsin Constitution, Part I," *Wisconsin Law Review* (1949): 648, and "Part II," *Wisconsin Law Review* (1952): 23. Wisconsin permitted suffrage for Indians who were citizens.

49. Frederick Douglass, "What to the Slave Is the Fourth of July?," oration at Rochester, N.Y., July 5, 1852, in *The Frederick Douglass Papers*, Series One: Speeches, Debates, and Interviews, vol. 2, 1847–54, ed. John W. Blassingame (New Haven: Yale University Press, 1982), 371.

50. Winthrop D. Jordan, *White over Black: American Attitudes toward the Negro, 1550–1812* (Chapel Hill: Institute of Early American History and Culture by University of North Carolina Press, 1968); Winthrop D. Jordan, *The White Man's Burden: Historical Origins of Racism in the United States* (New York: Oxford University Press, 1974), 50–54.

51. Samuel Sewall, *The Selling of Joseph: A Memorial* (Boston, 1700), 1, 3. Some Quakers took the same position in the 1688 "Germantown Protest." Katherine Gerbner, "Antislavery in Print: The Germantown Protest, the 'Exhortation,' and the Seventeenth-Century Quaker Debate on Slavery," *Early American Studies* 9 (2011): 564.

52. Jordan, *White over Black*, 199–200. Also Albert J. Von Frank, "John Saffin: Slavery and Racism in Colonial Massachusetts," *Early American Literature* 29 (1994): 252–72. Saffin (1626–1710) left Boston for Bristol, R.I., in 1687.

53. Sewall, *Selling of Joseph*, 2.

54. Jill Lepore, *New York Burning: Liberty, Slavery, and Conspiracy in Eighteenth-Century Manhattan* (New York: Alfred A. Knopf, 2005), 203, 205. Though the writer is anonymous, Lepore attributes the letter to Massachusetts jurist Benjamin Lynde. It compares the New York episode to Salem witchcraft prosecutions.

55. Arthur Lee, *An Essay in Vindication of the Continental Colonies of America, from a Censure of Mr. Adam Smith, in His Theory of Moral Sentiments* (London, 1764), 45, 37, 30.

56. Lee, *Essay in Vindication*, 45.

57. James Otis, *The Rights of the British Colonies Asserted and Proved* (Boston, 1764), 29. Otis anticipated the *Virginia Gazette* piece of Aug. 20, 1772 (see note 7, above), which said that color logic would leave "one free Man left, which will be the Man of the palest Complexion in the three Kingdoms!" Otis also seemed to accept the distinction that Edmund Pendleton made in the Virginia convention in 1776, namely that these rights belong to "every man out of society" (30). Otis did not explicitly say that people of color, free or slave, carry these rights into society, but presumably every free person, at least, did so.

58. Quoted in Alexander Saxton, *The Rise and Fall of the White Republic: Class Politics and Mass Culture in Nineteenth-Century America* (London: Verso, 1990), 30.

59. Quoted in Sweet, *Bodies Politic*, 108–9, 111, 114; for the Connecticut tavern talk, see Daniel R. Mandell, *Tribe, Race, History: Native Americans in Southern New England, 1780–1880* (Baltimore: Johns Hopkins University Press, 2007), 193, 438n3; Thomas N. Ingersoll, *To Intermix with Our White Brothers: Indian Mixed Bloods in the United States from the Earliest Times to the Indian Removals* (Albuquerque: University of New Mexico Press, 2005).

60. Jacqueline Barbara Carr, *After the Siege: A Social History of Boston* (Boston: Northeastern University Press, 2005), 232–33.

61. Sweet, *Bodies Politic*, provides the most thorough examination of this subject.

62. James Sidbury, *Ploughshares into Swords: Race, Rebellion and Identity in Gabriel's Virginia, 1730–1810* (Cambridge: Cambridge University Press, 1997), 33–34; Andrew Levy, *The First Emancipator: Slavery, Religion and the Quiet Revolution of Robert Carter* (New York: Random House, 2005), 180.

63. Robert Pleasants to George Washington, "Curles," Dec. 11, 1785, in *Papers of George Washington*, ed. W. W. Abbot and Dorothy Twohig et al., Confederation Series, vol. 3, *May 1785–March 1786* (Charlottesville: University Press of Virginia, 1994), 449–50.

64. Elias Boudinot of New Jersey, Mar. 22, 1790, in *The Negro in the Congressional Record*, comp. and ed. Peter M. Bergman and Jean McCarroll, vol. 2, *1789–1801* (New York: Bergman, 1969), 38.

65. Petition of Jacob Nicholson, Jupiter Nicholson, Job Albert, and Thomas Pritchet, Philadelphia, Jan. 23, 1797, in Bergman and McCarroll, *Negro in the Congressional Record*, 130–31.

66. Proceedings of Jan. 30, 1797, in Bergman and McCarroll, *Negro in the Congressional Record*, 132. On Swanwick, see Roland M. Baumann, "John Swanwick: Spokesman for 'Merchant-Republicanism' in Philadelphia, 1790–1798," *Pennsylvania Magazine of History and Biography* 97 (1973): 131–82. Swanwick, born in England in 1760, was brought as child to Pennsylvania. His Loyalist father returned to England during the War for Independence. Swanwick stayed in Pennsylvania, fought as a Patriot, and used his connections with Robert Morris to rise afterward. He was an Episcopalian, but his mother and sister were Roman Catholic.

67. Proceedings of Jan. 30, 1797, 132.

68. Proceedings of Jan. 30, 1797, 133.

69. Proceedings of Jan. 30, 1797, 134.

70. Mason, *Slavery and Politics*, 15, 19.

71. Thomas Jefferson, *Notes on the State of Virginia*, intro. Thomas Perkins Abernethy (New York: Harper and Row, 1964), 155, 156; Bruce Dain, *A Hideous Monster of the Mind: American Race Theory in the Early Republic* (Cambridge, Mass.: Harvard University Press, 2002), chap. 1, "The Face of Nature"; Peter Onuf, "'To Declare Them a Free and Independent People': Race, Slavery and National Identity in Jefferson's Thought," *Journal of the Early Republic* 18 (1998): 1–46, explains Jefferson's commitment to black colonization.

72. Jefferson to Benjamin Banneker, Philadelphia, Aug. 30, 1791, in *The Portable Thomas Jefferson*, ed. Merrill D. Peterson (New York: Viking, 1975), 454; Madison to Jedidiah Morse, Mar. 14, 1824, in *Writings of James Madison*, ed. Gaillard Hunt, vol. 9 (New York: G. P. Putnam's Sons, 1910), 134.

73. Jefferson to the Abbé Henri Grégoire, Washington, Feb. 25, 1809, in Peterson, *Portable Jefferson*, 517.

74. Bradburn, *Citizenship Revolution*, 235–36.

75. Jefferson to Edward Coles, Monticello, Aug. 24, 1814, in Peterson, *Portable Jefferson*, 546.

76. Mark A. Graber, *Dred Scott and the Problem of Constitutional Evil* (New York: Cambridge University Press, 2006), 31; [Prudence Crandall], *Report of the Arguments of Counsel, in the Case of Prudence Crandell, Plff. in Error, vs. State of Connecticut, before the Supreme Court of Errors, at Their Session at Brooklyn, July term, 1834. . . .* (Boston: Garrison and Knapp, 1834), 5, 6; Scott v. Sandford, 60 U.S. 393 (1857) at 393. Taney's own views changed during his career. In 1819 Taney argued the principles of the Declaration of Independence ought to end slavery. Timothy S. Huebner, "Roger B. Taney and the Slavery Issue: Looking beyond—and before—*Dred Scott*," *Journal of American History* 97 (2010): 17–38. See also Dain, *Hideous Monster of the Mind*, chap. 7, "The New Ethnology."

77. *Scott v. Sandford* at 139. Calhoun in Wilentz, *Rise of American Democracy*, 612. According to William Goodell, *Our National Charters: For the Millions* (New York, 1863), 15, 133–34, of the thirteen original states, eleven at first allowed people of color to vote.

78. *Scott v. Sandford* at 188, 189 (Custis); Graber, *Dred Scott*, 47. Paul Polgar treats this tangled history: "Immediate, Not Gradual: Achieving African American Freedom during the First Emancipation," Society of Historians of the Early American Republic, Philadelphia, July 2014, and his "'To Raise them to an Equal Participation': Early National Abolitionism, Gradual Emancipation, and the Promise of African American Citizenship," *Journal of the Early Republic* 31 (2011): 229–58.

79. [Crandall], *Report of the Arguments*, v; *Scott v. Sandford* at 18 (quotation), 21 (Daggett).

80. Robert Pierce Forbes, *The Missouri Compromise and Its Aftermath: Slavery and the Meaning of America* (Chapel Hill: University of North Carolina Press, 2007), 286–91; Eric Foner, *Free Soil, Free Labor, Free Men: The Ideology of the Republican Party before the Civil War* (New York: Oxford University Press, 1970), 97–98; Holzer, *Lincoln-Douglas Debates*, 356.

81. Holzer, *Lincoln-Douglas Debates*, 189; Foner, *Free Soil*, 291–93. This discussion is informed by Eric Foner, *The Fiery Trial: Abraham Lincoln and Slavery* (New York: W. W. Norton, 2010), 98–104.

82. Holzer, *Lincoln-Douglas*, 285.

83. Holzer, *Lincoln-Douglas*, 244–45.

84. Holzer, *Lincoln-Douglas*, 224, 244, 247.

85. Holzer, *Lincoln-Douglas*, 243–44.

86. *Scott v. Sandford* at 393, 407, 410.

87. Douglass, "What to the Slave Is the Fourth of July?"; David Thomas Konig, "Constitutional Law and the Legitimation of History: The Enduring Force of Roger Taney's 'Opinion of the Court,'" in *The Dred Scott Case: Historical and Contempo-*

rary Perspectives on Race and Law, ed. David Thomas Konig, Paul Finkelman, and Christopher Alan Bracey (Athens: Ohio University Press, 2010), 11–18.

Chapter Five. People of Color and Equal Rights

Epigraph: *Report of the Arguments of Counsel, in the Case of Prudence Crandall, Plff. in Error, vs. State of Connecticut, before the Superior Court of Errors, at Their Session at Brooklyn, July Term, 1834* (Boston: Garrison and Knapp, 1834), 6, 22.

1. John W. Sweet, *Bodies Politic: Negotiating Race in the American North, 1730–1830* (Baltimore: Johns Hopkins University Press, 2003), 252, reports the 1795 judgment of the Reverend Jeremy Belknap of Boston, that Massachusetts slavery was "abolished by public opinion; which began to be established about 30 years ago." This opinion is set in context by Margot Minardi, *Making Slavery History: Abolitionism and the Politics of Memory in Massachusetts* (New York: Oxford University Press, 2010), 16–20.

2. Howard W. Allen and Jerome M. Clubb, *Race, Class, and the Death Penalty: Capital Punishment in American History* (Albany: State University of New York Press, 2008), fig. 1.3, 20, 29–31; see also table 2.1, 30. Allen and Clubb note that the proportions are skewed by twenty whites executed for witchcraft at Salem in 1692, so the predisposition to execute people of color may have been even greater. See also David V. Baker, "Black Female Executions in Historical Context," *Criminal Justice Review* 33 (2008): 64–88. For other regions 1606–95, statistics are too small or unreliable for meaningful comparisons. Blacks and Indians, usually nonliterate, could rarely claim "benefit of clergy" to escape hanging.

3. Daniel Allen Hearn, *Legal Executions in New England, 1623–1960* (Jefferson, N.C.: McFarland, 1999), 52; Samuel Green, *Life of Samuel Green, Executed at Boston, April 25, 1822, for the Murder of Billy Williams, a Fellow Convict with Green at the State Prison* (Boston, 1822); Allen and Clubb, *Race, Class, and the Death Penalty,* 31–37, tables 2.1, 2.2, 2.4; Richard Slotkin, "Narratives of Negro Crime in New England, 1675–1800," *American Quarterly* 25 (1973): 3–31.

4. Zephaniah Swift, *A System of the State of Laws of Connecticut,* vol. 2 (Windham, Conn., 1795), 368.

5. Arthur Koestler, *Reflections on Hanging* (New York: Macmillan, 1957), 13, 14, 15; Negley K. Teeters and Jack H. Hedblom, *"Hang by the Neck": The Legal Use of Scaffold and Noose, Gibbet, Stake, and Firing Squad from Colonial Times to the Present* (Springfield, Ill.: Charles C. Thomas, 1967), 13, 15, 18, 19. Teeters and Hedblom erroneously state that Guild's victim was his mistress. Daniel Allen Hearn, *Legal Executions in New Jersey, 1691–1963* (Jefferson, N.C.: McFarland, 2005), 75–76, 80–81, 85–86, describes cases in detail: Guild's victim was a white neighbor aged over sixty years. The convict was aged twelve years, five months, at the time of the murder and thirteen years, seven months, at execution. Huff killed her sixty-

two-year-old mistress, Sarah Hight, and Rosanne Keen murdered her employer, Enos Seeley.

6. Henry Channing, *God Admonishing His People of Their Duty, as Parents and Masters; A Sermon Preached at New-London, December 20th, 1786; Occasioned by the Execution of Hannah Ocuish, a Mulatto Girl, Aged 12 Years and 9 Months; For the Murder of Eunice Bolles, Aged 6 Years and 6 Months*, 2nd ed. (New-London, 1787), 29 (on mother), 5 (on her ignorance). Nancy Hathaway Steenburg, *Children and the Criminal Law in Connecticut, 1635–1855* (New York: Routledge, 2005), 69–70.

7. Channing, *God Admonishing*, 5, 6.

8. Channing, *God Admonishing*, 29, 30.

9. Channing, *God Admonishing*, 5, 23. Sweet, *Bodies Politic*, 295–96, treats Ocuish and Channing's sermon: "Americans in the early Republic struggled with competing impulses: to emphasize the leveling capacity of education, and to categorize and rank the varieties of humankind." Frances Manwaring Caulkins, *History of New London, Connecticut* (New London: Published by the author, 1852), 576.

10. *Windham (Conn.) Herald*, Nov. 21, 1795, 3; *Connecticut Gazette* (New London), Mar. 17, 1796, 3; Connecticut Superior Court Records, 30, 157–58, Connecticut State Library. In 1813 a New Jersey court sentenced a thirteen-year-old slave, Ann Hitchens, to seven years' imprisonment for nonfatal poisoning of her master and mistress. James J. Gigantino II, *The Ragged Road to Abolition: Slavery and Freedom in New Jersey, 1775–1865* (Philadelphia: University of Pennsylvania Press, 2015), 124.

11. Robert L. Hale, *A Review of Judicial Executions in America* (Lewiston, N.Y.: Edwin Mellen Press, 1997), 62–63; William Halsted, *Reports of Cases Argued and Determined in the Supreme Court, and, at Law, in the Court of Errors and Appeals of the State of New Jersey*, vol. 5 (Trenton, 1829), 163–90, esp. 174, 189, 190, quotation on 178. For the legislature's rejection of commutation bill, see *Baltimore Gazette and Daily Advertiser*, Nov. 14, 1828, 2. The *Trenton Federalist*, Nov. 28, 1828, 1:4, calls Guild "the black boy."

12. Huff's and Keen's crimes in Hearn, *Legal Executions in New Jersey*, 80–81, 85–86. For Keen and Hitchens, see also Gigantino, *Ragged Road to Abolition*, 124. Holly Brewer, *By Birth or Consent: Children, Law, and the Anglo-American Revolution in Authority* (Chapel Hill: University of North Carolina Press for the Omohundro Institute of Early American History and Culture, 2005), 222–25, discusses the Guild and Ocuish cases, concluding: "One is left finally with the puzzling logic that allowed these two young nonwhite children to be convicted when white children of the same age were not." Yet Brewer's counterexample (220–21) of the acquittal of a white child of twelve or thirteen years, Mary Doherty, concerns a very different murder: Doherty's victim was not an unrelated little girl or an old neighbor woman but her abusive, alcoholic father who, the child said, killed her mother. "Horrid Murder!! Knoxville, April 25," *Hampshire Federalist* (Springfield, Mass.), June 3, 1806, 2:2–3. Available facts are limited, but Doherty's murder resembles an abused

wife murdering a husband. The family lived in an isolated log house, and none of the children attended school. As the eldest with three younger siblings, Mary Doherty served as a surrogate mother and possibly as her father's sexual prey. State v. Mary Doherty, 2 *Overton's Tenn. Reports* 80 (1806). Brewer does not mention the 1796 case of Ann, the black girl judged guilty of manslaughter, the 1813 case of Ann Hitchens, who was sentenced to seven years in prison for poisoning her master and mistress, or Huff's and Keen's cases. Punishment for petty treason, restated in a 1725 English legal work, is explained in J. M. Beattie, *Crime and the Courts in England, 1660–1800* (Princeton, N.J.: Princeton University Press, 1986), 79n10. For the Boston burning in 1755, see Hearn, *Legal Executions in New England,* 142–43. For the 1806 Virginia case, see Sidbury, *Ploughshares into Swords,* 220–21.

13. Sweet, *Bodies Politic,* 167–71.

14. *Report of the Trial of Susanna, a Coloured Woman: Before the Hon. Ambrose Spencer, Esq. at a Court of Oyer and Terminer, and Gaol Delivery, Held at the City of Schenectady, on the 23d October, on a Charge of Having Murdered Her Infant Male Bastard Child, on the Night of the 22d June, 1810; Taken in Short Hand by Henry W. Warner* (Troy, N.Y., 1810), 39.

15. *Trial of Susanna,* 50.

16. Sweet, *Bodies Politic,* 154.

17. Cesare di Beccaria, *An Essay on Crimes and Punishments; Translated from the Italian; with a Commentary, Attributed to M. de Voltaire, Translated from the French* (New York: Stephen Gould, 1809), 137–38. From its initial 1764 Milan publication to 1810, dozens of editions were published throughout Europe, including at least two dozen in Britain and the United States.

18. In 1803 Deborah Stevens, convicted of murdering her three-year-old daughter in Massachusetts, was not executed. After three years' incarceration she was granted a full pardon. Irene Q. Brown and Richard D. Brown, *The Hanging of Ephraim Wheeler: A Story of Rape, Incest, and Justice in Early America* (Cambridge, Mass.: Harvard University Press, 2003), 209. Slave Jenny's 1767–68 Rhode Island case resembles Susanna's. Jenny was convicted of murdering her newborn, but a petition to King George led to pardon. Jenny had an owner; so execution would destroy his property. Sweet, *Bodies Politic,* 155–56.

19. Peggy Facto, a Roman Catholic, was executed Mar. 18, 1825, in Plattsburgh, N.Y. For newspaper coverage, see *Franklin (N.Y.) Telegraph,* Jan. 27, Mar. 24, 31, 1825, and *Plattsburgh Republican,* Jan. 29, Mar. 24, Apr. 23, 1825. For a history of infanticide laws and prosecutions, see Peter C. Hoffer and N. E. H. Hull, *Murdering Mothers: Infanticide in England and New England, 1558–1803* (New York: New York University Press, 1981); and Dana Y. Rabin, *Crime and Legal Responsibility in Eighteenth-Century England* (Basingstoke, U.K.: Palgrave Macmillan, 2004).

20. *Trial of Susanna,* 19, 20, 49.

21. *Trial of Susanna,* 29, 30.

22. John L. Brooke, *Columbia Rising: Civil Life on the Upper Hudson from the Revolution to the Age of Jackson* (Chapel Hill: University of North Carolina Press for Omohundro Institute of Early American History and Culture, 2010), 246–48, 266.

23. *Trial of Susanna*, 48, 44, 45.

24. Jarvis (1748–1807), son of a great merchant, graduated Harvard in 1766. He was a medical apprentice in Boston and London and a Patriot leader in the Revolution, active in the 1780 Massachusetts Constitutional Convention. Jarvis was Boston representative to the legislature, 1788–97, and a founding member of the Massachusetts Medical Society and the American Academy of Arts and Sciences. Initially Federalist, he supported the French Revolution even after the Terror; he ended as a Democratic-Republican allied with Samuel Adams. Clifford K. Shipton, *Sibley's Harvard Graduates*, vol. 16, *Biographical Sketches of Those Who Attended Harvard College in the Classes 1764–1767* (Boston: Massachusetts Historical Society, 1972), 376–83.

25. *Sketch of the Proceedings and Trial of William Hardy, on an Indictment for the Murder of an Infant, November 27, 1806, before the Supreme Judicial Court, Holden at Boston, in and for the Counties of Suffolk and Nantucket, in the Commonwealth of Massachusetts, on the Second Tuesday of March, in the Year of Our Lord 1807* (Boston: Oliver and Munroe, 1807), 6, 7, 21.

26. "Proceeding against William Hardy," Supreme Judicial Court, Suffolk County, November 1806 volume, Massachusetts Archives.

27. William Bentley, *Diary of William Bentley, D.D.: Pastor of the East Church, Salem, Massachusetts*, 4 vols. (1905–14; reprint, Gloucester, Mass.: Peter Smith, 1962), 3:266.

28. Brown and Brown, *Hanging of Ephraim Wheeler*, 206–9.

29. *Trial of William Hardy*, 10, 11. Blake refers to "Miss Talbot" at 28. On Bridget and Dominic Daley, see Richard D. Brown, "'Tried, Convicted, and Condemned, in Almost Every Bar-room and Barber's Shop': Anti-Irish Prejudice in the Trial of Dominic Daley and James Halligan, Northampton, Massachusetts, 1806," *New England Quarterly* 84 (June 2011): 205–33.

30. *Trial of William Hardy*, 6. That Valpy was white is evident from Blake's reference to Valpy as Hardy's "fair enamorata" at 18.

31. *Trial of William Hardy*, 8, 10, 11, 12. Jarvis's wife, Mary Pepperell Sparhawk (1754–1815), was the niece of the wealthy merchant and Loyalist Sir William Pepperell, as was her first cousin Harriet Hirst Sparhawk (1781–1871). *The Trial of William Hardy* identifies her as Harriet Hurst Sparhawk. Providing baby linens as evidence of the mother's desire for a live infant was an established defense ("benefit of linen") against infanticide in Anglo-American law. Hoffer and Hull, *Murdering Mothers*, 69–70; Rabin, *Crime and Legal Responsibility*, 95–96.

32. *Trial of William Hardy*, 27, 28–29, 32, 42.

33. *Trial of William Hardy*, 11, 12, 32, 34, 35, 42. Rabin, *Crime and Legal Responsibility*, chap. 4, "Bodies of Evidence, States of Mind: Infanticide, Emotion, and Sensibility," 95–110.

34. *Trial of William Hardy*, 11, 26, 34; first group of words, 17, 20, 22, 27; "poor and destitute," 20; "Blackman," 18, 27, 30, 37; play on "black bastard," 20, 23. Mrs. Jarvis was unable to attend the second trial, so the court allowed the chief justice's "minutes' of previous testimony to be read.

35. *Trial of William Hardy*, 42, 43. Advertisements for *Report of the Trial of Dominic Daley and James Halligan, for the Murder of Marcus Lyon, before the Supreme Judicial Court, Begun and Holden at Northampton, within and for the County of Hampshire, in the Commonwealth of Massachusetts, on the Fourth Tuesday of April, 1806* (Northampton, Mass.: S. and E. Butler, 1806) in the *Repertory* (Boston), Mar. 17, 24, 1807, 4. First published in May 1806 and advertised in western Massachusetts and Vermont, May–June 1806, this trial report first advertised in Boston when Hardy's trial brought Bridget Daley notoriety.

36. *Trial of William Hardy*, 42, 46.

37. *Trial of William Hardy*, 47.

38. *Trial of William Hardy*, 47

39. Sidbury, *Ploughshares into Swords*, 176–78, recounts the case of Angela or Angelica Barnet (or Barnett), a freeborn black convicted in 1793 for killing a white man who entered her house at night, threatening to take her into slavery. The jury ruled her guilty but stayed execution owing to her pregnancy; during that time prominent, Richmond, Va., gentlemen (including U.S. Supreme Court Chief Justice John Marshall) took up her cause by petition, winning a full pardon because she killed intruder into her "own home."

40. *Acts and Laws, Passed by the General Court of Massachusetts at the Session Begun and Held at Boston, in the County of Suffolk, on Thursday, the Seventeenth Day of January, Anno Domini, 1805* (Boston, 1805), 613.

41. "Proceeding against William Hardy," 170–71.

42. *Independent Chronicle* (Boston), Dec. 22, 1806, 3.

43. Charles Warren, *Jacobin and Junto; or, Early American Politics as Viewed in the Diary of Dr. Nathaniel Ames, 1758–1822* (Cambridge, Mass.: Harvard University Press, 1931), 198. Anecdote in *Independent Chronicle* (Boston), Dec. 15, 1806, 2:4, and the *Democrat* (Boston), Dec. 14, 1806, 3. William Bentley recorded the anecdote on Dec. 10, 1806. Bentley, *Diary*, 266.

44. *Trial of Thomas O. Selfridge, Counsellor at Law: before the Hon. Isaac Parker, Esquire; for Killing Charles Austin; on the Public Exchange; in Boston, August 4th, 1806* (Boston: Russell and Cutler, 1807), 157; Warren, *Jacobin and Junto*, 197.

45. *Independent Chronicle* (Boston), May 5, 1807, 2; Apr. 4, 1807, Bentley, *Diary*, 287.

46. For example: "Negro Ann," charged with murder of Martha Clark, tried at Windham, Conn., March 1796, convicted for manslaughter, not murder. The case was

covered in a hundred words in the *Connecticut Gazette* (New London), Mar. 17, 1796, 3.

47. *The Confession of John Battus a Mulatto, Aged 19 Years and 7 Months, Who Was Executed at Dedham, November 8, 1804, for the Crimes of a Most Cruel Rape and Murder on the Body of Salome Talbott, of Canton, in the 14th Year of Her Age to Which Is Added, His Writing [about?] His Imprisonment* (Dedham, Mass.?, 1804?); Ephraim Williams, *Reports of Cases Argued and Determined in the Supreme Judicial Court, of the State of Massachusetts from September 1804 to June 1805 — Both Inclusive* (Northampton, Mass.: S. and E. Butler, 1805), 95–96; Beattie, *Crime and the Courts*, 336.

48. Samuel Freeman, Connecticut Archives, Hartford, Windham County, Superior Court file, box 193 (1805 Sept.). Moses C. Welch, *The Gospel to Be Preached to All Men, Illustrated in a Sermon, Delivered, in Windham, at the Execution of Samuel Freeman, a Mulatto, November 6, A.D. 1805, for the Murder of Hannah Simons; Together with an Appendix, Containing, Memoirs of His Life, a Sketch of His Trial, His Appearance after Condemnation, Confessions, &c.* (Windham, Conn.: John Byrne, 1805). Byrne, Windham's only printer, published the *Windham Herald*.

49. U.S. Census, *Return of the Whole Number of Persons . . . of the United States, 2d Census* (Washington, D.C., 1801).

50. Welch, *Gospel to Be Preached . . . Samuel Freeman*, 19–23.

51. *Biographical Directory of the United States Congress, 1774–Present*, s.v. "Goddard, Calvin."

52. Samuel Freeman, "Complaint, Justices Court, Arrest Warrant & Charges," true copy of record, dated Aug. 1, 1805, originals dated May 31, 1805; "Indictment for murder of Hannah Simons & Judgment, Oct. 4, 1805," Connecticut Archives.

53. Welch, *Gospel to Be Preached . . . Samuel Freeman*, 24, 26, 30.

54. *Courier* (Norwich, Conn.), Nov. 13, 1805, 2.

55. Daniel A. Cohen, *Pillars of Salt, Monuments of Grace: New England Crime Literature and the Origins of American Popular Culture* (New York: Oxford University Press, 1993), 111–12, notes that some execution sermons stressed the fairness and legitimacy of the legal system, in part defending capital punishment. Cohen quotes the Rev. Moses C. Welch.

56. Samuel J. May, *Some Recollections of Our Antislavery Conflict* (Boston: Fields, Osgood, 1869), 40, 50. Donald E. Williams Jr., *Prudence Crandall's Legacy: The Fight for Equality in the 1830s, Dred Scott, and Brown v. Board of Education* (Middletown, Conn.: Wesleyan University Press, 2014), provides a thorough account. Peter Hinks, "Connecting Prudence Crandall: Black Education and Antislavery in Southeastern Connecticut before 1833," Association for the Study of Connecticut History, Pomfret, Conn., Nov. 2, 2013, reports Elisha Niles teaching black and white students together, 1795–1805, and the opening of a "colored" school in 1805 that was operating under a black teacher, Prince Saunders, 1806–8. He reports that Norwich, Conn., was another center of black education.

57. May, *Some Recollections*, 47, 71; Marvis Olive Welch, *Prudence Crandall: A Biography* (Manchester, Conn.: Jason, 1983), chap. 3.

58. American Board of Commissioners for Foreign Missions, *Extracts from the Report of the agents of the Foreign Mission School to the American Board of Commissioners for Foreign Missions, September 1817* (Hartford: Hudson, 1818), 3; John Demos, *The Heathen School: A Story of Hope and Betrayal in the Age of the Early Republic* (New York: Vintage, 2014). This pattern was the reverse image of the history of "Moor's Indian School" (reborn as Dartmouth College), which was failing in the late 1760s. Accordingly the Reverend Eleazar Wheelock opened the school to whites in 1771, an experiment in integrated education that lasted until 1776, when white students ousted the remaining Indians. Sweet, *Bodies Politic*, 119.

59. James Brewer Stewart, "The New Haven Negro College and the Meanings of Race in New England, 1776–1870," *New England Quarterly* 76 (2003): 323–55; Stewart, "The Emergence of Racial Modernity and the Rise of the White North," *Journal of the Early Republic* 18 (1998): 203–4.

60. David B. Potts, *Wesleyan University, 1831–1910* (New Haven: Yale University Press, 1992), 53–55. See also May, *Some Recollections*, 267–68.

61. David Grimsted, "Rioting in Its Jacksonian Setting," *American Historical Review* 77 (1972): 361–97; Paul Gilje, *Rioting in America* (Bloomington: Indiana University Press, 1996), 64–91.

62. *A Statement of Facts, Respecting the School for Colored Females, in Canterbury, Ct. Together with a Report of the Late Trial of Miss Prudence Crandall* (Brooklyn, Conn.: Advertiser Press, 1833); *New-London Gazette and General Advertiser*, July 10, 1833, 2.

63. [Prudence Crandall], *Report of the Arguments of Counsel, in the Case of Prudence Crandell, Plff. in Error, vs. State of Connecticut, before the Supreme Court of Errors, at Their Session at Brooklyn, July Term, 1834; By a Member of the Bar* (Boston: Garrison and Knapp, 1834), 15, 22, 23.

64. [Crandall], *Report of the Arguments*, 17, 18.

65. May, *Some Recollections*, 59.

66. [Crandall], *Report of the Arguments*, 5, 6.

67. [Crandall], *Report of the Arguments*, 6.

68. [Crandall], *Report of the Arguments*, 8, 9.

69. [Crandall], *Report of the Arguments*, 24–34. Matthew Mason, *Slavery and Politics in the Early American Republic* (Chapel Hill: University of North Carolina Press, 2006), chap. 8, "The Missouri Crisis"; Robert Pierce Forbes, *The Missouri Compromise and Its Aftermath: Slavery and the Meaning of America* (Chapel Hill: University of North Carolina Press, 2007), 118.

70. [Crandall], *Report of the Arguments*, v.

71. May, *Some Recollections*, 70; Williams, *Prudence Crandall's Legacy*, 144–46, 200–202.

72. May, *Some Recollections*, 70, 71; Philip Pearl, a Whig lawyer from neighboring Hampton, chaired the legislative committee that recommended the law. Theodore Weld to Lewis Tappan, Hartford, Conn., June 8, 1837, in *Letters of Theodore Dwight Weld, Angelina Grimké Weld and Sarah Grimké Weld, 1822–1844*, ed. Gilbert H. Barnes and Dwight L. Dumond, vol. 1 (New York: Appleton-Century, 1934), 397–98. On diminishing northern racism after 1840, see Jeffrey Bolster, "'To Feel Like a Man': Black Seamen in the Northern States, 1800–1860," *Journal of American History* 76 (1990): 1173–99.

73. Sweet, *Bodies Politic*, 331; Samuel J. May, *Right of Colored People to Education: Letters to Andrew Judson, Esq., and Others in Canterbury, Remonstrating with Them on Their Unjust and Unjustifiable Procedure Relative to Miss Crandall and Her School for Colored Females* (Brooklyn, Conn.: Advertiser Press, 1833), 6 (Mar. 29, 1833); on May's ouster, see Paul Goodman, *Of One Blood: Abolitionism and the Origins of Racial Equality* (Berkeley: University of California Press, 1998), 92; *General Laws of Massachusetts*, 1855, chap. 256, sec. 1. In 1843, after twelve years' agitation, Massachusetts repealed the ban on interracial marriage. Daniel R. Mandell, *Tribe, Race, History: Native Americans in Southern New England, 1780–1880* (Baltimore: Johns Hopkins University Press, 2008), 318, 320.

74. Kent (1763–1847) quotation from 6th ed. (1848), quoted in Williams, *Prudence Crandall's Legacy*, 203. Taney's own views changed during his career. In 1819 Taney argued that the principles of the Declaration of Independence ought to end slavery. Timothy S. Huebner, "Roger B. Taney and the Slavery Issue: Looking beyond—and before—Dred Scott," *Journal of American History* 97 (2010): 17–38; Bruce Dain, *A Hideous Monster of the Mind: American Race Theory in the Early Republic* (Cambridge, Mass.: Harvard University Press, 2002), chap. 7, "The New Ethnology."

Chapter Six. Subordinate Citizens

1. Henry Steele Commager and Milton Cantor, eds., *Documents of American History*, vol. 1, *To 1898*, 10th ed. (Englewood Cliffs, N.J.: Prentice Hall, 1988), 103–4; Abigail Adams to John Adams, Braintree, Mass., Mar. 31, 1776, John's response to Abigail, n.p. [Philadelphia], Apr. 14, 1774, in *The Adams Papers: Digital Edition, Adams Family Correspondence*, vol. 1, http://www.masshist.org/publications/apde/portia.php?id=ADMS-04-01-02-0248. Edith B. Gelles, *Portia: The World of Abigail Adams* (Bloomington: Indiana University Press, 1992), 24–26. Michaela Dobošiová, "Marriage and Human Relationships in the Eighteenth-Century Britain" (Ph.D. diss., Masaryk University, 2006).

2. Rosemary Zagarri, *Revolutionary Backlash: Women and Politics in the Early American Republic* (Philadelphia: University of Pennsylvania Press, 2007), 31–33. Zagarri includes newspaper quotations. For the Independence Day orator, see Elias Boudi-

not, *An Oration, Delivered at Elizabeth-Town, New-Jersey, Agreeably to a Resolution of the State Society of Cincinnati, on the Fourth of July, M.DCC.XCIII; Being the Seventeenth Anniversary of the Independence of America* (Elizabeth-Town, N.J., 1793), 24.

3. Zagarri, *Revolutionary Backlash*, 33–36.

4. Elaine Forman Crane, "Political Dialogue and the Spring of Abigail's Discontent," *William and Mary Quarterly*, 3rd Ser., 56 (1999): 744–74; James Otis, *Rights of the British Colonies Asserted and Proved* (Boston, 1764), 4, 6. See Linda K. Kerber, "The Republican Mother: Women and the Enlightenment—An American Perspective," in *Toward an Intellectual History of Women: Essays by Linda K. Kerber* (Chapel Hill: University of North Carolina Press, 1997), 41–62.

5. John Adams to Abigail Adams, n.p., Apr. 14, 1776, in *Adams Family Correspondence*, vol. 1, *December 1761–May 1776*, ed. L. H. Butterfield and Marc Friedlaender (Cambridge, Mass.: Harvard University Press, 1963), 382–83. The sequence of John Adams's words has been altered in two cases for clarity.

6. John Adams to James Sullivan, Philadelphia, May 26, 1776; in a letter to Mercy Otis Warren, Apr. 16, 1776, Adams claimed that women were more principled than men in politics because they were more honest and considered issues "more cooly." Robert J. Taylor, ed., *Papers of John Adams*, vol. 4, *February–August 1776* (Cambridge, Mass.: Harvard University Press, 1979), 123–25, 208–12; Zagarri, *Revolutionary Backlash*, 29–30; Linda K. Kerber, "'Ourselves and Our Daughters Forever': Women and the Constitution, 1787–1876," in *One Woman, One Vote: Rediscovering the Woman Suffrage Movement*, ed. Marjorie Spruill Wheeler (Troutdale, Ore.: NewSage, 1995), 24–27.

7. Charles Brockden Brown, *Alcuin: A Dialogue* (New York, 1798), 54–57, 59, 69, 70, quotations out of order. See Bryan Waterman, *Republic of Intellect: The Friendly Club of New York City and the Making of American Literature* (Baltimore: Johns Hopkins University Press, 2007), 110–16, chap. 3.

8. Zagarri, *Revolutionary Backlash*, 29.

9. Benjamin Rush, *Thoughts upon Female Education Accommodated to the Present State of Society, Manners, and Government, in the United States of America . . . ,* ed. Michael Meranze (Schenectady, N.Y.: Union College Press, 1988), 45, 47–49, 54, italics added. Rush's collected essays were first published in 1798; the modern edition follows the 1806 edition. *Thoughts upon Female Education* was originally published in Philadelphia and Boston in 1787; the second Boston edition was published in 1791.

10. Lucia McMahon, *Mere Equals: The Paradox of Educated Women in the Early Republic* (Ithaca, N.Y.: Cornell University Press, 2012), 164. Italics added to quotation from "On the Happy Influence of Female Society," *American Museum* (Philadelphia), 1 (January 1787): 63. Taken from William Alexander, *The History of Women from Earliest Antiquity to the Present Time* (London, 1782); Zagarri, *Revolutionary*

Backlash, 168–69; Linda K. Kerber, *Women of the Republic: Intellect and Ideology in Revolutionary America* (Chapel Hill: University of North Carolina Press for the Institute of Early American History and Culture, 1980); Jan Lewis, "The Republican Wife: Virtue and Seduction in the Early Republic," *William and Mary Quarterly*, 3rd Ser., 44 (1987): 689–721.

11. Mary Kelley, *Learning to Stand and Speak: Women, Education, and Public Life in America's Republic* (Chapel Hill: University of North Carolina Press, 2006), 2.

12. Kelley, *Learning to Stand*, 39.

13. Hannah Mather Crocker, *Observations on the Real Rights of Women, with Their Appropriate Duties, Agreeable to Scripture, Reason and Common Sense* (Boston: Printed for the Author, 1818), in Hannah Mather Crocker, *Observations on the Real Rights of Women and Other Writings*, ed. Constance J. Post (Lincoln: University of Nebraska Press, 2011), 117. Post says that Crocker quoted and borrowed from English sources including Wollstonecraft. Kelley, *Learning to Stand*, 10, 121–22.

14. E. Jennifer Monaghan, *Learning to Read and Write in Colonial America* (Amherst: University of Massachusetts Press, 2005), 374–78; Kenneth A. Lockridge, *Literacy in Colonial New England* (New York: W. W. Norton, 1974); Kelley, *Learning to Stand*, 23, 56. Joanne Dobson and Sandra A. Zagarell, "Women Writing in the Early Republic," in *A History of the Book in America*, ed. Robert A. Gross and Mary Kelley (Chapel Hill: American Antiquarian Society and University of North Carolina Press, 2010), chap. 2 ("An Extensive Republic: Print Culture, and Society in the New Nation, 1790–1840"), 364–81. Hawthorne's letter was not his whole view of women writers; quoted in James D. Wallace, "Hawthorne and the Scribbling Women," *American Literature* 62 (June 1990): 204.

15. Townshend Act protest including eight signed broadsides, Oct. 28, 1767, Houghton Library, Harvard University; available online at: http://pds.lib.harvard.edu/pds/view/46431739; Mary Beth Norton, *Liberty's Daughters: The Revolutionary Experience of American Women, 1750–1800* (Boston: Little, Brown, 1980), 156–61.

16. Nancy F. Cott, *Bonds of Womanhood: "Woman's Sphere" in New England, 1780–1835* (New Haven: Yale University Press, 1977).

17. Abigail's "all Men would be tyrants if they could" quoted her husband's unpublished 1763 essay "On Man's Lust for Power"; Edith B. Gelles, *Abigail and John: Portrait of a Marriage* (New York: HarperCollins, 2009), 78. Abigail Adams to John Adams, n.p., June 17, 1782, in *Adams Family Correspondence*, ed. L. H. Butterfield and Marc Friedlaender, vol. 4, *October 1780–September 1782* (Cambridge, Mass.: Harvard University Press, 1973), 328; William Blackstone, *Commentaries on the Laws of England*, vol. 1 (London, 1765), 442–43.

18. Blackstone, *Commentaries*, 443–45; Hendrik Hartog, *Man and Wife in America: A History* (Cambridge, Mass.: Harvard University Press, 2000), 105, 150, 151. For "legitimate" child beating that became excessive: Alan Taylor, "'The Unhappy Stephen Arnold': An Episode of Murder and Penitence in the Early Republic,"

in *Through a Glass Darkly: Reflections on Personal Identity in Early America*, ed. Ronald Hoffman, Mechal Sobel, and Fredrika Teute (Chapel Hill: University of North Carolina Press for the Omohundro Institute of Early American History and Culture, 1997), 96–121. Francis W. Edmonds, "The New Scholar," 1850, cited in Elizabeth Johns, *American Genre Painting: The Politics of Everyday Life* (New Haven: Yale University Press, 1993), 155–56.

19. Cesare di Beccaria, *An Essay on Crimes and Punishments* [1764] (London: J. Almon, 1767). John Adams cited Beccaria in the Boston Massacre trial in 1770. Washington and Jefferson owned Beccaria, and it shaped Jefferson's proposed revisions of Virginia penal code, 1777–78. See Paul M. Spurlin, "Beccaria's Essay on Crimes and Punishments in Eighteenth-Century America," *Studies in Voltaire and the Eighteenth Century* 27 (1963): 1489–504, esp. 1494 ff. After the Revolution Beccaria was excerpted and quoted repeatedly in the American press, e.g., *Pennsylvania Evening Herald and the American Monitor* (Philadelphia), Feb. 2, 1786; *Loudon's New-York Packet*, Dec. 1, 1786; and *Pennsylvania Mercury* (Philadelphia), Oct. 21, 1788. *On Crimes and Punishments* in *New Haven Gazette and Connecticut Magazine*, Mar. 2–May 11, 1786; Harold D. Langley, *Social Reform in the U.S. Navy, 1798–1862* (Urbana: University of Illinois Press, 1967), 170–208; Leo F. S. Horan, "Flogging in the United States Navy: Unfamiliar Facts regarding Its Origin and Abolition," *U.S. Naval Institute Proceedings* 76, no. 9 (September 1950): 969–75.

20. Zephaniah Swift, *A System of the Laws of Connecticut; in Six Books*, 2 vols. (Windham, Conn.: John Byrne, 1795), 1:184, 202; Hartog, *Man and Wife*, 105.

21. Cornelia Hughes Dayton, *Women before the Bar: Gender, Law, and Society in Connecticut, 1639–1789* (Chapel Hill: University of North Carolina Press for the Omohundro Institute of Early American History and Culture, 1995).

22. Tapping Reeve, *The Law of Baron [Husband] and Femme [Wife]; of Parent and Child; of Guardian and Ward; of Master and Servant . . .* (New Haven: Oliver Steele, 1816), 1, and following 494, first page of "Contents." Woody Holton, *Abigail Adams* (New York: Free Press, 2009); Laurel Thatcher Ulrich, *Good Wives: Image and Reality in the Lives of Women in Northern New England, 1650–1750* (New York: Oxford University Press, 1982), chap. 2, "Deputy Husbands." On the general topic, see Marylynn Salmon, *Women and the Law of Property in Early America* (Chapel Hill: University of North Carolina Press, 1986).

23. Reeve, *Law of Baron and Femme*, 60–63, 66.

24. Peter King, *Crime, Justice, and Discretion in England, 1740–1820* (Oxford: Oxford University Press, 2000), 200; Reeve, *Law of Baron and Femme*, 67, 72–74.

25. Lee Virginia Chambers-Schiller, *Liberty a Better Husband: Single Women in America, the Generations of 1780–1840* (New Haven: Yale University Press, 1984). Hannah Mather Crocker (1752–1829) married in 1779 and was widowed in 1797; she bore ten children, 1780–95.

26. Thomas E. Buckley, *"The Great Catastrophe of My Life": Divorce in the Old Dominion* (Chapel Hill: University of North Carolina Press, 2002), 1, 4. One-third of divorce requests were enacted. For comparable statistics for Maryland and North Carolina, see Glenda Riley, *Divorce: An American Tradition* (New York: Oxford University Press, 1991), 35–36. On Pennsylvania, see Merril D. Smith, *Breaking the Bonds: Marital Discord in Pennsylvania, 1730–1830* (New York: New York University Press, 1991); and Reeve, *Law of Baron and Femme*, 205–6.

27. This was Connecticut law since 1667. Dayton, *Women before the Bar*, 112 and chap. 3, "Divorce: The Limits of a Puritan Remedy," 105–56. Vermont followed Connecticut; see Mary Beth Sievens, *Stray Wives: Marital Conflict in Early National New England* (New York: New York University Press, 2005), 24.

28. Swift, *System of the Laws of Connecticut*, 327–28. In 1707 Lord Chief Justice John Holt described sexual relations with another man's wife as "the highest invasion of property."

29. Buckley, *"The Great Catastrophe of My Life,"* 168; Kelly A. Ryan, "'The Spirit of Contradiction': Wife Abuse in New England, 1780–1820," *Early American Studies* 13 (2015): 586–625.

30. John Adams to Abigail Adams, n.p., Apr. 14, 1776, and Abigail Adams to John Adams, Braintree, Mass., Mar. 31, 1776, in Butterfield and Friedlaender, *Adams Family Correspondence*, 1:370, 382–83. On husbands' power, see Sharon Block, *Rape and Sexual Power in Early America* (Chapel Hill, N.C.: University of North Carolina Press for the Omohundro Institute of Early American History and Culture, 2006), esp. 114. On changing understandings of divorce, see Norma Basch, *Framing American Divorce: From the Revolutionary Generation to the Victorians* (Berkeley: University of California Press, 1999).

31. For Ann Parker Cowper's marital history, see Buckley, *"The Great Catastrophe of My Life,"* 155–67. The four sons' births are recorded online at: http://wc.rootsweb .ancestry.com/cgi-bin/igm.cgi?op=GET&db=jmljr&id=I6316.

32. Buckley, *"The Great Catastrophe of My Life,"* 156–57. At this time botanical abortifacients (e.g., tansy, pennyroyal) and various "mechanical" techniques were used. Like childbirth, all were risky.

33. Buckley, *"The Great Catastrophe of My Life,"* 155–59, 161, 165, 177, 296n48.

34. Benjamin Trumbull, *An Appeal to the Public, with Respect to the Unlawfulness of Divorces, in All Cases, Excepting Those of Incontinency* (New Haven, 1788), 40, 43; Connecticut data from Dayton, *Women before the Bar*, 113n15, 131; Virginia data from Buckley, *"The Great Catastrophe of My Life,"* 271, appendix, table A.4, "Legislative Divorces Granted."

35. Swift, *System of the Laws of Connecticut*, 202; Reeve, *Law of Baron and Femme*, 141; Hartog, *Man and Wife*, 105; Dayton, *Women before the Bar*, 33, 137, 154–55; Nancy Isenberg's analysis brought Shaw's case to my attention: see *Sex and Citizen-*

ship in Antebellum America (Chapel Hill: University of North Carolina Press, 1998), 163. See also Ryan, "'Spirit of Contradiction,'" 593–94, 616–17.

36. Marriage reported: *Connecticut Courant* (Hartford), Dec. 4, 1826, 3, and *Connecticut Herald* (New Haven), Dec. 5, 1826, 3; http://sharonhist.org/geneology/people-index/; Emeline Shaw, "Petition to the General Assembly at New Haven, First Wednesday of May 1846," Connecticut State Archives, Hartford, RG 002, Assembly Papers 1846, box 45, doc. 54B. Daniel T. Shaw's $150, which the court found "he expended upon the Dwelling House & real Estate in which the said Emiline had a life Estate," in Connecticut State Archives, Litchfield County Superior Court, box 326, Divorces, Shaw v. Shaw, Pt., for divorce mss.

37. Nancy E. Schott, *Barbour Collection of Connecticut Town Vital Records*, gen. ed. Lorraine Cook White (Baltimore: Genealogical Publishing, 2000), 38, 315. Emeline Shaw, "Petition to the General Assembly at New Haven, First Wednesday of May 1846," Connecticut State Archives, RG 002, Assembly Papers 1846, box 45, doc. 45A. Information on pregnancy from death record of "Shaw, Catharine F., dau. of Daniel T. and Emily B., d. Sept. 22, 1848, ae. 6 yrs., 1 mo., dys.," http://sharonhist.org/geneology/people-index/.

38. Thomas Day, *Reports of Cases Argued and Determined in the Supreme Court of Errors of the State of Connecticut . . .* , 17 (Hartford, 1847), 189–91.

39. Day, *Reports of Cases*, 17, 191.

40. Day, *Reports of Cases*, 17, 192–93.

41. Shaw v. Shaw, Pt., for divorce mss.; Day, *Reports of Cases*, 193–97. Church (1785–1854), a native and lifelong resident of Salisbury, graduated Yale in 1803. During 1821–31 he served eight years as representative and senator in the legislature. An Episcopalian, he was Connecticut Supreme Court justice, 1833–47, and chief justice, 1847–54. The court's restrictive reading of the law differed from Tapping Reeve's formulation thirty years earlier that "adultery, cruelty, and a well-grounded fear of bodily hurt" justified divorce. Reeve, *Law of Baron and Femme*, 205.

42. Sedgwick (1795–1882), a Congregationalist, graduated Williams College, 1813, and, after operating a school in Sharon, was admitted to the Connecticut bar in 1820; he practiced law in Sharon until death. Seymour (1804–81), a Litchfield native, lived there until death. An 1824 Yale graduate, he served in Connecticut's House of Representatives, including as Democratic Speaker in 1850, and in the U.S. Congress (1851–55). He was chief justice of the Connecticut Supreme Court, 1873–74.

43. Shaw, "Petition to the General Assembly at New Haven."

44. Compiled from Connecticut General Assembly, *Roll of State Officers and Members of General Assembly of Connecticut, from 1776 to 1881* (Hartford, 1881), 315–17; and *Resolutions and Private Acts, Passed by the General Assembly of the State of Connecticut, May Session, 1846* (New Haven, 1846), 17, 18.

45. Connecticut State Archives, RG002, Assembly Papers 1846, box 45, doc. 55D, "Schedule A" (Emeline Shaw inventory). Analysis by Jack Larkin, author of *The Reshaping of Everyday Life, 1790–1840* (New York: Harper and Row, 1988), in e-mail to author, Oct. 30, 2012; death record of "Shaw, Catharine F." The U.S. Census of 1850 records two 1826 residents of Sharon named Berry, Amanda and Asa. Amanda may have been Emeline and Charles Berry's daughter.

46. *Shaw v. Shaw* in Day, *Reports of Cases,* 193.

47. Christopher Collier, "The Campaign for Women's Property Rights: Sarah Banks's Story," *American Journal of Legal History* 54 (2014): 378–428.

48. Reeve, *Law of Baron and Femme,* 64, 205–6; Hartog, *Man and Wife,* 137. See also Jerome Nadelhaft, "'The Public Eye and the Prying Eye': The South and the Privacy Doctrine in Nineteenth-Century Wife Abuse Cases," *Cardozo Journal of Law and Gender* 14 (2008): 549–607; Hartog, *Man and Wife,* 153; Post, *Hannah Mather Crocker,* 118.

49. Arthur J. Larsen, ed., *Crusader and Feminist: Letters of Jane Grey Swisshelm, 1858–1865* (1934; reprint, Westport, Conn.: Hyperion, 1976), 1–3; Sylvia D. Hoffert, *Jane Grey Swisshelm: An Unconventional Life, 1815–1884* (Chapel Hill: University of North Carolina Press, 2004), 20–23; Jane Grey Swisshelm, *Half a Century* (Chicago: Jansen, McClurg, 1880), 41–42. The New Testament directs wives to obey husbands: Col. 3:18, Eph. 5:22, 1 Pet. 3:1; http://www.mnopedia.org/person/swisshelm-jane-grey-1815–1884. Swisshelm later advocated against divorce. Riley, *Divorce,* 77.

50. Ilyon Woo, *The Great Divorce* (New York: Atlantic Monthly, 2010), 12–30. According to Woo, *Great Divorce,* 17, the couple married in Brooklyn (17); however, Eunice Chapman reported the location as New-Durham, Greene County, N.Y., in her *An Account of the People Called Shakers: in the case of Eunice Chapman and her children,* since her husband became acquainted with that people and joined that society. Eunice Chapman, *An Account of the People Called Shakers* (Albany: Published by the Authoress, 1817), iii. Also second, expanded edition: Eunice Chapman, *An Account of the Conduct of the Shakers, in the Case of Eunice Chapman & Her Children Written by Herself; Also, a Refutation of the Shakers' Remonstrance to the Proceedings of the Legislature of New-York, in 1817, by Thomas Brown; To Which Are Added, the Deposition of Mary Dyer, Who Petitioned the Legislature of the State of New-Hampshire, for Relief in a Similar Case; Also, Depositions of Others Who Have Been Members of the Shaker Society; Also, the Proceedings of the Legislature of the State of New-York, in the Case of Eunice Chapman* ([Lebanon, Ohio]: Van Vleet and Camron, 1818). For a similar case, see Elizabeth A. DeWolfe, *Shaking the Faith: Women, Family, and Mary Marshall Dyer's Anti-Shaker Campaign* (New York: Palgrave Macmillan, 2002). See also Glendyne R. Wergland, *Shaker Women and Equality of the Sexes* (Amherst: University of Massachusetts Press, 2011).

51. Chapman, *Account of the People Called Shakers,* iv–v.

52. Woo, *Great Divorce*, 108–9; Riley, *Divorce*, 68.

53. Woo, *Great Divorce*, 153, 168–69; Chapman, *Account of the People Called Shakers*, iv–v.

54. Chapman, *Account of the People Called Shakers*, vi–vii.

55. Woo, *Great Divorce*, 252, 253–54, 258–59, 280, 392n; Hartog, *Man and Wife*, 123–24, 153.

56. Woo, *Great Divorce*, 233–34.

57. Dayton, *Women before the Bar*, 164–72; data compiled from works by Daniel Allen Hearn: *Legal Executions in New York State, 1639–1963* (Jefferson, N.C.: McFarland, 1997), *Legal Executions in New England, 1623–1960* (Jefferson, N.C.: McFarland, 1999), and *Legal Executions in New Jersey, 1691–1963* (Jefferson, N.C.: McFarland, 2005). Crime not recorded in one New York case, Ann Bowen, a white woman executed in 1708. Records for the murder of husbands may be scarce because poisoning, perhaps the most common method, was difficult to detect until forensic autopsies became routine in the first half of nineteenth century, leading to more convictions.

58. U.S. Bureau of the Census, *Historical Statistics of the United States, Colonial Times to 1970*, 2 vols. (Washington, D.C.: U.S. Department of Commerce, Bureau of the Census, 1975), 1:25, 29, 31, 32, 34, 2:1168.

59. Data compiled from Hearn, *Legal Executions in New York State*, *Legal Executions in New England*, and *Legal Executions in New Jersey*.

60. Data from Hearn, *Legal Executions in New York State*, *Legal Executions in New England*, and *Legal Executions in New Jersey*. See also Peter C. Hoffer and N. E. H. Hull, *Murdering Mothers: Infanticide in England and New England, 1558–1803* (New York: New York University Press, 1981), 47–48.

61. G. S. Rowe, "Infanticide, Its Judicial Resolution, and Criminal Code Revision in Early Pennsylvania," *Proceedings of the American Philosophical Society* 135 (1991): 200–232, esp. 207–9.

62. Proceeding against "negro fornication" in Edward W. Hanson's notes on "Supreme Judicial Court Criminal Cases, 1776–1800, 41, compiled for Hanson's edition of Robert Treat Paine Papers, generously shared, March 2011; Doron Ben-Atar and Richard D. Brown, *Taming Lust: Crimes against Nature in the Early Republic* (Philadelphia: University of Pennsylvania Press, 2014), 90; Dayton, *Women before the Bar*, 161 182–83. See also Hoffer and Hull, *Murdering Mothers*, 39, fig. 2.1, "Convictions for Infanticide in Massachusetts, 1670–1780." South Carolina information from Michael Stephen Hindus, *Prison and Plantation: Crime, Justice, and Authority in Massachusetts and South Carolina* (Chapel Hill: University of North Carolina Press, 1980), 51.

63. See note 19, above. *Pennsylvania Evening Herald and the American Monitor of Philadelphia* printed Beccaria's entire chapter "On the Punishment of Death," Feb. 25, 1786, vol. 3, issue 10, p. 40, cols. 1–4. *New Haven Gazette, and Connecticut*

Magazine published the entire work serially: Mar. 2, 9, 16, 23, 30, Apr. 27, May 4, 11, 1786 (vol. 1, issues 3–7, 11–13). Connecticut jurist Zephaniah Swift quoted Beccaria in his *System of Laws*, 295, 308.

64. *An Essay on Crimes and Punishments; Written by the Marquis Beccaria of Milan; With a Commentary Attributed to Monsieur de Voltaire* (Philadelphia: R. Bell, 1778), 191–92. A study of English courts similarly shows a dramatic reduction in infanticide cases. In the Chester Court of Great Sessions, 1650–1800, sixty-three cases, 1650–99, fell to thirty-one cases in 1700–1749 and to eighteen cases in 1750–1800, with a reduction of women hanged from twenty to four to three. Mark Jackson, *New-Born Child Murder: Women, Illegitimacy and the Courts in Eighteenth-Century England* (Manchester, U.K.: Manchester University Press, 1996), 38.

65. Dayton, *Women before the Bar*, 250.

66. Rowe, "Infanticide in Early Pennsylvania," 227; Dayton, *Women before the Bar*, 248; Hoffer and Hull, *Murdering Mothers*, chap. 3.

67. On Hannah Pegin (Peggin, Pegion), see Hearn, *Legal Executions in New England*, 169, 411, and *Connecticut Courant* (Hartford), Aug. 1, 1785, 3:2. On Abiah Converse, see Hearn, *Legal Executions in New England*, 174, 412, and *Hampshire Gazette* (Northampton, Mass.), Apr. 16, 1788, 3:2, July 23, 1788, 3:1. Sex prosecutions in western Massachusetts from Edward W. Hanson's notes on "Supreme Judicial Court Criminal Cases, 1776–1800" (note 62, above); Ben-Atar and Brown, *Taming Lust*, 91, 184n38. Hoffer and Hull, *Murdering Mothers*, omit these cases. They fall outside period for N. E. H. Hull, *Female Felons: Women and Serious Crime in Colonial Massachusetts* (Urbana: University of Illinois Press, 1987).

68. [Elizabeth Wilson], *A Faithful Narrative of Elizabeth Wilson; Who Was Executed at Chester, Jan. 3, 1786; Charged with the Murder of Her Twin Infants* (Philadelphia: William Glendinning, Preacher of the Gospel, [1786?]), reprinted in Philadelphia, New Haven, and Hudson, N.Y., 1786, and in Philadelphia, 1807. Between February and June 1786, the Wilson pamphlet was advertised in eleven newspapers from Baltimore to Boston. Edited versions appeared in nine more papers, from Charleston, South Carolina, to Windsor, Vermont.

69. *Independent Gazetteer* (Philadelphia), May 30, 1787, 3. Rowe, "Infanticide in Early Pennsylvania," 202–3, 223, 227–30.

70. Beccaria, *Essay on Crimes and Punishments*, 132; Hull, *Female Felons*, 34. Lydia Maria Child's 1847 fact-based story "Elizabeth Wilson," *Fact and Fiction: A Collection of Stories* (New York: C. S. Francis, 1847), 126–48, treated Wilson as a victim.

71. *Courier* (Norwich, Conn.), Jan. 27, 1808, 3:3. [John Milton Earle], *Report to the Governor and Council concerning the Indians of the Commonwealth under the Act of April 6, 1859* (Boston: William White, 1861). This was Senate Report No. 96, listing eight persons named Ockry at Mashpee, Mass., and one named Ockray at New Bedford.

72. *Courier* (Norwich, Conn.), Feb. 3, 1808, 2:1–3.

73. "Memorials of Connecticut Judges and Attorneys," *Connecticut Reports*, vol. 14, app., 21–22.

74. Clarissa Ockry's petition, May 1808, Connecticut Archives, Crimes and Misdemeanors, 2nd Ser., 4:92.

75. Lawrence B. Goodheart, *The Solemn Sentence of Death: Capital Punishment in Connecticut* (Amherst: University of Massachusetts Press, 2011), 76–77, and his "Changing Legal Culture in the Early Republic: Connecticut, Neonaticide and the Case of Clarissa Ockry," *Connecticut History Review* 53 (Spring 2014): 3–15; Nancy Hathaway Steenburg, *Children and the Criminal Law in Connecticut, 1635–1855* (New York: Routledge, 2005), 54, identifies infant's sex.

76. Goodheart, *Solemn Sentence of Death*, 77. Goodheart notes (78) that in 1816 Connecticut ended the death penalty for adultery, a 1672 statute. The 1810 case of Susanna in New York, covered in chapter 4, is similar to the Clifton and Ockry cases in that a young black woman was tried for infanticide but not executed. Susanna certainly killed her infant and hid the corpse, but her behavior permitted a successful non compos mentis defense.

77. Steenburg, *Children and the Criminal Law*, 69–70.

78. *Phenix or Windham (Conn.) Herald*, Nov. 21, 1795, 3, Mar. 5, 1796, 3.

79. Stuart Banner, *The Death Penalty: An American History* (Cambridge, Mass.: Harvard University Press, 2002), 98.

80. [Rachel Wall], *Life, Last Words and Dying Confession, of Rachel Wall, Who, with William Smith and William Dunogan, were executed at Boston, on Thursday, October 8, 1789, for High-Way Robbery* (n.p., n.d.). American Antiquarian Society copy; Richard D. Brown, "Hanging Rachel Wall: Massachusetts' Last Female Execution, 1789," unpublished paper delivered at Old South Meeting House for Bostonian Society, Nov. 1, 2001.

81. F[rancis]. W. Dana, Simeon Strong, Theodore Sedgwick, Samuel Sewall, and Geo[rge]. Thatcher to His Excellency Governor Strong, Boston, Apr. 7, 1804, in Records of the Governor's Council, Pardons Granted File, Massachusetts Archive. Stevens was pardoned on May 29, 1806. See also Supreme Judicial Court records, November 1806 term, 169. Stevens's racial identification from *Columbian Centinel and Massachusetts Federalist* (Boston), Nov. 23, 1803, 2:3 ("On Monday at the Supreme Judicial Court now sitting in this town, a mulatto was convicted of the murder of her infant child"). See also Brown and Brown, *Hanging of Ephraim Wheeler*, 209.

82. Karen Halttunen, *Murder Most Foul: The Killer and the American Gothic Imagination* (Cambridge, Mass.: Harvard University Press, 1998), 151–56. Notwithstanding substantial testimony implicating Elsie Whipple as accessary in her husband's murder—she was in an affair with Jesse Strang, who was convicted and executed—Whipple was acquitted. See *Trial and Acquittal of Mrs. Whipple, as Accessary to the Murder of Her Husband, John Whipple; With a Brief Sketch of Her Life*

(New York, 1827). For the Thirza Mansfield conviction, see *New Haven (Conn.) Pilot*, Aug. 21, 1824, reprinted in *National Gazette and Literary Register* (Philadelphia), Aug. 26, 1824, 3. For the commutation, see *Connecticut Herald* (New Haven), May 31, 1825, 3, with letter from "E" opposing commutation. Per capita calculations are based on executions compiled in Daniel Allen Hearn's volumes on legal executions in New York, New Jersey and New England and averages of census data from the relevant colonies and states (note 57, above). On American patterns as roughly similar to those of England, see King, *Crime, Justice, and Discretion*, 278–87. For Massachusetts, New York, and Pennsylvania, see William Francis Kuntz, *Criminal Sentencing in Three Nineteenth-Century Cities: Social History of Punishment in New York, Boston, and Philadelphia, 1830–1880* (New York: Garland, 1988). In Ohio in the 1850s nearly half of all women convicts (47 percent) served less than one-year prison terms and were pardoned; the longest woman's sentence was three years. In succeeding decades sentences increased and percentage of pardons fell. L. Marra Dodge, *"Whores and Thieves of the Worst Kind": A Study of Women, Crime, and Prisons, 1835–2000* (DeKalb: Northern Illinois University Press, 2002), 56, table 1. For England, see King, *Crime, Justice, and Discretion*, chap. 8, "Sentencing Policy and the Impact of Gender and Age." Kerry Seagrave, *Women and Capital Punishment in America, 1840–1899: Death Sentences and Executions in the United States and Canada* (Jefferson, N.C.: McFarland, 2008), 4, reports that after 1870 women were convicted of 10 percent of murders but were executed at rate much lower than men.

83. Holly Brewer, *By Birth or Consent: Children, Law, and the Revolution in Authority* (Chapel Hill: University of North Carolina Press for the Omohundro Institute of Early American History and Culture, 2005), 1, 23. The early modern European understanding of children as "little adults" is expounded by Philippe Ariès, *Centuries of Childhood: A Social History of Family Life* (New York: Anchor, 1965).

84. Brewer, *By Birth or Consent*, 1, 9, 26–27. By end of the eighteenth century, or earlier, British sentiment almost entirely turned away from executing children: King, *Crime, Justice, and Discretion*, 255–56. See also Robert L. Hale, *A Review of Juvenile Executions in America* (Lewiston, N.Y.: Edwin Mellen, 1997).

85. The age of consent, ten years, in [Samuel Sewall and Nathan Dane], *Communication from the Hon. Samuel Sewall, Esq. and the Hon Nathan Dane, Esq. Accompanied with Several Bills for the Regulation of the State Prison and an Alteration of the Criminal Laws of the Commonwealth* (Boston: Young and Minns, 1805), 36–37. For the age of testimony, see Joseph Chitty, *A Practical Treatise on the Criminal Law . . . With Additional Notes . . . by Richard Peters, Jr.*, vol. 2 (Philadelphia: Isaac Riley, 1819), 575. For example, see the Ephraim Wheeler Jr. testimony in Brown and Brown, *Hanging of Ephraim Wheeler*, 75–76.

86. Irene Quenzler Brown and Richard D. Brown, "Pardons Won and Pardons Lost: Narratives from Massachusetts, 1780–1820," paper presented at a meeting of the

American Historical Association, Boston, Jan. 5, 2001; Brown and Brown, *Hanging of Ephraim Wheeler*, 206–9, 211–12.

87. *Pennsylvania Mercury and Universal Advertiser*, Sept. 30, 1785, 2.

88. [Boston] *Palladium* [New-England Palladium], Dec. 14, 1813, 2:4.

89. [Boston] *Palladium* [New-England Palladium], Dec. 14, 1813, 2:4; Daniel A. Cohen, *Pillars of Salt, Monuments of Grace: New England Crime Literature and the Origins of American Popular Culture, 1674–1860* (New York: Oxford University Press, 1993), 89–94.

90. [Thomas C. Cushing], *Account of the Short Life and Ignominious Death of Stephen Merrill Clark, Who Was Executed at Salem on Thursday the Tenth day of May, 1821; at the Early Age of 16 Years and 9 Months, for the Crime of Arson* (Salem, Mass.: T. C. Cushing 1821), 4, 5. Clark's middle name was spelled "Merril" at trial.

91. Angier March to Russell and Cutler, printers of *Boston Gazette*, June 3, 1811, 2; *Independent Chronicle* (Boston), June 3, 1811, 2; *An Account of the GREAT FIRE which destroyed about 250 buildings in Newburyport, on the Night of the 31st of May, 1811* (Newburyport, Mass., 1811), 22–23, reports that on July 24, 1811, "a youth of about 15 years of age was apprehended and examined before a magistrate, on a charge of setting fire to the barn of Capt. Thompson." The youth, who confessed setting fire to two other barns and "was learning the baker's trade," was to be tried before Supreme Judicial Court the following November. *Thomas's Massachusetts Spy, or Worcester Gazette*, June 5, 1811, 3, cites 280 buildings.

92. *Newburyport Herald*, Aug. 22, 1820, 3.

93. [Stephen Merril Clark], *Report of the Evidence, Arguments of Counsel, Charge, and Sentence, at the Trial of Stephen Merril Clark, for Arson, before the Supreme Judicial Court, February 15, 16 & 17 . . . 1821* (Salem, Mass.: T. C. Cushing and W. Palfray, 1821), 16 (testimony of William Woart, Esq.); [Cushing], *Short Life and Ignominious Death of Stephen Merrill Clark*, 6.

94. [Clark], *Report of the Evidence . . . Trial of Stephen Merril Clark*, 3.

95. John Pickering (1777–1846), son of prominent Federalist Timothy Pickering and a specialist in languages, also served in the Massachusetts House and Senate. William Thomas Davis, *The Bench and Bar of the Commonwealth of Massachusetts*, 2 vols. (Boston: Boston History, 1895), 1:279; John Glen King (1787–1857), student of Joseph Story, also served in the state house and senate. Davis, *Bench and Bar*, 2:203.

96. [Clark], *Report of the Evidence . . . Trial of Stephen Merril Clark*, 19, 32, 33, 34, 37, 39, 41, 42, 44, 45.

97. [Cushing], *Short Life and Ignominious Death*, 6.

98. [Clark], *Report of the Evidence . . . Trial of Stephen Merril Clark*, 12. Clark's father, Moses Clark Sr., also complained to selectmen about Hannah Downes, 16.

99. [Clark], *Report of the Evidence . . . Trial of Stephen Merril Clark*, 36, 40–41.

100. [Clark], *Report of the Evidence . . . Trial of Stephen Merril Clark*, 29, 39, italics added to "unfortunate boy." *Salem [Essex] Register*, May 12, 1821, reprinted in *Baltimore Patriot and Mercantile Advertiser*, May 18, 1821, 2.

101. [Clark], *Report of the Evidence . . . Trial of Stephen Merril Clark*, 14, 16.

102. [Clark], *Report of the Evidence . . . Trial of Stephen Merril Clark*, 48–50, 56.

103. [Clark], *Report of the Evidence . . . Trial of Stephen Merril Clark*, 59, 60.

104. [Clark], *Report of the Evidence . . . Trial of Stephen Merril Clark*, 61, 62.

105. [Clark], *Report of the Evidence . . . Trial of Stephen Merril Clark*, 63.

106. [Cushing], *Short Life and Ignominious Death*, 9, 10. Brooks characterized in David Hackett Fischer, *The Revolution of American Conservatism: The Federalist Party in the Era of Jeffersonian Democracy* (New York: Harper and Row, 1965), 246.

107. [Cushing], *Short Life and Ignominious Death*, 6–7, 10.

108. [Clark], *Report of the Evidence . . . Trial of Stephen Merril Clark*, 49.

109. Massachusetts Archives, Council Records (Records of the Governor's Executive Council, 1819–1822), GC3/329X, 1819–1822, 256, 258, 259, 268; [Cushing], *Short Life and Ignominious Death*, 10. The reprieve lasted from the original execution date, April 26, 1821, to the actual date, May 10, 1821.

110. [Cushing], *Short Life and Ignominious Death*, 10, 11.

111. [Cushing], *Short Life and Ignominious Death*, 13, 14.

112. [Cushing], *Short Life and Ignominious Death*, 3, 16. *Essex (Mass.) Register*, May 9, 1821, 3.

113. The cases of Ocuish and two of the New Jersey children are treated in chapter 4. The third New Jersey child was Roseanne Keen, who poisoned her employers, July 23, 1843, and was executed, April 26, 1844, after efforts to spare her life failed. Hearn, *Legal Executions in New Jersey*, 85–86; Thomas Cushing and Charles E. Sheppard, *History of the Counties of Gloucester, Salem, and Cumberland New Jersey* (Philadelphia: Everts and Peck, 1883), 85–86. For John Tuhi, see [John Tuhi], *Life and Confession of John Tuhi, (a Youth of 17 Years,) Who Was Executed at Utica, (N.Y.) on Friday, July 25th, 1817, for the Murder of His Brother, Joseph Tuhi* (n.p., n.d.), and broadside: *The Life and Confession of John Tuhi, an Indian of the Brothertown Tribe, While under Sentence of Death for the Murder of His Brother, Joseph Tuhi, as Taken from His Own Mouth, in Prison at Whitestown, Oneida County, State of New-York, a Few Days Previous to His Execution which Took Place at Utica, July 25th, 1817*. The Tuhi brothers were alcoholics. In 1848 Massachusetts tried the fourteen-year-old white girl Sarah Jane Pinkerton for the poisoning murder of her mother. The jury acquitted her on the ground that the girl thought that the arsenic would only sicken her mother. *Trial of Sarah Jane Pinkerton, for the Murder of Her Mother, Sarah Cain, by Poison, before the Supreme Judicial Court at Boston* [Boston? 1848?]. The crime and execution of Michael Jennings in New Haven, Connecticut, was reported in Hearn, *Legal Executions in New England*, 234–35. After 1860 regional and racial differences increasingly set North and South apart, with South Carolina executing the black fourteen-year-old George

Stinney Jr. in 1944 as punishment for the murder of two white girls, aged seven and eleven years.

114. *Newburyport (Mass.) Herald*, Nov. 12, 1830, 2:4–6.

115. "Trial for Arson," *New Hampshire Gazette* (Portsmouth), June 20, 1837, 2; *Gloucester (Mass.) Telegraph*, July 12, 1837, 2. The court that convicted Monahon acquitted his ten-year-old accomplice, Michael Whaling [Whalen]. Wiley S. Sanders, ed., *Juvenile Offenders for a Thousand Years: Selected Readings from Anglo-Saxon Times to 1900* (Chapel Hill: University of North Carolina Press, 1970), 337–38, reprints a different account of the trial from the *Southern Citizen* (Ashborough, N.C.), July 15, 1837. This account mentions Chief Justice Shaw's charge to the jury "that notwithstanding their age they must suffer the punishment of the law (death) if it appeared that they wilfully and maliciously committed the act charged."

116. Linda K. Kerber, *No Constitutional Right to Be Ladies: Women and the Obligations of Citizenship* (New York: Hill and Wang, 1998), 27, points to the 1805 case of *Martin v. Commonwealth of Massachusetts*, where Martin's attorney, George Blake, argued that the legislature classed "feme covert and infants" together. See also Corinne T. Field, *The Struggle for Equal Adulthood: Gender, Race, Age, and the Fight for Citizenship in the Antebellum United States* (Chapel Hill: University of North Carolina Press, 2014), esp. chaps. 3–5; and Rogers M. Smith, "'One United People': Second-Class Female Citizenship and the American Quest for Community," *Yale Journal of Law and the Humanities* 1 (1989): 229, 255.

117. Teresa Anne Murphy, *Citizenship and the Origins of Women's History in the United States* (Philadelphia: University of Pennsylvania Press, 2013).

118. See note 20, above; Norton, *Liberty's Daughters*, 157–63.

119. Thomas Weston, *History of the Town of Middleboro, Massachusetts* (Boston: Houghton, Mifflin, 1906), 455–56; Franklin B. Dexter, *Biographical Sketches of the Graduates of Yale College*, vol. 3, *May 1763 to July 1778* (New York: Henry Holt, 1903), 473–74.

120. Abigail Adams to John Adams, n.p., June 17, 1782, in Butterfield and Friedlaender, *Adams Family Correspondence*, 4:328; Alexander Keyssar, *The Right to Vote: The Contested History of Democracy in the United States* (New York: Basic Books, 2000); Sean Wilentz, *The Rise of American Democracy: From Jefferson to Lincoln* (New York: W. W. Norton, 2005).

121. Zagarri, *Revolutionary Backlash*, 151.

122. *Richmond Enquirer*, Oct. 20, 1829, in Zagarri, *Revolutionary Backlash*, 153. On the characterization of Daniel Webster, see Fischer, *Revolution of American Conservatism*, 295. Definition, italics added, from *An American Dictionary of the English Language* (New York: S. Converse, 1828), discussed in Zagarri, *Revolutionary Backlash*, 157.

123. Susan Zaeske, *Signatures of Citizenship: Petitioning, Antislavery, and Women's Political Identity* (Chapel Hill: University of North Carolina Press, 2003), 23.

124. Alisse Portnoy, *Their Right to Speak: Women's Activism in the Indian and Slave Debates* (Cambridge, Mass.: Harvard University Press, 2005), 43–46; Catharine E. Beecher, *Educational Reminiscences and Suggestions* (New York: J. B. Ford, 1874), 63–65.

125. "Circular: Addressed to Benevolent Ladies of the U. States," *Christian Advocate and Journal and Zion's Herald* (New York), Dec. 25, 1829, 65–66; Portnoy, *Their Right to Speak*, 47; Zaeske, *Signatures of Citizenship*, 24–26; Mary Hershberger, "Mobilizing Women, Anticipating Abolition: The Struggle against Indian Removal in the 1830s," *Journal of American History* 86 (1999): 15–40. Hershberger reports that the largest single petition carried 670 signatures from the women of Pittsburgh.

126. Zaeske, *Signatures of Citizenship*, 27, 173–74. Zaeske explains that no precise signature count is possible because many petitions were destroyed in the nineteenth century.

127. Senator Thomas Hart Benton (Missouri), *Gales and Seaton's Register of Debates of Congress [Senate]*, 21st Congress, 1st Session, Feb. 2, 1830, 109; Rep. William Drayton (South Carolina), *Gales & Seaton's Register of Debates of Congress [H. of R.]*, 21st Congress, 1st Session, Jan. 11, 1830, 508; Zaeske, *Signatures of Citizenship*, 27.

128. Christopher Leslie Brown, *Moral Capital: Foundations of British Abolitionism* (Chapel Hill: University of North Carolina Press for the Omohundro Institute of Early American History and Culture, 2006), 422–23; Zaeske, *Signatures of Citizenship*, 173.

129. Zaeske, *Signatures of Citizenship*, 120–21.

130. Zaeske, *Signatures of Citizenship*, 129–30.

131. Jefferson to Samuel Kercheval, Sept. 5, 1816, in *The Writings of Thomas Jefferson*, ed. Paul Leicester Ford, vol. 10 (New York: G. P. Putnam's Sons, 1899), 45n–46n, in Zaeske, *Signatures of Citizenship*, 129. Catharine E. Beecher, *An Essay on Slavery and Abolitionism, with Reference to the Duty of American Females* (Philadelphia: Henry Perkins, 1837), 99–100, 104.

132. Zaeske, *Signatures of Citizenship*, 140–42.

133. Paulina W. Davis, *A History of the National Woman's Rights Movement, for Twenty Years . . . from 1850 to 1870* (1871; reprint, New York: Kraus, 1971), 10–11, 11n.

134. Isenberg, *Sex and Citizenship*, 172; Carole Shammas, "Re-Assessing the Married Women's Property Acts," *Journal of Women's History* 6 (Spring 1994): 16.

135. Shammas, "Re-Assessing the Married Women's Property Acts," 16, 20–22.

136. On the growing number of single women, see Chambers-Schiller, *Liberty, a Better Husband*, 5; Hartog, *Man and Wife*, 118.

137. Although several women served as postmasters at the beginning of the Republic, and one in the decades before 1860, the 1810 postal act used male-gendered language to describe the office and women were effectively excluded. Lydia Maria Child, *Letters from New York* [1843], 11th ed. (New York: C. S. Francis, 1850), 220–21. John C. Colt, brother of Samuel Colt, the inventor of a revolving pistol and

firearms company founder, killed the printer Samuel Adams with a hatchet. He committed suicide before his scheduled hanging. Thomas McDade, *The Annals of Murder: A Bibliography of Books and Pamphlets on American Murders from Colonial Times to 1900* (Norman: University of Oklahoma Press, 1961), 62–63.

138. Elizabeth R. Varon, *We Mean to Be Counted: White Women and Politics in Antebellum Virginia* (Chapel Hill: University of North Carolina Press, 1998), 3–4; Zagarri, *Revolutionary Backlash*, 163–64, on Whig rallies.

139. Elisha P. Hurlbut, *Essays on Human Rights and Their Political Guaranties* (New York: Fowlers and Wells, 1848), 109–11. When Hurlbut speaks of "our race," as he does on p. 109, he appears to mean the human race because New York law at the time admitted blacks to vote (albeit with higher residency and property requirements) and Hurlbut is seeking to enlarge voting rights in New York. Biographical information on Hurlbut from George Anson Hardin, *History of Herkimer County, N.Y.* (Syracuse, N.Y.: D. Mason, 1893), 148.

140. Hurlbut, *Essays on Human Rights*, 112, 113–16, 118, 119, 120–23.

141. "Declaration of Sentiments and Resolutions. Women's Rights Convention, Held at Seneca Falls, 19–20 July 1848," Elizabeth Cady Stanton and Susan B. Anthony Papers Project, Rutgers University, http://ecssba.rutgers.edu/docs/seneca.html.

142. "Declaration of Sentiments."

143. "Declaration of Sentiments."

144. "Declaration of Sentiments."

145. "Declaration of Sentiments."

146. "Declaration of Sentiments," Signers at Women's Rights National Historical Park website: http://www.nps.gov/wori/historyculture/signers-of-the-declaration-of-sentiments.htm.

147. Kerber, *No Constitutional Right to Be Ladies*, 38–42; Paulina W. Davis, *History of National Woman's Rights Movement for Twenty Years: With the Proceedings of the Decade Meeting Held at Apollo Hall, October 20, 1870, with an Appendix Containing the History of the Movement during the Winter of 1871, in the National Capitol* (New York: Journeymen Printers, 1871), 8–11, 13, 15, 21. For another example of woman's equal rights based on the Declaration of Independence, see *The Proceedings of the Woman's Rights Convention, Held at Akron, Ohio, May 28 and 29, 1851* (Cincinnati: Ben Franklin Book and Job Office, 1851), 8. Jane Swisshelm was among the speakers supporting the resolutions.

148. Davis, *History of National Woman's Rights Movement*, 23, 24, 25, 33, 43–45, 47, 49, 51.

149. Ellen Carol DuBois, *Feminism and Suffrage: The Emergence of an Independent Women's Movement in America, 1848–1869* (Ithaca, N.Y.: Cornell University Press, 1978), chap. 3.

150. For the Fourteenth Amendment, see Cornell University Law School, Legal Information Institute, http://www.law.cornell.edu/constitution/amendmentxiv.

151. DuBois, *Feminism and Suffrage*, 174–75.

152. Isenberg, *Sex and Citizenship*, 194.

153. Isenberg, *Sex and Citizenship*, 202–3, treats the Bradwell case. Bradley's words are from Bradwell v. State of Illinois, 83 U.S. 130 (1873). See also Richard L. Aynes, "Bradwell v. Illinois: Chief Justice Chase's Dissent and the 'Sphere of Women's Work,'" *Louisiana Law Review* 59 (1999): 520–41. Aynes supplies the "high honors" quotation (525) and reports that Chase supported women's suffrage.

154. Keyssar, *Right to Vote*, 277. For a full discussion of the age requirement, see Wendell W. Cultice, *Youth's Battle for the Ballot: A History of Voting Age in America* (Westport, Conn.: Greenwood, 1992), 4–14.

155. Davis, *History of National Woman's Rights Movement*, 47.

156. "Report of the Committee on the Judiciary, January 30, 1871, . . . the Memorial of Victoria C. Woodhull," in Davis, *History of the National Woman's Rights Movement*, 99.

157. See Ann Russo and Cheris Kramarae, eds., *The Radical Women's Press of the 1850s* (New York: Routledge, 1991).

Chapter Seven. Equal Rights and Unequal People

1. Alexis de Tocqueville, *Democracy in America*, trans. and ed. Harvey C. Mansfield and Delba Winthrop (Chicago: University of Chicago Press, 2000), bk. 1, chap. 2, 44–45, 245 (epigraph).

2. C. B. Macpherson, *The Political Theory of Possessive Individualism: Hobbes to Locke* (Oxford: Clarendon Press, 1962).

3. John Adams to James Sullivan, Philadelphia, May 26, 1776, in *Papers of John Adams*, vol. 4, *February–August 1776*, ed. Robert J. Taylor (Cambridge, Mass.: Harvard University Press, 1979), 208–12; in the first quotation, the order of sentences is reversed before and after the ellipses; "An Address . . . to Their Constituents," *Journal of the Convention for Framing a Constitution of Government for the State of Massachusetts Bay . . . September 1, 1779 to . . . June 16, 1780* (Boston, 1832), 216, 218, italics added.

4. Mansfield, Bristol County, Mass., in Elisha P. Douglass, *Rebels and Democrats: The Struggle for Equal Political Rights and Majority Rule during the American Revolution* (Chapel Hill: University of North Carolina Press, 1955), 204.

5. Douglass, *Rebels and Democrats*, 205–6.

6. Douglass, *Rebels and Democrats*, 207.

7. Alexander Hamilton, John Jay, and James Madison, *The Federalist*, ed. Benjamin F. Wright (Cambridge, Mass.: Harvard University Press, 1961), 131.

8. *The People the Best Governors; or, A Plan of Government Founded on the Just Principles of Natural Freedom* (n.p., 1776), 6.

9. *People the Best Governors*, 7, 9, 10.

10. Gordon S. Wood, *The Creation of the American Republic* (Chapel Hill: University of North Carolina Press for the Institute of Early American History and Culture, 1969), 70–71.

11. Wood, *Creation*, 89.

12. James Madison in "Parties," *National Gazette* [Philadelphia], Jan. 23, 1792, issue 25, 99.

13. "Mr. Trumbull," *Norwich (Conn.) Packet*, Sept. 9, 1791, 1 (John Trumbull was the printer-editor of the *Packet*); Ruth Bogin, "Petitioning and the New Moral Economy of Post-Revolutionary America," *William and Mary Quarterly*, 3rd Ser., 45 (1988): 391–425.

14. James Madison to W. T. Barry, Aug. 4, 1822, in *Writings of James Madison*, ed. Gaillard Hunt, vol. 9 (New York: G. P. Putnam's Sons, 1910), 103.

15. "Mr. Trumbull," *Norwich (Conn.) Packet*, Sept. 9, 1791, 1.

16. "A Freeman of the State," *Norwich (Conn.) Packet*, June 28, 1792; Bogin, "Petitioning and the New Moral Economy of Post-Revolutionary America," 391, 413.

17. Alexander Keyssar, *The Right to Vote: The Contested History of Democracy in the United States* (New York: Basic Books, 2000), 348–49; Bruce P. Stark, "Universal Suffrage, the 'Stand-Up Law,' and the Wallingford Election Controversy, 1791–1818," *Connecticut History Review* 53 (Spring 2014): 16–44.

18. Elias Boudinot, *An Oration, Delivered at Elizabeth-Town, New-Jersey; Agreeably to a Resolution of the State Society of Cincinnati, on the Fourth of July, M.DCC.XCIII; Being the Seventeenth Anniversary of the Independence of America* (Elizabeth-Town, N.J., 1793), 22, 23, 24.

19. William Manning, *The Key of Liberty: The Life and Democratic Writings of William Manning, "a Laborer," 1747–1814*, ed. Michael Merrill and Sean Wilentz (Cambridge, Mass.: Harvard University Press, 1993), 31, 138, 141, 153–55.

20. Manning, *Key of Liberty*, 4, 138–39, 157.

21. The Ohio Constitution of 1851 provided suffrage for adult white men resident for one year. The convention rejected nonwhite and women's suffrage. Keyssar, *Right to Vote*, 30, 33, 55, 61, 62 (Wisconsin allowed paupers suffrage), 83, table A.3, 348, table A.4, 349–53.

22. Keyssar, *Right to Vote*, 23, 30, 38, 39, 41, 44, 46.

23. Keyssar, *Right to Vote*, 86.

24. Michael Vorenberg, *Final Freedom: The Civil War, the Abolition of Slavery, and the Thirteenth Amendment* (Cambridge: Cambridge University Press, 2001); Robert J. Cottrol, "The Thirteenth Amendment and the North's Overlooked Egalitarian Heritage," *National Black Law Journal* 11 (1989): 198–211; Keyssar, *Right to Vote*, 89; Robert R. Dykstra and Harlan Hahn, "Northern Voters and Negro Suffrage: The Case of Iowa," in *Voters, Parties, and Elections*, ed. Joel H. Silbey and Samuel T. McSeveney (Lexington, Mass.: Xerox College, 1972), 155–66. Dykstra and Hahn

note (163) that Irish and German immigrants opposed black suffrage, whereas American-born voters from the upper Ohio Valley supported equal rights. An 1857 Iowa referendum defeated black suffrage.

25. Bruce Mann, *Republic of Debtors: Bankruptcy in the Age of American Independence* (Cambridge, Mass.: Harvard University Press, 2002), 26, 53–60, 67, 77, 82, 105, 106, 212.

26. "Treaty of Peace with Great Britain," in *Documents of American History*, vol. 1, *To 1898*, ed. Henry Steele Commager and Milton Cantor, 10th ed. (Englewood Cliffs, N.J.: Prentice-Hall, 1988), art. 4, 118.

27. Mann, *Republic of Debtors*, 89, 101, 163, 179,

28. U.S. Constitution, art. 2, sec. 8, 4th para., in Commager and Cantor, *Documents of American History*, 1:141.

29. Mann, *Republic of Debtors*, 202.

30. Mann, *Republic of Debtors*, 203.

31. Mann, *Republic of Debtors*, 100–101.

32. Mann, *Republic of Debtors*, 100–101; Julian Ursyn Niemcewicz, *Under Their Vine and Fig Tree: Travels through America in 1797–1799, 1805, with Some Further Account of Life in New Jersey*, ed. and trans. Mechie J. E. Budka, in *Collections of the New Jersey Historical Society* (Elizabeth, N.J., 1965), 14, 17.

33. Mann, *Republic of Debtors*, 168, 203, 204.

34. Mann, *Republic of Debtors*, 214.

35. Mann, *Republic of Debtors*, 214–19, 222.

36. Mann, *Republic of Debtors*, 248, 255.

37. Mann, *Republic of Debtors*, 104–5; *The Forlorn Hope* (Prison, New York), vol. 1, no. 1, Mar. 24, 1800, 2.

38. Supreme Court U.S. (June 29, 1970), Williams v. Illinois, 399 U.S. 235 (1970); Supreme Court U.S. (May 24, 1983), Bearden v. Georgia, 461 U.S. 660 (1983). See Robert Kuttner, *Debtors' Prison: The Politics of Austerity versus Possibility* (New York: Alfred A. Knopf, 2013).

39. Douglas Hay et al., *Albion's Fatal Tree: Crime and Society in Eighteenth-Century England* (New York: Pantheon, 1975), 32–34; V. A. C. Gatrell, *The Hanging Tree: Execution and the English People, 1770–1868* (Oxford: Oxford University Press, 1996), 292–94; J. Burke, "Crime and Punishment in 1777: The Execution of the Reverend Dr. William Dodd and Its Impact upon His Contemporaries," in *Executions and the British Experience from the 17th to the 20th Century*, ed. W. B. Thesing (Jefferson, N.C.: McFarland, 1990), 59–76; Cynthia B. Herrup, *A House in Gross Disorder: Sex, Law, and the Second Earl of Castlehaven* (Oxford: Oxford University Press, 2001).

40. Samuel Johnson, *London: A Poem in Imitation of the Third Satire of Juvenal* (Dublin, 1738), 12, 13, ll. 159–60.

41. [Jason Fairbanks], *Report of the Trial of Jason Fairbanks on an Indictment for the Murder of Elizabeth Fales; At the Supreme Court, Holden at Dedham, in the County of Norfolk, on Thursday the 6th, and Friday the 7th days of August, 1801* (Boston, 1801). Context in Daniel A. Cohen, *Pillars of Salt, Monuments of Grace: New England Crime Literature and the Origins of American Popular Culture, 1674–1860* (New York: Oxford University Press, 1993), chap. 8, "The Story of Jason Fairbanks: Trial Reports and the Rise of Sentimental Fiction," 167–94.

42. [Fairbanks], *Report of the Trial*, 64, 72, 81, 82.

43. *Report of the Trial of Joel Clough, on an Indictment for the Murder of Mrs. Mary W. Hamilton, before Chief Justice Hornblower, and Four Associate Judges, at Mount Holly, New Jersey, in June 1833* (Boston: Beals, Homer, 1833), 32 ("respectable"), 47; Karen Halttunen, *Murder Most Foul: The Killer and the American Gothic Imagination* (Cambridge, Mass.: Harvard University Press, 1998), 179; Daniel Allen Hearn, *Legal Executions in New Jersey, 1691–1963* (Jefferson, N.C.: McFarland, 2005), 76–77. Estelle Fox Kleiger, *The Trial of Levi Weeks or the Manhattan Well Mystery* (Chicago: Academy Chicago, 1989), recounts Weeks's trial for 1800 murder of Gugliema [Elma] Sands. Murderer and victim from respectable families. After corpse found in well, Weeks accused of murder to avoid marriage. Weeks defended by Alexander Hamilton and Aaron Burr and acquitted. Trial testimony left suspicion of Weeks, but social class, distinguished defenders, and insufficient evidence freed him.

44. William Bentley, *Diary of William Bentley, D.D.: Pastor of the East Church, Salem, Massachusetts*, 4 vols. (1905–1914; reprint, Gloucester, Mass.: Peter Smith, 1962), 4:301–2 (Dec. 15, 1814), 335 (Jun. 16, 1815), 421–22 (Nov. 21, 1816), 495–96 (Jan. 15, 1818), 586 (Apr. 8, 1819). When the mother (Mary Derby Crowninshield) of the brothers died at age seventy-six in 1813, Bentley remarked: "She was indeed an extraordinary woman & maintained with a dignity of person, a dignity of action, which was assisted with the purest manners. In her family we have had nothing like her." Bentley, *Diary*, 4:217 (Nov. 26, 1813). For Richard's marriage to an Irish hotel maid in New York City, see Howard A. Bradley and James A. Winans, *Daniel Webster and the Salem Murder* (Columbia, Mo.: Artcraft, 1956), 17.

45. Bradley and Winans, *Webster and the Salem Murder*, 16. On the relationship of Joseph Knapp Sr. to Captain White, see Robert Booth, *Death of an Empire: The Rise and Murderous Fall of Salem, America's Richest City* (New York: St. Martin's, 2011), 199.

46. Bentley, *Diary*, 1:104 (Sept. 23, 1788), 105–6 (Sept. 28, 1788), 216 (Dec. 5, 1790); George Henry Moore, *Notes on the History of Slavery in Massachusetts* (1866; reprint, New York: Negro Universities Press, 1968), 225–27.

47. Bradley and Winans, *Webster and the Salem Murder*, 16, 17.

48. Booth, *Death of an Empire*, 199.

49. Bradley and Winans, *Webster and the Salem Murder*, 46; Bentley, *Diary*, 1:123 (May 13, 1789).
50. Bradley and Winans, *Webster and the Salem Murder*, passim.
51. Booth, *Death of an Empire*, 224; "Speech at the Trial of John [sic] F. Knapp for Murder, at Salem, Massachusetts," in Samuel M. Smucker, *The Life, Speeches, and Memorials of Daniel Webster . . .* (Philadelphia: Duane Rulison, 1861), 347–417. There are many editions of Webster's speech; see Harold D. Moser, *Daniel Webster: A Bibliography* (Westport, Conn.: Greenwood, 2005), 201, item 1585.
52. *Newburyport (Mass.) Herald*, Aug. 13, 1830, 3.
53. *Boston Courier*, quoted in Bradley and Winans, *Webster and the Salem Murder*, 98, 99; *Newburyport (Mass.) Herald*, Aug. 13, 1830, 2.
54. Booth, *Death of an Empire*, 223; Bradley and Winans, *Webster and the Salem Murder*, 110, 159.
55. *Boston Commercial Gazette*, Nov. 15, 1830, 1; Bradley and Winans, *Webster and the Salem Murder*, 221–24. Bradley and Winans argue (221–22) that Webster falsely denied receiving payment for the Joseph Knapp Jr. prosecution, and they present a facsimile of the receipt signed by him. They misread the receipt, which refers only to the defense of "Jno. [John] F. Knapp." Webster claimed that he was not paid for this trial work.
56. At first the J. F. Knapp trial, Webster said, "There is no refuge from confession, but suicide,—and suicide is confession," quoted in "Attempted Suicide as Evidence of Guilt in Criminal Cases: The Legal and Psychological Views," *Washington University Law Quarterly* 204 (1964): 204–13. Webster's remarks are in *Commonwealth v. Knapp*, 26 Mass. 496 (1830). The full text is in *American State Trials*, vol. 7 (1916), 395.
57. Bradley and Winans, *Webster and the Salem Murder*, 22, 23, 69, 226; Booth, *Death of an Empire*, 161; *Salem (Mass.) Gazette*, Nov. 16, 1830, 2:5.
58. "Trial of George Crowninshield," *Boston Evening Transcript*, in *Newburyport (Mass.) Herald*, Nov. 19, 1830, 2. Both Morton and Congressman Crowninshield were Democrats.
59. "Trial of George Crowninshield, for Misprison of Felony," *Newburyport (Mass.) Herald*, Nov. 30, 1830, 2.
60. *Boston Commercial Gazette*, Nov. 18, 1830, 4, from *Salem Gazette*, Nov. 16, 1830. Richard Crowninshield's letter is dated "Salem, June 15, 1830," and was found with his corpse in jail cell; on William Ward, friend of John Francis Knapp, see Bradley and Winans, *Webster and the Salem Murder*, 226; for letter to John Dikes, September 1831, see Bradley and Winans, *Webster and the Salem Murder*, 229.
61. Helen Thomson, *Murder at Harvard* (Boston: Houghton Mifflin, 1971), 28–29.
62. Thomson, *Murder at Harvard*, 42, 43, 90, 91; Oliver Wendell Holmes, *The Benefactors of the Harvard Medical School: With a Biographical Sketch of the Late Dr. George Parkman* (Boston: Ticknor, Reed, and Fields, 1850), 24, 25, 35.

63. Webster was the grandson of Hannah Webster Foster, author of *The Coquette*. *Biography of Prof. John W. Webster; Containing a Full Account of His Imprisonment, Confession, and Last Moments on the Scaffold; By a Member of His Class* (Boston: Hotchkiss, 1850), 5, reports an annual income of two to three thousand dollars and does not mention inheritance.

64. Thomson, *Murder at Harvard*, 250, 251.

65. Thomson, *Murder at Harvard*, 62, 251, 252.

66. Thomson, *Murder at Harvard*, 44, 252.

67. Richard B. Morris, *Fair Trial: Fourteen Who Stood Accused from Anne Hutchinson to Alger Hiss* (1952; reprint, New York: Harper and Row, 1967), 165.

68. W. E. Bigelow, *An Expose of the Evidence in the Case of the Parkman Murder!* (Boston: n.p., 1850), 19, 20, 21, 22, 28, 29, 32; Thomson, *Murder at Harvard*, 140–42.

69. Thomson, *Murder at Harvard*, 196–206.

70. Alan Rogers, *Murder and the Death Penalty in Massachusetts* (Amherst: University of Massachusetts Press, 2008), 96; Morris, *Fair Trial*, 168.

71. Thomson, *Murder at Harvard*, 171–72. The claim of sixty thousand spectators seems inflated and may count some people several times.

72. Rogers, *Murder and the Death Penalty*, 99–101; Halttunen, *Murder Most Foul*, 130.

73. Morris, *Fair Trial*, 193; Robert Sullivan, *The Disappearance of Dr. Parkman* (Boston: Little, Brown, 1971), 169.

74. Thomson, *Murder at Harvard*, 260; Sullivan, *Disappearance of Dr. Parkman*, 169, 170; *Biography of Prof. John W. Webster*, 14, 23.

75. On Kelley, see Wayne W. Wright, comp., *The Cooper Genealogy Library Notes*, New York State Historical Society, 1983, with additions and corrections by Hugh C. MacDougall (James Fenimore Cooper Society, online August 2002, updated July 2005); Levi Kelley, "Last Will and Testament," Cooperstown, Otsego County, New York, filed Jan. 1, 1828 (Family Search, Church of Latter-Day Saints), New York Probate Records, 1629–1971, Otsego County, Wills and Administrations, 1823–1830, vol. G–H, images 178–81; [Levi Kelley], *Trial of Levi Kelley, for the Murder of Abraham Spafard, on the Evening of 3d Sept. 1827; Before a Special Court of Oyer and Terminer, Held at the Court-House in the County of Oswego, in Pursuance of a Commission for That Purpose, on the 21st of November, 1827* (Cooperstown, N.Y., 1827), 15 for "clock." For the description of Kelley as "a reputable farmer in easy circumstances," see *Albany (N.Y.) Argus*, Sept. 12, 1827, 2. Records of Kelley's real estate transactions are in Otsego County office building, Cooperstown, N.Y. He was listed as a "cabinet-maker and joiner" in his first purchase.

76. Jeremiah Spofford, *Genealogical Record: Including Two Generations in Female Lines of Families Spelling Their Name Spofford, Spafford, Spafard, and Spafard; Descendants of John Spofford and Elizabeth Scott, Who Emigrated in 1638, from Yorkshire, England and settled at Rowley, Essex County, Mass.* (Boston: Heliotype, 1888), 84. Multiple households: *Trial of Levi Kelley*, 6.

77. *Trial of Levi Kelley*, 6, 7.

78. *Trial of Levi Kelley*, 3, 12, 17, 18.

79. *Trial of Levi Kelley*, 20, 21; *Middlesex Gazette* (Middletown, Conn.), Sept. 9, 1827, 2. Another newspaper, calling Kelley a "reputable farmer in easy circumstances," reported that ten days before attacking Spafard, Kelley witnessed Jesse Strang's hanging for murder. *Saratoga (N.Y.) Sentinel*, Sept. 18, 1827, 2, editorialized that this "goes to show that public executions do not deter from crime."

80. *New York Herald*, May 9, 1856, 4; *Daily National Intelligencer* (Washington, D.C.), May 16, 1856, 2, July 24, 1856, 3, July 25, 1856, 3; *Daily Evening Bulletin* (San Francisco), June 16, 1856, 1; *Sun* (Baltimore), July 29, 1856, 1.

81. *New York Herald*, May 9, 1856, 4.

82. William P. Preston, Esq., *An Argument in the Case of the United States versus Philemon T. Herbert, Tried for the Murder of Thomas Keating. Delivered in the Criminal Court of the United States for the District of Columbia, on the Twenty-Fourth of July, 1856: by William P. Preston, Esq. Taken in Short-Hand by P. B. Templeton, Stenographer* (Washington, D.C.: C. Alexander, 1856), 3, 4, 5. Philip Barton Key was the son of Francis Scott Key, author of "The Star Spangled Banner," and the nephew of Chief Justice Roger B. Taney.

83. See Preston Papers, University of Maryland Archives digital collections: http://digital.lib.umd.edu/archivesum/actions.DisplayEADDoc.do?source=MdU.ead.histms.0124.xml&style=ead#series4.a.

84. Preston, *Argument in the Case*, 5.

85. Preston, *Argument in the Case*, 14, 15, 19, 36.

86. Preston, *Argument in the Case*, 19, 20, 37.

87. *National Era* (Washington, D.C.), July 31, 1856, 122; "Mariposa gambler," *Annapolis (Md.) Gazette*, July 24, 1856, 2.

88. *National Era* (Washington, D.C.), Aug. 14, 1856, 131; *Albany (N.Y.) Evening Journal*, Aug. 5, 1856, 2.

89. *Daily Globe* (Washington, D.C.), Oct. 14, 1856, 3.

90. *National Era* (Washington, D.C.), July 31, 1856, 122.

91. *New York Daily Tribune*, July 28, 1856, 4, July 29, 1856, 4. Matt F. Ward killed Professor W. G. H. Butler in Louisville in 1853, and the trial was held in 1854; see *Boston Evening Transcript*, Apr. 29, 1854, 2, headline "KENTUCKY DISGRACED"; and *Salem (Mass.) Register*, May 1, 1854, 1, headline "THE KENTUCKY FARCE. In 1791, by contrast, Berkeley County, Virginia, twenty-four-year-old gentleman John Crane was convicted and executed for the murder of farmer Abraham Vanhorn. Crane's father was connected to elite families and vainly sought a pardon for his son. See *Hampshire Chronicle* (Springfield, Mass.), Aug. 8, 1791, for coroner's inquest, and *Baltimore Evening Post*, July 26, 1792, 3, for Crane's execution. On the legitimacy of honor killing as greater in the midcentury South than earlier, see Edward L.

Ayers, *Vengeance and Justice: Crime and Punishment in the Nineteenth-Century American South* (New York: Oxford University Press, 1984); *Washington (Pa.) Review and Examiner,* Aug. 2, 1856, 2.

92. Richard P. Robinson's concocted alibi compared to Matt F. Ward's in *Boston Evening Transcript,* Apr. 29, 1854, 2, under headline "KENTUCKY DISGRACED."

93. Benjamin F. Hallett, *A Full Report of the Trial of Ephraim K. Avery, Charged with the Murder of Sara M. Cornell, before the Supreme Court of Rhode Island, at a Special Term in Newport, Held in May 1833, with the Arguments of Counsel* (Boston: Daily Commercial Gazette, 1833), 14, 15, 18.

94. Richard Hildreth, *Report of the Trial of Ephraim K. Avery before the Supreme Judicial Court of Rhode Island, on an Indictment for the Murder of Sarah Maria Cornell,* 2nd ed. (Boston: Russell, Odiorne, 1833), 143.

95. *American Repertory* (St. Albans, Vt.), June 20, 1833, 4, reported the five hundred dollars from the *New Bedford (Mass.) Gazette.*

96. Halttunen, *Murder Most Foul,* 195–96.

97. Hallett, *Full Report,* 114, 117.

98. Hallett, *Full Report,* 110, 112, 113–18.

99. Thomas M. McDade, comp., *The Annals of Murder: A Bibliography of Books and Pamphlets on American Murders from Colonial Times to 1900* (Norman: University of Oklahoma Press, 1961), 13–18, items 33–47, 49–53; *Republican* (Newport, R.I.), June 12, 1833, 2. The paper is also identified as the *Rhode-Island Republican.*

100. *Report of a Committee of the New England Conference of the M. E. Church, on the Case of Rev. E. K. Avery, a Member of Said Conference* (Boston: David H. Ela, 1833). *American Sentinel* (Middletown, Conn.), extracts, June 19, 1833, 3. The *Newburyport (Mass.) Herald,* June 18, 1833, 6, argued that if a person was declared "not guilty" in court, "innocence is to be presumed." The *Catskill (N.Y.) Recorder* (reprinted in the *Jamestown [N.Y.] Journal,* June 19, 1833, 2) rejected the idea of innocence but said that "the evidence appears to us wholly insufficient to justify a conviction."

101. *Lowell (Mass.) Mercury,* Dec. 27, 1833, 3.

102. *Weekly Eastern Argus* (Portland, Me.), June 14, 1836. The episode is thoroughly explored in Patricia Cline Cohen, *The Murder of Helen Jewett: The Life and Death of a Prostitute in Nineteenth-Century New York* (New York: Alfred A. Knopf, 1998); chap. 15 (291–320) covers trial.

103. *Public Ledger* (Philadelphia), June 10, 1836, 1.

104. Cohen, *Murder of Helen Jewett,* 317; *Newburyport (Mass.) Herald,* June 10, 1836, 3. From second edition of *New York Evening Star.*

105. Cohen, *Murder of Helen Jewett,* chap. 16.

106. Cohen, *Murder of Helen Jewett,* 326. *Middletown (Conn.) Advocate,* reprinted in *Newburyport (Mass.) Herald,* June 21, 1836, 2.

107. Cohen, *Pillars of Salt*, 205, 216.

108. Cohen, *Pillars of Salt*, 219–28.

109. Cohen, *Pillars of Salt*, 230.

110. Kelly A. Ryan, *Regulating Passion: Sexuality and Patriarchal Rule in Massachusetts, 1700–1830* (New York: Oxford University Press, 2014), chap. 6 and Conclusion.

111. [George Coombs], *Sketch of the Trial of George Coombs for the Murder of Maria Henry, Alias Maria Coombs, on the 15th of June, 1816 Conducted on Tuesday, 3d December, before the Supreme Judicial Court Now Sitting in This Town* (Boston: T. G. Bangs, 1816). Maria Henry was a Portsmouth, New Hampshire, prostitute who fornicated with whites and nonwhites, according to local gossip; see Jonathan Plummer, *Death of Tamar Ham! For the Unmarried Ladies of America, a New Psalm and a New Sermon, on the Death of Tamar Ham, Who Died in Boston, One Night in the Summer of the Year 1816, after Having Been Knocked Down and Stamped on the Day Before, If the Newspaper Account of the Matter Is True, by a Sailor with Whom She Lived without Being Married; The Name of This Man Is Coombs; He Had Been Sometime Confined, but Had Not Had His Trial, When This Paper Went to Press* [Newburyport?, Mass., 1816].

112. *Sketch of the Trial of George Coombs*, 4, 5, 11–14, 15. John Gallison (1788–1820) was an 1807 Harvard College graduate and the nephew of Chief Justice Samuel Sewall (1757–1814).

113. *Boston Weekly Messenger*, Dec. 5, 1816, 1.

114. *Sketch of the Trial of George Coombs*, 21, italics added.

115. *Sketch of the Trial of George Coombs*, 21.

116. *Sketch of the Trial of George Coombs*, 12.

117. *Sketch of the Trial of George Coombs*, 12, 15. Coombs died less than two years later in Bath, Maine, "by a fall from the mast." *Boston Recorder*, July 7, 1818, 111.

118. Carl Edward Skeen, *1816: America Rising* (Lexington: University Press of Kentucky, 2003), treats the Peter Lung case, 175–77.

119. *Star* (Raleigh, N.C.), Oct. 13, 1815, 3, Nov. 10, 1815, 4, Nov. 17, 1815, 4; *Albany (N.Y.) Daily Advertiser*, Nov. 9, 1815, 2.

120. *A System of the Laws of the State of Connecticut*, 2 vols. (Hartford, Conn., 1795), 2:328. See Cornelia Hughes Dayton, *Women before the Bar: Gender, Law, and Society in Connecticut, 1639–1789* (Chapel Hill: University of North Carolina Press for the Institute of Early American History and Culture, 1995), chap. 4 ("The Eighteenth-Century Double Standard," 157–230) and chap. 5 ("Rape: The Problematics of a Woman's Word," 231–84).

121. Thomas Keneally, *American Scoundrel: The Life of the Notorious Civil War General Dan Sickles* (New York: Doubleday, 2002); W. A. Swanberg, *Sickles the Incredible: A Biography of Daniel Edgar Sickles* (New York: Scribner's, 1956).

122. *Biography of Prof. John W. Webster*, iv.

Chapter Eight. Equal Rights, Privilege, and the Pursuit of Inequality

Epigraph: Michael Vorenberg, *The Final Freedom: The Civil War, the Abolition of Slavery, and the Thirteenth Amendment* (Cambridge: Cambridge University Press, 2001), 131.

1. Elias Boudinot, *An Oration, Delivered at Elizabeth-Town, New-Jersey, Agreeable to a Resolution of the State Society of Cincinnati, on the Fourth of July, M.DCC.XCIII; Being the Seventeenth Anniversary of the Independence of America* (Elizabeth-Town, N.J.: Shepard Kollock, 1793), 22. Ironically he made this assertion before a hereditary honorific organization. Gordon S. Wood, *The Creation of the American Republic, 1776–1787* (Chapel Hill: University of North Carolina Press for the Institute of Early American History and Culture, 1969), 70–74. "La carrière ouverte aux talents" was promoted by Napoleon, though the idea goes back to classical antiquity and to ancient China.

2. Wood, *Creation*, 74; James Madison to W. T. Barry, Aug. 4, 1822, in *Writings of James Madison*, ed. Gaillard Hunt, vol. 9 (New York: G. P. Putnam's Sons, 1910), 106–7.

3. Bernard Bailyn, *The Ideological Origins of the American Revolution* (Cambridge, Mass.: Harvard University Press, 1967), titles his sixth chapter "The Contagion of Liberty" and treats slavery, religious establishments, democratic suffrage, and deference; Gordon S. Wood, *The Idea of America: Reflections on the Birth of the United States* (New York: Penguin, 2011), 225–26; John Cunliffe and Guido Erreygers, "Equal Inheritance and Equal Shares: A Reconsideration of Some Nineteenth-Century Reform Proposals," in *Inherited Wealth, Justice and Equality* (Abingdon, U.K.: Routledge, 2013), 60–63; Jens Beckert, *Inherited Wealth* (Princeton, N.J.: Princeton University Press, 2008), 172–73.

4. Alexis de Tocqueville, *Democracy in America*, trans. and ed. Harvey C. Mansfield and Delba Winthrop (Chicago: University of Chicago Press, 2000), 50.

5. Thomas Paine, *Collected Writings*, ed. Eric Foner (New York: Library of America, 1995), 23 ("Common Sense"); *Letters from an American Farmer; Describing Certain Provincial Situations, Manners, and Customs . . . of the British Colonies in North America* (London, 1782), 37, "Letter III, What Is an American."

6. *Appendix to the Congressional Globe, Senate,* 33rd Cong., 1st Sess., Feb. 20, 1854, 214; "Letter to the Maine Whig Committee," Boston, Aug. 9, 1856, in *The Works of Rufus Choate, with a Memoir of His Life*, ed. Samuel Gilman Brown, 2 vols. (Boston: Little, Brown, 1862), 1:215.

7. Richard D. Brown, "Sailors Learned to Adapt to Historic Change in the Navy," *Hartford Courant*, op-ed, Feb. 3, 1993.

8. Linda K. Kerber, *No Constitutional Right to Be Ladies: Women and the Obligations of Citizenship* (New York: Hill and Wang, 1999).

9. George M. Fredrickson, *The Comparative Imagination: On the History of Racism, Nationalism, and Social Movements* (Berkeley: University of California

Press, 1999), 4, 107, 110–11. Tocqueville was alert to these issues: see *Democracy in America*, 329–30ff.

10. One surviving statutory marker of class is imprisonment for those who cannot pay fines.

11. Wood, *Idea of America*, 225–26; Paine, *Collected Writings*, 401–2, 407–10 ("Agrarian Justice").

ACKNOWLEDGMENTS

I must first thank the University of Connecticut, which has, in my retirement, supplied a library carrel and word-processor support. The university's Homer Babbidge Library staff, and especially "Document Delivery," have cheerfully assisted the research. American Antiquarian Society staff, Vincent L. Golden, Lauren E. Hewes, Marie E. Lamoureux, Kimberly Melkey, Jaclyn Penny, Elizabeth Pope, and Laura Wasowicz, helped locate illustrations. Many scholars have contributed knowledge and insights in the decade or so since I began this work. At the outset John Demos encouraged me to pursue this sometimes daunting project. Later, Yale University Press asked Daniel A. Cohen and Frank Lambert to assess a half-completed draft, and each supplied highly informed, constructive, and insightful criticisms. Along the way Chris Beneke, Thomas E. Buckley, Daniel Dreisbach, Hendrik Hartog, Bruce Mann, Jack Rakove, Alan Rogers, and James Brewer Stewart offered suggestions in response to queries. My colleagues Fakhreddin Azimi, Christopher Clark, Cornelia Hughes Dayton, Robert A. Gross, R. Kent Newmyer, Nancy Shoemaker, and Altina Waller also shaped my thinking in numerous casual conversations, as has my wife and colleague, Irene Quenzler Brown. And when Linda Kerber visited University of Connecticut she provided important advice for the chapter on women and children. Seven other scholars very generously agreed to read and criticize particular chapters: Christopher Beneke, Christopher Bonner, Eric Foner, Mary Kelley, Alan Taylor, Gordon S. Wood, and Rosemary Zagarri. Two others read a draft of the entire manuscript for Yale University Press, adding valuable suggestions. Each of these readers influenced my interpretation and corrected inaccuracies. William Frucht, a Yale editor, has helped in numerous ways, as has Yale's manuscript editor Laura Jones Dooley. Remaining errors and wrong-headedness are mine.

Sentimental acknowledgments are not for me. That said, I must especially thank one truly rare person, Irene Quenzler Brown.

INDEX

Page numbers in *italics* indicate figures.

abolitionism. *See* slavery
Act for the Relief of Eunice Chapman, 201
"An Act Providing for the Public Worship of God" (Massachusetts), 52
"Act to establish an uniform Rule of Naturalization" (Continental Congress), 67
Adams, Abigail, 24, 168–69, 172–73, *173*, 175–76, 179–81, 225–26, 300, 306
Adams, Charles Francis, 271
Adams, John: class consciousness of, 6, 24, 246; immigration and, 70–71, 76–77; Massachusetts Declaration of Rights and, 21; race and, 9, 17, 125; religious liberty and, 48–49, 59–60; women's rights and, 169–72, 174–75, 189
Adams, John Quincy, 230
Adams, Samuel, 29, 49, 55, 153, 247
"Address on Slavery" (Lee), 6–7
adultery, 185–86, 197, 202, 206. *See also* marriage
adults. *See* age; children
African Americans: criminal trials and, 140–59, 223; education and, 159–67; equality and, 27, 106–8, 110–11, 113, 124–25, 164; Haitian Revolution and, 115, 117; Northwest Territory states and, 118–23; prejudice against, 120–21, 124–31, 143–51; Revolutionary War participation by, 66; scientific inferiority of,

15–16, 123–31; state-by-state variance and, 112–18, 124–31; suffrage and, 113–15, 121–22, 132–33, 165, 171, 226, 238–39, 253. *See also* race; slavery
age, x–xi, 24–25, 169, 357n91. *See also* children
Alien and Sedition Acts, 76, 83, 93
Allen, Howard W., 339n2
American Bloody Register, 81
American Museum, 177
Ames, Fisher, 70
Anabaptists, 42
Anglicans, 18–20, 29–30, 34, 36, 45. *See also* Church of England; Protestants; religion
Ann (defendant), 143–47, 210, 340n12, 343n46
Anthony, Susan B., 238
"Anti-Catholic Doings" (Johnston), 56
aristocracy, 5–6, 24–25, 68–70, 245, 249–50, 261–62, 298, 300. *See also* Britain; class (social); property rights
asylum tradition, 70–74, 78–79, 93, 303
Austin, Charles, 153
Avery, Ephraim, 282–86, 288, 290–91, 295–96

Babcock, Primus, 165
Bache, Benjamin, 259
Backus, Isaac, 47–48
bail, 162, 245, 268. *See also* class (social)